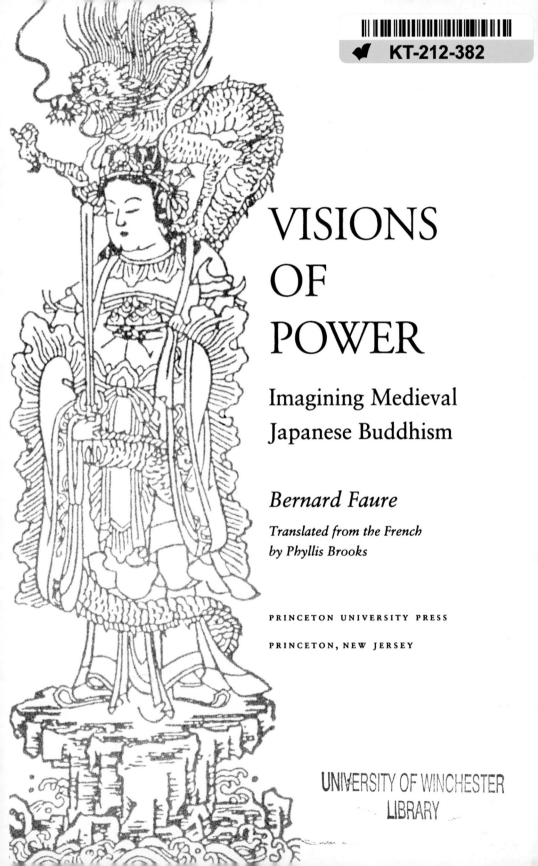

VISIONS
OF
POWER

Imagining Medieval
Japanese Buddhism

Bernard Faure

*Translated from the French
by Phyllis Brooks*

PRINCETON UNIVERSITY PRESS

PRINCETON, NEW JERSEY

Copyright © 1996 by Princeton University Press
Published by Princeton University Press, 41 William Street
Princeton, New Jersey 08540
In the United Kingdom: Princeton University Press, Chichester,
West Sussex
All Rights Reserved

Second printing, and first paperback printing, 2000

Paperback ISBN 0-691-02941-5

The Library of Congress has cataloged the cloth edition of this book as follows
Faure, Bernard.
[Fragments de l'imaginaire bouddhique. English]
Visions of power : imagining medieval Japanese Buddhism /
Bernard Faure ; translated from the French by Phyllis Brooks.
p. cm.
Includes bibliographical references and index.
ISBN 0-691-03758-2 (alk. paper)
1. Keizan, 1268–1325. 2. Sōtōshū—Rituals. 3. Buddhist art
and symbolism—Japan. I. Title.
BQ9449.S547F3813   1996
294.3'927—dc20
95-37197

This book has been composed in Sabon

The paper used in this publication meets the minimum requirements of ANSI/NISO
Z39.48-1992 (R1997) (*Permanence of Paper*)

http://pup.princeton.edu

Printed in the United States of America

10 9 8 7 6 5 4 3 2

To Michel Strickmann

CONTENTS

ILLUSTRATIONS

Illustrations by Zuikō Chingyū and Daiken Hōju, *Teiho Kenzeiki zue* (1806), in *Sōtōshū zensho*, 17, *Shiden*, 2, rev. ed. (Tokyo: Sōtōshū shūmuchō, 1970–73).

ACKNOWLEDGMENTS

THIS BOOK was first written in French, with a French audience in mind. For this reason, it uses some of the same materials covered in my earlier books, *The Rhetoric of Immediacy* and *Chan Insights and Oversights*. I hope that the reader will find them complementary, not redundant. The originally French context of the book also explains why its argument revolves around the notion of the *imaginaire* —with therefore none of the plot development that could be expected if this had been an intellectual biography of the traditional kind. Unfortunately, as *imaginary* has not (yet) acquired a substantive meaning in English, the semantic field of the *imaginaire* was partially lost in translation. Although the term is beginning to gain some currency in recent scholarly discourse, it still belongs to psychoanalytical jargon. We have therefore tried, the translator and myself, to find other equivalents, but we had to use this neologism at times, when no other translation seemed to work.

I have greatly benefited from the pioneering work of Ishikawa Rikizan on *kirigami*, that of his student William Bodiford on the Sōtō Zen tradition, and, of course, that of Yanagida Seizan on Chan/Zen in general. On the theoretical level, the influence of Marcel Mauss and Jacques Derrida is significant. Among other friends and colleagues to whom I am indebted for suggestions, criticisms, encouragement, and friendship, I would like to single out Carl Bielefeldt, James Dobbins, Hubert Durt, Bernard Frank, Louis Frédéric, Francine Hérail, François Jullien, Kuo Li-ying, Robert Sharf, and Michael Wenger. My graduate students at Stanford and the anonymous readers of the manuscript also deserve credit for helping me to experiment with and reformulate a number of ideas.

The production of this book would not have been possible without the good will and excellent advice of the editor, Ann Himmelberger Wald, and the expertise of the Princeton University Press staff. Phyllis Brooks, the translator, had the unrewarding task of rendering into fluid English the rather convoluted French prose of the original. The translation cost was covered by a grant from the Stanford Center for East Asian Studies. I want to thank in particular Theodore Foss for his support over the years. Finally, the Stanford Japan Center provided me with an ideal setting and technical support to do the final revisions, and I am grateful to the director, Terry MacDougall, and his staff for their kind support.

One of the last persons with whom I discussed various themes of this book during the summer of 1994 was Michel Strickmann. With his untimely death, I have lost not only a friend and a model of scholarship, but one of my most demanding (and rewarding) readers. It is to him that this book is dedicated, with the hope that it may serve in some ways as a stepping stone to his *magnum opus* on Chinese Tantrism, *Mantras et mandarins.*

Despite all the (not always intentional) loose ends, there is indeed a certain sense of closure, as I ritually and quite arbitrarily decide to put an end to a book whose initial project grew during my last stay in Japan in 1987–1988. But it is precisely when the cycle seems completed, *lorsque la boucle est bouclée,* to use one of the root metaphors of this book, that the dissemination may at last begin. In this I cannot hope for more than appropriating Ernest Larousse's famous motto, "Je sème à tout vent."

Kyoto, Christmas 1994

ABBREVIATIONS

PRIMARY SOURCES

BEFEO   *Bulletin de l'Ecole Française d'Extrême-Orient.* Paris: Ecole
        Française d'Extrême-Orient.
DNBZ   *Dai Nihon bukkyō zensho.* 151 vols. Tokyo: Bussho
        kankōkai, 1911–22.
DZ   *Dōgen zenji zenshū.* Ōkubo Dōshū, ed. 2 vols. Tokyo:
        Chikuma shobō, 1969–70.
DZZ   *Dōgen zenji zenshū.* Ōkubo Dōshū, ed. Tokyo: Chikuma
        shobō, 1969–70.
HJAS   *Harvard Journal of Asiatic Studies.*
IBK   *Indogaku bukkyōgaku kenkyū.*
JAOS   *Journal of the American Oriental Society*
JDZ   *Jōsai daishi zenshū.* Kohō Chisan, ed. 1937. Rpt.
        Yokohama: Daihonzan Sōjiji, 1976.
JIABS   *Journal of the International Association of Buddhist
        Studies*
KDBK   *Komazawa daigaku bukkyō gakubu kenkyū kiyō.* Tokyo:
        Komazawa University.
KDBR   *Komazawa daigaku bukkyō gakubu ronshū.* Tokyo:
        Komazawa University.
SZ   *Sōtōshū zensho.* Sōtōshū kankōkai, ed. 1929–35 Re-ed. 18.
        vols. Tokyo: Sōtōshū shūmuchō, 1970–73.
T.   *Taishō shinshū daizōkyō.* Takakusu Junjirō and Watanabe
        Kaigyoku, eds. 85 vols. Tokyo: Taishō issaikyō
        kankōkai, 1924–34.
ZZ   *Dai Nihon zokuzōkyō.* Nakano Tatsue, ed. 750 vols.
        Kyoto: Zōkyō shoin, 1905–12. Rpt. Taibei, Xinwenfeng,
        1968–70.

MISCELLANEOUS

attr.   attributed
c.   century
Ch.   Chinese
d.   died
d.u.   date(s) unknown

fl.	flourished
J.	Japanese
litt.	litterally
n.d.	no date
n.p.	no publisher
Skt.	Sanskrit
var.	variant

VISIONS OF POWER

INTRODUCTION

> Behind Moses, who touched the bare rock, stood the whole
> nation of Israel, and while Moses may have felt some
> doubts, Israel certainly did not.
>
> *Marcel Mauss*

WE ARE EMBARKING on an outline of the mental world of a Zen monk of the beginning of the fourteenth century, Keizan Jōkin (1268–1325), the third generation in succession from Dōgen (1200–1253). Dōgen is usually considered to be the founder of the Japanese Sōtō Zen sect, while Keizan has the ambivalent distinction of having reformed this sect, which would henceforth become one of the most flourishing schools in Japanese Buddhism. Popular opinion has it that this prosperity, encouraged by active proselytizing, was also accompanied by a certain amount of deviation from the ideal, "pure" Chan line imported from China by Dōgen. The Sōtō school is known to pride itself on the direct transmission of the esoteric teachings of the Buddha Śākyamuni, a transmission allegedly accomplished by the Indian patriarch Bodhidharma at the beginning of the sixth century in China. Much could be said about the assumptions behind this notion of a Chan/Zen that was originally pure but quickly contaminated by popular superstition. Here my aim is to define the "Zen imagination," the way beliefs are rendered in images, a concept often referred to in French contexts by the term *imaginaire*. I do not intend to promote, in the wake of D. T. Suzuki (1870–1966) and others, a Zen that is largely imaginary because of its fundamentally ideological nature; a Zen that is at best a secondary, more recent form of this *imaginaire*. Keizan was certainly an original thinker, but I will draw on his writings mostly for what appears to me to reflect the emergence or the continuation of certain mental structures. These structures have been largely misunderstood by Japanese scholars who have studied Keizan. Excessively concerned with seeing Sōtō Zen as a single, unified school, they have concealed the contradictions and ambiguities within it. On an even wider level, they have been hesitant to consider any evidence that might question the uniqueness of Zen as a whole. Here, therefore, we will stress what one may call, as opposed to highly mystical transports, "ordinary" Zen, which is far from ordinary in the general (or Western) sense of that word. The *imaginaire* constitutes the warp on which is woven, or rather the backdrop against which is erected, the theoretical discourse of the "sudden teaching" of Chan.

In spite of his status as "second founder" and "fourth patriarch" of the Japanese Sōtō "sect," Keizan, far from being a narrowly sectarian figure, stands at the crossroads of various traditions. Of course he is first and foremost a Zen monk, and his references in this regard are impeccable, and consequently relatively trite. He quotes and comments on the eponymous masters of the Sōtō (Chinese Caodong) tradition: Dongshan Liangjie (807–869) and Caoshan Benji (840–901). But he also likes to be seen as an *ujiko*, a "clan child" of Hakusan, a name designating both the mountain range that dominates and separates the three prefectures of Fukui, Ishikawa, and Gifu, and its protective deity, Hakusan Myōri Daigongen. Unlike Dōgen, Keizan was completely immersed in local cults and legends from the time of his childhood. His entire work reflects and maintains this tension between two fundamentally opposed realms of thought. This ambiguity is usually glossed over by Japanese historians or else attributed to efforts at proselytizing on the part of a reformer consciously adapting his teachings to local conditions. But it actually expresses what the Buddhists have called the "two truths": ultimate truth and conventional truth. This hermeneutic strategy of the "twofold truth" is critical in Chan/Zen Buddhism, but its role is problematic in that it seeks to diminish tensions rather than let them play against each other, and eventually covers up rather than reveals the reality of the practices. If this pattern of discourse cannot be discarded, one must at least avoid replicating it. To do this, an anthropologico-historical approach seems useful. We are working in a domain that is still little studied, one largely dominated by the teleological concepts of an entire tradition that sees Zen as the final outcome of the history of Buddhism and, at the same time, the zenith of Japanese culture. Thus any attempt of the kind made in this book is fraught with difficulties, and our conclusions will remain tentative.

Sources

The main document behind this study is a relatively short text that has been largely neglected in the Sōtō tradition because of its seemingly unorthodox nature; its compilation was begun by Keizan and continued by his disciples. Its name, *Tōkokki* (var. *Tōkoku ki,* "The Record of Tōkoku"), comes from the spot where Keizan founded Yōkōji (the Eternal Light Monastery)—a place at the bottom of the Noto Peninsula, near the town of Hagui in Ishikawa prefecture. It is a chronicle tracing the foundation and early development of this monastery in the first half of the fourteenth century.[1]

The text of the *Record of Tōkoku* is made up of three parts.[2] First there is a section covering the years 1312 to 1324, the period from the giving of the land for Yōkōji to the death of Keizan. This section contains an account of the origins of the monastery, Keizan's autobiography, and the biographies of his four predecessors, along with various poems, sayings, and sermons of Keizan. I have used most of this section here, with the exception of the biographies (well-known in other editions) and the collection of sayings (clearly a later addition). It should be noted that the *okibumi* (record of intent) concerning the future of Yōkōji does not appear in the "secret edition" of Daijōji. The second section contains documents from various sources, all dating from after the death of Keizan. These include extracts from Yōkōji monastic rule and directions for rituals like the offering to the Arhats. This section is very brief in the "secret edition." The third section consists of three collections that originated after the rupture in 1415 between the Meihō Sotetsu and Gasan Jōseki branches. These collections are preceded in the "secret edition" by a "collection of the sayings" of Keizan, put together by an acolyte named

[1] Tōkoku is the name given by Keizan to the place donated to him in 1312 by a couple of laypeople. This name is based on that of Dongshan (Jap. Tōzan), the mountain where the Chan master Liangjie (807–869), founder of the Caodong (Sōtō) school, lived. But the word *mountain* (Chinese *shan*, Japanese *san* or *zan*) is replaced here by *valley* (*koku*).

[2] The *Tōkoku ki* is currently known from five manuscript editions: 1) the edition in the collection at Daijōji, copied in 1432 by a monk named Eiji; 2) the edition in the collection at Eifukuan (near Fukui), copied by Menzan Zuihō in 1714; 3) the Daijōji edition, edited in 1718 by Chitō Shōgen; 4) The Yōkōji edition (undated); 5) The edition in the library of Komazawa University in Tokyo (undated).

The five editions show significant variants. The one that seems closest to being a basic text is the first, known as the "secret edition of Daijōji." The third seems to be only a revision of this text, copied yet again in the fourth. The fifth seems to constitute a later version of the text. The text of the *Record of Tōkoku* has appeared in two published forms: in the *Collection of Texts of the Sōtō Sect* (*Sōtōshū zensho*, hereafter SZ, published in 1930 and republished in 1971) and in the *Complete Works of the Grand Master Jōsai* [i.e., Keizan] (*Jōsai daishi zenshū*, hereafter JDZ, published in 1937, republished in 1967). Apparently these two editions contain many interpolated passages. But it is possible that some of these passages, although added later, were actually drawn up by Keizan himself; the "secret edition" of Daijōji, on the other hand, has been reworked and should not be accepted uncritically as being entirely from the hand of Keizan. This said, and without delving into specialists' quarrels over the authenticity of this passage or that (but rejecting any parts that are clearly later additions), it is this Daijōji text that I am using to establish Keizan's pattern of thought. A critical edition of the 1432 manuscript was also produced by Ōtani Teppu in the journal *Shūgaku kenkyū* in 1974, but I have not had access to it. I have also not been able to use the modern translation by Kōchi Eigaku in *Keizan no Zen*, vol. 8 (Tokyo: Sankibō Busshorin, 1985).

Genso. Even the first section itself is not entirely the work of Keizan. In the colophon to the "secret edition" (dated 1432), there is mention of a monk named Eijū, about whom almost nothing is known. He is supposed to have copied a holograph text, but it is not clear that the writer of that text was Keizan himself. It might well have been Kikudō Sōei, a fourth-generation successor to Meihō Sotetsu. As for the third section, it seems to have been added in order to authenticate the lineage of Meihō Sotetsu and Kikudō Sōei at the expense of the claims of Gasan Jōseki. Thus the *Record of Tōkoku*, in its revised and expanded form, had become by 1415 a sectarian work of propaganda, and its statements must sometimes be accepted with caution, one that extends even to the autobiographical sections apparently composed by Keizan himself; these may well have been extensively revised by overzealous copyists.

Nevertheless, for the purposes of this work, the discrepancies between the various versions of the text do not pose problems, even if, *horresco referens*, we are faced with interpolations, as the historians of the Sōtō tradition piously point out. In fact, whether the suspect passages are really the work of Keizan or of his disciples does not make much difference, since in either case we can draw useful information from them concerning the mindset of medieval monks, among whom Keizan is only one example, albeit both representative and atypical.

Another extensively used set of sources are initiation documents, *kirigami* (literally, "cut leaves").[3] These are documents varying in length from one to several pages, sometimes gathered together into bound volumes. They contain secret information of all kinds, most often related to ritual but sometimes also to various doctrinal points considered to be secret. Their use is not limited to the Sōtō sect; they are actually found in most Buddhist schools and traditions, whether religious or artistic, based on a secret oral transmission from master to disciple. Zen *kirigami* may be characterized by their reliance on the dialogical style of the *kōan* and by their use of certain types of diagram (the swastika and its variants, circles, and the like). Possession of such documents, along with various others, constituted proof of transmission and supplemented the teachings about ritual and doctrinal matters furnished by monastic codes and "recorded sayings," or Zen funeral sermons. Although the documents that

---

[3] According to the *Daikanwa jiten*, the reading is *kirigami*, but the *Kojien* has *kirikami*. The latter term seems to be more specific to the Sōtō school, but I have retained the more general reading to emphasize the cross-sectarian nature of the phenomenon. On these documents, see Ishikawa 1983–94, and in particular ibid. (1) for a tentative typology. See also Sugimoto 1938, and the catalog given by Menzan Zuihō (1683–1769) in his *Tōjō shitsunai danshi kenpi shiki*. Menzan lists 145 types of *danshi* (his word for *kirigami*). Another interesting collection is the *Bukke ichi daiji yawa* preserved at Ryūtakuji (Gifu prefecture) and edited in Ishikawa 1983–94.

have come down to us date to a time later than that of Keizan (mostly from the early part of the Edo period, 1600–1868), they have been accepted here as evidence of a long-term development of ways of thinking, or rather what French historians call *mentalités*, a development whose origins must go back to the very beginnings of the Sōtō sect, if not even earlier. They show particularly well the general shape of a tradition that encompasses both oral and written teachings, one that may be termed "diagrammatic Buddhism" from its very sophisticated use of an occult graphic symbolism. These documents also provide a vast amount of information on aspects of monastic life as it must have gone on at Yōkōji. It is also significant that one of the main collections of *kirigami*, still largely untapped by Japanese scholars, is precisely the one from Yōkōji, where these documents are still kept today.

There is one last source that I have turned to in order to shed light on the social context of the foundation of Yōkōji: the so-called *okibumi*, documents that record instructions left by Keizan for his disciples but are not counted as legally valid testamentary texts. The most important among these were inserted into the *Record of Tōkoku* at the end of the chronicle proper.

Yōkōji

After Yōkōji, Keizan founded another monastery, Sōjiji, in the northern part of the Noto peninsula. It would become, along with Eiheiji, which was founded by Dōgen, one of the two major centers of Sōtō Zen.[4] According to tradition, in 1322 a decree from Emperor Go-Daigo, who had received from Keizan the Bodhisattva Precepts, made Sōjiji into an officially recognized monastery. Two years later Keizan passed the direction of this monastery on to his disciple Gasan Jōseki while he himself went back to Yōkōji to spend his remaining days, according to the wish he had expressed in the *Record of Tōkoku*.

In 1325, when Keizan died, his disciple Meihō Sotetsu (1277–1350) became the second abbot of Yōkōji. Later the monastery received the protection of powerful patrons, not only that of estate stewards [*jitō*] and other prominent local officials, but even that of emperors (Go-Daigo, Go-Murakami) and Ashikaga shōguns (Takauji, Tadayoshi). Unfortunately, during the Ōnin war, in 1468, the monastery was heavily damaged by fire. By 1579 there remained nothing but Dentōin, a memorial hall dedicated to the five Sōtō patriarchs. The monastery was partially reconstructed during the period 1634–1637 but was once again destroyed

---

[4] Other monastic institutions founded by or placed under the direction of Keizan include Enzūin, Hōōji, Kōkōji, Hōshōji, Jōjūji, and Daijōji.

in 1674, this time by a typhoon. Internal conflicts also pitted Sōjiji, Dai-jōji, and Jōjūji against each other. It was not until the Meiji period, in 1883, that Kōhō Hakugen, with the help of a famous layman, the artist Yamaoka Tesshō, was able to rebuild the main buildings, but he was unable to restore the monastery's former prosperity.

Thus, despite Keizan's high hopes for Yōkōji, it was another of his foundations, Sōjiji, that would prosper after his death, thanks to Gasan Jōseki and his disciples. In spite of efforts at restoration undertaken at the end of the last century (efforts that still continue), Yōkōji remains a barren spot. On the other hand, Sōjiji, which during Keizan's lifetime was only a branch of Yōkōji, began to eclipse it within a century after the founder's death and ended up even more important than Dōgen's Eiheiji. The entire history of the Sōtō school from the fifteenth to the nineteenth century is bound up with the rivalry between Sōjiji (with its two locations in Noto and Yokohama) and Eiheiji.

KEIZAN'S TWO TRUTHS

The path that we are going to follow begins from a simple but surprising observation: the doctrine that Keizan followed was, as is all monasticism if we are to believe Max Weber, fundamentally rationalist and de-mythologizing. Furthermore, the religious experience that inspires Chan/Zen is, paradoxically, not very "religious" (in the Western sense of the word), since it relies on an immediate perception of reality, in its initial "thusness," prior to all thinking processes and imagination. Thus Chan/Zen takes as its position the rejection of all imagination. But the universe in which Keizan lived was no less impregnated with the mar-velous, structured by the imaginary than that of his contemporary Dante Alighieri. This contradiction is only one surface sign, one manifestation of a deep tension that we shall meet again and again. Keizan's Zen is, as we might expect, aporetic and therefore paradoxical: it is at the same time elitist and popular, idealistic and realistic, sudden and gradual (or, if you like, immediate and mediate), unlocalized and localized, obsessed with the idea of unity and besotted with multiplicity. Keizan's thought develops around these polarities and doubtless owes its vitality to this tension. As he says in one of his dialogues, "In the doctrine of emptiness we can finally detect neither heights nor depths, neither for nor against." We thus have a fusion within supreme awakening of the two orders of reality which give rise to dreams and to waking life. But this absolute standpoint (a contradiction in terms) results in only a theoretical dis-avowal of multiplicity. In practice things are very different, as we can see, for example, in the importance that Keizan attached to visions of all sorts, or his interest in the concrete details of monastic life. Thus, in a dialogue with his benefactress-turned-disciple, Sonin, Keizan alludes to the cosmic order, the conventional truth according to which the seasons succeed each other on the branches of trees, only to hear her reply that a tree "without shade" (the tree in its absolute reality) does not have "seasonal knots."[5] This realization of the eternal present does not prevent the two interlocutors, apparently concerned for the future, from leaving detailed instructions for their descendants.

Let us continue with this line of thought. Chan/Zen theory, in its orthodox immediacy, presents itself as completely rejecting all mediation: rejecting the *imaginaire* as an intermediary or "imaginal" world, dismissive of cosmologies, symbols, images—in other words, traditional beliefs and belief in general. It goes without saying that practice looks somewhat different: when we look at them closely, the fine theoretical certainties of Chan start unraveling, replaced by a game in which practically all kinds of mediation are allowed. Reminiscent of the writer described by Roland Barthes, the Chan master is a divided subject because he participates "at the same time and in a contradictory way in the deep pleasure of all culture . . . and the destruction of that culture. He enjoys the strength of his own self . . . (in this lies his pleasure) and tries to lose it (in this lies his enjoyment)."[6]

Keizan is consistent in his contradictions; they make up a system. His theoretical statements almost always stand in opposition to his actual practice—at least insofar as this latter can be reconstructed. This divergence is not accidental, and we may speak without too much fear of exaggeration, of a systematic effect characterizing Chan/Zen discourse. Instances of denials in principle may even serve as indicators; they reveal the dual nature of this discourse. Practice is "contained" by them (in every meaning of the word: included, enclosed, protected, prevented from spreading). The divergence between representations and actual practices is thus constitutive—it defines the very domain of the *imaginaire*.

Is practice then a kind of "controlled catastrophe," and the awakening that crowns it a self-possessed madness—a foundry in which all false notions are melted away—an emptiness of spirit suggesting a move beyond all mental functions, and thus beyond all meanings, words, and images? This attitude would explain iconoclasm and the "senseless" attitudes of the "Chan madmen" and other eccentric mystics. No more images, and thus no more *imaginaire*? Perhaps. But as far as we can tell, in almost all Chan texts we are in the presence of a normative vision of

---

[5] JDZ, 401. The term *jisetsu*, translated here literally, is an allusion to an expression often used by Dōgen, *jisetsu innen*, the "temporal causes and conditions" of awakening.

[6] See Barthes 1973: 26.

awakening rather than a simple description, a program that passes itself off as a simple inventory (*état des lieux*)—or rather an account of the non-place (*non-lieu*) called the arena of awakening (Skt. *bodhimaṇḍa*). This kind of awakening is still part of the Chan *imaginaire*, an imagination that has certainly been purified but one that cannot pride itself on any ontological or epistemological superiority over the image-rich imagination of local religion which it disavows. The desire to surpass and go beyond the ideological and the imaginary is also part of the ideological and the imaginary.

THE ZEN *IMAGINAIRE*

What do we mean here by the *imaginaire*? We shall take as our point of departure the definition put forward by Jacques Le Goff, one that has the merit of adhering to etymology and emphasizing the primacy of images. After reminding us that literary and artistic works of art (and, in the case of a religion, ritual practices) do not represent any eternal, unitary reality but rather are the products of the imagination of those who produce them, Le Goff stresses that "the phenomena of the imagination are embodied in words. . . . Every idea is expressed in words, and every word reflects some reality. When terms appear or disappear or change their meaning, the course of history stands revealed."[7] In his work he draws strict lines between the imaginary and the symbolic or ideological.

However, the distinction between the imaginary on the one hand, and the symbolic and ideological on the other, is not always clear, and in our examination of Keizan's thought the line that separates them will be blithely crossed over and over again. It seems, in fact, that we have here different aspects of a single phenomenon, or various stages in a dialectical process. In some cases the ideological and symbolic apparently shape the *imaginaire*: so it was that, in order for Keizan and his coreligionists to be able to reach, through dreams of ascent, Tuṣita Heaven, the "Pure Land" of the future Buddha Maitreya, this paradise still had to be set precisely within the Buddhist cosmology. Similarly, how do we distinguish, in the case of a mythical animal like the dragon, between the imaginary, the symbolic, and the emblematic? Dragons appear in legends, on screens, and even in the names of Buddhist temples. In various cases they are associated with tigers or snakes as representatives of autochthonous culture; they also symbolize heavenly energy—and thus awakening; as heraldic animals emblematic of the eastern direction, they share all the qualities associated with that compass direction in the Yin-Yang cos-

[7] Le Goff 1988, vol. 3, 12.

mological theory. All these meanings are not mutually exclusive; they intertwine and we pass constantly from one register to another.

It is thus impossible to deal with the pure *imaginaire*: as we approach different sides of the imaginary—those of place, body, images, but also from various points of view: Indian, Buddhist, Chinese, Japanese—we find ourselves undertaking side trips into the symbolic, utopian, ideological. There is, however, a "purely" Zen form of imagination, a reservoir of images and *exempla* specific to Chan. They were collected in the texts such as the *Biyan lu* (Emerald Cliff record) or the *Sanbyaku soku* (Three Hundred Cases), which would provide the Chinese matrix for Dōgen's *Shōbōgenzō* (Treasury of the True Dharma Eye) and Keizan's *Denkōroku* (Record of the Transmission of the Light].[8] More than "cases" (*kōan*) or mechanisms triggering awakening, they are *topoi*, mnemonic devices (like the mantras and *dhāraṇī* of esoteric Buddhism) helping in the memorization of essential points of Chan doctrine. Thus we have the episode in which the Buddha Śākyamuni, showing a flower to his assembled disciples, transmits the Law to Mahākāśyapa; or the classic examples of awakening among the Chan masters of the ninth century—that of Lingyun Zhiqin (d.u.) when he saw peach tree blossoms, of Xiangyan Zhixian (d. 898) at the sound of a pebble hitting a bamboo, of Linji Yixuan (d. 867) under the blows of the rod wielded by his master Huangbo Xiyun. These are matrix images that tend to replace the more philosophical matrices of early Chan—abstract formulas like "This very mind is the Buddha (*jixin shifo*)." The Chan of the Song period, strongly influenced by Chinese literary circles, embodies the main import of its message in textual images or metaphors.

If we follow Le Goff's distinction among three types of imagination— miraculous, magic, and marvelous—we note that Buddhism does not have any true miracles since the Buddhist universe is always governed by laws, no matter how strange these may sometimes seem. In a sense, only awakening itself can be termed miraculous, or unconceivable—insofar as it transcends all causality.

Buddhism is split between the ideology of karmic retribution and that of Emptiness. From the first unfolds an *imaginaire* made up of rebirths and metamorphoses determined by karma, a whole world peopled by spirits who, like the old fox who became the disciple of Baizhang Huaihai (720–814), even come to monasteries in search of deliverance from the cycle of births and deaths.[9] The second ideology seems to block the path to the imaginary, but it constitutes in itself a "purified" form of imagining—that of empty space. Karmic retribution is the mechanism by

---

[8] See *T. 82*, 2582 and 2585.
[9] See Heine 1994: 127–29.

which we can explain knowledge of past lives and which brings together the imagination and the memory. Thus Keizan could recall his many past lives and convinced himself that one of his favorite disciples, the nun Sonin, was the reincarnation of a female disciple of Dōgen. It is true that the importance of karmic bonds sometimes seems difficult to justify in the context of an idealistic doctrine in which all is illusion, but Keizan and his contemporaries did not seem to be concerned by this. To them, the knowledge of past lives was a power conferred by the practice of contemplation and for this reason deserved to be granted a certain degree of reality.

The reality of any *imaginaire* is predominantly historical and localized. It is "at the same time inscribed deep within each human being and inherent in social relations; it is through it that a society can express its identity without having to elaborate any formal doctrine, as the individual incorporates into himself those rules of conduct transmitted by his ancestors and that he must observe."[10] It is thus a matter of grasping all its ins and outs, to the greatest possible extent. This *imaginaire* is not only tied to a single epoch and social milieu—in our case the Zen monastic institution of the end of Kamakura; it is closely bound up with a specific place, Yōkōji, and understanding Keizan requires first an acquaintance with this place. It will thus be necessary to demonstrate the local nature of a way of thought that sees itself ultimately as unlocalized, and so to question its ideological nature—the *utopian* (in the etymological sense; atopical, unlocalized) ideal being precisely one of the features of ideology.

Keizan is, of course, much more than a simple case of medieval *mentalités*; he remains an exceptional individual. His *imaginaire* does not draw simply on the mindset of the collective; it is also in many respects idiosyncratic, and we must guard against any hasty generalization that might unduly privilege the type at the expense of the individual. If the *imaginaire* is never neutral or universal, it is perhaps impossible to discern a Zen imaginary or a medieval imagination. Certain motifs do recur, however, above and beyond idiosyncrasies and sectarian divisions, and we can try, in a preliminary fashion, to discern them.

When we come to Keizan's case, we are faced with a masculine *imaginaire* in which the mother and the idealized woman play a large role. As we shall see, in Keizan the constellation of the *imaginaire* seems to organize itself around poles like awakening, dreams, places, gods and their icons, Chan/Zen masters and their relics, stūpas, texts and talismans, lineage, and symbols of transmission. We need to determine whether his discourse constitutes a simple apology for the *imaginaire* or a passage through signs and images that ultimately denies it. Should we take at face

---

[10] See Schmitt 1990: 305.

value his typically Zen criticism of "superstitions," or should we see this only as a kind of *pro forma* statement? This question is perhaps inappropriate, but we can decide this only when we have completed our investigation.

CONSTITUENT IMAGINATION

Zen is often described as a form of introspection, a Buddhist variation on the "Know thyself" theme. But Keizan *imagines* himself more than he knows himself, or rather comes to know himself by imagining himself. He entrusts himself to what might be termed creative or constituent imagination. In him we find something analogous to what the Greeks defined as a tension between the *hieron*, the proper domain of the sacred from the point of view of official religion, and the *hosios*, liberation from the sacred through mystical experience.[11] In Chan the gradual/sudden paradigm refers to this kind of tension and the system established by its two poles.

Theoretically the strictly acosmological nature of Chan/Zen clearly sets this religious movement apart from traditional Buddhism as well as from Daoism and local religions. These latter are characterized by an extremely complex cosmology—which takes the form of the description of a universe that may be called, in a term used by Henri Corbin, "monde imaginal," an *imaginal* world.[12] For Corbin, the imaginal world is a domain that, although not yet based on a purely intellectual understanding of things, is no longer based only on empirical observation. In this intermediary domain, immanence and transcendence blend together, and "the non-corporeal becomes corporeal." This formulation reminds us in some ways of the visions of Mahāyāna and the atmosphere of the Dharma Assemblies as they are described in texts like the *Lotus Sūtra*. During these assemblies, in order to preach the Dharma to the Bodhisattvas and his other disciples, the Buddha takes on his "retribution body" (Skt. *saṃbhogakāya*). As Paul Mus has emphasized, the apparently acosmological nature of Nirvāṇa in early Mahāyāna presupposes an entire cosmology: in fact, it constituted a reversal of this cosmology and did not simply discount its existence.[13]

However, we cannot exclude the hypothesis that belief in the inter-

---

[11] See Vernant 1965, vol. 2, 81.

[12] See, among others, Corbin 1958: 7.

[13] See Mus 1935: 60–84. Admittedly, as Paul Harrison has argued, Mus tends to hypostasize the dharma body (*dharmakāya*). However, in the later Japanese context, strongly influenced by esoteric Buddhism, his insights remain heuristically useful. See Harrison 1992: 78–79.

mediary world may be one of those pseudo-beliefs well known to anthropologists: informants may unanimously confirm, for example, that "formerly we believed in masks," but that "formerly" seems, like the horizon, to move farther and farther backward the more one tries to get close to it. Such a stated belief may never have had anything but a virtual reality.[14]

For those who admit its truth, access to and participation in the *mundus imaginalis* are achieved through creative imagination and its symbols. According to Corbin, imagination is indeed a "truly central and mediating function due to the median and mediating position of the *mundus imaginalis*." What about the status of imagination in Chinese and Japanese Buddhism, and more specifically in Chan/Zen?

At first sight Chan is characterized by a denial of ontophanic or "constituent" imagination of the kind manifested in the visualization techniques of the Indian *dhyāna*. As in Hinduism, these practices were intended to achieve identification with the deity visualized, and they "thus turn realizing imagination into a spiritual organ of making present."[15] At the very heart of Chan, we actually find a cleavage analogous to that in Hinduism between the Vedantic way, "in which the brahman's meditation is realized indirectly, by means of symbolic meditations taking as their object symbols that become more and more transparent but that are never completely eliminated," and the method prescribed by the *Yogāvasiṣṭha*, in which one tries to "free oneself from the tyranny of perceived forms by denying the apparent substantiality of this world." As François Chenet has stressed, in Hinduism but also in Buddhism "to imagine is never to absent oneself but rather to reactivate the evidence of a presence."[16] But this presence must eventually be able to do without any images at all.

In the Chinese and Japanese traditions, it seems that, although images involve more than *mimesis*, this latter is nonetheless important to catch the essence of the real: this can be seen in the case of the fake money used in offerings and other ritual simulacra. However, the effectiveness of some rites seems to be even greater when *mimesis* is not strictly observed, and we may wonder whether the nonanthropomorphic icon does not have some kind of logical priority (and not simply a historical one) over the anthropomorphic one. We shall return to this question in Chapter 11.

It is important, finally, as Wittgenstein has stressed, to remember that "this imagination is not like a painted picture or a three-dimensional model, but a complicated structure of heterogeneous elements: words

---

[14] See Mannoni 1969: 14.
[15] See Chenet 1990: 159.
[16] See ibid.: 166.

and pictures. We shall then not think of operating with written or oral signs as something to be contrasted with the operation with 'mental images' of the events."[17] We must therefore, as Wittgenstein advises, "plough over the whole of language."[18]

Symbolic Mediation

Are we not doing violence to the Western schema of the mediating imagination when we try to apply it to Chinese or Japanese Buddhist contexts? It has often been noted that Chinese ontology does not recognize the Platonic division between being and thinking, feeling and knowing, and that it thus has no need for any Aristotelian mediation by means of the imagination. According to Marc Augé, "pagan thought" (a term he uses in a positive sense to cover all non-Christian religious thought) is characterized by its lack of division of the universe into the visible and the invisible.[19] In the same way, we are often told that the Chinese did not divide the real into physical and nonphysical, visible and invisible, rational and nonrational, human and divine, true and illusory. Without polarities of this type, symbols have no function since by essence they imply an "other scene," one that was not supposed to exist in China, or at least not until late in its history. The Chinese indeed possess a hermeneutic and symbolic tradition, represented among others by the *Yi jing* (Book of Changes). Nevertheless, the trigrams or hexagrams that interweave along this strand (the first meaning of *jing*) were seen as full-fledged realities rather than mere symbolic "representations." Henri Maspero stresses that "the hexagram was not a symbolic representation of the thing; it was the thing itself in its reality."[20] Since that which is "beyond representation" is revealed precisely through representation, such a representation cannot refer to a different reality. All of nature thus becomes an "ontophany," reality revealing itself, even if in this case there is nothing behind, prior to, or beyond the phenomena. Whoever perceives the Dao sees the real in its "thusness," and its "true nature" stands revealed. According to François Jullien, at this level the distinction be-

[17] Wittgenstein 1979: 7e.
[18] Ibid.
[19] See Augé 1982.
[20] See Maspero 1955: 446. However, the stratified structure that characterizes the symbol remains, since, a little further, Maspero underscores that the reality of these hexagrammatic "things" is not the same as that of ordinary things, inasmuch as they belong to an ideal (*idéel*) world, that of divination, which matches and duplicates the phenomena of the empirical world. The paradox is that the ideal (*idéel*) and the real have the same degree of reality. The hexagrams are therefore both things and symbols, signified and signifier [ibid.: 480].

tween an abstract signification and its concrete representation is no longer relevant since nothing refers to anything, nothing represents anything. Conditions making possible any symbolic activity are thus eliminated.[21]

Without denying the overall accuracy of this analysis, we must qualify it. It is true that symbols in China are never purely "representational" but must be understood in an etymological sense as a "constituent part" of the reality they invoke. Still, what we call a "symbolic" dimension is present, especially in Buddhism and ways of thinking that derive from Buddhism. The Buddhists' use of symbols to represent reality expresses the deep intuition that "things are not as they seem." Thus we find, in Chinese and Japanese Buddhism, a whole "allegorical" hermeneutic recalling that of the four meanings of biblical scripture. It is also true that the development of the nondualist Mahāyāna philosophy in China and Japan did modify slightly this perception of reality. We can thus define the theory of a "fundamental awakening" as "a way of collapsing the distance between ordinary mind and enlightened mind and, thus, abolishing the dualism that is itself the stuff of delusion."[22] However, far from being truly a cultural given, this nondualism actually remains an ideal very difficult, if at all possible, to achieve. In this sphere we often tend to take representations as the reality itself. Although these representations also constitute part of reality, and can sometimes modify it, the distance between the two is still considerable.

Ordinary people in Asia as in the West do not live constantly and consciously in the realm of the void or the absolute. Only Zhuangzi's perfect sage, who can "play around all day within the Dao," or the ideal Buddhist layman Vimalakīrti, who has fully comprehended the nonduality of the passions and awakening, can enjoy such a privilege. Far from being innocent, the "renewed simplicity" of Zen (whose desire to escape the "prevarication of meaning" and the domination of symbols was so admired by Barthes)[23] is first of all an aesthetic position and we may well wonder what strategic moves are concealed behind this "mediated immediacy."[24]

Two concepts of the real stand in opposition to each other within Chan/Zen (and thus in Keizan's thinking), reflecting the opposition between Chan orthodoxy on the one hand and popular Buddhism and local

---

[21] See Jullien 1984.

[22] See LaFleur 1983: 21.

[23] See Barthes 1989: 73.

[24] For a similar analysis, see William LaFleur, "Too Easy a Simplicity," *The Eastern Buddhist* 13, 1 (1980): 116–27; for a different viewpoint, see Gary L. Ebersole, "The Buddhist Ritual Use of Linked Poetry in Medieval Japan," *The Eastern Buddhist* (n.s.) 16, 2, (1983): 50–71.

religions on the other. The orthodox view is that the everyday world of sensory appearances and the higher, unseen world are clearly distinct from each other, even if the distance between them is less than it is in the West. The other view, which may remind us of what Hegel calls the "inverted world," holds that the world we see coincides exactly with the higher, unseen world: as the Buddhist expression goes, "*Saṃsāra is* Nirvāṇa."[25] This second view, which Chan/Zen derives from Mahāyāna, amounts to a paradoxical affirmation that the real lies completely within objective reality, transmuted by an epistemological reversal and perceived as *such*, as "thus," or Thusness. It ends up by reducing the importance of the invisible world, emptying it of all content, and at the same time by demythologizing Chan and denying the *imaginaire*—which served in popular Buddhism, as it did for Aristotle, as a middle term and mediator between the visible and the invisible. Henceforth sensory impressions are no longer a veil behind which lies the real, they do not constitute a world of illusion we must go beyond in order to reach the Pure Land of ultimate reality: they are the real itself, in its entirety. The world, stripped of these worlds beyond, does lose some depth but gains reality. As Linji puts it, "As I see it, there isn't much to do. Just be ordinary: put on your robes, eat your food, and pass the time doing nothing. You who come here from every quarter all have the idea of seeking Buddha, seeking Dharma, seeking emancipation, seeking to get out of the three realms. Foolish fellows! When you've left the three realms where would you go?"[26]

But coincidence does not entail identity: the "supplement of copula" (the "is" that connects Nirvāṇa and *saṃsāra*) unites in a paradoxical fashion the two levels of reality but also is enough to induce a tension, to introduce the "uneasiness" of duality (a nondual duality, of course) into the very heart of the real, to blow it apart. It prevents the Chan adept from relaxing fully in the plenitude of emptiness, which remains an ideal state constantly threatened from within. Keizan, like so many others, feels constrained to oscillate between these poles, divided between two irreconcilable and supplementary conceptions of the real (supplementary rather than complementary, since complementarity implies a stable whole).

Chan pushed to an extreme the Mahāyānist theory of the "two truths," which maintained a certain hierarchy between transcendence and immanence, and reinterpreted it into one of a paradoxical "transcendent immanence." Finally, perhaps under the influence of Confucianism, Chan ended up with a quasi-immanence, which renders useless any mediation between levels of reality and no longer gives "conventional truth"

[25] Regarding Hegel, see Rosset 1976: 69.
[26] See Sasaki 1975: 26.

and "skilfull means" (*upāya*) any degree of reality that could justify their usefulness. Believers in Chan subitism could have taken as their slogan Jean-Jacques Rousseau's statement, "For me there has never been any intermediary between everything and nothing."[27] But this position, by denying all traditional forms of mediation and the reality of a world beyond the senses, was doomed to remain purely theoretical.[28] It constituted no more than a denial, a powerless exorcism, in the face of a worldly reality that remained stubbornly sovereign. Although Chan practitioners were no longer able to go through to the "other side of the mirror," to transfer themselves truly into the "other scene" in an *excessus mentis* as sudden as it is understandable, they still ritually invoked the beyond on this human scene. Paradoxically this "hierophany," this capture of the sacred achieved by ritual, is at the same time an impoverishment—since it implies that beyond ritual time and space, in the unseen world, there exist more refined realities—and an enrichment, insofar as it brings into the current ritual space and time some of these realities—that of the Buddha as he manifested himself *in illo tempore* or that of other deities in their eternal, metaphysical present—which come to coincide or communicate with the real life of the officiants.

IMAGES

Insofar as the imaginary derives ultimately from images, it is appropriate to consider the status of images in Chan/Zen. As we shall see later, there was in Chan a theoretical rejection of iconism. But were traditional Chan masters blind men in the kingdom of images? Was Keizan himself only one-eyed, like Linji?[29] Chan/Zen advocates the passage through images into their beyond. In the *Denkōroku*, for example, Keizan seems to move

[27] Jean-Jacques Rousseau, *Les Confessions*, in *Oeuvres complètes*, vol. 1, Bibliothèque de la Pléiade (Paris: Gallimard, 1956), 332.

[28] The difficulty of maintaining this position is well illustrated by the Zen master Mujū Ichien (1226–1312) in the humorous anecdote of the scholar-monk who, having been cheated by a salt vendor, sought revenge the next day on a lumber dealer. When his disciples told him that he was making a mistake, he rebuked them, arguing that, although a salt vendor and a lumber dealer may differ from the viewpoint of conventional truth, from that of ultimate truth they are one and the same. Says Mujū: "Our scholar misunderstood the notion of the Undifferentiated. If he is speaking of phenomenal identity in the light of the absolute, then how can he show the identity only between salt-vendor and lumber-dealer? The monk, those who lived with him, and his retainers are all identical in this sense. . . . But if, in the light of the phenomenal truth,' we consider the phenomenal aspect of things, then the salt-vendor and the lumber-dealer are separate beings. Why should he suppress this side of it? Needless to say, his views were biased." See Morrell 1985: 157–58.

[29] See the comment of the Chan eccentric Puhua concerning Linji Yixuan: "That fellow is one-eyed!" *Jingde chuandeng lu*, T. 51, 2076: 280b.

beyond the imaginary as he devalorizes images in favor of empty space. But doesn't this void itself come from Zen's cultural imagination? Is it anything more than a symbol itself? And is not the discourse of going beyond images finally ideological?

The *imaginaire* seems able to retain only images, just as the mind needs, in its "memory palace," symbols or images that are easier to retain than what Thomas Aquinas termed "intentions." However, even if the imagination works mainly on images, these have no value except through the invisible efficacy (Ch. *ling*) that supports them and that they communicate. One secret may hide another: although an image can to a certain extent "make the invisible visible," the secret that it reveals (and betrays) in this way risks, by its very visibility, concealing something even more essential, the invisible source from which it springs. Such is the case with the mimetic and aesthetic conceptions of art historians who overlook and make others overlook—for lack of the ability to think about it—the ritual nature and the invisible part of every religious image.

A Buddhist image is not, as is a Western one, caught between *mimesis* and invention but derives from a problematic of the double, a concept also present in ancient Greece, as Jean-Pierre Vernant has shown. The image is in no way an "unreal non-being": an image of the Buddha *is* the Buddha, just as a portrait of Caesar was Caesar. We don't have, as in the Platonic mimetic conception, "Cratylus and the image of Cratylus that resembles him"; we are in the presence of an image-double.[30]

According to a fairly widespread logic, the formless (Chinese *wuxiang*, the absence of all forms, marks, or characteristics) is conceived of as the source of the forms, of empirical multiplicity. Laozi said that "the great image is without image"—which may mean that the invisible rules within the visible, or on the contrary that the image rules beyond the visible. In any case, while in traditional Buddhism the forms go back to the formless, by a return motion which is also that of the Dao, in Chan no *meta*-morphosis is possible: forms cannot theoretically lead to anything beyond themselves; they lead merely to a bogging down in illusion, an entrapment in forms and images. They must therefore be rejected completely, as the sixth patriarch Huineng did in his famous (and apocryphal) "subitist" verse: "Fundamentally there is not one thing." What good, then, is there in cultivating religious practices? This really is the meaning of radical subitism, for which all religious experience, however "sudden" it may be, is still gradual insofar as it forms part, even paradoxically, of a soteriological process. This theoretical subitism dismisses both the "practical" subitism of breaking through and gradualism—which conversely does not imply any solution of continuity. The true

---

[30] Plato, *The Sophist* 240a,b; *Cratylus* 432a.

fault line is thus not so much between subitism and gradualism as between the rejection on principle of all images and going beyond images (*per visibilia ad invisibilia*), between the fundamental absence of thought (Ch. *wunian*) and going beyond thought (*linian*). As Shenhui, the apostle of subitism, said approximately, the true mirror (viz., the fundamental spirit) is that which reflects no images. But this is in itself an image, showing clearly the aporia of sudden teaching, which is thus doomed to remain an ideal, or even an alibi. Paradoxically, the literary style of so-called classical Chan, while claiming the most radical subitism, becomes more and more image-ridden: theoretically removed from practice, the image returns in discourse. It is not limited to discourse, however: Chan/Zen monasteries, despite their apparent simplicity, have always been filled with images and symbolic objects.

THE PROBLEM OF BELIEF

As a Zen master respectful of his predecessors, Keizan has to reveal a critical spirit, even lay claim to an iconoclastic lack of belief. Nevertheless he had frequent visions that he clearly took very seriously.[31] Meditation or dreams let him move into a dimension that could almost be termed hallucinatory, where the marvelous and the strange appeared normal. The multiplication of points of passage between the human and animal realms ends up in a blurring of boundaries, a breakdown of notions of nature and culture. In this "floating world" where the boundary between human and animal, real and unreal, shifts, a fox or an ox sometimes become human, and vice versa.[32] Relics of the Buddha turn into gems or rice, a tree spirit is reborn in human form. It is a world of marvels where anything is possible: magical transformations and powers, apparitions of gods and spirits, animal and human metamorphoses. To simplify, we may distinguish two forms of the marvelous in Buddhism: the first, based on temporal Buddhist logic, consists mainly of stories of karmic retribution; the second is a supernatural based on a spatial logic, that of local cults, founded on an acute awareness of the ambivalence of the sacred, of the danger lying in sites imbued with power.

In this context Buddhism can also be interpreted as a response to fear: fear of ghosts, of death, of mysterious *kami*. It provides a set of protective

[31] On this question see the following works: de Certeau 1985: 192–202; Georges Dumézil, "Credo et Fides," in *Idées romaines* (Paris: Gallimard, 1969), 47–59; Benveniste 1969, vol. 1, 171–79; Bazin 1991: 492–511; Mannoni 1969: Boureau 1991: 512–26.

[32] On people being reborn as oxes for labor for having stolen property, see Nakamura 1973: 122, 131, 173, 203.

exorcisms, an apotropaic teaching. The Buddhist priest is protected by efficient techniques, but he always runs the danger of being captivated by them: he must believe in them to a certain extent and thus in the reality of the power of the demons that they let him conquer. In this sense we may say that the Buddhist theory of emptiness itself constitutes a form of exorcism, a protection, a denial of reality, when it comes to the dangers of the *mundus imaginalis*. Philosophy, just like relics, often serves as a magical talisman. It represents the parade of the "enlightenment" against enchantments, nocturnal ghosts, and threatening other worlds, a reassuring and more prestigious discourse no doubt, but also one working toward the same "uncanny" effects as that of the gross materialism of ordinary awareness (that is, illusion).

Buddhist universalism brought a message of uniformization and of deculturation. Well before the modern era, it humanized animals and all sentient beings—which are all so many potential or actual Buddhas. Is it not said that an inch-long worm possesses an inch-long Buddha nature? In China Buddhism became the ally of Confucianism and Daoism in their criticism of animal sacrifices and their efforts to break down local cults, but it also remained open to all the effects of acculturation.

Despite the relative flexibility of a system of karmic retribution that seems to promote a kind of ontological mobility resulting in a vast brotherhood among all living beings, the Japanese caste system managed to keep resolutely apart the *hinin*, or "nonhumans," individuals sullied by their professional status or their physical and moral degeneracy. This discrimination, which continues to a lesser degree in today's Japan, was especially marked in funeral rites, a specialty of the Sōtō school. These rites were among other things intended to protect the living against ghosts, of which some of the most dangerous are the tormented spirits of the *hinin*, pariahs with whom one must thus cut all karmic bonds.[33] This is, in a way, the perverse result of *karma*, a theory that legitimizes present human misery by explaining it as punishment for past sins. There were

[33] See Ishikawa 1983–94 (4). One *kirigami*, entitled "Kawara konpon no kirigami," explains as follows the mythical origin of the *hinin* (or *kawaramono*): Formerly, on a mountain near Tiantong shan (the Chinese cradle of Sōtō Zen), there was a small tree under which grew a nameless grass. One day, the future Arhat Subhūti climbed that tree and satisfied a sexual urge. His semen fell on the grass, and eventually a male child was born. This child was named "Kawaramono" because he grew up on the riverbank near Tiantongsi, where Chan master Rujing was serving as abbot. Having heard that he was Subhūti's offspring, Rujing authorized the young man and his wife to listen to his sermons. When the couple died without children, they were cremated and their possessions given to the monastery. Later, Subhūti took their relics to Japan, and these relics, when they fell on the ground and scattered, gave birth to the *kawaramono* (outcasts). See Ishikawa, ibid., 164–65; and 1989: 71–72. On *hinin*, see also Amino 1978: 153–63.

many *hinin* in and around Buddhist temples, where they performed most of the maintenance work.[34] We should note that Keizan, when he received the donation of the Tōkoku land, insisted on having complete freedom to make of this place what he deemed good, including a refuge for *hinin*. Keizan, after all, did have a very clear memory, if we are to believe his own testimony, of his own nonhuman past. Besides, monks like him, pioneers and ascetics, are in a sense on the frontiers of humanity (and of the rational universe implied by life in society). To convert (or be converted) to Buddhism implies shifting to another logic.

However, as a monastic community developed, the rational tended to reassert itself. Thus Keizan was sometimes skeptical, even about his own Zen tradition. For example, he refused to credit the legend about the Indian patriarch Bodhidharma crossing the Yangtze river on a reed. This did not prevent him at another time from peddling, after Dōgen, the story of the poisoning of Bodhidharma by two rivals, and even adding unattested details to it: thus we learn that the two monks who planned to assassinate Bodhidharma first shattered his teeth with stones. Buddhism, the reputedly nonviolent religion. . . .

This constant wavering between belief and critical detachment may well represent only a linguistic phenomenon, the movement from one enunciatory position to another. Or it may represent a change in epistemological level: as if awareness unrolled along a double band, in a double flow, and as if it could move from one register, one "truth program," to another.[35] We obviously risk reading too much into people's minds when we impute to them too hastily the beliefs that seem to be indicated by their actions. As Jean Bazin has emphasized, "Belief is a relationship that the subject enters into not with a fact but with a representation."[36] A state of belief does not imply necessarily a theory of the objective world; most of the time belief neither nullifies nor confirms knowledge.[37] It would be better to insist on the "pragmatic" or "perlocutionary" nature of belief: it defines a community of believers, and its content is perhaps not the most important thing about it. As Musō Soseki and other Zen masters have pointed out, the teaching of Zen is a skillfull means "comparable to the calling of the maid Xiaoyu by her mistress."[38]

---

[34] See Nishiguchi 1987: 145–53.

[35] On these two models, see Favret-Saada 1980: 291; and Veyne 1988: 21–22.

[36] Bazin 1991: 504–5.

[37] Ibid.: 507.

[38] Xiaoyu was the name of a servant whom her mistress called out to raise the screens, thereby to let her lover know that she was aware of his presence outside the house. See for instance *Muchū mondō*, quoted in Kenneth Kraft, "Musō Kokushi's *Dialogues in a Dream*," *The Eastern Buddhist* 14, 1 (1981): 91; or Ikkyū's allusions to Chan master

Thus the fact that Keizan makes constant use of Chan doctrinal and hagiographic *topoi* does not mean that he believes firmly in everything they say, nor that his belief is merely a form of "individual bad faith maintained and supported by collective bad faith,"[39] but simply that he asserts himself as part of a certain tradition. This is a sincere form of belief, but not one that necessarily makes up the basis of his worldview, a view that in the final reckoning would superficially appear to be contradicted by "superstitious" acts. Systems of thought can contradict each other, but actions, even if they derive from these systems, have a certain autonomy from them. We can even hold, as does Wittgenstein, that they do not derive from them at all. "We can only say: where that practice and these views go together, the practice does not spring from the view, but both of them are there."[40] Michel de Certeau argues that belief, unlike vision, introduces a temporal nature to the relation with the other. It must be considered then as a form of praxis (social alliance) and not only as a representation.[41] Creeds, as etymology suggests (*croyance* = "credence"), are first of all claims—on other people and on the future.[42]

In spite, or perhaps because of, his denials, Keizan is without question a believer: we may even say that he believes more than he believes. Does he not search constantly for signs of his mission (marvels such as the appearance of a fox, a serpent, dreams of an Arhat or a kami)? Is he not convinced that the world is seeking him out to address him directly? These messages are not of the same tenor as the more orthodox ones of the "preaching of the nonsentient" (*mujō seppō*) dear to Dōgen; they have their roots deep in the "*imaginaire* of the place." Keizan is always ready to believe, insofar as he is ceaselessly listening to himself and to the world, listening to the signs that an intelligent reality (which conceals itself by unveiling itself) sends to him. As Bazin says, "The Other is real insofar as it sends messages to a believing subject."[43] For such a believer,

---

Wuzu's "little love song," in Sonja Arntzen, *Ikkyū and the Crazy Cloud Anthology: A Zen Poet of Medieval Japan* (Tokyo: University of Tokyo Press, 1986), 42–43: "She often called her maid for no reason at all, / Just so her lover would recognize her voice."

[39] Pierre Bourdieu, "Genèse et structure du champ religieux," *Revue française de Sociologie* 12 (1971): 318.

[40] Wittgenstein 1979: 2e.

[41] According to Michel de Certeau, the fact that beliefs, which in Greece or Rome had the form of practices, "have been considered as *representations* capable or not of enjoying an individual or collective assent (of the type: "I believe in it" or "we do not believe in it") is, in part, an effect of historical interpretation, based on *utterances* that survive practices that have now disappeared. See Certeau 1985: 196.

[42] Cf. "Créance et croyance," in Benveniste 1969, vol. 1, 171–77.

[43] Bazin 1991: 509.

everything becomes a personal message, everything has a meaning. Unlike Madame du Deffand, who was afraid of ghosts without believing in them, Keizan was not afraid of spirits but he really seems to have believed in them.

Keizan was always ready to single out fragments of everyday life and interpret them as auspicious "signs." Thus, just after the founding of Enzūin, a nunnery adjacent to Yōkōji, one of his disciples heard mysterious voices reciting the scriptures at night, at some distance from the monastery. Keizan immediately interpreted this as a supernatural confirmation of the new institution. In the same way, when someone witnessed an ox from the village, one being used for work at Yōkōji, turning into a man, or when a fox came to die at the foot of the monks' building, Keizan reached the conclusion that the monastery—along with the mountain that formed its natural extension, both metonymically and metaphorically—were sacred places that could purify from their previous karma all those who took refuge there.

Assuming the reality of belief(s), to what extent should we take seriously, literally, the beliefs of historical actors? Does the content of belief have a value in and of itself, or does its value lie elsewhere? Often what is presented as a belief is only a matter of some kind of expressive convention, not to be accepted as absolute truth.[44] But sometimes the invitation to believe, or one's feelings that things have another side, become so compelling as to make "the reality of reality" waver. We seem then to be in a forked "logic" of the "I know, but still . . ." kind.[45] In the case of an elite dreamer like Keizan, we may also think of the title of the Pirandello play *I'm Dreaming (but Perhaps I'm Not).*[46] Among some of the most famous examples of users of such logic, or of what Jon Elster calls "higher order beliefs" or "beliefs about beliefs," we can cite at random the Quesalid of Lévi-Strauss, the Hopi and their belief in Kachina spirits, Casanova overcome by panic when a storm struck during a black mass, Madame du Deffand and her ghosts, Niels Bohr and his horseshoe that brings luck "even to those who don't believe in it."[47] According to Octave Mannoni, we are dealing here with the Freudian logic of the *Verlügnung,* a denial of

[44] Boureau 1991: 526.

[45] This form of logic has been analyzed, among others, by Octave Mannoni and Jeanne Favret-Saada. According to Favret-Saada, logical and prelogical thinking are not the characteristics of two different categories of people, but of linguistic positions that any individual can occupy at various times. See Favret-Saada 1980: 291. Paul Veyne has used a similar notion, that of alternating "programs of truth." See Veyne, 1988: 21–22.

[46] See Pirandello, 1977–85.

[47] See Niels Bohr, quoted in Elster 1983: 5, and Umberto Eco's variant, "Superstition brings good luck," in exergue of *Foucault's Pendulum* (San Diego: Harcourt, Brace, Jovanovich, 1989). See also "The Sorcerer and his Magic," in Lévi-Strauss 1963: 167–85; Mannoni 1969; Bazin 1991.

reality whose paradigm would be fetishism and which is not the same thing as a simple negation because it implies a transformation of belief.[48] Nevertheless, the Freudian "cleavage of the self" seems to rest on an essentialist conception of the human personality. I prefer the idea of a speaking and thinking subject moving through various enunciatory stances—a passage that implies only a minimum of residual memory, but still sufficient to raise a problem. We must indeed take into account the tension between the two parts of the proposition "I know, but still. . . ." Most interpreters try to rely only on the first part of the proposition, seeing the "but still . . ." as an annoying residue that must be discarded.

We should keep in mind another important point stressed by Octave Mannoni: children (noninitiates) provide a support for the belief of adults (initiates). Indeed, "beliefs are based first of all on the credulity of children. . . . The child, as an external, present figure, can play a significant role as he takes on our beliefs even after we have repudiated them."[49] The pleasure of belief (and the superior feeling we get from nonbelief) persists because it continues to exist among others (children, rustics). As in a play, "everything seems to be set up to produce belief, but in someone else, as if we were in collusion with the actors."[50] The mistake of an individualistic approach would be to think that Keizan's belief is only that of the individual, and essentially rational, being who bears the name Keizan, whereas the group of noninitiates provides a basis for a more diffuse kind of belief that gives Keizan the possibility of believing without really believing he does. Another possible approach might be to consider that Chan/Zen masters, like Lévi-Strauss's shamans, are situated outside the system and called on by the group to "represent certain forms of compromise which are not realizable on the collective plane."[51]

I have suggested that the Buddhist *imaginaire* constitutes a system. But maybe the system does not exist in the case of Keizan, maybe it is never— as with Madame du Deffand—anything but fragmentary, erratic, made up of bits and pieces of belief, of cultural debris. Still, we must distinguish between belief and superstition: if, according to Emile Benveniste's definition, superstition is everything that "survives," it cannot really be identified with belief, or even with beliefs since in the *imaginaire*, as in popular religion, "nothing survives; everything continues to live, or else it disappears."[52]

Let us at least recall Pierre Bourdieu's statement that "when one dis-

---

[48] Mannoni 1969.

[49] Ibid.: 18.

[50] Ibid.: 164.

[51] Lévi-Strauss 1987: 18.

[52] Jean-Claude Schmitt, "'Religion populaire' et culture folklorique," *Annales E.S.C.* 31, 5 (1976): 941–53; Benveniste 1969: vol. 2, 273–79.

covers the theoretical error that consists in presenting the *theoretical view* of practice as the *practical relation* to practice, and more precisely in setting up the model that has to be constructed to give an account of practice as the principle of practice, then simultaneously one sees that at the root of this error is the antinomy between the time of science and the time of action, which tends to destroy practice by imposing on it the intemporal time of science."[53] In other words, what I discover when I say that there is a system to the *imaginaire* constitutes a model by which I can then examine Keizan's practice, but this model does not lie behind Keizan's practice. Let us go a little further: this system will never be anything but virtual. It is, after all, the result of an attempt on the part of the analyst to find coherence. The observer never finds belief in its pure, native state, but only traces of it: "In the past people believed that. . . ." Whatever the case may be, in Keizan belief continues to exist—even if only in a latent state—at the level of praxis. It can be read behind body gestures, belying the skepticism and disbelief (or inverted belief) expressed in his discourse. Disbelief is coupled with belief; it is, so to speak, another face of belief.

BELIEF AND PRACTICE

Once we accept this paradoxical coexistence of opposed beliefs, we need to look at the problem of the relation, and at times the conflict, between beliefs and practices. We may, as Wittgenstein has done, see the formulation of problem itself as problematic, by considering that there is no necessary congruence, nor even any relation, between praxis and belief, and thus no need to explain the one by the other. Thus at one stroke there would no longer be any reason to wonder about the gap between theory and practice since this gap, presupposing a nonexistent relationship, is itself null and void. Reacting rightly against the "causal superstition" that leads us to assume the existence of a belief behind every act, Wittgenstein ends up by denying any symbolic meaning behind acts that can be seen as ritual:

> Burning in effigy. Kissing the picture of a loved one. This is obviously *not* based on a belief that it will have a definite effect on the object which the picture represents. It aims at some satisfaction and it achieves it. Or rather, it does not *aim* at anything; we act in this way and then feel satisfied. . . . The same savage who, apparently in order to kill his enemy, sticks his knife through a picture of him, really does build his hut of wood and cuts his arrow with skill and not in effigy.[54]

53 Bourdieu 1990: 81.
54 Wittgenstein 1979: 4e.

This way of cutting the Gordian knot has the merit of eliminating a lot of almost sterile rationalist or functionalist hypotheses and shows that traditional symbolic systems have often been elaborated after the fact, to justify an existing practice. We are reminded of Plutarch's story of the Greek priestess who, when asked for a drink by the mule drivers who had transported the sacred vessels, refused out of fear that this apparently meaningless act might get into the ritual—a ritual that exegetes would then feel obliged to justify by all kinds of theological subtleties.[55] Still, even if we reject all causal relations between beliefs and practices, this does not mean that we should not study beliefs as such. Furthermore, Wittgenstein tends to forget that autochthonous explanations, unlike those of anthropologists who fortunately have little retroactive effect, can come to make *a posteriori* changes to praxis and end up by motivating it, by making it aware of itself.

In his desire to react against the hermeneutic of "everything making sense," Wittgenstein falls back into a kind of functionalism, where the subject is denied any intent, any full understanding of his/her acts. Although it may be true that a rite does not always have a meaning, or in any case the meaning that the observer generously grants to it (not without usury), although a rite can become mechanical, it is still significant that what one burns is an effigy, or what one kisses is a portrait. The fact that the picture of the beloved may be replaced by his or her name does not change the problem fundamentally. Although there is no need to actualize consciously an entire representational system to do this, the power of the affect that accompanies these gestures nevertheless implies the existence, or even the repression, of such a system. Wittgenstein's example of the savage who knows how to distinguish between magical activities (stabbing the image of his enemy) and practical activities (building a house, making an arrow) may show, before Lévi-Strauss's critique of Lévy-Bruhl, the error of reducing the *pensée sauvage* to a prelogical way of thinking that confounds different orders of reality. But it does not explain the presence of the effigy in the first place. When he disavows the purely "magical" nature of the ritual act, Wittgenstein avoids the question of the passage from the magical to the rational rather than examining how it takes place—and this from a thinker who has written elsewhere, "We must retain the profundity of magic. Yes, the elimination of magic here looks like magic itself."[56]

At any rate Chan/Zen praxis is sufficiently formalized by text to produce two kinds of theoretical thought: doctrinal and ritual. These constitute two symbolic systems that stand in opposition to each other and that must both be considered. For this reason we must, first of all, try to

---

[55] See Plutarch, *De vitioso pudore*, 534C, quoted in Smith 1982: 53.
[56] Quoted by Jacques Bouveresse, in Wittgenstein 1982: 12.

reconstruct what these systems actually consisted of, at least so that we can understand certain of the internal constraints that drive the actions derived from them, even when they have been taken up again or reinscribed in other cultural or individual logics or pseudo-logics.

The paradoxical coexistence, most often repressed, of these two modes of reality or thought is precisely, according to Freud, what produces the sense of "the uncanny" ("das Unheimliche"), an effect that seems to be practically unknown to Keizan. Freud points out that "this disturbing strangeness has no hold over the person who has definitively wiped out his animist convictions."[57] We could argue that the same is true for anyone who, like Keizan, admits the equal reality of the two modes—for anyone who does not try, as do Freud and Wittgenstein, to go beyond them, to "liquidate" them, but rather simply accepts them.

This seems to be, finally, the aporia personified by Keizan. We cannot bypass the "twofold truth" that both he and Zen adhere to. It is, on the contrary, important to linger over it—and that is what we shall do in this study. But unlike more traditional studies, we shall take the point of view of the *imaginaire* and symbolic mediation.

THE QUESTION OF THE GENRE

In Zen discourse we see two opposing tendencies, even two mental or cultural universes. Zen theoretical discourse seems almost impervious to the discourse of local religion. This is less true, however, with Keizan than with Dōgen: even in Keizan's *Denkōroku*, the *imaginaire* looms large, but it is an Indian *imaginaire*, doubly imaginary because it is exotic. But the reality (or rather the imaginary) revealed in the *Record of Tōkoku* differs vastly from the theoretical discourse of the *Denkōroku*. In both cases we run up against the question of literary genres and themes.

In many ways, the *Record of Tōkoku* is a counterpart not only to the *Denkōroku* but also to the *Tōkoku shingi* ["Pure Rule of Tōkoku," a work better known under the title *Keizan shingi*, the "Pure Rule of Keizan"]. This work, as its first title indicates, is a presentation of the rules of behavior and the liturgy that guided the daily life of the monks at Yōkōji, while the *Denkōroku* consists of sermons that Keizan made during a summer retreat at Daijōji and later repeated at Yōkōji. Although belonging to completely different genres, the three works profit from being studied together. Up to now, however, Japanese researchers have paid attention almost exclusively to the *Denkōroku*, which is not surprising

[57] See "The Uncanny" [*Das Unheimliche*, 1912], in Sigmund Freud, *Collected Papers*, (London: Hogarth, 1924–50), vol. 4, 368–407.

since it belongs to the pure tradition of Zen "histories of the lamp" and establishes itself precisely because of its orthodoxy (just as the *Tōkoku shingi* does because of its orthopraxy).[58] The *Denkōroku* was first presented during a summer retreat, for a small group of practitioners. This is not true of the *Record of Tōkoku*, which gives a very different view of Keizan's thought, even though at certain points it recalls and is connected with the other two texts. Nevertheless, the *Record of Tōkoku* is also bound by the restraints of a genre, those of the *engi*, or "narration of origins," and cannot be considered in this respect as "more authentic" than the others.

What conclusions can we draw? On the one hand, there is a discontinuity between the various genres that Keizan uses, but there is no pure genre because every one is subverted by intertextuality. The *Record of Tōkoku* is thus "tainted" by the monastic rules and "dialogues" that make up most of the *Tōkoku shingi* and the *Denkōroku*. There are probable interpolations that have been left out in the translation, even though their presence indicates, from a textual point of view, the impossibility of treating one genre to the exclusion of others. We must never lose sight of the constant dialectic between the different points of view they express, between the *imaginaire* and ideology, syncretism (local) and the sectarian spirit (paradoxically "universalist").

The various points of view adopted by Keizan thus result in part from the literary genres that influenced his discourse and even, within a single discursive genre, from the different enunciatory stances he finds himself obliged to adopt. All at once we see that there is no "last instance" position: all pronouncements are equally sincere—or equally insincere. It is precisely in the differential discrepancy among these texts that the discursive system of Keizan can be perceived and his truth or truths be located.

[58] Other works of Keizan include the *Shinjinmei nentei* [T. 82, 2587], a typical Zen commentary on the *Xinxin ming* (a "classic" attributed to the third patriarch Sengcan), and two meditation manuals, the *Zazen yōjinki* [T. 82, 2586] and the *Sankon zazensetsu*. See *JDZ*, 243–52.

Chapter One

AUTOBIOGRAPHICAL IMAGINATION

ONE OF THE CHARACTERISTIC features of the *Record of Tōkoku* is its autobiographical element. Unfortunately this autobiographical fragment deals only with the later part of Keizan's life, the years he spent at Yōkōji and not the earlier period when he lived at Daijōji. Nevertheless it is still important in the way it documents the emergence of an individual from the matrix of Japanese feudal society—at least as important as the private diaries that have survived from the period. The way that Keizan saw himself is, however, quite unusual and reveals certain interesting—and less well-known—features of the medieval imagination. For example, he could casually announce to his disciples that he was the reincarnation of a tree spirit, a chimera-like being who lived in the Himalayas and who had been converted to Buddhism, achieving the exalted status of an Arhat:

> As for me, it was in the past, at the time of the Buddha Vipaśyin, that I realized the fruit of Arhatship. I was living on the Himalayas, to the north of Mount Sumeru. At that time I was the deity of a Kuvala tree. With the head of a dog, the body of a kite, and the belly and tail of a serpent, I was a four-footed animal. Although I was only a humble tree deity, I nonetheless received the fruit [of Arhatship]. From that time on, I lived on the Himalayas, in the northern continent of Uttarakuru, with Suvinda, the fourth Arhat. This is why I am now reincarnated here [in the north of Japan]. Owing to my karmic affinities with the [northern] regions, I managed to be reborn as an *ujiko* of Hakusan. . . . Since achieving the fruit of Arhatship, I have been reincarnated through five hundred existences in order to spread the Dharma and bring profit to all beings. [*JDZ*, 395]

However, unlike the protagonist of a famous Chan dialogue—a monk who had to be reborn five hundred times as a fox in order to pay off a karmic debt and was finally delivered by the words of the master Baizhang Huaihai—the future Keizan had achieved awakening before his long series of reincarnations. The number five hundred is highly symbolic. It is associated most often with the five hundred Arhats, and it is precisely with one of these great disciples of the Buddha, the Arhat Suvinda, that Keizan tells us that he spent his time. After this brief mention of his previous existences, which reminds us of the style of the *Jātaka*, tales of the former lives of the Buddha Śākyamuni, Keizan gives a brief chronological account of his monastic career and spiritual journey:

At eight years old I received the tonsure and went to live in the community of the master Gikai, who was then the abbot of Eiheiji. At thirteen I became a monk under the Reverend Ejō, the former abbot [of Eiheiji] and the successor to Eihei [Dōgen]. At eighteen I made a firm resolve to seek awakening. At nineteen I went to consult Jakuen, the guardian of [Dōgen's] stūpa. Having already produced the thought of awakening, I reached the level of non-backsliding. At twenty-two I obtained awakening as I heard a sound. At twenty-five, emulating Kannon, I produced the universal wish of the great Icchantika. At twenty-eight I became the superior of Jōmanji in Umibe, in Awa province. At twenty-nine, I received the ritual of ordination from Master Gien of Eiheiji, and during the winter of the same year I began to administer the Precepts. I ordained at first five people. At thirty-one I had already ordained more than seventy people. At thirty-two I went to consult the Reverend Gikai, founder of Daijōji in Kaga province, and I inherited his Dharma. I became his main disciple, and I was the first vice-abbot (hanza) of Daijōji.[1] I had the right to private meals, and I received a propitious name for my quarters. I was assured that I had the stuff to be an eminent master. At thirty-three I was named rissō nisshitsu.[2] At thirty-five I ascended alone the preaching chair of Daijō[ji] and I was named second-generation abbot. At the end of fifteen years of preaching, I came to settle on this mountain [Tōkokuzan] in order to found a monastery here. [JDZ, 395–96]

As we can see, taking the tonsure at the age of eight, Keizan first served Gikai (1219–1309) at Eiheiji. He was then ordained as a novice when he was thirteen, receiving complete ordination at eighteen. Once he was a monk, he left the service of Ejō (1198–1280) and went to Jakuen (Ch. Jiyuan, 1207–1299), one of Dōgen's Chinese disciples, from whom he received a first inkling of the truth, followed three years later by a more profound awakening. At twenty-eight he became the superior at Jōmanji in Kaifu and the following year he received from Gien (d. 1314), then the superior at Eiheiji, his own authorization to ordain. He immediately made use of this power, ordaining more than seventy monks over the next two years. At thirty-two he went back to Gikai, who had left Eiheiji to found a new community farther north, Daijōji in Kaga. He became Gikai's main disciple, the inheritor of his Dharma, and three years later succeeded him as abbot of Daijōji. After staying fifteen years in this monastery, he left to take possession of a parcel of land at Tōkoku and founded his own monastery, Yōkōji.

[1] The term hanza, deriving from the story according to which Śākyamuni shared his seat with Kāśyapa, came to designate in Zen the shuso ("chief seat") who is authorized to preach instead of the master. See Azuma 1974: 105.

[2] The meaning of these two functions (rissō and nisshitsu) is not entirely clear, but they designated monks who stood out among the main disciples of a Zen master and were authorized to "enter his cell" (nisshitsu). See ibid.: 106–7.

Keizan goes on by telling the initiatory dream during which he achieved awakening.

> Bodhidharma appeared in my dream and bathed me in pure water that sprang from the stones under his seat, in a pure, cold lake. As I was naked, he gave me a monk's robe and I then produced the thought [of awakening].
>
> Maitreya appeared in my dream and gave me a blue lotus seat. I was reborn three times, and then I was carried through space. The deva, playing music, escorted me before Maitreya. He led me into the Inner Court of Tuṣita. Then I achieved the status of non-backsliding.
>
> Śākyamuni appeared in my dream, revealing himself in his body from the time of the preaching of the *Ratnakūṭa-sūtra*. He expounded the doctrine of the Three Deliverances—deliverance from time, mind, and phenomena—during a period of fifty-eight years [*JDZ*, 396].

The three mythic characters who initiated him—Bodhidharma, Maitreya, and Śākyamuni—helped him, respectively, to produce the thought of awakening, to reach the state of nonreturn, and finally to fulfill the doctrine of the triple deliverance, the crowning of the career of a Bodhisattva. These three stages had already been mentioned in more or less the same terms in the chronological section preceding the account of the dream. Keizan apparently went through them during his eighteenth, nineteenth, and twenty-second years. Thus it is possible that what is presented here as a single dream in three phases actually constitutes the memory of three separate dreams, coming some years apart. The autobiography in the strict sense of the term ends there. Autobiographical details show up elsewhere in the work, however, and when he is giving various details about Yōkōji, Keizan supplies some of the most meaningful information about himself, his way of thinking, and his dreams.

Keizan's "autobiography" fits the standard pattern of the genre and we should not be too quick to accept the biographical data supplied in it. In spite of their apparent sincerity, Buddhist autobiographies often constitute no more than subjective projections of the life of the Buddha himself. Behind the apparently objective framework of facts, the imagination plays a great part. The "imitation" of the paradigm provided by the life of the crown prince Śākyamuni is a fundamental element of monastic life. It may take various forms, depending on whether the practitioner holds to an intransigent subitist position or one of various forms of gradualism. From the subitist point of view, the only "biographical" motifs that stand out are the Buddha's awakening and final entry into Nirvāṇa. So the "lives" of the Chan masters, at least as they show up in hagiographic literature, are essentially reduced to these two important occasions. The meager biographical information provided is there only insofar as it is needed to back up this imperative of spiritual transcendence. From traditional Buddhism's gradualist point of view, to which Keizan remains clearly indebted despite his theoretical subitism, the life of the Buddha forms a whole, in which each significant event, even if still building toward the pinnacle of awakening, is in itself a sign of transcendence— following the logic of *pars pro toto*. The main actions of Śākyamuni become paradigms from a mythico-ritual repertoire. Thus the flight of the young prince from his father's palace, a dramatic rejection of the bonds of blood, is replayed mentally by each postulant on the occasion of his own "leaving the family" (J. *shukke*), a term that designates monastic ordination. This ordination then comes to be considered as a real initiation, an entry by adoption into the "lineage of the Buddha," a saving affiliation into the Chan patriarchal lineage. Equally important is the practice of asceticism: we know that the Buddha practiced the most extreme mortifications of the flesh for a period of six years before achieving the "Middle Path," midway between rigorous asceticism and hedonism. Despite this rejection of extreme asceticism, the image of an emaciated Śākyamuni, reduced almost to the condition of a living corpse, would continue to haunt the Buddhist imagination and would come to justify monastic poverty, and even more extreme forms of "rejecting the self." Here is Keizan's description of this ascesis in his *Denkōroku*: "One night when he was nineteen years old, Śākyamuni left his palace and shaved off his hair. After this he spent six years practicing ascesis. He sat on an indestructible seat, so still that he had spider webs on his eyelashes, a bird's nest on his head, and grass grew through his meditation mat. He remained seated like this for six years."[3]

Another critical moment in the life of the Buddha, this time after the Awakening, was that of the transmission of the Dharma from master to disciple, an essential concept for a school like Chan which, by rejecting canonical tradition, had deprived itself of traditional criteria for orthodoxy. This transmission was achieved by Śākyamuni's holding up of a flower in front of his disciples, a gesture understood only by Kāśyapa (better known as Mahākāśyapa, "Kāśyapa the Great"). Keizan had this model in mind each time he designated a successor.

As a result of the growing ritualization of monastic life after Dōgen, however, it was the entire life of the Buddha that became the ritual paradigm and engaged the imagination of the monks. Speaking of the donation of the land for the future Yōkōji, Keizan writes, "King Bimbisāra once offered the Bamboo Grove park to the Buddha. In the same way, when one enters this place with a pure faith, one sees one's desires lessen and one's good karma increase" [*JDZ*, 394]. The pious lay donor is thus promoted to the dignity of a king, and Keizan to that of the Buddha.

---

[3] See *Denkōroku*, T. 82, 2585: 344b.

We can also see in the description Keizan gives of his first years at Tōkoku all the tropes of monastic poverty: "To welcome visitors I used pine needles in water instead of tea, and I used cedar leaves to put in the recipients" [*JDZ*, 398]. But how far was this ideal of poverty and renunciation actually put into practice? From reading the *Record of Tōkoku* alone, it is difficult to make any clearcut decisions. Although we cannot doubt Keizan's reforming zeal and sincerity, the close relations that he maintained with his benefactors lead us to think that he must have had to make some compromises.

Whatever the case, this imaginary projection into a mythical time was not purely individual. It did not involve simply the reproduction for oneself of the awakening and life of the Buddha, identifying oneself with him individually; within the communal utopia the primordial Buddhist community also had to be recreated. The Buddha had to be brought back to life not just by himself but in close symbiosis with the community of his disciples, the Buddhist *saṃgha*. As a result the career of the Buddha was followed as if it consisted of two stages: first a time of individuation, and then that of collectivization. This communal ideal is present from the very first pages of the *Record of Tōkoku*

WOMEN IN KEIZAN'S LIFE

Keizan's biography is not entirely spiritual. His life is portrayed within a very real framework of relationships and power structures. If the imagination of the Chan tradition and of the cult of relics connects Keizan with a masculine universe, the iconic and mythological imagination of Buddhism (dominated by the Bodhisattva Kannon) seems to connect him to a feminine universe. Is Keizan not at the same time the spiritual son of Gikai, the birth son of Ekan (and, symbolically, of Kannon), and the child (*ujiko*) of the tutelary god of the Hakusan (itself a manifestation of Kannon)?

When we read the *Record of Tōkoku*, we are struck by the large part played by women in the life of Keizan. Yet this "woman's man" had nothing but sublimated relationships with the opposite sex. Although he "left the family" at an early age, in one sense he never left it at all. He saw in his disciple Sonin, a lay benefactor turned nun, a reincarnation of his grandmother Myōchi, one of the first female disciples of Dōgen: "Now this lady Taira *no uji* is none other than the reincarnation of Myōchi, a lay disciple of the Master Dōgen during the time when he lived at Kenninji."[4]

[4] *JDZ*, 394. According to the *Nihon Tōjō rentōroku*, Keizan had this realization when

Keizan's mother Ekan lavished advice on him, along with her prayers, during most of his monastic career. Although the father is generally absent, the mother occupies a central place in the biographies of many Buddhist monks, and Keizan's autobiography proves to be no exception. He tells us how he managed to overcome many karmic obstacles by means of prayers addressed by his mother to Kannon (another female figure, at least in China and Japan), and how he received through her his faith in this Bodhisattva.

Moreover, when she was thirty-seven, my merciful mother dreamed that she was swallowing the warmth of the morning light, and when she woke up she found she was pregnant.[5] She then addressed the following prayer to the Venerated [Kannon]: "Let the child I am carrying become a holy man, or a spiritual guide. If he is to become a benefit to men and *deva*, give me an easy delivery. If not, O Kannon, use your great divine power to make the insides of my womb rot and wither away." With this prayer on her lips, for seven months she prostrated herself 1333 times each day, and recited the *Kannon Sūtra*.[6] At the end of this time, she had a natural, painless childbirth. Thus I was born in a property belonging to the Kannon Temple of Tane, in Echizen Province. Later, all the events that marked my life were determined by maternal prayers to the Venerated [Kannon]. I was able to reach adulthood without any problems, leave my family and study letters, cultivate the Way and produce wisdom, and finally inherit the Dharma and become an abbot, and come to the aid of men and *deva*—all this due to the prayers [that my mother addressed] to Kannon. Furthermore, during my youth I was especially irritable and bitter, and everything seemed useless. This is why my merciful mother addressed the Venerated [Kannon] again and said, "If his anger continues to grow like this, this monk will not be of any use to men or *deva*, no matter how great his abilities, intelligence, and wisdom. I beg you, in accord with your vow of great compassion, to give him the power to calm his anger." At that very moment, the winter of my eighteenth year, I produced the thought of awakening. During the autumn of my nineteenth year, I became determined to seek the way. Once I was named as superintendent, I

Sonin came to ask for ordination. The night before, he had dreamed that Dōgen, when he was at Kenninji, had ordained his grandmother, the *upāsikā* Myōchi. He then told Sonin that she must be Myōchi's reincarnation and ordained her. See *DNBZ* 110: 234a.

[5] This is a topos of Buddhist hagiography, beginning with the legend of the Buddha. In the Sōtō tradition, the mother of Gasan Jōseki, Keizan's disciple, prayed to the Boshisattva Monju (Mañjuśrī) to obtain a "child of wisdom" and became pregnant after dreaming that she had swallowed a "sharp sword." The mother of his disciple Gennō Shinshō was also granted a handsome boy in response to her prayers to Kannon. See *Nihon Tōjō shosoden*, in *DNBZ* 110: 13b, 17b.

[6] Other sources give the variants "nine months," "3,333 times" and "333 times." The latter seem symbolically more appropriate (thirty-three, or a multiple of it, is the traditional number of Kannon's manifestations). See *DNBZ* 110: 11a.

excelled at monastery administration. Everyone was pleased with me. But it was at that time that someone maligned me. My anger started to grow, and I was on the verge of committing a great sin. Then, in a sudden spurt of repentance, I reflected as follows: "Since my earliest years I have been set apart from the common herd. Now, having produced the thought [of awakening], I have achieved this position. My greatest desire is to become the roofbeam of Buddhist Law in order to convert and guide men and *deva*. This is my great wish. If I commit a sin, this body will surely become good for nothing. Thus, I shall never again become angry. Once I have become naturally mellowed and harmonized by compassion, I shall become a great spiritual guide." All this I owe to the fervor of my merciful mother's prayers. [*JDZ*, 405–406]

In memory of his mother, Keizan founded Enzūin, a convent dedicated to Kannon and the salvation of all women.[7] Ekan preceded Keizan on the Buddhist path, and she had even, during the lifetime of Gikai, become the abbess of a convent of Sōtō nuns. Although she was very much absorbed in her son's destiny, he had been taken from her very early on and was raised by his grandmother until he was eight years old. This experience may have given rise to his ambivalent attitude toward his mother. There is a clear cleavage between the ideal of autonomy regarding to the mother, which Keizan derived from role models like Dongshan Liangjie and Huangbo Xiyun, and the psychological or emotional reality.[8] In one sense, although he was early on severed from maternal care, Keizan long remained mentally dependent on his mother.[9]

Ekan always monitored very closely the spiritual and monastic career of her son, whose destiny she believed exceptional. As we just noted, according to Keizan's own testimony, it was his mother's prayers and the admonitions she lavished on him until the very hour of her death that helped him, from the time of his first achievements, to overcome his tendencies toward arrogance and to turn away the jealousy of others. When he in turn reached the twilight of his life, Keizan testified to the eternal gratitude he bore for her transforming influence. In one of two "adamantine vows" made at the end of his life, he said:

The second vow is to respect the final words of my merciful mother, the elder sister Ekan. She was a Boddhisattva who worked for the well-being of women, and I would not dare disappoint her. I must dedicate myself to her last wishes and respect them. May all the Buddhas of the three periods, the patriarch-masters of all generations, as well as [the Buddhas of] the *Shuryōgon-kyō*

---

[7] Similar foundation for the Kamakura period include Myōe's Zenmyōji, near Kōzanji at Takao, and Tōkeiji in Kamakura. See Brock 1990; Kaneko and Morrel 1983.

[8] On this question, see Faure 1994: 142–43.

[9] See "Jōkin hotsuganmon," in *Sōtōshū komonjo*, vol. 1, 125–26.

[*Shouleng'yan jing*] and all the other sūtras, help me to preserve the spirit of my two adamantine vows. [*JDZ* 432–33]

Although Keizan's relations with his mother are full of filial piety, we can see how they are affected by the "double bind" of familial ideology versus the monastic ideal. The theme of the abandoned mother haunts Buddhist literature. Accusations of a lack of filial piety have been leveled against Chinese Buddhists for centuries. Not only did the monks abandon their parents but, by refusing to provide grandchildren for them, they cut the chain of ancestral rites. Already in Indian Vinaya we have the case of a mother begging her son to return home or at least to produce one child with the wife he so shamelessly abandoned in order to take Buddhist orders. The Buddhists thought they could counter Confucianist criticisms by claiming that "leaving the family," or ordination, was more efficacious and ecumenical than their detractors' filial piety since it ensured the salvation of nine generations of ancestors. Besides, didn't the Buddha himself watch over the salvation of his parents, especially when he went up into the Trāyastriṃṣa Heaven (Heaven of the Thirty-three Gods) in order to preach the Dharma to his mother Māya? Another famous case of Buddhist filial piety is that of his disciple Maudgalyāyana (Ch. Mulian, J. Mokuren), who did not hesitate to go down into hell to save his mother. We know that the legend of Mulian lies behind the festival of "universal deliverance" (Ch. *pudu*) of the souls of the dead, which contributed to the successful transplanting of Buddhism into Chinese and Japanese society.[10] Unlike the Confucianist ancestor cult, centered on the paternal line, Buddhism seems to pay most attention to female ancestors. But this seems to have been an afterthought rather than a radical change, because the Chan "ancestor cult" remains patriarchal.

Salvation of one's mother remained just a pious wish in many cases. Often maternal love was actually sacrificed by the son on the altar of awakening. In a society as centered on the family as is the Chinese society, that did not happen without some intense feelings of sorrow and guilt. The hesitations of a young monk are well expressed in a tearful song, "Farewell, Mother," the text of which was found at Dunhuang.[11] In Chan/Zen literature in particular, the tragic fate of the mother seems above all to strengthen the steadfast virtue of the son. Linji Yixuan's call for spiritual murder—"If you meet your parents, kill them!"—had a strong impact, at least in Chan/Zen hagiography. Monks rarely seem to be concerned about their fathers, but they have a hard time "killing their mothers." This "murder" is often represented in Chan stories. Thus the

---

[10] On this question see Teiser 1990.
[11] See Demiéville 1973c.

blind mother of Huangbo Xiyun drowns herself in a river as she tries to follow her son, whom she recognized when he was making a begging tour through his native village.[12] Huineng (d. 713) also abandoned his aged mother, whose sole support he was, to go and study with the fifth patriarch, Hongren.[13] Outside Chan/Zen hagiography, a particularly eloquent example of maternal grief is found in the poetic journal left by the mother of Jōjin when her son left in 1072 for China, where he died nine years later. An interesting detail is that she compares this abandonment to that of the *father* of Śākyamuni when his son "left the family"; after all, the mother of the future Buddha had died shortly after his birth and never had time to become attached to him.[14]

In the *Denkōroku* Keizan tells in great detail the searing tale of Dongshan Liangjie's mother. Separated from her son, the mother was reduced to begging. When she finally traced him, she went to visit him but he refused to see her. She died of grief on his doorstep. Dongshan picked up the rice she had with her and mixed it into the breakfast gruel of the community as a funerary offering. Shortly afterward, his mother appeared to him in a dream, thanking him for having given such proof of his steadfastness because thanks to that she had been able to put an end to her illusory attachment and be reborn in heaven. Keizan comments: "Although all masters and patriarchs excel in virtue, Dongshan, the founder of our school, contributed especially to promote its style. This is due to the power he achieved by forsaking his parents and keeping his purpose."[15] Likewise, in the *Shōbōgenzō Zuimonki*, Dōgen advises one disciple, in a rather hypocritical fashion, to abandon his old mother: "The point is: How can you waste an opportunity for eternal bliss by clinging to this temporary, fleeting body? Consider this thoroughly on your own."[16] In the *Denkōroku* Keizan also tells a significant story concerning Ejō and Dōgen. When Ejō's mother was dying, she asked her son to stay at her side. Since Ejō had already taken all the leaves of absence he was entitled to, he had no other alternative than to break the rule to fulfill his filial duties. Although he had made up his mind, he decided to ask the advice of his fellow monks. They unanimously told him to leave immediately. However, after consulting Dōgen, he decided not to listen to them. True filial piety in this case meant not leaving: obeying the rule of the Buddha is more important than yielding to human feelings. Keizan,

---

[12] See Fujii 1977: 3.

[13] Hongren himself had, according to legend, abandoned his mother at seven. See *Denkōroku*, T. 82, 2585: 380c.

[14] See Frank 1989: 480–81; Takagi 1988: 257–69.

[15] See T. 82, 2585: 388b–c; and *JDZ*, 733.

[16] See *Shōbōgenzō zuimonki*, 4–14; DZZ 2: 466–67.

who obviously agrees, continues with a revealing description of the care with which Ejō attended Dōgen during the latter's illness—a typical case of transference from the mother to the master.[17]

We known that Keizan tried to emulate Dongshan Liangjie in every way, and it appears that he made use of Dongshan's dream to justify his own ambivalent attitude toward his mother. In fact he never actually managed to achieve an ideal detachment: even though he had "left the family," the monk Keizan remained closely attached to his mother and grandmother. After all, he dedicated Enzūin to his grandmother, Myōchi, and the main image worshiped in this temple was the statue of Kannon that his mother had commissioned and that she worshiped all her life. We shall come back to the influence of Kannon on Keizan. Here let us simply note that we may see in this Bodhisattva, who had become a compassionate female figure in China, the sublimated double of all women and mothers, just as the Arhat is in a sense the double of all monks (and Śākyamuni, paradigm of the Chan master, the double of all fathers).

Unlike the other mothers mentioned above, Keizan's mother was also his spiritual guide. The relations between Keizan and Ekan remind us of those between Augustine and his mother Monica: it was thanks to her and her devotion to Kannon that he left the family and managed to correct his youthful faults. Like Dōgen (and many others), Keizan had the feeling that he was destined for greatness, but especially as the *mōshigo* of Kannon, a child whose destiny was fixed by the dreams and other karmic ties established by his mother. The analogy of the auspicious dream of the pregnant mother, a hagiographic *topos*, recalls the birth of the Buddha, but while the infant Śākyamuni was deprived of motherly love by the premature death of Māya, Keizan's mother, although assuming clerical functions, still behaves like a true Japanese mother, preoccupied with the proper education for her son, a future great man.[18] Born thanks to the compassion of Kannon, and in a domain belonging to a Kannon temple, Keizan had probably been dedicated to this Bodhisattva by his grateful mother. When Ekan died at age eighty-seven, she left him the statue of Kannon that was her most prized possession: another spiritual transmission—a matrilineal one at that. Keizan's identity as the "imaginary" child of Kannon is shown during the inauguration of Enzūin when he enclosed in the base of the statue of Kannon the hair taken from his head when he was born and his umbilical cord, carefully preserved by his mother. We have here a case of preposthumous relics, giving

[17] See *Denkōroku*, T. 82, 2585: 409c–410a.

[18] Japanese Buddhist hagiography contains many stories of eminent monks whose birth was due to Kannon's compassion. Such is, for instance, the case of Jōkei (Gedatsu Shōnin, 1155–1213).

life to the statue of Kannon and strengthened by the power of the latter. But we may also see in this act a kind of sublimated (but somewhat incestuous) impregnation of Keizan's mother, a symbolic reenactment of Keizan's virgin birth from his mother Ekan/ Kannon.

The Ideal Woman

Another woman plays a prominent role in Keizan's career. Even a very superficial reading of the *Record of Tōkoku* reveals the omnipresence of the nun Mokufu Sonin.[19] Of course a text dedicated to the origins of Yōkōji may be expected to include many references to one of the two donors who made possible the building of the monastery. But obviously Sonin held a very special place in Keizan's mind, one not justified entirely by her role as a generous benefactor. Keizan even went so far as to consider her a reincarnation of his grandmother, who was apparently a disciple of Dōgen. Talking of his relations with Sonin, Keizan, perhaps without realizing how daring the metaphor was, states, "We are as close as the magnet and iron—as master and benefactor, and as master and disciple" [*JDZ*: 395].

Who was this Sonin? Keizan reveals almost nothing about her except that she was the wife of Shigeno Nobunao, lord of Shinshū, and the daughter of Yorichika, steward (*jitō*) of the domain of Nakagawa.[20] Yorichika's wife, Sonin's mother, also became a nun under Keizan, taking the religious name of Shōzen. Following the marital politics of the time, Sonin was married by her family to Nobunao when she had just entered puberty. She became a woman at the age of thirteen—just the age when Keizan became a novice. Their two fates were very different, but they shared the experience of an early break from their family circle. In 1312 it was at the suggestion of his wife that Shigeno Nobunao issued an invitation to Keizan and gave him part of his landholdings. Here is how Keizan, at the beginning of the *Record of Tōkoku*, reports this event—to which he will refer several times:

> "During the springtime of the first Shōwa year [1312], *mizunoe ne*, they both produced the thought of awakening and made me a gift of this mountain. In their statement they said: "By giving this mountain, our only hope is that the Reverend will settle there for the rest of his life. He may do with it as he sees fit; it matters not whether he observes or transgresses the Precepts, or even if he gives it over to outcasts or beggars. Once we have given this mountain to the

---

[19] The Yōkōji library still possesses a scroll showing the two nuns Ekan and Sonin, as abbesses of Enzūin, seated side by side under an icon of Kannon.

[20] Sonin's biography, in *Nihon Tōjō rentōroku*, has very little to add to the *Tōkoku ki*. See *DNBZ* 110: 66a–b.

Reverend, we do not wish to retain any rights over it. We make this gift in perpetuity, in a spirit of renunciation, and not with any hope of profit." [*JDZ*, 392]

But Keizan did not come to live at Tōkoku until 1317, perhaps because of financial difficulties that prevented Sonin and her husband from making the donations needed for his upkeep. Perhaps Shigeno Nobunao did not hold a sufficiently important position. It is apparently the death of his benefactress's elder brother that allowed her to keep her promise:

In the first Bunpō year [1317], *hinoto no mi*, at the death of the *jitō* of Nakagawa Sakawa [Sakō] no Heihachi Yorimoto, older brother of the lady Taira *no uji*, he left her the home of their father Yorichika to be converted into a hermitage in memory of both Yorichika and himself. In the eighth month, in the autumn of the same year, I took up residence there in order to build a cell. On the second day of the tenth month disciples moved in and we carried out a formal inauguration ceremony [*JDZ*, 393]

In passages referring to events prior to Sonin's ordination in 1319, Keizan does not give the personal, lay name of his benefactress, designating her simply as "Taira no uji" or "Shigeno no uji." This should not surprise us, since women at that period were simply identified by the name of their clan and not by personal names; it was only at the time of ordination—either while they were still alive or at their funeral services—that they obtained a personal religious name.

We may note in passing the large number of widows who at that period became nuns and so succeeded in achieving a certain degree of power.[21] On the death of her husband, a wife could actually inherit a part of his property of which she had the usufruct during her lifetime but which she was obliged to leave to a son designated by her husband. She might also inherit another part that she could dispose of as she wished. She could also hold the status of executor of her husband's will. In addi-

---

[21] On this question see Mass 1989. Mass translates the deeds by which Taira *no uji* bestowed land to Keizan. See Document 131, dated "2nd year of Bunpō [1318], 10th month, 15th day," and bearing the "Taira no ujime seal" [Ibid.: 265]:

Commended: mountain fields and upland within Sakai *ho*, Noto Province. Boundaries appear in the deed of alienation (*hōken*) of Toshitada and Noritane. Taira *no uji*, the daughter of Sakawa Hachirō Yorichika, petitioned for and was granted edicts of confirmation over the said mountain fields and paddy upland, in accordance with the deeds of alienation by Sakai Jurō saemon Toshitada and by Sakai Yuzō Noritane. She possesses [these holdings] as private lands [*shiryō*]. Nevertheless, in order to promote the wisdom of Buddha [*mujō-bodai*], Taira no uji bestows them in perpetuity to the priest (*oshō*] Jōkin, along with the two edicts of confirmation, the two alienation deeds, and copies of the original holder's sequence of documents. Let our descendants create no disturbance. For the future, this instrument of commendation is thus.

tion to the spiritual motivations that pushed Sonin into holy orders, certain strictly material factors may also have played a part. If a widow remarried, she had to hand over all she had inherited to the children of her new husband. Expecting the early death of an aging husband, Sonin was perhaps better off putting herself under the care of a Buddhist institution, represented in this case by a young and charismatic priest, Keizan. At the end of the Kamakura period, women are not usually mentioned in wills. Although more and more of them left their worldly goods to temples, these gifts were not always officially registered as in the present case. Such transfers were made by means of a special type of document, the *okibumi*, which Keizan also used a great deal.

As we may expect, Keizan leaves out any information about Sonin that is not strictly connected to his monastery. We can only conjecture about Sonin's life. But Keizan does insist on the spiritual progress made by Sonin, "whose pure acts every day increase in number, while her thought of awakening is steadily refining itself and ripening. Having received the Buddhist Precepts and become aware of the spiritual essence, she has cut through and rejected all passions and thoughts of desire, and she is intent on the pure practice of those who have 'left the family.'" Toward the end of the year 1321, Keizan makes reference to a "dialogue" in the course of which Sonin pronounced her "first extraordinary words," preliminary signs of awakening: "The same day I asked Sonin, 'The year is coming to an end, the springtime is arriving. There is an order in this. What is it?' [Sonin replied,] 'On the branches of a shadeless tree, how could there be any seasonal knots?' These were her first extraordinary words. I noted them down for future generations."[22]

In 1322, when Keizan built a nunnery on Yōkōji land, it was Sonin who was charged with running it. This convent fulfilled several functions: it was a place of prayer for the soul of Keizan's grandmother and, in accordance with the wishes of Ekan, a place of prayer for the salvation of women at the same time as for the success of Keizan's conversion work. In 1325, just before his death, Keizan named Sonin the mother superior of Hōōji, in Kaga province. She survived him by some years and died when she was over eighty. Her tombstone was recently found, along with several others, near Yōkōji.

Given the documentation now at our disposal, it would be premature to talk of a sublimated love between Keizan and Sonin, but it is certain

---

[22] Here the *Nihon Tōjō rentōroku* is a little more detailed. We learn that Sonin, having been asked by Keizan about her understanding of "temporal conditions" (*jisetsu innen*), was at first unable to answer. Afterward she eventually had an insight and went to see Keizan in his cell. This is when the above exchange supposedly took place. After Sonin's reply, Keizan asked, "At such time, what about it?" upon which Sonin bowed. Keizan then transmitted his Dharma-robe to her. See *DNBZ* 110: 234a-b.

that this woman played a crucial role in his thinking and his career. It was no doubt due in part to her presence that Keizan put into practice the theory of equality between men and women about which various Chan/Zen masters like Dahui Zonggao (1089–1163) and Dōgen had already preached, but without any great effort at practicing it. The importance for Keizan of the themes of the mother, the soul sister, and the intercession of Kannon cannot but recall other cases like those of Myōe and Shinran.[23] We may also think of Ikkyū Sōjun, whose story of love late in life for a blind singer is widely talked of in Buddhist chronicles.[24] We may draw some conclusions about Keizan on the basis of the indications in the biographies of these monks.

THE RHETORIC OF EQUALITY

Chan/Zen texts offer many passages insisting on equality between men and women, especially in matters concerned with the ultimate goal, awakening.[25] This was at a time when the position of women in society was, as we have just seen, completely subordinate. Such protestations of equality should not be taken too literally, however, and they rarely translated into practice. In this matter reference is often made to the statements of principle by Dahui and Dōgen. Speaking of one of his female lay students, Dahui stated: "Can one say that she is a woman and that women have no share in the awakening? Know that [awakening] has nothing to do with being male or female, old or young. Ours is an egalitarian Dharma-gate that has only one flavor."[26]

Buddhism seems to have attracted women who were trying to avoid their otherwise inevitable fate as mothers and wives. Although Chan/Zen, unlike other religious movements such as Daoism, did not assert the value of femininity, it seems from its beginnings to have attracted a fairly large number of noble women. Chan egalitarianism may therefore derive more from its need for aristocratic support than from theoretical premises. The sudden increase in references to women in Dahui's sermons may be explained in part by the fact that these were addressed to nuns or influential laywomen. Dahui named five nuns and one laywoman among

---

[23] Several scholars have described Myōe's idealization of the mother figure in his worship of the female deity Butsugen butsumo, the "mother of all Buddhas." See for instance Tanabe 1992: 55–57. As to Shinran, there is the well-known dream in which Kannon appeared to him at Rokkakudō to tell him that she would become his lifelong companion and sexual object. Incidentally, the motif of Kannon leading men to salvation through carnal love was already widespread in China. See Stein 1986.

[24] See James Sanford, *Zen-Man Ikkyū* (Chico, CA: Scholars Press, 1981).

[25] On this rhetoric of equality, see Levering 1982 and Faure 1994: 130–37.

[26] *Dahui pushuo*, in ZZ 1, 31, 5: 455a; quoted in Levering 1982: 20.

his fifty-four successors, but none of them appears in the official lineage of his school.

At the beginning of his preaching career, Dōgen also stressed sexual equality. In the *Shōbōgenzō* he states: "What demerit is there in the fact of being a woman? What merit in being a man? There are bad men and good women. If you want to hear the Dharma and put an end to suffering and confusion, abandon ideas like male and female. As long as illusions have not been eliminated, neither men nor women are free from them. When they are eliminated and reality is perceived, there is no longer any distinction between male and female."[27]

We may suspect that this equality discourse reflects a typically masculine point of view. However that may be, as initial proselytism was succeeded by administrative preoccupations regarding his monastery, equality of the sexes, along with equality of monks and laymen, disappeared from Dōgen's discourse. He apparently had some female disciples, and it may have been that he put together some of his sermons for them. But like his ideal Śākyamuni—as it is presented to us in the Vinaya tradition—Dōgen remained, if not fundamentally misogynist, at least very aware of the dangers that a feminine presence could bring to his community.

Keizan inherits the Mahāyāna discourse about nonduality.[28] However, he seems to have been more ready to take a few risks in order to bring to pass this equality of the sexes, in particular when he founded the nunnery at Tōkoku.[29] Women were not excluded from his "mountain," as was the case in many other mountain temples.[30] But the nuns remained on the margins of the masculine monastic community of Yōkōji. Despite her importance in his life, and her awakening, to which he duly testified, Sonin does not figure among the successors named by Keizan. Only one late source, the *Nihon Tōjō rentōroku*, attests that Sonin really had received the robe of the Dharma (thus the succession) from Keizan. We see a significant gap between the hagiography of the Sōtō tradition and certain of Keizan's *okibumi*, whose purpose is to establish a pairing, to make official the marriage of two "lineages," to organize the coordination of two social units, two "houses," even if it is not intended, as in the Western medieval society, to set up a unit of comparable form.[31]

Sōtō hagiography has not given much attention to Sonin, despite the

27 *Shōbōgenzō* "Raihai tokuzui," T. 82, 2582: 36c.
28 See for instance *Denkōroku*, T. 82, 2585: 392b, 403a.
29 On Keizan and women, see Ishikawa 1993; Aotatsu Sōji, "Keizan Jōkin no nyonin sonjū shisō ni tsuite," *Shūgaku kenkyū* 16 (March 1974); and Sōtōshū Nisōshi Hensankai 1955.
30 See Nishiguchi 1987: 22–42.
31 See Duby 1988: 11.

special status that Keizan tried to give her by making her the "author of the fundamental vow," and thereby the spiritual mother of the Yōkōji community.[32] We cannot but be surprised at the complete absence of any biographical information about this woman who, rather than care for her own family line, chose to give birth rather to spiritual sons and daughters by associating herself, even before the death of her husband, with the priest Keizan. In spite of the status she would later enjoy as abbess of Enzūin, by doing this she was actually simply passing from one form of masculine tutelage to another, from a physical lineage to a spiritual one. It should be noted that most of the women who gathered around Keizan and Sonin were already fairly advanced in years and had reproduced; and we may wonder whether, as in Western medieval society, we might have here evidence of women rejected by their lineage once they were deemed useless.[33] In the absence of more precise documentation, this can be no more than a hypothesis.

But the fact does remain that most of the legends in the Sōtō tradition concern male monks. In a masculine tradition, Keizan's example, a man devoted to his matrilineal lineage, may appear to be an exception.[34] Keizan got from his mother his devotion to the cause of women; for example, he transcribed into Japanese the Chinese commentary by Dōgen on the Buddhist Precepts so that they would be accessible to one of his disciples, the nun Ekyū. The inspiration on this point was perhaps not so much the Buddha as Ānanda, the third Indian patriarch. We know that even if the Buddha ended up, in spite of himself, accepting women into his community, beginning with his own aunt Gautami, his motive was not so much recognition of the woman who had been his stepmother but rather the insistence of his cousin Ānanda, son of Gautami, in order to avoid upsetting this much-beloved disciple. However, for Keizan, as a representative of the clerical culture, the blood bonds attaching him to

[32] The *Nihon Tōjō rentōroku*, however, counts Sonin and Ekyū among Keizan's seven Dharma-heirs and gives Sonin's biography. See *DNBZ* 111: 60a and 66a–67a. Another woman who played an important role was Enkan Myōshō, who became abbess (*unshū*) of Enzūin after the death of Sonin. In the *Record of Tōkoku*, at the date of 4/10/1325, we are told that she was appointed to Hōōji of Kaga (temple founded by Keizan for the *bodhi* of his mother Ekan), and that on this occasion she was authorized to copy the ordination manual for Bodhisattvas (*Busso shōden bosatsukai sahō*). Like Sonin, she seems to have been autonomous as practitioner. Hōōji was apparently the first independent nunnery in Sōtō, and Myōshō its first abbess. She was succeeded by Ekyū at the head of Enzūin. In 1223, according to the *Record of Tōkoku*, Ekyū received succession documents from Keizan. He wrote specially the ordination manual in *kana* for her. This means that she could confer ordination herself. She receives special treatment also when Keizan decides what funeral services will be offered to nuns. A large part of the financial support of Yōkōji was reserved for nuns.

[33] Duby, 1988: 59.

[34] There were, however, other similar cases. See Nishiguchi 1987: 146–62, 184–218.

his matrilineal line always was less important than the spiritual line, which remains purely male.

The *Record of Tōkoku* can also be read as a kind of oneirical autobiography, which suggests that the rise of the autobiographical genre in Japan was permitted not only by the discovery of interiority, the affirmation of a self that was denied at the doctrinal level, but also by the gradual shift of the dreams from the public to the private sphere. The dream world of Keizan, as we will see, was nurtured by the feminine, maternal realm, a realm symbolized above all by the Bodhisattva Kannon.

Chapter Two

IMAGINED LINEAGES

HISTORIANS SEE KEIZAN above all as the reformer of the Sōtō tradition, and thus we should examine his position within that context.[1] The Sōtō tradition was brought to Japan by Dōgen (1200–1253), who in 1243 went on to found Eiheiji (Monastery of Eternal Peace) in Echizen province (today's Fukui prefecture). Unlike his contemporary and rival, the Rinzai master Enni Ben'en (1202–1280), Dōgen rejected the doctrinal syncretism that then reigned in Zen (and in Chinese Chan) and preached "pure" Zen. This was also the position of his successor Koun Ejō (1198–1280). But after the latter's death, the Eiheiji community is said to have split over Dōgen's succession, during what came to be called the third-generation controversy,[2] a conflict that seems to have involved conservative elements, partisans of a strict adherence to Dōgen's "purism," and those who, with Ejō's successor, Gikai (1219–1309), advocated an openness to esoteric Buddhism and local cults. Gikai was evicted from Eiheiji and took refuge in a monastery in Kaga province, Daijōji (in Ishikawa prefecture). Keizan, the disciple and successor of Gikai, thus belonged to this dissident branch of the Sōtō sect which, thanks to him and his disciples, would become the majority party and by the same token, for a long time, the party of orthodoxy.

The syncretism of Gikai and Keizan, however, also reflects their adherence to another Zen tendency little understood until recently, referred to as the Dharma school (Darumashū).[3] This school, named after the legendary founder of Chan/Zen, the Indian monk Bodhidharma, was apparently founded by a monk named Dainichi (var. Dainichibō) Nōnin even before the official introduction of Zen into Japan by Yōsai (var. Eisai, 1141–1215) and Dōgen. Unlike these figures, Nōnin had never visited China; he achieved awakening by himself, with no spiritual guide. It was only much later, in response to criticisms, that he obtained, through two disciples, the transmission of the Chan master Fozhao, alias Zhuoan Deguang. This detail, as we shall see, is not without significance. The suc-

---

[1] What Lévi-Strauss says of physical lineages (kinship) seems even truer of spiritual lineages: "A kinship system does not consist in the objective ties of descent or consanguinity between individuals. It exists only in human consciousness; it is an arbitrary system of representations, not the spontaneous development of a real situation." See Lévi-Strauss 1963: 50.

[2] On this question, see Bodiford 1993: 70–80.

[3] See Ishii 1974; Faure 1987b.

cess of the Darumashū provoked strong reactions, sometimes motivated by doctrinal disagreements and sometimes by envy. Among Nōnin's detractors were several prominent monks of the time, such as the Kegon master Myōe (1173–1232), but also Yōsai and Dōgen themselves. Dōgen had private reasons to oppose Nōnin and his doctrine, even if, unlike Yōsai, he did this only indirectly. His main disciples, beginning with Ejō and Gikai, were essentially breakaway members of this school. While Ejō's conversion to Dōgen's teaching was wholehearted, that of his co-disciples was more ambivalent. In spite of his diatribes against the school of Linji (Rinzai), Dōgen could never succeed completely in persuading his disciples to renounce their former affiliation. In the very heart of the new Japanese Sōtō school, the Rinzai ideas and lineage of the Darumashū continued, finding a synthesis and outcome in the thought of Keizan.

On this point as on others, Keizan's attitude is ambiguous. Sometimes, like Dōgen in his hardly veiled criticism of the Darumashū, he insists on the importance of a face-to-face transmission between master and disciple, authenticated by a certificate of succession. At other times he seems to admit the possibility of "awakening alone, without a master" (*mushi dokugo*), as Nōnin was said to have done. In his *Denkōroku* he treats Dōgen as the heir to the Rinzai master Myōzen (1184–1225), a disciple of Yōsai whom Dōgen had accompanied to China and whose relics he brought back to Japan.[4] According to Keizan, Dōgen had inherited Myōzen's robe and bowl along with his esoteric teachings and rituals. Thus he was Myōzen's sole legitimate heir, from whom he received the true lines of the three schools: exoteric, esoteric, and Zen. If we are to believe Keizan's account, Dōgen too was an eclectic teacher.[5]

Keizan may be projecting his own situation onto Dōgen. He combined in his own person two very different lines, one that would represent Zen orthodoxy and the other, heterodoxy.[6] This tension between lineages re-

[4] See *Denkōroku*, T. 82, 2585: 405c; and Dōgen, *Shari sōdenki*, in DZZ 2: 395.

[5] See *Denkōroku*, ibid. Keizan also emphasizes that Dōgen had the privilege of seeing several transmission documents while in China. However, he eventually claims that Dōgen was the first one to transmit "pure Zen" in Japan. See ibid., 406c–407c.

[6] Keizan emphasizes in a passage of the *Record of Tōkoku* that he is heir to Dayang Jingxuan's lineage. In the *Denkōroku* he explains at some length how Dayang transmitted the Sōtō lineage to Fushan, although the latter had also inherited the Linji lineage. Keizan comments, "At this point it should be realized that the lineages of Qingyuan [Sōtō] and Nanyue [Rinzai] are basically not separate" [T. 82, 2585: 396a]. Keizan's position on this point is very different from that of the later Dōgen, although he also claims to have inherited his "pure" Zen. That all Sōtō monks were not as eclectic as Keizan is well illustrated by the story in which Ejō returns as a ghost to haunt a monk who has shifted to the Rinzai school, or by the case of Chūgan Engetsu (1300–1375), who was attacked as a heretic and even physically wounded by a former fellow-monk in Kamakura after he left the Chinese Sōtō master Dongming Huiri to follow the Rinzai master Dongyang Dehui. See Pollack 1986: 119.

flects another, deeper tension—at the level of ideas or even of world-views. We return to this second tension later in this chapter. For now, we linger a moment on the idea of the patriarchal tradition. As is well known, the transmission of the Dharma is essential in Chan/Zen. From at least the time of the sixth patriarch Huineng (died 713), if not before, this transmission, considered to take place "outside scriptural teaching," "from mind to mind," was verified by the transmission of the patriarchal robe.[7] The Dharma robe of Huineng, the emblem of the patriarchate "invented" by his alleged disciple Shenhui (684–758), was coveted by many parties. During the Tang the Chinese emperors even considered it as a sort of dynastic treasure (*bao*) whose presence in the imperial palace, even if only temporary, helped to legitimize a new reign. Later other relics played a similar role. At the time of Dōgen, and at his insistence, the certificates of succession (*shisho*) became more important. Just as Shenhui resorted to the symbol of the patriarchal robe in order to prove the legitimacy of his master Huineng (and his own at the same time), Dōgen came to insist on the requirement of the certificate of succession, doubtless to invalidate the claims of freelancers like Nōnin. On this point Keizan is more easygoing than Dōgen, considering that both types of transmission are authentic even if they are not completely equal in weight.

There is one more lineage to which Keizan seems very close, even if he cannot truly be called its heir. This is the Hottō branch, named after Hottō kokushi (National Master Hottō, posthumous title of Shinchi Kakushin, 1207–1298). This lineage was heavily influenced by Shingon esotericism, which Kakushin had studied at Kōyasan before he went to China to study the Chan of the Linji (Rinzai) school. Kakushin's eclecticism was shared by Keizan. We know that the latter, in his youth, studied in various Tendai and Rinzai monasteries. But the affinities between Kakushin and Keizan did not prevent a rivalry between the two branches in certain situations. Thus, when Keizan succeeded his master Gikai at Daijōji, he was soon replaced, on the insistence of the lay patrons of the monastery, by a monk from the Hottō branch, Kyōō Unryō (1267–1341). In a document dated 1323, Keizan writes:

> Daijōji is the monastery where my late master [Gikai] first preached the Dharma. Among his disciples there were some worthy of becoming abbots, but the person who holds administrative power there at the moment is a monk who does not follow my way of thinking. Yet what motivated the founder [Gikai] was the hope of revitalizing our sect. This is why, when the patrons [of Daijōji] come back to the right principle, the worthies of our sect should once again reside there. Furthermore, since the relics of three generations of Eiheiji

---

[7] On this question see Anna Seidel, "Den'e," *Hōbōgirin* 9 (forthcoming).

[abbots] have been deposited there, this is a monastery that we must work to restore. Disciples, see that you observe my wishes.[8]

Of course we must not exaggerate Keizan's feelings of rivalry. After all, the new abbot of Daijōji, Kyōō Unryō, had studied for some time under his supervision, and Keizan himself sent his two main disciples, Meihō Sotetsu and Gasan Jōseki, to study in turn at Daijōji.[9]

THE PATRIARCHAL TRADITION

What, then, was this patriarchal tradition that Keizan claimed to belong to? It was not a matter of a simple transmission from master to disciple, already so well known in China and Japan, but the transmission par excellence, that of the ultimate truth or *shōbōgenzō*, the "Treasure of the True Dharma Eye" transmitted by the Buddha to his disciple Mahā-kāśyapa, and, through the intervening Chinese and Japanese patriarchs, to Dōgen and Keizan. The hieratic nature of this transmission is under-scored by the fact that, in certain Chan manuscripts uncovered at Dun-huang, it is considered to operate on a suprahistorical level, in the *Vajradhātu*, or Adamantine Realm, between two patriarchs who are no longer simply flesh-and-blood people but metaphysical beings. Its histo-ricity is thus of a special kind reminiscent of the Christian Church, un-rolling in a time of a higher order, the *aevum*. Questions of transmission that seem strictly sectarian to us expressed, to Dōgen, Keizan, and their contemporaries, the highest truth, the very essence of their world. Their sectarianism carried them, so to speak, to the heart of things.

THE FIVE ELDERS

Keizan constructed the main buildings of Yōkōji according to an archi-tectural tradition that was well established, at least in China. But then he became innovative, building, on a hill overlooking the monastery, a fu-nerary mound that he called Gorōhō [Peak of the Five Elders] and a memorial called Dentōin [Pavilion of the Transmission of the Lamp]. Like some imperial tombs in Korea and Japan, the mound over the course of centuries blended into the landscape and today it is covered with vegetation. It is about five meters high and ten meters across. Its name, the Peak of the Five Elders, was perhaps borrowed from a famous peak of Mount Lu, in Jiangxi. What concerns us particularly is that Kei-zan buried in it various relics of these Five Elders, among whom he

[8] *Sansō iseki jiji okibumi*, in *JDZ*, 416–18.
[9] See also Keizan's short work on the transmission of Dōgen's robe, *Hōe sōden sho*, in *JDZ*, 485–86.

counted himself: the *Recorded Sayings* of Rujing (Dōgen's Chinese master), the "sacred bones" of Dōgen, a *sūtra* that Ejō had copied in his own blood, Gikai's documents of succession, and Mahāyāna scriptures copied by Keizan himself. The *Record of Tōkoku* itself, like Yōkōji, contains a memorial—in this case a literary one—entitled "Short Notices of the Deeds and Kōans of Awakening of the Five Elders of Dentōin at Tōkoku." Concluding the fourth notice (and actually last, despite the title), that of his master Gikai, Keizan writes: "Now I respectfully deposit on this mountain the relics of Samantabhadra preserved by the Six patriarchs and transmitted in the school of Nanyue [Huairang], the frontal bone of my late master, and the Scriptures of the Five Sections of Mahāyāna copied in my own hand." And he signs: "Jōkin of Tōkoku, heir of the Dharma at the fifty-fourth generation from Śākyamuni."[10]

In this way Keizan built up, parallel to the continuing, open lineage of the Indian, Chinese, and Japanese patriarchs that had preceded him, a new series that formed a closed whole and that recapitulated, even eclipsed, the former in the collective memory of the Sōtō sect. Short-circuiting the classical list, this new patriarchal tradition also subtly adulterated the "pure Zen" of Dōgen by including among the new cult objects certain relics inherited, through Gikai, from the Rinzai lineage of the Darumashū school. Dōgen, the "founder" of the Japanese Sōtō sect, occupies only the second place in this condensed patriarchal line. Keizan chose to go back, beyond his Japanese predecessors, to the Chinese master Rujing. At the same stroke, Yōkōji now became more important than Eiheiji because the latter held only the mausoleum of the "second patriarch," Dōgen. We discuss farther on in this chapter the central place of the cult of relics in the Sōtō tradition as reformed by Keizan.

It is also possible that the relics of the Five Elders were arranged, as were their funerary tablets in Dentōin, in accordance with a spatial schema involving the five points (center and cardinal directions). Referring to the custom of depositing relics in Buddhist stūpas in India, Paul Mus argues that "their regular arrangement in an oriented space reveals . . . the circulation of their power, passing from one to the next according to a spatial schema of time, and because of this fact their grouping contains a messianic promise."[11] Thus at Gorōhō we may have

---

[10] Note also the importance of naming for an identification (in the strong sense), an affiliation with the tradition. In the *kechimyaku*, the naming of new adepts brings about *ipso facto* their affiliation. Keizan multiplies speech-acts that identify him (by affiliation): he names Tōkoku through a paradigmatic variation of Tōzan (Dongshan), Yōkōji by reference to the posthumous title of Dayang Jingxuan (Ming'an dashi, "Great Master Bright Peace," 943–1027), Saishōden by reference to the *Saishōōkyō*, a sūtra said to have been preached by Kannon and Kokūzō, the two acolytes of Shaka at Yōkōji, etc.

[11] See Mus 1935: 434.

the "pentarchy" of Yōkōji: five patriarchs forming a collective ancestor and not simply five successive generations.

As we have seen above, Dentōin contains statues of the Five Elders along with the funerary tablets of Keizan and the four later "patriarchs" (Meihō Sotetsu, Mugai Chikō, Gasan Jōseki, and Koan Shikan), along with those of Keizan's mother (Ekan) and paternal grandmother (Myō-chi), and those of the main patrons of Yōkōji: the nun Sonin and her husband, Unno Saburō (ordained under the religious name of Myōjō). Above the tablets there are icons of the masters and disciples, with the exception of Myōjō. Sonin is shown twice: once as a benefactress of the monastery and once as the abbess of Dentōin. The importance of the patriarchal line is further underscored by a horizontal plaque, carved by Sōan Shien, sixth abbot of Yōkōji, on the basis of a calligraphy by Keizan dated 1323, listing the fifty-four generations from Mahākāśyapa to Kei-zan. The spatial arrangement of the tablets is suggestive. Beginning from Rujing, in the central position, one proceeds from side to side, in ever larger sweeps, toward the right (Dōgen), to the left (Ejō), back to the right (Gikai), and once again to the left (Keizan).[12] We are apparently in a mausoleum organized on the model of the Chinese ancestor cult, with the five "ancestors" of Yōkōji constituting a collective entity.

Before he died, Keizan named six successors: Meihō Sotetsu (1277–1350), who succeeded him as head of Yōkōji; Gasan Jōseki (1276–1366), to whom he entrusted Sōjiji; Mugai Chikō (died in 1351), Koan Shikan (died in 1341), Kohō Kakumyō (1271–1361), and Genshō Chin-san (dates unknown). Only Meihō and Gasan played an important part in the later development of the Sōtō school and their schools quickly became rivals, as shown in a late passage in the *Record of Tōkoku*. Al-though the funerary tablets of the four first-named among the successors are arranged in pairs on each side of those of the Five Elders, the other two are missing.

Kohō Kakumyō deserves special mention among these successors. His inheritance was jointly from the Zen of Shinchi Kakushin, and so he was strongly influenced by Shingon esoterism. He shares with Keizan (and many other monks of that period) another trait: the importance he assigns to dreams. In Chapter 5 we look in some detail at the role of dreams in medieval Zen. Let us note here that dreams are closely associ-ated with spiritual transmission. As already noted, it was during an one-iric experience that Keizan received the transmission from the Buddhist triad of Bodhidharma, Śākyamuni, and Maitreya. Śākyamuni and Bodhidharma appear at two of the most significant times in the Chan/Zen transmission, in India and in China. The presence of Mai-

---

[12] On the arrangement of Chan/Zen ancestral halls, see Foulk and Sharf 1993.

treya, the Buddha of the future, is a little more surprising because he is not very important in Chan/Zen and Keizan could have been influenced by a Maitreyic trend.[13]

This triad, which gave Keizan his supernatural legitimization, helps him to pass through in a single leap (a single dream?) the three main stages in the career of a Bodhisattva: production of the first thought of awakening, stage of nonretreat, achievement of the triple deliverance. These three stages reflect on the oneiric level those that Keizan had actually gone through, according to the autobiographical section of the *Record of Tōkoku*, at the ages of eighteen, nineteen, and twenty-two. We may note in passing that it was with Jakuen (Ch. Jiyuan), Dōgen's Chinese disciple, that he reached the second stage. In another dream connected with Keizan's spiritual lineage, Gien appeared to him. Gien was the leader of the conservative faction at Eiheiji, opposed to the reforms introduced by Gikai. He had been instrumental in Gikai's eviction from the monastery.

> On the twenty-second of the same month, during the night, I dreamed that I held the post of acolyte of the second rank to Master Gien of Eiheiji and that I wanted to ascend the hall in his place. But Gien moved forward and ascended the hall, saying, "If one lights only one lamp, it can illuminate [as far as] the shutters, but the darkness will not leave the mountain even in twenty years." After he came down from his seat, I said, "Has the Reverend vowed not to leave the mountain?" Gien said, "That is so. I am delighted that you, alone among thousands of men, have understood the depths of my heart." I made a note of this as a model for future generations. It was also a sign that the benevolent spirit [of Gien] would accompany me throughout my life. This happy omen showed that I should live in retirement on this mountain until the end [of my days] [*JDZ*, 401].

By reporting Gien's favorable comments about him, Keizan reconciled to his own benefit the two antagonistic tendencies within the Sōtō school. Let us also note the eponymous ancestors of Tōkoku and Yōkōji:

> As the sixteenth-generation heir to the founding patriarch Tōzan [Dongshan Liangjie], I revere his style. This is why I named this mountain "Tōkoku," simply replacing [the character] "Mount" [*san*] with [that of] "Valley" [*koku*], just as Sōzan [Caoshan, i.e., Caoshan Benji] was derived from a change in Sōkei [Caoxi, i.e., Huineng]. And as I am the eleventh-generation heir to the founding patriarch Dayang [Jingxuan], I inspired myself from his [posthumous] title ["Great Sun"] and named this monastery Yōkōji, "Monastery of Eternal Light." [*JDZ*, 395].

---

[13] On Maitreya messianism in East Asia, see Sponberg and Hardacre 1988.

The importance for Keizan of the patriarchal tradition is shown by his main work, the *Denkōroku* (Record of the Transmission of the Light), a chronicle of the transmission of the Dharma through the ages, from the Buddha Śākyamuni to the fifty-third patriarch (here Ejō, not Gikai). The *Denkōroku* consists of sermons given by Keizan while he was still the abbot of Daijōji. We know that Keizan repeated these lectures at Yōkōji, but his ideas may have been modified slightly in the interim, with the erection of Gorōhō. As noted above, for the consecration of this funerary monument, Keizan compiled a textual memorial, the biographies of the Five Elders (actually four), which he inserted into the *Record of Tōkoku*. Although he still considered himself to be the fifty-fourth patriarch in the Chan/Zen tradition, the only authentic lineage in his eyes, he tended to shift his emphasis to the series of Five Patriarchs of the Sōtō school, of whom he is, in a way, the "seal" that authenticates and closes it.

If we are to believe Linji and various masters of "classical" Chan, nothing in Chan can be transmitted. Thus we have the paradox of a tradition that claims to be without *tradita*. We do find within this school some strong-minded individuals who criticize the very notion of a tradition. Nevertheless, *tradita* are only absent in a very superficial fashion; in reality they abound, and this abundance sometimes overwhelms the tradition that they nourish.

The patriarchs belong to a mythic time, and Keizan places himself, in his own lifetime, in that mythic time. We are reminded in this case of what Pierre Bourdieu has said about manipulations of lineages and the gap that grows up between the imaginary lineage (theoretical and official) and the reality of lineage strategies.[14] Nevertheless, even if the tradition that Keizan speaks of actually derives mostly from sectarian strategies, we cannot dispense with interpreting the symbolism of the lineage.

For Keizan the history of the world tends to be reduced to a mere reflection of that of the patriarchal tradition. This tradition serves a double function because it is at the same time historical (thus belonging to linear time and so introducing temporal linearity into the heart of the cyclic time of the liturgy) and also cyclic. Each awakening goes back to the awakening *in illo tempore* of the Buddha, to the "eternal solstice." The same scheme is found, in diagrammatic form, in various Sōtō *kirigami*. Keizan thus lived, in his imagination at least, in a "Zen world" that constitutes, at the level of discourse, a self-contained realm, a sort of discursive utopia.

[14] See Bourdieu 1977: 35.

THE BLOOD LINEAGE (KECHIMYAKU)

Along with the transmission of the Dharma, which is usually identified with the patriarchal tradition, we should also note the central role played by the transmission of the Precepts, described as being a "blood lineage" (kechimyaku). The Sōtō sect had received the privilege of granting its own ordinations. This is how Keizan could obtain full ordination without leaving his native province while his master Gikai, like Dōgen before him, had to go to the ordination platform of Enryakuji, on Mount Hiei, the center of the Tendai school. The transmission of the "One-Mind Precepts" (isshinkai), inherited from the Northern school of Chan, was important for Yōsai, Dōgen, and later in the Sōtō sect during the Edo period.[15] This transmission of the Precepts, which the transmission of the Dharma in a way completed, sometimes contradicts the latter: the logic of the supplement establishes between the two lines an interplay that can encourage syncretic tendencies. Saichō (767–822), the founder of the Japanese Tendai school, cites the four lineages (Tiantai, esoteric Buddhism, Vinaya, and Chan) that he inherited from his stay in China. We also know that in 1295 Keizan received the transmission of the Precepts from Gien, Gikai's rival, three years before receiving from Gikai himself the transmission of the Dharma. He then returned immediately to his rural temple in Awa and ordained, in the space of two years, the seventy monks who would form the nucleus of his community at Yōkōji. In the same way, at the inauguration of the hall of Sōjiji in 1324, he ordained twenty-eight monks.

Sometimes transmission could be very complex, involving all sorts of strategic moves. Thus Gikai received the tonsure at the hands of the Darumashū master Ekan (d. ca 1251), the successor to Nōnin at Hajakuji (in Echizen); he then went to receive full ordination on Mount Hiei. He followed Ekan when the latter went to join Dōgen's community in 1241, along with other adepts from the Darumashū. But Ekan died without inheriting from the Dharma line of Dōgen, and he could transmit to Gikai only his Darumashū lineage and the lineage of the Bodhisattva Precepts. It was through Ejō that Gikai succeeded in obtaining, at long last, the transmission of the Dharma. In the document that mentions this transmission, Ejō states: "These are secret matters and oral initiations. These things, which have never before been confided to anyone else, concern the mental attitude of the abbot, the monastery rituals, and the ceremony that confers the Bodhisattva Precepts. [Dōgen has said:] 'All of this

---

[15] See Faure 1988: 149–54.

can be transmitted only to one's Dharma heir.' This is why I alone, Ejō, have received this instruction."[16]

The discrepancy between the line of transmission of the Bodhisattva Precepts and that of the Dharma Law is striking: the Zen Precepts (*zenkai*, also known as the "One-Mind Precepts," *isshinkai*) were transmitted to Japan through the Northern School, the same school that, toward the middle of the eighth century in China, was accused by Shenhui of gradualism and of being a collateral lineage. It was in fact from this school that Saichō inherited the tradition of the Bodhisattva Precepts, and after him Yōsai and the entire Sōtō tradition. This discrepancy forced Kōshū, a Tendai scholar of the fourteenth century, to explain away the fact that Saichō (767–822) was a distant heir to Shenxiu (606–706), the leader of the Northern School, in spite of the latter's defeat in the poetry contest that pitted him against Huineng, the future "sixth patriarch" of Chan and the presumed founder of the Southern School. In what will remain a fine example of Buddhist casuistry, this scholar claims that, although Shenxiu had not yet achieved the same awakening as had his rival at that time, he did get it eventually. Once that had happened, there was no reason why Saichō and the Tendai school could not claim to have received the Bodhisattva Precepts via Shenxiu and the Northern School.[17]

During the time of Keizan, the transmission of the Dharma and of the Precepts went together in the Sōtō sect, by means of two documents: a certificate of succession (*shisho*) and a "blood lineage" document (*kechimyaku*). Many different *kirigami* provide details on these transmission rituals.[18] A *kechimyaku* actually constitutes a set of procedures for the transmission of the Precepts. It was usually transmitted in the ritual area where ordination and de-ordination (if someone was returning to lay life) took place, during collective ceremonies of passing on the Precepts (after Kamakura), and at postmortem ordinations. Despite these different settings, the *kechimyaku* are basically identical. They are also transmitted as a preliminary to the transmission of certificates of succession, even though there is no new transmission of the Precepts on such occasions. The two lines transmitted in Sōtō are those of the Rinzai "Zen Precepts"

[16] See *DZZ* 2: 502.

[17] See Kōshū, *Keiran shūyōshū*, T. 76, 2410: 534a.

[18] In the Edo period the transmission consists of "three things": the document of succession (*shisho*), the lineage chart (*kechimyaku*), and an epitome of the esoteric tradition in the form of a dialogue between master and disciple (*daiji*). In the thirteenth century, however, the third document is not yet used, but several other *sacra* are transmitted, such as the Dharma robe (*kesa*), the alms bowl (*hatsuu*), the staff (*shūjō*), the bamboo scepter (*shippei*), the fly-whisk (*hossu*), or the portrait of the master (*chinsō*), as well as certain canonical scriptures and various secret texts. See Ishikawa 1983–94 (13): 163; Bodiford 1993: 17; 1991.

(leading to Yōsai, Myōzen, and Dōgen), and those of Sōtō proper, transmitted by Rujing to Dōgen.

TRANSMISSION OF THE DHARMA

The *Record of Tōkoku* describes a meeting, toward the middle of 1323, during which Keizan transmitted to Meihō Sotetsu the Dharma robe of Dōgen and the *shippei*:

> The twenty-fifth of the same month, the *shuso* [So]tetsu was promoted to the status of *rissō nisshitsu*,[19] and the Dharma robe and *shippei* were transmitted in the same interview. As he received the Robe of the Law he [Sotetsu] said, "The Robe of the Law of Eihei [Dōgen] has been transmitted as [a token of] faith from one generation to the next during a private encounter between master and disciple. The *shuso* Sotetsu, receiving it respectfully in his turn, declares, 'This mountain range, who said that one could not move it? I have succeeded in doing it. I have now come to the door, and it opened.'" The same day, after a sermon, I had him come to my room. It was not like promoting an ordinary *rissō*. When he ascended the hall, gave a sermon, or entered into my cell, it was as a complete preacher. On Vulture Peak and at Caoxi there were the *shuso* Kāśyapa and Qingyuan. At Daijōji and at Tōkoku we have the *shuso* [Keizan] Jōkin and [Meihō] Sotetsu" [*JDZ*, 410].

Thus Keizan compares this transmission to the ones in India on Vulture Peak (from Śākyamuni to Mahākāśyapa) and at Caoxi in Southern China (from Huineng, the sixth patriarch, to Qingyuan Xingsi, the ancestor of the Sōtō lineage). Strangely he omits another important occasion in the patriarchal transmission, the transmission from the first "Chinese" patriarch Bodhidharma to his disciple Huike. Toward the middle of the year 1324, Keizan transmits his Dharma robe to Gasan Jōseki, whom he promotes by the same token to the position of abbot of his newly founded monastery, Sōjiji:

> On the seventh of the seventh month I handed over to the *shuso* Gasan Jōseki the position of abbot of Sōjiji, and I transmitted to him the Dharma robe. During the opening ceremony, I also transmitted to him the staff [*shūjō*], the fly-whisk [*hossu*], and the certificate of ordination. That very day the new abbot and the old one met for the first time and transmitted from one to the other the three-inch *shippei* of Kōshō[ji], the first that ever existed in Japan. It is the *shippei* [that gives] access to the [master's] cell. For the next three days auspicious events kept happening. [*JDZ*, 430]

[19] Concerning these functions, which were those of Keizan at Daijōji, see above, Chap. 1, note 2; and Mujaku 1963: 225.

To judge from the metaphors used to describe these events, the succession from master to disciple boils down to the question of finding the "right vein" (*shōmyaku*). Symbolically speaking, the transmission is a blood transfusion that makes the donor and receiver identical in nature. The life blood of the Buddhist Law circulates metaphorically from the master's body to that of the disciple. The concurrent metaphor of transmitting a flame suggests a symbolic equivalence between blood and fire.

In the symbolism of the transmission, the circle functions as a ritual shifter. Some of the *kirigami* contain a diagram of the transmission of the Precepts which derives from a synthesis of Buddhist cosmology and that of the *Yi jing*. In this diagram the circle corresponds to the lotus world, from which emerge humans, animals, plants, Buddhas, and Bodhisattvas. The base of the lotus is the character *shin* (mind, heart), because all phenomena emerge from the mind (the circle) and return to it.[20] The name of Śākyamuni and then those of the patriarchs are written on the lotus itself.

> From the great pinnacle emerge the two emblems (Yin and Yang), the four sacred animals, the eight trigrams—from which derive the sixty-four hexagrams and the 12520 specific divinatory cases. Laymen [. . .] the frontal bone of Śākyamuni indicates that they have achieved the fruit of Buddhahood, the deep awakening that transcends life and death, the highest level without beginning or end. This is what the circle symbolizes. . . . The layman [who has just received the transmission of the Precepts] differs in no way from the [past] Buddha Vipaśyin, and living eyes open in his body. Although he may have been born into an age of decline, his fleshly body does not show this, [because] the light of ten thousand years has its source in a time before Śākyamuni.[21]

The certificate of succession (*shisho*) shows a somewhat different kind of diagram, one with the complete list of the names of the patriarchs laid out in a circle. As a general rule, it includes also the names of the master and the disciple and contains a ritual dialogue stressing their perfect identity. In the *Denkōroku* Keizan expresses, through images, the eternal present (and circular nature) of transmission:

> Wishing to express [the true Dharma, [Śākyamuni] held up a flower to reveal permanence, and [Kāśyapa] smiled to reveal longevity. Thus, master and disciple face each other and the life blood circulates [. . . .] [Kāśyapa] correctly cut through his conceptual faculty and withdrew to Mount Kukkuṭpāda to await the coming of Maitreya. This is why he has not yet entered Nirvāṇa [. . . .]

[20] This symbolism seems to extend to the "eye." See for instance the *Denkōroku*: "However diverse the mountains, rivers, land, and all things may appear, they are all reflected in the eye of Gautama Buddha. And you too are standing in the eye of Gautama Buddha. And it is not simply that you are standing there, the eye has become you. Gautama's eyeball has become everyone's whole body, each standing tall." *T*. 82, 2585: 344c.

[21] See Ishikawa, 1983–94 (14): 122.

Therefore you should not long for a past of two thousand years ago. If you study the Way now, you won't have to go to Mount Kukkuṭpāda: Kāśyapa will be able to appear in Japan. Thus, Śākyamuni's flesh-body is still warm, Kāśyapa's smile will return. When you reach this state, you will succeed to Kāśyapa, and Kāśyapa will be your heir.[22]

In another passage Keizan writes:

Once you have become your own master, you will understand that Mahā-kāśyapa can wriggle his toes in your straw sandals. Just when Gautama raised his eyebrows and blinked his eyes, he passed completely away; just when Kāśyapa smiled, he reached awakening.[23]

This identity between master and disciple may be specific to Chan/Zen. For instance, according to the canonical translator and Yo-gācāra master Xuanzang (600–664), Mahākāśyapa does not wear the Buddha's robe but carries it respectfully in his arms.[24] While Chan makes this Arhat-patriarch and the patriarchs who follow him into equals of the Buddha, whose robe they therefore wear, Xuanzang maintains a clear hierarchical distinction: Śākyamuni's robe can be worn only by the next Buddha, Maitreya.[25]

The ritual of Dharma transmission deserves more of our attention. The ritual sequence can be more or less complete, and here we will give only the main elements. After purifying himself, the disciple enters the mas-ter's cell. The master is standing, on the eastern side of his high chair, turned toward the west. The disciple faces him, turned toward the east. He prostrates himself nine times, and then master and disciple bow to-gether. The master then sits on the chair. The disciple advances toward him on his knees, after prostrating himself six more times. The master puts his hand on the disciple's head, sprinkles him with holy water, and recites three times the list of trigrams of the *Yi jing*. Then he gets down from his chair and takes up the succession document lying on a table in front of him. Master and disciple once again face each other, and the disciple prostrates himself as before. The master once again sits down, no longer in the meditation position but with his legs hanging down (Eu-ropean style). The disciple moves forward seven steps, on his knees, and nine times begs the master, in his great mercy, to grant him the transmis-sion and make him into a "new child" in the lineage of the Buddha-patriarchs. The master puts his hand on the disciple's head and says, "This Treasure of the True Dharma Eye, passed down to me from the

[22] See *Denkōroku*, T. 82, 2585: 345c–346a.
[23] Ibid. The story appears in many *kirigami*: see Ishikawa 1983–94 (16): 151–61.
[24] See de Visser 1923: 93.
[25] On this question, see Faure 1995: 339.

Buddha, I now transmit to you. Keep it carefully, and do not let the lineage of the Buddha die." He then lights two pine torches, opens the succession document and the lineage of the Precepts, and shows the disciple the names of the patriarchs and that of the disciple, now written at the end of the line. After new prostrations on the part of the disciple, he continues, "I have now found you, just as the Buddha found Kāśyapa." He repeats three times the command to never let the line of the Buddha die out, and the disciple prostrates himself six times.[26]

Sometimes the master then has the disciple sit on the chair and prostrates himself before him in turn. The disciple places his hand on the top of the master's head. The master picks up two mirrors set out on the table. He gives one to the disciple, who is facing him, and says, "I illuminate you." The disciple replies, "I do the same." The master then says, "[Thus] there are no reflections in the mirror."[27] To put it another way, there are only the "originals" that require each other for completion, like the two tallies of Chinese insignia. The transmission also recalls the Chinese system of vassalage, to which we return in Chapter 9. Finally, the transmission sometimes ends with a rite of blood mixing. The master and the disciple each prick a finger and squeeze out a drop of blood that they mix with purified water. In other cases they may seal the transmission document by each adding to it the character gō (union, covenant) written in their blood. We actually possess a kirigami from Yōkōji entitled Gō-fuin sahō, "Method for sealing the uniting of the tallies."[28] This "uniting of the tallies" is taken to mean transmission from mind to mind, the fusing of the minds of the master and the disciple. It is highly significant that this "spiritual" fusing is sealed by means of blood.

The general meaning of the ritual is clear. Beginning from a very hierarchical situation, the participants move to equality. At first, emphasis is placed on the superiority of the master over the disciple: the majestic pose of the master perched on his high chair and his gesture of putting his hand on the lowly disciple's head contrast to the humility of the kneeling disciple and his constant prostrations. Once the document of succession and the kechimyaku have been transmitted, everything changes and the disciple is now the equal of the master—at least in theory. Their identity is symbolized by the fusing of the two torches at the moment when the master invites the disciple to read the document—a fusing that will be found again in cremation rituals. The exchange of places, the reflections in the mirrors, and finally the mixture of their blood all stress the new relationship of equality that has been established. There is still a difference between them, however, marked by the disciples' repeated expres-

---

[26] See Ishikawa, 1983–94 (13): 164–66.

[27] Ibid., 165.

[28] Ibid. (14): 119.

sions of gratitude. Thus the transmission ritual transforms the master and the disciple into equals (in awakening) and at the same time a hierarchic pair (in the disciple's homage). This ritual is somewhat reminiscent of the Western ritual of vassalage described by Jacques Le Goff.[29]

There are other meaningful details. The sprinkling of water is the symbolic equivalent of the unction (*abhiṣeka*) found in esoteric Buddhism, a ritual based on that of Indian royal consecration. The recitation of the trigrams of the *Yi jing* during the aspersion is the equivalent of a mastering and purification of the eight directions symbolized by these trigrams. We can also see working the symbolism of the "three dots of the (Sanskrit) letter *i*," which will turn up again in funeral rites and the animation of icons. (See below, Chapters 6 and 10). The symbolism of the torch is the same as that of cremation: the transmission of the Dharma by Śākyamuni to Mahākāśyapa is elsewhere explicitly compared to setting light to a funerary pyre, with the officiant playing the role of the Buddha and the corpse that of Mahākāśyapa.[30] In both cases, as we shall see, the symbolism of the circle and of the three dots of the *i* is the equivalent of ritually producing a new Buddha.[31]

Just like the transmission from father to son in the Indian juridical system, Japanese Zen transmission is seen as a process of identification. According to a *kirigami* of the Sōtō sect: "When the transmission is completed, Kāśyapa is not distinct from Śākyamuni, Ānanda is not distinct from Kāśyapa. The disciple who has just received the Dharma is none other than the master who has just transmitted it. There is no beginning or end, no order of succession. Since there has been a constant transmission since Śākyamuni, they all occupy the same rank in a circle. All, at the moment of the *buddha-bodhi*, are undifferentiated."[32] The words *buddha-bodhi* are added to the name of each patriarch in the succession documents: Śākyamuni *buddha-bodhi*, Kāśyapa *buddha-bodhi*, Ānanda *buddha-bodhi*, and so on. According to oral tradition, *buddha* stands for the first awakening, the subject of the awakening, the master, and *bodhi* for achieved awakening, the content of the awakening, the disciple. The two terms also correspond to the Yin and the Yang, to the absolute and the relative, and to the father and the mother. The two parts making up the term *buddha-bodhi* are also considered to represent the two sides of the practitioner: disciple and master.[33] The explanation of these terms is shown diagrammatically by the schema of a quasi-Plotinian progression

---

[29] See Le Goff 1980: 237–87.

[30] See Ishikawa 1983–94 (13): 163.

[31] For more details, see Faure 1991: 195–201.

[32] See Ishikawa 1983–94 (14): 110. See also *Denkōroku*, T. 82, 2585: 348a: "Since now Ānanda has appeared in the world, Kāśyapa should fold up his banner: when one appears, the other disappears."

[33] See Ishikawa 1983–94 (14): 110.

from the one to the many: from two circles, black and red, that combine in various ways according to the symbolism of the Five Ranks of the absolute and the relative.[34]

The dominant symbol in all the *kirigami* is the circle/swastika. In the certificates of succession, the writing of the patriarchs' names in a circle indicates the eternal nature of a transmission without beginning and end, and the equality of status of all those who have achieved awakening. We sometimes see the circle of transmission explained in dialogue form: "The master says, 'When one draws a circle, what does the line mean that goes from the original master Śākyamuni to the latest recipient of the Precepts?' Reply, 'The monk who has just received the Precepts is none other than Śākyamuni himself.'"[35] The symbolism of the swastika is thought to add to that of the simple circle a temporal dimension (the three times) and a spatial one (the ten directions).

BLOOD BONDS

Blood symbolism plays an important role, as is attested by the role of the *kechimyaku*, literally "bloodline," the abbreviated name of a document describing the lineage of the Bodhisattva Precepts. One *kirigami* compares the *kechimyaku* of the Buddha-patriarchs and those of ordinary people, drowned in passions; but the comparison is made only to reaffirm their ultimate identity and the fact that, when ordinary people receive the Bodhisattva Precepts, they instantly become "sons of the Buddha" and are thus the equal of all the Buddhas.[36] Other *kirigami* interpret the two Sino-Japanese characters of the compound *kechi-myaku* as symbolizing the harmony between the two emblems Yin and Yang, the moon and the sun, the earth and the sky, female and male. Transmission from master to disciple thus takes on sexual overtones. It becomes an act of procreation that takes place within the framework of universal fertility and ensures the continuation of the Buddhist lineage (literally, "seed"). This ritual procreation, which perhaps reflects male monastic fantasies, is backed up by a complete cosmological terminology borrowed from the Japanese version of the Yin-Yang teaching (Onmyōdō). In China, where the Daoists thought that one could not achieve immortality unless one had received at birth the bones of an immortal, the symbolism is somewhat different: although there is a *Treatise on blood lineage* (*Xuemo lun*) attributed to Bodhidharma, it is his bone marrow and not his blood that he is thought to have transmitted symbolically to his disciple Huike.

[34] Ibid.: 114–15. On the Five Ranks, see Verdú, 1966.
[35] See Ishikawa 1983–94 (14): 112.
[36] Ibid.: 129.

In spite of all this lineage imagery, Keizan reports in the *Denkōroku* a legend according to which the fifth patriarch Hongren (601–674) was born without a father, and he explains it thus: "You should understand that people are not necessarily born only from the bloodline of their parents. Thus, although from the point of view of emotional attachments we receive our physical body, hair and skin, from our father and mother, we must realize that this body is not merely constituted of the five aggregates."[37] Was not Keizan himself a "miraculous" child, born thanks to the mercy of the Bodhisattva Kannon? The role of the father and of the male line is completely passed over in this virgin birth.

Although based on it, Chan patriarchal genealogy may also be seen as a rejection of one's parental genealogy. We know that, in China as in Vedic India, birth was regarded as a fundamental debt to gods and parents.[38] Chan tried to end this familial indebtedness (and also individual karmic debt), as well as all forms of credence and belief. The world of the absolute that it envisages is free of debt. We need only think of Linji and his rejection of filial piety as well as every other form of piety, a refusal going so far as the spiritual murder of parents, Buddha, and patriarchs—at exactly the moment when Chan was becoming a kind of ancestral cult. Paradoxically it was the monks, although they theoretically rejected their family lineage, who actually strengthened it by their funerary ceremonies, and metaphorically by their transmission ritual. We could doubtless say that inheritance is a form of symbolic murder: become your own father, become the Buddha—because it does not allow space for two. Maybe we should think back to the Indian concepts of transmission, where nothing is transmitted from father to son, from master to disciple, because the son simply becomes the father, the disciple becomes the master.

Funeral ritual establishes the perennial nature of the patriarchate beyond the death of individual patriarchs. There is thus a suprapersonal transmission from one patriarch to another. We are confronted with two differing models. The first is that of Indian-style transmission requiring the social death of the testator, in which the *sole* legatee (the disciple) becomes the father (the master). This is how we may interpret the poisoning that killed Bodhidharma once he had transmitted his Dharma to Huike, even though he had survived without difficulty several other murder attempts; this is also how we may interpret the death of Hongren three days after he transmitted the Dharma robe to Huineng. According to the other model, the Dharma is propagated by the master to *several* of his disciples, following the metaphor of the flame that is transmitted from one lamp to another without diminishing in the least.

[37] See *Denkōroku* 32, in *T.* 82, 2585: 381a.
[38] See Malamoud 1980: 57; Hou 1975.

Ordinations were not exclusively for aspirants to the monastic life. We see the rapid development, as was already the case with Shenhui, of ceremonies of mass ordination during which laypeople received *kechimyaku* or lineage diagrams whose value is in a sense magical.[39] The same nonexclusivity characterized funerals. During life or after death, the faithful laity could obtain from the Zen priest the distinct privilege of entering into the family of the Buddha by means of these same lineage diagrams. They were truly "signs that are more than just signs," since they bring into real existence the affiliations that they symbolize, create the very "blood bonds" for which they provide the written proof. Here is what one *kirigami* has to say on this subject:

> What is a *kechimyaku*? The *kechimyaku* of the Buddha-patriarchs and that of beings endowed with strong consciousness [of self] and illusory feelings are, in their true essence, non-dual and equal, of a single flavour. Since the Buddha-patriarchs are awakened, their awakening is like the moon shining in a cloudless sky; as ordinary men live in error, darkness covers the light for them. When ignorant men receive the Bodhisattva Precepts, the dust [that covers their spirit] immediately disappears and finally the spiritual light burgeons forth. This is why it is said that when beings receive the Buddhist Precepts, they immediately achieve the rank of Buddha, a rank identical to that of the Buddhas of great awakening. This is what it really means to receive [the title of] son of the Buddha.[40]

By the same token, the goal of the ordination ceremonies is radically modified, even denatured. It is no longer simply a matter of making vows to observe Buddhist morality but rather to incorporate oneself ritually, magically, into the dynastic lineage of the Buddha and draw from it, as an heir, the supreme successorial privilege, awakening. The lineage diagrams thus became magical talismans in which the name of the cleric or layperson was connected to those of past Buddhas by a red line, symbol of the blood (and spirit) lineage to which he or she was attaching him- or herself.[41] Awakening is no longer the *sine qua non* for transmission; on the contrary, it is ritual initiation that becomes the performative act par excellence, the symbolic realization of awakening recorded by the *kechimyaku*. For the people participating in this ritual, the moral content of the Precepts was less important than the magical transformation of karma that it was supposed to achieve.[42]

The transmission of the ordination ritual to a disciple—a transmission that must not be confused with a mere transmission of the Precepts, that

---

[39] See Bodiford 1993: 179–84; Ishikawa 1983–94 (6): 147.

[40] Ishikawa, ibid.

[41] See Bodiford, 1993.

[42] See "Kechimyaku no san," in Ishikawa 1983–94 (2), 1983: 144.

is, ordination—thus came to take precedence over, or at least to precede chronologically, the transmission of Dharma proper. The *Record of Tō-koku* mentions the two forms of transmission. Thus, toward the beginning of the year 1325, having heard that his cousin, the nun Myōshō, had been authorized (by Sonin?) to transmit the ordination ritual, Keizan decides to test her: "I asked: 'How do you understand the story of "Linji raising his whisk?"' She remained silent. I gave her my approval, saying: 'What you say is difficult to note with ink and paper.' She bowed and left. In this way she received the ordination ritual" [*JDZ*, 431].

One eventually reaches a paradoxical situation, in which the Dharma transmission can take place, whether or not the disciple has reached awakening, provided that he/she has formerly received the ordination ritual correctly.[43] The lineage has clearly taken precedence over religious experience, and it seems to indicate the triumph of the *hommes d'appareil* over the mystics, or rather the transformation of the mystics into *hommes d'appareil*, of personal charisma into institutional charisma.[44] We know that Bodhisattva Precepts (Skt. *bodhisattva-śīla*, Japanese *bosatsukai*) played an important role in the propagation of Mahāyāna among laypersons in China and in Japan—and more specifically, of Sōtō Zen during the medieval period. For instance, according to tradition, it is after receiving the Bodhisattva Precepts from Keizan that Emperor Go-Daigo (1288–1339) turned Sōjiji into an official monastery in 1322, on a par with Eiheiji and Nanzenji.

The lineage model finds its most developed expression in the dynastic lineage. Thus it is no surprise that the Chan patriarchal lineage presented itself from the outset as a spiritual dynastic lineage. In China as in Japan, Buddhists have attempted to underscore the parallelism between Buddhist Law and imperial or monarchic law. Most historians see this as a novelty compared to the Buddhist *saṃgha* in India, which was conceived as a community of renouncers. In Chan the dynastic notion goes at least as far back as the Northern school: the author of the funerary eulogy of Chan master Puji (651–739), for instance, compared the seven patriarchal generations with the seven generations of the Tang dynasty.[45]

During the Edo period, Manzan Dōhaku distinguished the "Dharma transmission," as it is recorded in the certificate of succession, and the transmission of the Precepts, as it is recorded in the *kechimyaku*.[46] The

---

[43] See Manzan Dōhaku, *Manzan oshō Tōmon ejoshū*, 7a, in *Eihei Shōbōgenzō shūsho taisai*, Daihonzan Eiheijinai Eihei Shōbōgenzō shūsho taisei kankōkai, ed. (Tokyo: Taishūkan shoten, 1974–82), vol. 20, 606; quoted in Bodiford 1993: 215.

[44] This importance of lineage might also indicate the resurfacing of an older, sacramental conception of the tradition and of religious experience.

[45] See *Quan Tang wen* 262, ed. Dong Gao (Taibei: Huawen shuju, 1965), 3360a.

[46] See Bodiford 1991.

first is still preferable, but insofar as this has become purely ritual, it is closer to the *kechimyaku*. This is the idea that Tenkei Denson (1648–1735) would come to criticize. He was a representative of a more individualistic tendency in which awakening remained the *sine qua non* condition for transmission. As early as the fourteenth century, Bassui Tokushō (1327–1387) rejected the Sōtō-style *kechimyaku* that his master Kohō Kakumyō (a monk of the Hottō school who had studied with Keizan) was giving out to laypeople for not always disinterested motives. According to Bassui, these documents are only material and therefore false representations of what should be a purely spiritual transmission.[47]

At times Keizan seems to merge the spiritual lineage with the family line, or at any rate to superimpose the one on the other. Did he not see his benefactor and disciple Sonin as a reincarnation of his paternal grandmother, who had herself been among the disciples of Dōgen? It is significant that, in Keizan's *okibumi*, the two lineages that are placed side by side are those of Keizan's disciples and the heirs of Sonin (even though it is nowhere recorded that she had any children). Thus, spiritual bonds are confounded with blood ties. Yōkōji turns out to be, in the literal as well as in the figurative sense, a family business. Participation in its activities (ordination and inheritance) is not so much a personal matter, based on conversion and religious experience, but rather a privilege devolving from transmission of a family inheritance. Thus a structure based on lineage replaces the individual's inner experience (or at least counterbalances it). It would be interesting to compare the strategies that control abbatial successions and those that determine, in aristocratic families, the transmission of the family's patrimony to the older sons and of various *apanages* to the younger ones.[48] We know that Japan saw significant changes in its social structures at around this time, and we may wonder whether Keizan was not caught between the two systems: that of his clan or family lineage and that of his Zen lineage. We will again encounter this opposition later on, in the disputes over succession that opposed the line established on the temple itself with that founded on the transmission of the Dharma.

The discussion of the *kechimyaku* shows the symbolic, metaphorical,

---

[47] See Tsūhō Meidō, *Bassui oshō gyōjitsu*, in *Zoku gunsho ruijū* 9: 638–39.

[48] A Buddhist priest had control over various properties: he first had rights over an estate, whether that of a Buddhist temple or of a shrine. Thus, Keizan had all rights over the estate that Taira *no uji* (the future Sonin) and her husband gave him. The same was true when an estate was inherited by a monk from his own relatives. He also had control over the land belonging to a temple. Finally, he could also transmit the functions of a temple, which he had inherited from his master or his parents. For the West, see Andrew Lewis, *Royal Succession in Capetian France: Studies on Familial Order and the State* (Cambridge, Mass.: Harvard University Press, 1981).

or imaginary importance of blood in what we might call "spiritual" transmission, and, more precisely, in the transmission of the Bodhisattva Precepts in Zen. The symbolism of blood does not play quite the same role in the Japanese imagination as it does in the West. On the one hand, it seems less important in family lineages: in the absence of a male heir, one could, without much difficulty, arrange the adoption of a son-in-law who would become a complete member of the lineage. On the other hand, at least in aristocratic society, blood ties were considered essential, above all when, copying the imperial line and its descent from the sun goddess Amaterasu, members of great families tried to trace their lineage back to a deity in the native mythology. Unlike the situation in Shin Buddhism (Jōdo shinshū) where blood ties became real and where we see the establishment of hereditary lineages, real dynasties that subvert the patriarchal tradition or identify themselves with it, the Sōtō "blood ties" remain metaphorical. But the reason is perhaps that, even in the case of family lineages to which one could become affiliated by adoption, blood itself played a primarily metaphorical role. To understand this, we should take a short detour into Shin Buddhism.

BLOOD LINE, DHARMA LINE

In Shin Buddhism the term *kechimyaku* does not mean, as it does in Zen, a transmission of the Bodhisattva Precepts. In his discussion of the lineages within Jōdo shinshū, Yamaori Tetsuo stresses the difference between "Dharma lineage" (*hōmyaku*) and "blood lineage" (*kechimyaku*).[49] The two terms originally referred to the same thing but came to represent two different types of lineage, even after they were reunited in the person of Kakunyo (1270–1351). In response to the claims of the alternative line descending through Nyoshin, Kakunyo compiled a work, the *Kudenshō*, to back up his double legitimacy, along with the legitimacy of Honganji where he was abbot or, more precisely the caretaker.[50] We know that Shinran (1173–1262), a disciple of Hōnen (1133–1212) and founder of Jōdo Shinshū, was married and had a son, Zenran, whom he had to disown in 1256.[51] Nyoshin was the son of Zenran, and thus the grandson of Shinran. Kakunyo himself was the grandson of the nun Kakushin, a sister of Zenran, and thus the great-grandson of Shinran, but in the female line. The bloodline that led to Shinran, and thence the legitimacy of Honganji, was weak because it passed through women. But Kakunyo tried to cover up this weakness by claiming that his legitimacy came not only through his grandmother's descent (*kechimyaku*), but also

---

[49] See Yamaori 1973: 327–44.
[50] See Dobbins, 1989: 81–88.
[51] Ibid., 40–43.

through the direct teaching he had received from Nyoshin (*hōmyaku*). It was the lineage of Honganji that continued from Kakunyo to Rennyo (1415–1499) and, with the help of the direct disciples of Shinran in the Kantō region, became guardian of the Ōtani mausoleum and of Shinran's tomb. Thus in Kakunyo's time there was no clear rule for the transmission of Shinran's doctrine.

However that may be, Dharma lineage and blood lineage were thenceforth seen as two different forms of legitimacy, even if they did come together in the person of Kakunyo. Blood lineage is no longer a metaphor in this case, but a biological reality. From that time forward, we see the development of a whole *imaginaire* based on the symbolic value of blood and on clan charisma. Rennyo had thirteen sons and fourteen daughters by five wives. These blood connections played an important role in the establishment of his power. We seem to have here what Max Weber called "lineage charisma," an expression that designates the transfer of lineage via blood bonds as opposed to "institutional charisma," in which charisma becomes part of an established social structure.[52]

ZEN TRADITA

In the *Record of Tōkoku*, Keizan records his first transmission on the twenty-ninth day of the seventh month of the year 1321, but he neglects to mention the name of the beneficiary. Meihō Sotetsu and Gasan Jōseki will have to wait until 1322 and 1324, respectively, to receive the official transmission. On the twenty-fifth of the eleventh month of the year 1321, at the time of the solstice, Keizan had asked Gasan to preach in his place, which suggests that he considered him worthy of succeeding him. One month later he seems to have transmitted the Dharma to Shikan, if one is to judge from the detailed fashion he reports the latter's statements in the *Record of Tōkoku*. At the beginning of 1323, he named Mugai Chikō as second abbot of Jōjūji in Kaga, the first having been an abbess, Ekan, his own mother (died in 1318). On this occasion he transmitted the Dharma robe to Mugai. In the sixth month of the same year, he transmitted the Dharma robe to Meihō, who had already received a kind of transmission as early as 1311 when Keizan, on the point of founding Yōkōji, handed over to him the administration of Daijōji. On the eighth of the eighth month of 1324, Keizan added an inscription to his portrait and gave it to Gasan. Two different portraits actually exist, with two different inscriptions—one dated 1319 and kept in Sōjiji, and the other at Tōryōji, in Ishikawa prefecture. As we can see, symbols of transmission are of various sorts: Dharma robe, portrait of the master (with or without in-

---

[52] Weber 1978: 1114.

scription), certificate of succession, and so on. The transmission of various ritual objects seems to have established a subtle spiritual hierarchy, but one that is never clearly enunciated. Here we will concern ourselves only with examining the major "symbol" of the passing on of powers, the Dharma robe (*kāṣāya*). Designating originally a Buddhist stole of red or brown color (*kāṣāya*), made of pieced-together strips, the term *kāṣāya* came later to refer to a liturgical vestment worn over ordinary clothing.

This robe acquired its high reputation in Chan with the story of the establishment of the sixth patriarch, Huineng. This story is so well known that we need not linger over it. Suffice it to say that the Dharma robe (and the begging bowl) were not simply the proof of transmission but were also, as we shall see later, types of dynastic relics and talismans. The robe is taken usually as a simple symbol, a "token of transmission" that "expresses the faith," but a token is already more than a simple sign because it has a performative value, it commits the future. Thus, the importance of the robe in the Chan *imaginaire* goes far beyond that of a simple symbol of transmission. It constitutes the Buddhist equivalent of a dynastic treasure (*bao*): this explains the physical weight of Huineng's robe, which was so heavy that when one of his jealous co-disciples tried to take it from him, he could not lift it. We know that the weight of dynastic treasures is a function of the worthiness of their possessors.[53] The Dharma robe and the Dharma itself are complementary, interdependent, forming a single bipartite reality. By metonymy we come to the idea that there really is an identity between the robe and the Dharma. As a consequence, those who wear the Buddhist *kāṣāya*, the Dharma robe, acquire Buddha bodies.[54]

ABBATIAL SUCCESSION

In the Sōtō school another principle of transmission came to play an important role, to the point of competing with traditional methods: a rotating succession of abbots, which Keizan was among the first to implement, would allow each of his disciples to become abbot of Yōkōji in turn.[55] The question of succession as abbot had already come up with some acuteness at Eiheiji, with the death of Dōgen, and it was probably

[53] See Seidel 1983.

[54] See Ishikawa 1983–94 (6): 106.

[55] On this question, see Bodiford, 1991: 441. During the Edo period, this principle led to the widespread practice of abbots abandoning their Dharma-lineage for the monastery lineage. This practice was denounced by Manzan Dōhaku, himself the heir to the Dharma-lineage of Meihō Sotetsu at Daijōji, for whom correct transmission meant one single Dharma-lineage and a face-to-face transmission. One of Manzan's opponents, Jōzan Ryōkō (d. 1736), emphasized the fundamentally atemporal nature of transmission—the true master is always Śākyamuni, the disciple is always Kāśyapa.

with this lesson in mind that Keizan chose the new system. But this question would recur at Yōkōji after Keizan's death, despite all of his testamentary precautions.

Yōkōji remained the head monastery of the branch of Sōtō under the leadership of Keizan's immediate disciples. Meihō was the second abbot from 1325 to 1339, at which date he returned to Daijōji. Yōkōji was administered in turn by Mugai, Gasan, and Koan, as Keizan had wished. During Mugai's term as abbot, a three-story stūpa was built at the request of the Shogunate, one of the stūpas for the benefit of all beings (*rishōtō*) set up in each province. The fact that Yōkōji was chosen for this stūpa reveals its high status. The prestige of the stūpa brought new revenues and led to the construction of new buildings: a new monks' hall in 1338, a network of corridors in 1339, a belfry. A list of Yōkōji properties, dated 1379, reveals the existence of four sub-temples on its grounds, one for each of the disciples' lineages (Meihō, Mugai, Gasan, and Koan). Although the abbacy system devised by Keizan ensured the prosperity of Yōkōji in early years, it is clear that by 1379 things were going awry. After the schism that divided the disciples of Gasan from those of Meihō, all the abbots of Yōkōji belonged to the latter line. The rivalry between Yōkōji and Sōjiji would last until the Tokugawa period, and it is difficult to untangle the true course of events since each side presented its own version. Even the final sections of the *Record of Tōkoku* should be read with caution since they tend to confirm the superiority of Yōkōji. Later the partisans of the Meihō branch tried to strengthen their position at Daijōji, while those of the Gasan branch did the same at Sōjiji, thus abandoning Yōkōji.

To sum up, Keizan was the point of encounter, and of tension, between various lineages: of the Precepts (*kechimyaku*) and of the Dharma, but also of relics, which we examine below. For now suffice it to say that the dissemination of relics created a dynastic *genus* within which transmission by the direct line was achieved through possession of certain privileged regalia. The problem is that there was no agreement as to exactly what comprised these regalia—robe, portrait, text, or bodily relics—and still less about the order of precedence among them. Keizan's religious personality takes shape as a function of these various affiliations; it constitutes a nodal point at the intersection of these lineages, which sometimes reinforce and sometimes contradict each other, thus making up a kind of differential network that determines the various sectarian stakes. Such is the force field within which his teaching unfolds.

Chapter Three

IMAGINING POWERS

GENNŌ SHINSHŌ, a successor of Keizan at the second generation, is famous for having exorcised, during one of his peregrinations, the "killing stone" (*sesshōseki*). According to tradition, this mortiferous rock on Mount Nasu was the dwelling of the
malevolent soul of a nine-tailed fox, an extremely powerful spirit that, in
one of his former incarnations, had been a courtesan by the name of
Tamamo no mae ("Jewel Maiden").[1] After being pacified by Gennō, it
was sculpted into an image of the Bodhisattva Jizō, which is today worshiped at Shinnyodō in Kyoto.[2] The *Nihon Tōjō rentōroku* gives a somewhat different account: "One day, the master, holding his staff, went
there. Knocking three times on the stone he said: "You are after all just a
stone. Whence comes your nature, whence your powers (*rei*, Ch. *ling*)?
The stone began to sweat and to tremble, and cracked and dissolved.
Suddenly a strange man appeared, and bowed, saying: 'I am the spirit of
this stone. Thanks to the master's teaching, I have suddenly escaped the
evil path, and was reborn in heaven.' Having thus spoken, he disappeared."[3] This account is strongly reminiscent of the story of the encounter between the Chan master Pozao Duo ("Duo the Stove-Breaker") and
the Stove God (Zaojun). There was on Song shan a shrine dedicated to
the Stove God. Duo visited it and struck the stove, saying: "Whence
comes the deity? Where are his miraculous powers?" Then a young layman in a blue robe appeared and bowed respectfully to Duo, saying:
"I have suffered many afflictions here. Now by virtue of your discourse
on the teaching of non-birth, I have been reborn in heaven. I cannot
repay your kindness." Having said this, he departed.[4] In the *Shasekishū*'s version of this story, the emphasis is on the animal sacrifices
made to the god, while the violence of Pozao Duo's action is downplayed:
"At the foot of a certain mountain in China was a shrine with miraculous

---

[1] This story became the theme of a Nō play, *Sesshōseki*, and was also illustrated by the
ukiyoe artist Yoshitoshi ("Nasu no hara sesshōseki no zu"). See John Stevenson,
Yoshitoshi's Thirty-six Ghosts (Seattle: University of Washington Press, 1983), 64–65.

[2] See Kobayashi Gesshi, *Gennō Zenji dengenshutsu to Shinnyodō shinkō* (Kyoto: Shinnyodō kenkyūkai, 1988). Yet, according to touristic guides, the "killing stone" stills exists
on location and is still potent enough to kill insects (due to the poisonous gas emitted
through its porous structure). See Bodiford 1993–94: 273n.19.

[3] See *Nihon Tōjō rentōroku*, in DNBZ 110: 245a–b.

[4] There are several variants of the story. See for instance *Song gaoseng zhuan*, T. 50,
2061: 828b.

powers which the people of the countries venerated with offering of cattle, sheep, fish and birds. The shrine deity was only an old pot. Now it happened that a Zen master came and struck the pot, saying, 'Whence comes the deity? Where are the miraculous powers?' And he completely demolished it." Then the god comes, as in the Chinese version, to pay his respects to the self-righteous vandal. And Mujū concludes with the following comment: "It has been stated that when the gods receive offerings of slain creatures, their lot is pain; but when the pure nectar of the Law is offered up in profound discourse, then they experience happiness."[5] Keizan uses the same hagiographical topos in his section on the patriarch Haklenayaśas, in the Denkōroku: "When he was seven years old, Haklenayaśas went from village to village, and saw people performing illicit cults. He went into a shrine and scolded the god, saying, 'You are deluding people by randomly distributing calamity and fortune. Every year you require animals for your sacrifices, and cause extreme harm.' Upon these words, the shrine suddenly collapsed."[6]

Often, the mere presence of a virtuous Buddhist master is sufficient to exorcise a haunted place or to pacify the wilderness. The first Chan masters were supposedly able to overcome local gods or spirits, as well as their manifestations in the form of wild animals (tigers, snakes, dragons).[7] To give just an example, Xuanzong, a monk of the Northern school, lived in isolation on a mountain infested with tigers. One day an old man came to pay his homage to him and told him, "I was a man-eating tiger, but thanks to your teaching, I have reformed and have been able to be reborn as a *deva*. I've come to thank you."[8] Sometimes the encounter between a monk and the genius loci is staged in Buddhist hagiography in a more dramatic fashion. Thus, on another occasion, Gennō heard that a dragon who dwelt in a pond at the foot of a mountain used to attack people and to destroy crops. When Gennō, answering the villagers' prayers, came near the pond, the wind arose suddenly and the surface of the water began to seethe. The dragon emerged from the pond and moved toward Gennō, who started to recite scriptures. Under the spell of these powerful incantations, the dragon, we are told, turned into the Bodhisattva Kannon and disappeared in the sky. The next day the pond itself was gone, and a monastery, Taikyūji, was erected on that spot for Gennō.[9] Sometimes, however, the spirit is a little more recalcitrant, and the monk is forced to use all his spiritual resources and to resort to greater violence.

[5] See Morrell 1985: 93–94.
[6] Denkōroku, T. 82, 2585: 372a.
[7] On this question, see Faure 1993: 155–74.
[8] See Shenseng zhuan, T. 50, 2064: 1002.
[9] Quoted in Bodiford 1993: 176; see also Kelsey 1981: 109.

Keizan and his disciples were very close to the Shugendō movement, a branch of esoteric Buddhism characterized by worship of mountains and deeply concerned with supernatural powers—one aspect of which is the power to tame chthonian forces. Unlike popular tradition, Sōtō orthodoxy has played down this relationship and the fact that Keizan and his disciples at times almost identified with this trend. The sectarian attempt to expurgate Keizan's thought of any esoteric taint was permitted by the hermetic (in the sense of "sealed off") nature of the Zen literary genres he resorted to. The sparse references to supernatural powers in Keizan's writings may not represent all of his thinking on the matter. In each of his works, he follows the conventions of the traditional literary genres he is using. His writings thus resemble other works in the same genre more than they do each other, to the extent that without prior knowledge it would be hard to recognize that the Record of Tōkoku is by the same author as the Denkōroku. There are no echoes from the one in the other. This close fidelity to the constraints of genre means that in the Denkōroku, a chronicle of Zen transmission, Keizan refrains from any reference to Japanese popular beliefs and downplays the ritual or mythological aspects of traditional Buddhism. He restricts himself to typically Chan/Zen anecdotes and seems completely unaware of the rest of Chinese and Japanese culture. Such is not the case with the Record of Tōkoku. If we ignore these structural constraints, we risk misunderstanding Keizan's thought and reducing it to a single, monolithic discourse, a variant of Zen ideology as it was edited and corrected by Dōgen.

Buddhist thaumaturges are believed to possess six supranormal powers.[10] Usually seen as deriving from meditation, these powers make up one of the main mechanisms for converting others. Only the last of the six powers, however, is specifically Buddhist, insofar as it derives from the realm of the formless. Buddhist cosmology, as is well known, distinguishes three levels of reality: the worlds of desire, subtle form, and the formless. The first five powers belong to the domain of form and are thus held to be impure states.

The attitude of the early Buddhists toward supernormal powers and their use is not without ambiguity. Although the Buddha himself performed miracles on several occasions, we know that he criticized his dis-

---

[10] The traditional list of these powers is the following: 1) Miraculous powers properly speaking, which allow the Bodhisattva to pass through obstacles, to fly, to tame wild animals and transform himself at his will; 2) The divine eye, which allows him to see the death and rebirth of all beings; 3) The divine ear, which allows him to hear all the sounds of the universe; 4) Discerning the mind of others; 5) The memory of his past lives and those of others; 6) The knowledge of the destruction of all defilements, the end of ignorance that occurs in the formless realm and marks the attainment of Buddhahood. Among the many sources, see in particular Lamotte 1944–80: vol. 1, 328.

ciple Piṇḍola for having displayed his powers in front of common people. Without entering into detail, we can say that the argument against the use of miraculous powers should be set in its sociohistorical context, and more precisely in a sectarian one.[11] Since such powers were found in certain rival religious movements (Hinduism and Daoism), the Buddhists either laid claim to a different, superior type of power, or else, what amounted to the same thing, downplayed the very idea of supranormal powers in the name of the principle of emptiness. What at first sight appears to be a form of demystification is often only a tactical maneuver that is still part of the same mythic discourse: the doctrine of emptiness, in spite of all the philosophical interpretations that the exegetes are always too ready to accept at face value, operated essentially as a "superpower."

The existence of this tradition does not mean that in early Buddhism there was not a rationalist strain that viewed such powers as illusory. But this line of thinking, although it received the lion's share in the Pāli canon, was neither the only one nor the main one. The development of Mahāyāna increased ambivalence about thaumaturgy. On the one hand, its conception of Buddhas and Bodhisattvas as working marvels led to Mahāyāna scriptures, like the *Lotus Sūtra*, describing scenes in which the Indian predilection for marvels sometimes goes wild. At least this is what the first Western commentators thought, in the wake of Eugène Burnouf, the French translator of the *Lotus*. On the other hand, the logic of emptiness tended to rid these marvels of their content and convert them into illusions, magical tricks that at first astonish the readers but end up leaving them indifferent. Unlike the false magic of heretics, the magic of the Buddha, we are told, is the right magic, since he has fully realized that the entire reality is but magic.[12] So the achievement of emptiness is perceived as the supreme supernatural "power," but it is also the negation of all powers, since it embraces them and renders them null and void at the same time. The achievement of emptiness, like a sort of return to the "source of power," recalls Marcel Mauss's description of *mana* as immersion in the Brahman.[13]

The Sanskrit term *abhijñā*, used for these powers, is usually rendered by two Sino-Japanese characters (read as *shentong* in Chinese and *jinzū* in Japanese) that mean something like "spiritual penetration." This compound, with its Daoist resonance, contributed to the frequent identification between Buddhist thaumaturgists and the Immortals. The best-known example is that of Bodhidharma, who revealed his immortal nature by achieving the "deliverance from his corpse," a Daoist method

---

[11] For a more detailed account, see Faure 1991: 96–114.
[12] See Lamotte 1994–80: vol. 1, 16, citing the *Bhadramāyākāra*.
[13] See Tambiah 1985: 338.

that consisted of only appearing to die, leaving in the tomb only an imitation of the corpse. According to the later Chan tradition, Bodhidharma
was really an avatar of the Bodhisattva Guanyin (Japanese Kannon).
When Keizan took up the question of supranormal powers in his exchange of letters with Emperor Go-Daigo, it is obvious that he had in
mind the legendary story of the interview between Bodhidharma and Emperor Wu of the Liang (r. 502–549). During this interview, famous in the
annals of Chan, Bodhidharma alienated his interlocutor by refusing to
acknowledge the least merit in the latter's pious works. Finally Baozhi
(418–514), a character also considered to be an avatar of Guanyin, revealed Bodhidharma's true identity to the puzzled emperor, but by that
time Bodhidharma had disappeared. Thus the tradition stands revealed
in all its ambivalence: it is a thaumaturge who denounces belief in the
supranormal and all the cults growing out of it, and another thaumaturge
who lets the cat out of the bag. We are told that, when Go-Daigo asked
Keizan to explain to him how the "ordinary man" Bodhidharma could
have such "powers," Keizan replied: "The Buddhist patriarchs all have
supernatural powers. In the case of Bodhidharma, even though he was
born a prince, he was actually the incarnation of the Bodhisattva Kannon. How should he not have had supranormal powers? However, in
Zen no emphasis is placed on such powers."[14] As we can see, Keizan's
attitude is completely characteristic of Chan/Zen in general, in which
ambivalence leads to a double discourse: a disparagement of powers on a
theoretical level; a changing fortune of the image of the thaumaturgist in
hagiography, an image particularly esteemed in early Chan and then in
Japan with the spread of the Sōtō sect beginning with Keizan. As a counterpoint, one observes the growth of a particular category of powers,
those conferred by the Buddhist ordination, an ordination perceived as a
magical ritual. Already in the Heian period, the ordination was used as a
way to ensure "wordly gains" such as longevity: it was for instance conferred on women of the aristocracy at times of childbirth or serious
illness.[15]

The success of Buddhism in China and Japan depended more on its
prestige as a way of obtaining "powers" than on its philosophical excellence. Meditation (dhyāna), from which Chan derived its name, was first
of all a method for obtaining supranormal powers, and the biographies
of thaumaturgists make up a large part of the first hagiographical collections in Chinese Buddhism. Their success was partly a response to the
desire of the faithful for marvels. Although Chan does constitute, on the
whole, a reaction against this occult use of meditation, condemned as

---

[14] See T. 82, 2588: 422.
[15] See Ishida Mizumaro, "Kitō to shite no jukai," in Nihon bukkyō kenkyūkai 1991:
67–81.

"demoniac *dhyāna*," it did not give it up completely. The Indian translator Guṇabhadra, whom one early Chan chronicle tries to make into the "first patriarch" of Chan, was careful to warn his listeners against those who "use demons and spirits to learn about the acts of others." Still he was nonetheless revered himself as a powerful wonder-worker.[16]

Chan discourse on the subject of supranormal powers is fairly consistent. The official position is that Chan "does not make very much of these powers, to which it prefers the clarity of spiritual vision." This position is expressed in plain language in many "dialogues." Here is one that presents the Chan master Yangshan Huiji (ca. 807–883) and an Indian wonder-worker:

> One day a strange monk came down from the sky, greeted [Huiji], and stood there. The master asked him, "Where do you come from?" "From India," was the reply. "Why do you remain in this world?" "To stroll in the mountains and valleys." Huiji then said, "It's not that in the Buddha Dharma we scorn the subtle function of *abhijñā*, but one must wait until he is an old monk in order to acquire it." The monk said, "I came specially to the Eastern Land to pay homage to Mañjuśrī; and instead I have met a little Śākyamuni!"[17]

One of the powers most often mentioned is that of telepathy, the ability to receive and send mental images. The *Abhidharmakośa* shows how, by means of mental images, one can gain access to what other people are thinking:

> The ascetic who wants to know what other people are thinking first considers, in his own series, the characteristics of his body and thoughts. . . . In the same way, considering someone else's series, he arrives at the characteristics of his body and thought. Thus he can know what the other's thoughts consist of, and *abhijñā* [spiritual penetration] arrives. When *abhijñā* is achieved, the ascetic no longer considers the body, the form; he knows the thoughts directly.[18]

This form of telepathy should have been naturally honored in a school that preaches a transmission "from mind to mind," or rather "of the mind through the mind" (*yixin chuanxin*). Still, reading other people's thoughts is often disparaged in Chan. Many stories tell how a Chan master is put to the test by a Western monk from India or Central Asia who is endowed with the ability to read thoughts. The Chan master at first meets setbacks and seems unable to prevent the other from reading his thoughts; but he ends up by overcoming when he takes refuge in the absence of all thought (*wunian*) a domain where the other cannot follow him. These stories have their prototype in the works of the Daoist

---

[16] See *Lengqie shizi ji*, in *T.* 85, 2837: 1283c, 1284c.

[17] *Liandeng huiyao*, quoted in Mujaku Dōchū, *Kinben shigai*, ms., Coll. Hanazono University, chap. 13.

[18] *Abhidharmakośa-śāstra* vii, 102, quoted in Lamotte 1944–80: vol. 1, 333.

thinkers Zhuangzi and Liezi, and we may see in their resurgence a claim for the superiority of Chinese (non-)thought over Indian thinking. They tend in any case to show that, while psychic reading remains dependent on images and forms, non-thinking, by insisting on the formless, achieves a return to the source of power, which is pure potentiality. It is therefore intrinsically superior to any "manifestation" of psychic powers and allows the practitioner to dispense with them.

There is one accepted "power" that does rely on images: the ability to remember past lives. In Tang China there was a tendency to criticize this type of clairvoyance which led to eschatological claims and social troubles. According to Paul Demiéville, "Far from being an indication of sanctity, the memory of past existences . . . became in Chinese superstition a dangerous faculty against which every human being should be protected.[19] This gave rise to the popular belief that the dead drank, as in Plato's myth, the draught of forgetfulness poured for them by the goddess Mengpo. We have seen that Keizan remembered perfectly his past lives.

The other tactic adopted by Chan Buddhists against their rivals consisted in claiming for awakening the status of an "extraordinary" power. The story of the conversion of the god of Mount Song by the Chan master Yuangui is meaningful in this respect. When the god appeared to him in the middle of the night and threatened to punish him for his lack of respect, Yuangui replied, "Given that I am [fundamentally] non-born, how can you kill me? My body is empty and I see no difference between me and you: how can you destroy emptiness without destroying yourself?" This argument seems to have convinced the god, since he became Yuangui's disciple. After having conferred on him the Bodhisattva Precepts, Yuangui explained to him that the one true "power" is emptiness: "The fact that there is neither Dharma nor master is what is called nonthinking. For those who understand this, the Buddha himself has no powers. He can only, by non-thinking, penetrate all things."[20] This in itself is worth more than all other powers. As we can see, supranormal powers are by a single gesture both confirmed and denied, and the true wonder-worker is the one who knows how to go beyond "ordinary" powers. Likewise, Gennō Shinshō exorcized the "killing stone" when he struck it with his staff, shouting, "*Genjō kōan* is the great difficulty!"[21] In his gesture, the physical violence of the exorcism and the magical power of his staff are combined with the preaching of the ultimate principle (*genjō kōan*, "the actualized *kōan*"), which tames the malevolent spirit by enlightening it.

[19] See Demiéville 1927: 298.
[20] See *Song gaoseng zhuan*, T. 50, 2061: 994b.
[21] See Tenkai Kūkō, *Hōō Nōshō zenji tōmei*, in *SZ*, vol. 17, *Shiden*, 2: 278a; quoted in Bodiford 1993: 173.

With Chinese masters like Linji Yixuan, these powers have become purely metaphorical and only illustrate the total freedom of the Chan adept who knows how to use all conditions. The paradigm is provided by Layman Pang, an ordinary-looking man, not even ordained: "To carry water and cut wood—those are real powers!" In his description of the virtues of Tōkoku, Keizan takes up the same theme: "Both the fundamental spirit and everyday acts contribute to the work of the Buddha. Drawing water, carting wood—everything derives from the marvelous efficacy of spiritual powers; harvesting vegetables, gathering fruit—all this contributes to the turning of the wheel of the profound Dharma" [JDZ, 401].

We may see in the Chan/Zen masters' criticism of extraordinary powers an attempt to explain away their own inability to perform marvels. Thus, when a monk asked Yōsai why he did not have the powers of the masters of the past, the latter cited the story of the Arhat Piṇḍola, chastised by the Buddha for having made a display of his powers. In a chapter of the Shōbōgenzō entitled "Jinzū" [Supranormal Powers], Dōgen treats the question in detail: after having opposed true and false powers (with the latter for him meaning those of non-Buddhists as well as of traditional Buddhism: Hīnayāna, scholastic Abhidharma), he praises as true powers "ordinary activities like drinking tea or eating rice." Despite his ritualist bent, he here looks a lot like the "man with nothing to do" praised by his rival Linji, for whom Buddhist practice consisted simply of "moving one's bowels, pissing, getting dressed, eating one's rice, and lying down when one gets tired."[22] Dōgen even comes to reject as inferior the purely physical marvels accomplished by the Buddha—for example, making water gush out of his body (not to be confused with Linji's description mentioned above)—in comparison with the great "meta-physical" power that consists, if we may cite again the poem of Layman Pang, in "drawing water."[23]

In the Denkōroku, Keizan reports several anecdotes in which supranormal powers play an important role. In this sense the work is a breviary rather than a "history" of Chan/Zen. It recites (and at the same time confirms) the litany of the victories of Buddhist emptiness over the many forms of profane illusion (of which the most aggressive is that of wild animals who threaten the solitary monk). One of these stories presents the patriarch Aśvaghoṣa and his future disciple Kapimala. Kapimala at the outset is a powerful demon with whom Aśvaghoṣa had predicted he would have a confrontation. The demon appeared in the form of a golden dragon and made the mountains shake, but he could not move the patriarch. At the end of a week, he changed into a tiny insect

[22] See Watson 1993: 31.
[23] Shōbōgenzō, "Jinzū," T. 82, 2582: 112b.

and hid under Aśvaghoṣa's chair. But the patriarch picked up the insect and showed it to his disciples, saying, "Here is an avatar of the demon who has come secretly to listen to my teaching." When he released him, the demon could no longer move. Aśvaghoṣa then said, "If you take refuge in the Three Jewels, you will achieve supranormal powers." The demon resumed his original form, saluted him, and repented. "What is your name," asked Aśvaghoṣa, "and how many disciples do you have?" The demon replied, "My name is Kapimala and I have three thousand disciples." Aśvaghoṣa asked him about the extent of his powers. Kapimala said, "To produce an ocean is nothing for me." Aśvaghoṣa asked, "Can you produce the ocean of the [Buddha] nature?" Kapimala had never heard of anything like this. Aśvaghoṣa then explained to him what he was talking about: "The mounts, rivers, and earth all rest on this ocean; the three wisdoms and the six supranormal powers arise from it." Then Kapimala understood and asked to become Aśvaghoṣa's disciple. Keizan makes this commentary on the story:

> Even if he could, as a non-Buddhist, perform prodigious transformations, [. . .] Kapimala did not know that all these were [mere waves on] the ocean of the [Buddha] nature. This is why he had doubts about himself, and came to be suspicious of others too. Furthermore, since he did not know all beings, he was no match for someone who understood the origin [of things]. This is why, when his magical powers came to an end, he became unable to perform prodigious transformations. He finally had to surrender and become the disciple of someone else.[24]

After a prolonged eclipse in Chan after the Tang, the figure of the wonder-worker reappears more lively than ever in Japanese Zen. The hagiographies of the Sōtō school contain many stories in which monks succeed, thanks to powers that they derive from the practice, in pacifying all kinds of supernatural beings. We find in these stories themes that were already widespread in the early days of Chan, and in every case it seems that we are dealing with a more or less conscious proselytizing effort on the part of the monks. This tendency shows up, for example, in the Darumashū and in the Hottō branch of Shinchi Kakushin (1207–1298), but it also becomes particularly flourishing in Keizan's line, with Gasan Jōseki (1275–1365) and his disciples.

Worldly Gains

Access to the other world and "profits in this world" (*genze riyaku*) constitute the two sides of supranormal powers. The distinction between the

---

[24] See *Denkōroku*, in *T*. 82, 2585: 359b–c.

living and the dead is not always as pertinent as it may appear: certain funeral rites, for example, are intended both to ensure the deliverance of the dead and to protect against the damage they can do as ghosts. Thus the *nenbutsu*, originally intended only to ensure for the dying person his rebirth in the Pure Land of the Amida Buddha, came to serve as a magical formula used to avoid the revenge of those whom one had killed, whether humans or animals. Finally the monks were asked to recite the *nenbutsu* to bring good harvests or success in hunting and fishing.[25] The formula had the advantage of killing two birds (or two fishes) with one stone: ensuring a good harvest or plenty of fish for the people, and the welfare within the Pure Land of the insects and fish who fall victim in this pious slaughter.

Moreover, if supranormal powers are themselves to be ranked among worldly, relative profits, they can sometimes translate into a loss of the absolute by becoming for the practitioner a stumbling block. The faithful often considered the achievement of ultimate deliverance too distant a prospect and preferred to think about improving their living conditions in this life or in the next. To satisfy their incessant demands, the monks were tempted, whether from a hope of proselytizing or out of compassion, to use the powers that they possessed or thought they possessed. It was in reaction to this tendency that Dōgen spoke out against practices intended to obtain spiritual powers and material or symbolic gains. According to him, "One should cultivate the Buddha Dharma for itself, and not to acquire spiritual power [*reiken*]."[26] On this point Dōgen was only returning to the orthodox doctrine of Indian Buddhism which has always tried, without much apparent success, to limit the use of magical incantations for materialistic purposes. However, within Sōtō itself many ceremonies, described by Keizan in his *Pure Rule of Tōkoku*, included laypeople in various parts of the cult, especially in the monthly recitation of the Precepts, which were considered to have the power to conquer evil.[27] These ceremonies were already going on at Eiheiji during Dōgen's life. One source, with a somewhat hagiographic tinge, reports that during one recitation of the Precepts, in 1247, some twenty laypeople saw multicolored clouds emerging from Dōgen's cell. They were so impressed that they decided to write down their experience as testimony for future generations.[28] The Chinese and Japanese monastic codes that inspired the *Pure Rule of Tōkoku* themselves contained many rituals for various events related to agricultural life: rites concerned with rain, sun, snow,

25 See Hōri Ichirō, "Nembutsu as Folk Religion," in *Folk Religion in Japan*, 1968: 117–27.

26 See *Gakudō yōjinshū*, T. 82, 2581:3b.

27 See *JDZ*, 288–95.

28 See *Sōtōshū komonjo* 1137–38, 2: 191–93; and ibid. 10, 1: 9.

and others for protection against insects or eclipses.[29] Still, as they carried out the ritual prayers, Chan/Zen monks, unlike the practitioners of esoteric Buddhism, did not appeal to the power of a Buddhist divinity but to the power deriving from their own meditation practices and their observance of monastic discipline.[30] If we are to judge from the huge popularity of the Precepts among the lay population, it seems as though these Precepts finally outranked meditation as a source of authority for Zen monks.

However, when they did not rely on the mediation of the monks, the faithful themselves often addressed their prayers to the gods. Keizan himself owed his birth to the prayers that his mother addressed to the Bodhisattva Kannon. Women and their prayers were very important in this kind of worship. A work put together by a Buddhist layman, Minamoto Tamenori, for the use of an imperial Princess, the *Sanbōekotoba*, mentions for example the existence of a cult dedicated to Ānanda, the Buddha's cousin and disciple, who was instrumental in the institution of female ordination. According to this source, when a woman worships him, Ānanda uses his supernatural powers to respond to her call, and he protects her and answers all her prayers.[31] As we will see later, these prayers were often part of an incubation ritual, in which the divine response was given in dreams. A divine response to prayers thus constitutes one of the major elements in the success of Zen at the beginning of the Kamakura period. It is significant that one of the recently rediscovered Darumashū texts, the *Jōtō shōgakuron*, contains one section entitled "All prayers are answered."[32] In a period beset by social troubles, fires, famines, and epidemics, the hope nourished by these formulas must have spread like wildfire. Keizan lived on the edges of this world haunted by hunger and horror. Although he himself never claimed any supranormal powers, and, true to the Chan/Zen spirit, he even tried to downplay these powers in his sermons to his monks, he was nevertheless well aware of the needs of his lay disciples. Thus, in a short text recording the origins of Sōjiji, a monastery dedicated to the Bodhisattva Kannon, Keizan insists on the miraculous powers of the two "Light-emitting Bodhisattvas," Kannon and Jizō. We should not be surprised if this Zen priest, who believed that he owed his birth to Kannon, deemed it appropriate to tell the story of a Chinese empress of the Tang who had prayed to this Bodhisattva for an easy childbirth and was granted a male child. Since then, Keizan adds, all Chinese and Japanese empresses have taken refuge in Kannon. But the Bodhisattva's compassion is not reserved for em-

---

[29] See *Chixiu Baizhang qinggui*, T. 48: 1, 115.
[30] See Hirose 1993: 423–81; Bodiford 1993: 178–79.
[31] Kamens 1988: 273.
[32] See Shinagawa 1974: vol. 1, 204.

presses: if the village women whom Keizan is addressing do the same, Kannon's miraculous powers will certainly operate.[33]

How far did Keizan participate in the popular *imaginaire*, and in particular did he share in the belief that Zen masters, including himself, were endowed with thaumaturgic power? It is difficult to make any firm statement on this point. Although Keizan himself apparently didn't indulge in such exploits (which came to be customary among his disciples and had even been the case with Dōgen—at least in hagiography), he did subscribe to the belief that knowledge of the Buddhist emptiness constitutes the supreme "power." As Wittgenstein has stressed, "This does not mean that the people believe that the master is endowed with these powers and that the master for his part knows very well that he does not have them. . . . On the contrary, the idea of his power establishes itself naturally in such a way that it can be seen as matching experience—that of the people and his own. It is correct to say that a certain hypocrisy plays a role in this only insofar as, in a general fashion, we can see such hypocrisy in practically all the acts of man."[34]

[33] See *Sōjiji chūkō engi,* in *JDZ,* 489. After Keizan, a number of Sōtō temples became important "prayer temples" (*kitō jiin*). The most famous are Saijōji, Kasuisai, and Myōgonji. Saijōji was founded by Ryōan Emyō, a disciple of Gasan Jōseki and Tsūgen Jakurei. Although he was himself quite a thaumaturge, he was superseded in popular belief by his disciple Dōryō. On the death of his master, Dōryō vowed to protect the temple and help the people and transformed into a Tengu riding a white fox. Kasuisai, founded by Jochū Tengin (d.u.), is a temple dedicated during Meiji to Akiba Sanshakubō Daigongen, a former Shugendō practitioner who obtained from Kannon the gift of flying and became a mythical bird, the Garuḍa; Myōgonji, founded by a disciple of Giin—a Sōtō master famous for his encounter with Dakiniten, the fox-riding goddess—is dedicated to Toyokawa Inari. See *Nihon shūkyō no genze riyaku,* 1991: 165, 170.

[34] Wittgenstein 1982: 28.

Chapter Four

MYTHICAL *IMAGINAIRE*

IN THE *RECORD OF TŌKOKU* Keizan mentions several classes of divine or supernatural beings.[1] In descending order they include the Buddha Śākyamuni; the Bodhisattvas Miroku (in Skt. Maitreya, the "future Buddha"); Kannon (Avalokiteśvara) and Kokūzō (Ākāśagarbha); the Arhats Suvinda and Vajraputra, protective deities of Indian or Chinese origin; Karaten [Mahākāla]; Bishamon [Vaiśravana], the dragon-king Shōhō Shichirō [Ch. Zhaobao Qilang); and finally Japanese *kami* like Inari, Hachiman, and the deity of Hakusan. The case of the Indian monk Bodhidharma is a special one: he is the first "Chinese" Chan patriarch, but in Keizan's dream he plays the role of a divine figure of the same status as the Buddha Śākyamuni and the Bodhisattva Maitreya, while in the popular tradition he is often included among the sixteen or eighteen Arhats.

But even for Yōkōji the list as given by Keizan is not complete. In any consideration of this subject, we should also include the protective deities of Yōkōji as they are present and represented in their images. Such figures come from several of the above-mentioned classes. From among the Bodhisattvas we have Monju (Mañjuśrī), the "holy monk" who presides over collective meditation, and his companion Fugen (Samantabhadra), of whom Keizan himself preserved a much-valued relic. In the other categories we see above all the Wisdom-king Ususama (Ucchuṣma) and the Arhat Battabara (Bhadrapāla), protectors respectively of the latrine and the bathhouse, along with omnipresent deities from Tantric ritual like the fire god (Katoku Shōkun).[2] Also to be noted, even if we cannot describe it, is the entire mental iconology that populates the monastery with imagined deities who are not always the same as those represented in images. However, Keizan only mentions some of them as protecting deities:

During the winter retreat of the same year, the prior [Shi]kan, the chief seat [Gen]ka, and the attendant in charge of cleaning, Kakujitsu, dreamed that Inari, the god of the mountain, told them in a kindly voice, "I am the ancient

---

[1] I use the conventional term *supernatural* despite the fact that in Buddhism even deities are part of nature, because they are subject to karmic retribution.

[2] On Ucchuṣma, "eater of impurities," see Iyanaga Nobumi, "Récits de la soumission de Maheśvara par Trailokyavijaya—d'après les sources chinoises et japonaises," in Strickmann 1985: vol. 3, 694–98. Bhadrapāla is a Buddhist layman who attained enlightenment through the contemplation of water while bathing.

lord of this mountain. Order the entire province to make offerings of salt and soy paste to me." With a "demon arrow," he subdued the western slope of the mountain. With another, he pacified the front of the mountain and the peaks behind it.

I had a dream in which the protective god of the province came to tell me, "Proclaim throughout the province that I am to be offered yet another vegetarian dish. Such is the mysterious oracle of the great tutelary deity Ichinomiya. In addition, under my direction you must construct from camphor [wood] a seated figure of Bishamon holding in his left hand the pearl that grants all wishes and making with his right hand the seal of the gift. Make this the *honzon* of the store-house." The protection of the Dharma was thus received in a dream. In addition, during the same winter, Karaten [Mahākāla] appeared to announce that he wished to serve [as protector].

In the springtime of the second Bunpō year [1318], *tsuchinoe uma*, someone named Kōei dreamed that Shōhō Shichirō entered into the mountain and announced to him, "I have received from your superior the order to reward and punish the monks and to guard the doors of this monastery." Thus the god of the mountain [Inari], Ichinomiya [the protector of the province], and Shōhō Shichirō were appointed as gods of the monastery, and they were made assistants [to the Buddha].

Since Kannon was formerly the *honzon* of this mountain, [this Bodhisattva] was made the principal acolyte [of the Buddha]. As for Kokūzō, since he dispensed the precious manna to the community, he was the one who was asked for favors. This is why we entrust ourselves to the three Jewels (the Buddha, the Dharma, and the saṃgha), to the two sages (Kanzeon and Kokūzō), and to the two *devas* (Bishamon and Karaten), as benefactors of the monastic community. [*JDZ*, 393–94]

To simplify this presentation, we shall reserve problems that most properly concern the realm of images for Chapter 10, which is dedicated to icons. Here we shall simply examine the mental representations (in the ordinary sense, not in the iconic sense of ritual visualization) that the Japanese Buddhists contemporary with Keizan had of Buddhist, Buddhicized, and non-Buddhist divinities.

BUDDHIST DIVINITIES

The "Main Worthy" (*honzon*) of Yōkōji is, as he should be, the Buddha Śākyamuni, the "historical" Buddha to whom the Zen sect was trying to return, as a reaction to the way that the Pure Land sects worship the Buddha Amida (Amitābha). He is flanked by two statues, of Kannon and Kokūzō. These three make up the primary objects of worship.[3] Keizan indicates first the origins of their icons:

[3] Let us note in passing that in the *kirigami* of the Sōtō tradition, Śākyamuni is more

The *honzon*, the Buddha Śākyamuni, was carved in wood thanks to the thirty strings [of silver] donated by the second lieutenant of the cavalry of the right, Umanojō Nakada, from Inoie village, for the thirteenth funeral service of his mother. I gave fifty strings for the decoration [of this statue]. The lefthand acolyte, the Bodhisattva Kanzeon, was carved in wood thanks to Hōgen Jōshin from Suruga, in Ōmiya, at the main crossroads of the capital, for the thirteenth funeral service of his father Hōgen Jōshū. The righthand acolyte, the Bodhisattva Kokūzō, was carved in wood thanks to Minamoto Jirō from Noichi, from the Tomigashi domain in Kaga province, to ensure the granting of his wishes. [*JDZ*, 395]

We might apply to the Japanese situation the distinction that Gérard Colas has found operative in the case of Indian statuary: a distinction between the main fixed image in a temple and the movable, "functional" images, with the first representing the all-pervading and unchanging aspect of the god, which is the object of a minimum of cult practice, while the others, representing its various manifestations, receive most of the everyday worship.[4] Despite his importance for the Zen sect, Śākyamuni remains a fairly remote deity who hardly appears at all in cult practice as such. He serves above all as a source of historical legitimacy, and it is usually the episode of the transmission of the "Treasure of the Eye of the True Dharma" (*shōbōgenzō*) to his disciple Mahākāśyapa, a relatively late invention, that appears in the Golden Legend of Zen.

In Keizan's mind, Kannon is not simply an acolyte of the Buddha. We have seen the special devotion that his mother held for this Bodhisattva, and how Keizan inherited from her the statue that would become the main object of worship (*honzon*) of Enzūin. This Bodhisattva, originally male like all his colleagues, had, during his Chinese acculturation, assumed a female appearance under circumstances that are still ill-understood.[5] Kannon seems to have become for Keizan and his contemporaries a sublimated figure of all women. Thus, in a chapel at Sennyūji, a Kyoto monastery founded by the Vinaya master Shunjō (1166–1227), a figure of Kannon has the features of the famous and unfortunate courtesan Yang Guifei, the concubine of the Tang emperor Xuanzong.

In his choice of Kannon, Keizan was obviously motivated by his devotion, following the example of his mother, to a Bodhisattva who had always protected him. Whatever he had become was all attributable to the kind protection that Kannon, in response to the fervent prayers of his mother, had deigned to bestow on him. At the age of twenty-five, he tells

---

often discussed in the context of transmission than as *honzon* of the Buddha Hall. He is ordinarily symbolized by a specific graphic form or by a complex form of the swastika. See for instance Ishikawa 1983–94 (7): 255.

[4] See Colas 1989: 135.

[5] The best study on this topic is A. Stein 1986.

us, following the model of this Bodhisattva, he made the "universal vow of the great *icchantika*," the vow to remain in this lower world as long as there were still beings to be saved.[6] But beyond this personal relationship with Kannon, Keizan was also influenced by a local tradition that had elevated this Bodhisattva to the position of protector of the mountain on which Yōkōji would be founded. In a note about the "ten places" of Tōkoku he writes, "Originally this mountain was called Shōrenji Valley. The reason is that formerly there was in this place a temple to Kannon called Shōrenji (Temple of the Magnificent Lotuses)." This was doubtless a little chapel built by the villagers, but it was sufficient for Keizan to consider Kannon as the owner of these lands. Kannon was also the true identity, the "essence" (*honji*) of the god of Hakusan, and as such played a prominent role in the Shugendō branch that grew up around the worship of this mountain. We will recall that in popular Chan, the patriarch Bodhidharma is also considered to be an avatar of this Bodhisattva. We also know that Kannon played a major role in the establishment of Sōjiji by inspiring in the abbot of this temple the dream that led to the transfer of powers to Keizan, and also Keizan's dream that justified the transformation of the temple into a Zen monastery.[7] The role of Kannon as provider of oracular dreams, as we will see in Chapter 5, is particularly relevant in Keizan's case.[8]

The presence of Kokūzō as another acolyte of Śākyamuni is more difficult to explain. Keizan reports that his master Gikai, after spending three years in China (1259 to 1262), asked the two Boddhisattvas Kannon and Kokūzō, esoteric deities of the "Womb Maṇḍala" (*taizōkai mandara*), to protect him on his voyage back to Japan. To win them over, he commissioned statues of them and promised them to decorate and consecrate these statues as soon as he had arrived in Japan (or only in some future life if he should drown).[9]

When he named the Buddha Hall of Yōkōji Saishōden, Keizan tells us he was inspired by the title of a *sūtra*, the *Saishōō-kyō* [*Suvarnaprabhāsa-*

---

[6] The term *icchantika*, "man without faith," usually designates a being unable to reach salvation due to his inferior nature. However, in certain cases like this one, *icchantika* designates a Bodhisattva who has made a vow not to enter Nirvāṇa before saving all sentient beings.

[7] In the *Sōjiji chūkō engi*, in *Sōtōshū komonjo* 1: 33–34. Keizan compares Sōjiji to Kiyomizudera, as temples devoted to Kannon.

[8] Alongside Keizan's personal devotion to Kannon, we must also mention this Bodhisattva's place in the erudite symbolism of the *kirigami*: thus the eleven faces of Jūichimen Kannon, the aspect of Kannon venerated by Keizan's mother, correspond to the three truths of the Tendai teaching. See Ishikawa 1983–94 (7): 262. In popular Buddhism, finally, Kannon is, like Jizō, present in each of the six karmic destinies, under the canonical form of the six Kannon.

[9] See *Daison gyōjiki*, in *SZ* 16, *Shiden*, vol. 1, 18.

sūtra],[10] during the preaching of which the Buddha had Kannon and Kokūzō as his acolytes. This Buddha hall was not completed until 1322, three years before his death, but already in 1318, as is shown by one passage in the *Record of Tōkoku*, his choice of a dedication was fixed: "Since Kannon is the former *honzon* of this mountain, [this Bodhisattva] was made the principal acolyte [of the Buddha]. As for Kokūzō, since he dispenses the precious manna to the community, he is the one who is asked for favors" [*JDZ*, 394]. But it seems that we are dealing here with a posteriori rationalizations, not true motivations. We also know that this Bodhisattva played a significant role in ordination ceremonies and in Shingon visualization techniques.[11] Another hypothesis is that this esoteric Bodhisattva was the central object of the local cult of Sekidōzan (Isurugiyama), a mountain on the Noto Peninsula. From its geographic position, Yōkōji was at the boundary between two important Shugendō cult centers, Sekidōzan and Hakusan, centered respectively on Kokūzō and Kannon. The choice of these two Bodhisattvas might thus reflect an attempt to reconcile the two symbolic systems, and at the same time to attract to Yōkōji the faithful of both branches.[12]

Usually in Sōtō monasteries the triad in the Buddha Hall is flanked by two further acolytes, whose altars are set somewhat to the rear, on each side of the principal altar. These are Bodhidharma and Daigenshuri, to whom we shall be returning. Maitreya is not usually represented. He nevertheless plays a significant role in the Zen *imaginaire*. Maitreya is not conceived of as an eschatological deity, the Buddha of the future, or as his Chinese avatar Budai, the potbellied Buddha who became popular as a gate-keeper in Chinese Chan monasteries. He is Maitreya as Boddhisattva, reigning in Tuṣita Heaven while he awaits his future descent to earth. An important feature of the "practice of dreams," as we see for example in Myōe, consists of a dream ascent to Tuṣita Heaven, anticipating thus a rebirth in this "Pure Land" of Maitreya.[13] However, the var-

---

[10] This sūtra was translated by Yijing. See *T*. 16, 665.

[11] Since the translation of *Xukongzang qiuwenchifa* [*T*. 1145] by Śubhakarasiṃha in 717, the mantra of Ākāśagarbha had become part of Buddhist esoteric practice, and it acquired importance in the conversion of Kūkai. See Hakeda 1972: 19–22. Concerning Ākāśagarbha's role in Buddhist repentance, see Kuo 1994: 64, 69–70, 136–38. On Kokūzō in *kirigami*, see Ishikawa, 1983–94 (7): 265.

[12] See Satō 1986–87.

[13] Maitreya's paradise is deemed inferior to that of Amida, from which there is no backsliding. This inferiority is manifested in the presence of women such as Māya, Śākyamuni's mother. However, there is an attempt to put the two paradises on a par in Mujū's *Shasekishū*: "In the Tuṣita Heaven the Inner and Outer Courts differ. In the Outer Court there is regression, but progress is possible. But among the forty-nine palaces of the Inner Court is the Pavilion of Everlasting Life which is the same as Amida's Pure Land of Supreme Bliss." See Morrell 1985: 117. It is in this Inner Court that Keizan is led by Maitreya in his dream.

ious functional aspects of this deity are never entirely separated from each other, and, in the cult of mummies in particular, the legend of Mahā-kāśyapa awaiting, deep in a state of *samādhi*, the arrival of the future Buddha in order to transmit to him the robe belonging to his master Śākyamuni, played an important role. But Maitreya remains, for Chan/Zen adepts, the spiritual guide whom one can reach without too much difficulty by means of meditation and who, more than any other Bodhisattva, can bestow visions or revelations to confirm the practitioner on his path. It was Maitreya, after all, who gave Keizan the ultimate confirmation during his dream ascent to Tuṣita Heaven. Another Bodhisattva who should be mentioned is the "holy monk" Mañjuśrī. His icon was installed in the meditation hall of Yōkōji in the spring of 1325, at the beginning of the summer retreat, a few months before Keizan's death.

The Cult of the Arhats

Alongside the Buddhas and Bodhisattvas, another group of figures from the Buddhist pantheon play an important role in Keizan's universe. These are the Arhats (Ch. *luohan*, J. *rakan*), disciples of the Buddha who, for one reason or another, did not follow him when he entered the final Nir-vāṇa and who remain in this world in order to bring enlightenment to later generations. On the model of the Daoist Immortals, they are elusive characters, living in between two worlds, which gives them the status of privileged intercessors. Although sometimes decried in the Buddhism of the Greater Vehicle as representing the ideal of personal salvation impor-tant in the Lesser Vehicle (an ideal considered as too narrow in compari-son with the Greater Vehicle's altruistic ideal of the Bodhisattva), they came to enjoy a great popularity in Chinese Buddhism, especially in Chan, and even competed with the Bodhisattvas. Their ambiguity emerges clearly from the little book used in the Sōtō ritual of offerings to the Arhats, in which it is said that the Arhats, although resembling super-ficially the Auditors (Skt. *śrāvaka*, adepts in the Lesser Vehicle), are really Bodhisattvas internally. In the *Record of Tōkoku*, Keizan often makes much of his meetings, during a former existence or in the course of dreams, with certain of these disciples of the Buddha. We may recall that he claimed to have been, during numerous past lives, the teratomorphous disciple of the Fourth Arhat Suvinda. However, it is the vision that he obtained from the Eighth Arhat Vajraputra that seems to have made the most durable impression on Keizan—judging from the way he constantly returns to it in his writings. I will quote here only one of these passages, toward the beginning of the *Record of Tōkoku*:

The eighth month of the second Shōwa year [1313], *mizunoto ushi*, I began to build a thatch hut that would serve temporarily as a refectory. That night I dreamed that the eighth Arhat [Vajraputra] came to tell me, "I have come here and have seen this mountain. Although from a distance it does not look like much, it is in fact an extremely propitious site, even more so than that of Eiheiji. At Eiheiji the abbot's hall was built in an enclosed space haunted by troublemaking spirits. This is why there have always been troubles there, since ancient times. The same will not be true of this mountain, where you can spread your teaching as much as you wish." [Indeed,] from the time I built my hermitage there, I never encountered the least difficulty. Since there was nothing there to interfere with [religious] practice, this prospered throughout the years. [*JDZ*, 392–93]

The appearance of the Arhat Vajraputra and his predictions about the future of Yōkōji testify that the past is not dead and that these beings, unimpeachable witnesses to a glorious past, are still present in today's world. They may still appear, in this time of the decline of the Dharma, to predict a glorious future. It is also notable that the appearance of Vajraputra sealed the alliance between Keizan and Sonin, who would henceforth dedicate herself to the worship of the Arhats.

Then she transformed her home, making it into a "place of awakening" (*bodhimaṇḍa*), and invited the sixteen Arhats to accept her offerings. Here is the proof that this is a propitious place, where the protection [of the Arhats] is secretly received. On the fifteenth day of the ninth month of the same year, the ceremony of offerings to the Arhats was inaugurated, and it was repeated on the fifteenth of each month since this is what they wanted. [*JDZ*, 395]

Keizan's attitude toward the Arhats is not unique. It is impossible to overestimate the role of these figures in Chan and Zen. Their importance for Zen during the Tokugawa period is clearly illustrated in statues, especially by the series of Arhats belonging to Manpukuji, principal monastery of the Ōbaku sect in Uji, to the south of the Kyoto. The Arhat cult seems to have developed first of all around the figure of Piṇḍola, the first of the sixteen or eighteen Arhats and one of the most individualized.[14] Piṇḍola was famous for his supernatural powers—and his gluttony. He was condemned to remain in this world after the Nirvāṇa of the Buddha and the other disciples because he used his powers to satisfy his greediness. In spite (or because) of his gluttony, Piṇḍola represents the ideal (or better, the double) of the monk, and his ritual role is revealed in his function as keeper of the kitchens and bathrooms. In China his cult seems to go back to the Vinaya master Daoxuan (596–667). In Japan Piṇḍola (J. Binzuru) became popular as a healing saint, and his image was associated

[14] See Strong 1979.

with those of Jizō and Yakushi as "gods of happiness." Despite recent attempts by the authorities to eliminate his cult for health reasons, in most of today's "prayer temples" he is the "Buddha one caresses" (*nadebotoke*): by fondling the statue's face (deformed from so much handling), or another part of its body, the worshiper communicates to the corresponding part of his own body the healing efficacy of the Arhat—according to a logic that we examine in more detail when we come to the subject of Buddhist icons in Chapter 10: that of the double or the substitute.

The cult of the Arhats as a group seems to derive from that of Piṇḍola. The incorporation of Piṇḍola's protective function into the schema of the four directions led, according to Lévi and Chavannes, to the idea of the "four great Arhats" (Mahākāśyapa, Kuṇḍopadhanīya, Piṇḍola, and Rāhula), and then, by a repetition of this process, to the appearance of the sixteen Arhats.[15] Their cult, which existed already in the fourth century, seems to have become widespread toward the end of the Tang after a monk artist by the name of Guanxiu (832–912) saw the Arhats in a dream and painted them in a group portrait that would become the basis of all later representations. According to legend, Guanxiu was surprised to see only fifteen Arhats in his dream but was told that he looked just like the sixteenth Arhat.[16] He therefore rounded out the number by including his own self-portrait. Another significant iconographic representation was by the painter Li Longmin (died in 1106). The cult of these Buddhist saints was intimately tied up with the emergence of Chan and took on a great importance in Japan during the Kamakura period. Around this time representations of the eighteen Arhats were placed in the monumental gates of all the great Zen monasteries. The addition of two new figures to the traditional list of sixteen Arhats seems to have come with the popularization of Chan.[17] The motif of five hundred Arhats, on the other hand, appears to have developed largely outside the Chan/Zen tradition.

During his stay in China, Shunjō (1166–1227), a Vinaya master and founder of Sennyūji, had received from a Chinese master a picture of the eighteen Arhats attributed to Guanxiu—supposedly because of his, Shunjō's, physical resemblance to the seventeenth Arhat. Another painting, this time attributed to Li Longmin, now the oldest in Japan, was brought from China by Chōnen (d. 1016), the superior at Seiryōji (a temple better known under the name of Shakadō, "Shaka Hall," from the famous image of Śākyamuni kept there), in Saga, to the west of

---

[15] See Lévi and Chavannes 1916: 273.

[16] See de Visser 1923: 110–11, quoting *The Nigu lu* by Chen Weiru (1558–1639).

[17] The two additions were emblematic figures of Chinese popular religion, the dragon tamer and the tiger tamer. See ibid. See also Menzan, *Rakan ōkenden*, vol. 3: 3.

Kyoto. Dōgen also brought back from China a picture of the sixteen Arhats attributed to Li Longmin.[18]

In spite of their cult importance in Chan/Zen, the Arhats were only rarely the object of doctrinal discussion in Zen texts. In a chapter of the *Shōbōgenzō* specifically titled "The Arhat" (*Arakan*), Dōgen makes of these figures emblems of authentic Buddhism, which is for him that of the Greater Vehicle, but he omits any mention of their mythological dimension.[19] The textual silence is broken, however, when we turn to hagiographical literature.

According to the preface of the *Treatise for the Protection of the State by the Encouragement of Zen (Kōzen gokokuron)*, Yōsai saw the image of an Arhat reflected in his tea bowl during his first visit to Mount Tiantai. After this vision he made an offering of tea to the five hundred Arhats. These famous Mount Tiantai Arhats had already been mentioned by the Japanese pilgrim Jōjin (1011–1081), who became himself well known for his "powers," his "Diary of dreams," and ultimately his mummification. According to Jōjin, the five hundred Arhats lived near a rock bridge, a natural arch that only "pure" monks could cross.[20] When Jōjin went on pilgrimage to Mount Tiantai in 1072, he remembered a dream, one he had recorded eleven years earlier, in which he had been able to cross the rock bridge with ease, proof that he had correctly produced the thought of awakening. Jōjin did not tell us, however, whether his dream was corroborated by a crossing of the actual bridge. We may doubt that this happened, since modern photographs show that the bridge is divided in the middle by a rocky barricade and the kingdom of the Arhats remains, as it should be, invisible to all those who cannot pass to the other side of this stony mirror. This does not seem to have troubled our Japanese pilgrims since, as a later Japanese commentator remarks, while eight or nine out of ten Chinese pilgrims had to give up on the effort, most of the Japanese succeeded in crossing.[21] This comment is followed by a eulogy of Chōgen (1121–1206), Yōsai's companion, who was apparently able to make the crossing. The text does not mention Yōsai himself, but we know from other sources that when Yōsai crossed the bridge he had a vision not of the Arhats (as one might expect) but of two "blue dragons," a vision followed by the revelation that he had been, during a previous existence, an Indian monk who lived in a monastery on Mount Tiantai, the Wanniansi, or Monastery of Ten Thousand Years.[22] According to the *Genkō shakusho*, "In 1168 Yōsai went to Mount Tian-

---

[18] See Michihata 1983.
[19] Dōgen, *Shōbōgenzō* "Arakan," *T*. 82, 2582: 152c–154a.
[20] See Morris 1970: 369.
[21] See Michihata 1983: 275.
[22] Ibid., 283.

tai and the sight of the great beauty of the mountains and streams filled him with joy. When he reached the stone bridge he burned incense and tea, and [so] worshipped the five hundred Arhats who live at this spot. A little later he returned to Japan."[23]

Furthermore, according to a later source, the Sōtō ceremony carried out in honor of the Arhats had been brought to Japan by Yōsai, who had been instructed in it by the Arhats themselves when he was on the rock bridge with Chōgen.[24] All this took place during the three days that Yōsai spent on Mount Tiantai during his first visit to China. During his second stay, twenty years later, Yōsai returned to Mount Tiantai and spent five years there. He restored several buildings there, including the stūpa of the founder of the Tiantai school, Zhiyi (538–597), and that of his own past reincarnation, the Indian monk Jixiangdan. There is no further mention of the Arhats in Yōsai's hagiography, even after his return to Japan. But it is clear that they continued to play a major role in Yōsai's life and in the liturgy of early Zen. We do know that Yōsai, in 1200, performed a ceremony to open the eyes of the statues of the sixteen Arhats commissioned by Hōjō Masako (1157–1225).

Dōgen was perfectly aware of these precedents. According to Sōtō tradition, he himself saw the Arhats when he visited Mount Tiantai and later at Eiheiji (see figure 1). In his commentary to Dōgen's biography, Menzan Zuihō (1683–1769) reports that during a ceremony dedicated to the Arhats, their images and statues emitted a glow indicating that they had accepted the offerings, as they had earlier at Mount Tiantai.[25] We also have a short text attributed to Dōgen himself that refers to this apparition. It is dated the morning of the first day of the first month of the year 1249. This vision came to Dōgen in his cell while he was meditating in front of a statue of the Buddha. He ends the account thus:

> As for other examples of the appearance of auspicious signs, apart from [the case of] the rock bridge of Mount Tiantai [in the province] of Taizhou, in the great kingdom of the Song, nowhere else to my knowledge has there been one to compare with this one. But on this mountain [Kichijōsan, the location of Eiheiji] many apparitions have already happened. This is truly a very auspicious sign showing that, in their deep compassion, [the Arhats] are protecting the men and the Dharma of this mountain. This is why it appeared to me.[26]

The sixteen Arhats also appeared on the branches of an ancient pine tree in front of Eiheiji.[27] The appearance of the Arhats was for Dōgen

---

[23] See de Visser 1923: 37.

[24] Michihata 1983: 283.

[25] Ibid.: 461.

[26] See DZZ, 399.

[27] This tree, known as the "Arhat pine tree" (Rakanshō), still exists today. See Michihata 1983: 212.

proof that Eiheiji was the only place in Japan where the Buddhist Dharma was being transmitted correctly and that this monastery was thus rivaled by no other, with the exception of that on Mount Tiantai in China.[28] This expression of Buddhist spiritualism should be taken to heart by those who persist in idealizing Dōgen as an "incomparable philosopher."

By an ironic turn of events, it was also the revelation of an Arhat—the Eighth Arhat Vajraputra—that allowed Keizan to claim that the site of Yōkōji, and by extension the branch of the sect that developed there, was superior to that at Eiheiji, its powerful rival. Thanks to the existence of many documents, we know of the importance of the Arhats in Keizan's life and the liturgy of Yōkōji and Sōjiji. The role played in Keizan's dreams by Vajraputra, a relatively obscure, rarely mentioned figure, remains intriguing.

Keizan's Zen teaching—and by extension the entire Sōtō sect—seems to owe its success to the protection of this Arhat. As noted earlier, a ceremony dedicated to the Arhats took place at Yōkōji on the fifteenth of each month, and it is carried on even today in the Sōtō sect, following the ritual established by Keizan rather than that transmitted by Yōsai and Dōgen.[29] During this ritual each of the sixteen Arhats is revered in turn, along with the five hundred Arhats of the rock bridge at Mount Tiantai, the four great Arhats, and a relic of the Buddha.[30]

Even though he supported a return to the "pure Zen" of Dōgen and a "demythologization" of the Sōtō tradition, Menzan dedicated an entire work, the *Rakan ōken den* [Chronicle of Miraculous Responses from the Arhats, 1754], to miracles worked by the Arhats in response to human solicitations. This work contains more than one hundred legends about the Arhats in China and Japan and is the best source on this subject. The first Japanese account is that of Nichira, a Korean general, who first served as tutor to the young prince Shōtoku and then became the tutelary god of Mount Atago (west of Kyoto) and in that role was considered a "manifestation" of the Bodhisattva Jizō in his martial aspect, "General Jizō" (Shōgun Jizō).[31] Menzan puns on his name, which he interprets as meaning the "Arhat of Japan" (*Nichi* being the first character of *Nihon*,

[28] Later, other Japanese Zen adepts made a pilgrimage to Mount Tiantai and made tea offerings to the Five Hundred Arhats: let us simply mention the cases of the Sōtō monk Giin (1217–1300) and the Rinzai monk Shōgen (1295–1364). On Giin, see *Nihon Tōjō rentō-roku*, in *DNBZ* 110: 225a.

[29] For a description of this ritual, see *Keizan shingi*, T. 82, 2589: 434–36; and de Visser, 1923: 182–96.

[30] *Keizan shingi*, T. 82; 2589: 434b.

[31] The Shōtoku Taishi biography, quoted by Menzan, presents Nichira as a Japanese, born in Higa province, who went to the Korean Kingdom of Paekche and became an official there, only to return to Japan at the invitation of Emperor Bidatsu. A more likely variant makes him a Korean. See Bouchy 1976: 9–48; and de Visser 1923: 85–92.

"Japan," and *ra* that of *rakan*, "Arhat").[32] Another pun of the same kind seems to be the source of the story that the arrival in Japan of the Chan master Wuxue Zuyuan (Japanese Mugaku Sogen, 1226–1286) was revealed in a dream to Hōjō Tokiyori by an Arhat: "Wuxue" is the Chinese translation of *aśaikṣa*, a Sanskrit term designating an Arhat.[33]

Menzan himself tells of his propitious meeting in a dream with an Arhat, just a few days before a summer retreat. Because it was inadequately publicized, he was afraid that this retreat would attract very few participants, and so he had begun a seven-day ceremony in honor of the eighteen Arhats. On the sixth night he dreamed that he was visited by a great Zen master, Ōbaku Kōsen, accompanied by more than twenty monks. After offering tea to his distinguished visitor, Menzan asked him, as was the custom, for a sample of his calligraphy. But he woke up just at the moment when an acolyte was beginning to prepare the ink. On the next day at the end of the ceremony, as Menzan was starting to put away the scrolls representing the Arhats, he was surprised to notice that the face of one of them was exactly that of the person with whom he had drunk tea in his dream. The Arhat even held a brush in his hand, while an acolyte prepared ink. Menzan then realized that his prayer had been heard. During the following days many monks arrived from the Rakanji ("Arhat Monastery") at Usa, in Bizen province.[34] Of course the retreat was a great success, thanks to the participation of sixty-eight worthy monks.[35]

In all these texts, and in the rituals described in some of them, the Arhat appears as a double of the monk, as well as a substitute for the Buddha. Ritually the Arhat is doubled by his icon, and sometimes by a monk who can also substitute for him. As indicated by the Vinaya master Daoxuan, "At present there are people who make an image of the holy monk Piṇḍola, set it up in a hall, and make offerings to it. This is one way of proceeding. But one must also set up, in another place, a cup and bowl in front of an empty seat. When the time comes for the monks to eat, an eminent monk is invited to receive the offerings by substitution."[36]

---

[32] See Menzan, *Rakan ōkenden*, ms. of Komazawa University Library, p. 26. Menzan also quotes Keizan's dream of the Eighth Arhat Vairaputra from the *Record of Tōkoku* and attributes the prosperity of the Sōtō school in Japan to the protection of this Arhat (ibid.: 2: 33).

[33] Ibid.: 2: 32.

[34] Rakanji was a well-known temple, which, after the model of Tiantai shan, boasted of a "very dangerous" rock bridge. De Visser, noting that it is a Rinzai temple, emphasizes that the cult of the five hundred Arhats, unlike that of the sixteen Arhats, played only a minor role in Sōtō because it originated in Southern China, whereas Sōtō represents Northern Chan. However, this identification of Sōtō with Northern Chan, and of the latter with Northern China, has no factual basis. See de Visser 1923, 57.

[35] See *Rakan ōkenden*, ibid.: 2: 37–38. On Rakanji, see also ibid.: 2: 32–33. See also Michihata 1983: 228.

[36] Lévi and Chavannes 1916: 214.

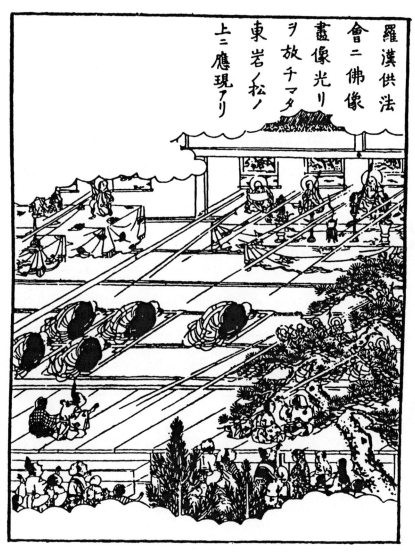

羅漢供法
會二佛像
畫像光リ
ヲ放チマタ
東岩ノ松ノ
上二應現アリ

FIGURE 1. The Arhat ceremony at Eiheiji, in Zuikō Chingyū and Daiken Hōju, eds., *Teiho kenzeiki zue* (1806), in *SZ*, 17, *Shiden*, 2, rev. ed. (Tokyo: Sōtōshū shūmuchō, 1970–73).

This "logic of the supplement" does not prevent Piṇḍola from coming down to participate personally in the ritual, whose success is determined by finding the impression made by the Arhat on the unoccupied seat cushion or his wet footprints at the edge of the bath.

The mediation of the Arhat makes possible the ritual projection *in illo tempore*, the "imaginary" connection between the officiating priest or the worshiper and the time and person of the Buddha. It makes it possible to reduce the sense of longing for this mythical time and the feeling of deprivation that overwhelms the faithful in this period of the last age of the Buddhist Dharma (*mappō*). Living in the intermediate space between this world (*saṃsāra*) and the higher realms, beings like Piṇḍola are emblems of the Buddhist *imaginaire*.

KEIZAN AND THE CULT OF THE KAMI

If the Arhats may be seen as idealized monks, the Buddhist deities appear sometimes as idealized laypeople, extraterrestrial doubles of ordinary lay folk. For example, the *Record of Tōkoku* calls Bishamon and Karaten "benefactors," a term ordinarily reserved for lay patrons. The gods must be converted, and in some cases even restrained by the monks, before becoming, as do powerful laypeople, the source of wealth and protection.

While the gods are, in principle if not always in practice, to be held accountable by virtue of the obligation that they have assumed by accepting the worship offered to them, the Buddhas, Bodhisattvas, and Arhats are freed from all such indebtedness; they are not accountable. They are not, consequently, bound to any necessary actions. It would therefore be presumptuous to try to increase their infinite stock of merits: they have been delivered from the cycle of rebirths, unlike the gods who are still subject to karma. As a result the benefits they bestow are seen as "freely given." Nevertheless they are often treated as gods. People try to sway them, win them over with promises of offerings, and thus involve them in the cycle of indebtedness. So Keizan's mother tried to twist one of Kannon's many arms by promising to provide a body for the carved head of Kannon she had found.

We recall that after a dream in which the tutelary god Ichinomiya of Keta shrine appeared to him, Keizan adopted as protecting deity Bishamon, an originally Hindu god converted to Buddhism. From the outset the syncretistic atmosphere in which Keizan lived is apparent. Likewise, the tutelary god Inari appeared to Keizan's disciples to require a cult. Keizan records in the *Record of Tōkoku* two oracles from Japanese *kami* that he received in a dream. The first oracle comes from the god Hachiman (Yahata no kami), a powerful deity considered to be the god of war.[37] The second oracle is not clearly attributed, but its content, as well as its archaic phonetic transcription, attest to its autochtonous origin and sacred nature.[38]

In spite of the efforts of some scholars to find in Japan some kind of

[37] On Hachiman, see Kanda 1985.
[38] See *JDZ*, 405, 409.

structuralist "mytho-logique," Japanese mythology seems at first glance less hierarchized, more ambivalent, less formalized or rationalized than the Greek, Indian, or Chinese mythologies. Thus Keizan's visions put all the apparitions therein of Bodhisattvas (Avalokiteśvara and Maitreya), Arhats, *kami* like Hachiman or Inari, as well as the ghosts of certain dead people, on the same level of reality. The *imaginaire*, in its leveling syncretism, undoes the discourse of Chan/Zen hierarchical and militant syncretism. The dream existence of the gods has to be acknowledged; otherwise one would have to deny the dream existence of the Bodhisattvas.

Despite his nativist bent and his increasing criticism of Chinese Buddhism, Dōgen is strangely silent on the subject of the Japanese *kami*. His attitude toward the lowest level of deities is clearly negative, an inheritance from the polemical spirit of the *Lotus Sūtra*. One of the rare passages in which he mentions them is a warning against being misled by them: "There are many people who, out of fear, seek refuge in gods of mountains, forests, trees, gardens, non-Buddhist sanctuaries, and so on. However, to seek refuge by this kind of divinity is worthless because it is impossible to free oneself from suffering in this way."[39] In another text, in which he lists the merits of ordination, Dōgen insists that simply by receiving the Buddhist Precepts the monk obtains the highest of merits and transcends the three levels of existence, and that, at the same stroke, the gods of heaven and earth become the protectors of the Dharma. Later Sōtō hagiography holds that the god Inari appeared to Dōgen when he was sick by the side of a road in Jiangxi and gave him a remedy (see figure 2).[40] This hagiography also claims that it was the deity of Hakusan (or the dragon-king Shōhō Shichirō) who helped Dōgen to recopy the *Biyan lu* on the eve of his departure from China, while Shōhō Shichirō protected him during his return crossing.[41]

Keizan's attitude seems different, even though his position with regard to local deities is not without its ambiguities. At the same time as he was elevating a textual monument, the *Denkōroku*, to the glory of Chan/Zen Buddhism, Keizan (unlike Dōgen and most of the Chan masters before him) recognized what Marc Augé has called the genius of paganism.[42]

[39] *Shōbōgenzō*. "Kie sanbō," in *T*. 82, 2582: 291c; see also Yokoi 1976: 130.

[40] Likewise, the goddess Dakiniten is said to have appeared to Dōgen's disciple Giin when the latter returned from his second trip to China. This Tantric deity, because of the fox symbolism that characterizes her cult, became associated with the god Inari in Japan.

[41] In the illustration of this scene in *Kenzei ki*, the deity of Hakusan is represented as an old man, and not as a young woman. As Susan Tyler points out, the nature of Japanese *kami* (and their representation) remains fluid: they can be seen as benevolent or malevolent (*nigimitama, aramitama*), singular or plural, female or male. See Tyler 1992: 64–66, 90–91.

[42] See Augé 1982. Augé's title is inspired by François-René Chateaubriand's famous work, *Génie du christianisme* (1802).

江西ノ路ニテ師病ヒ
アリ時ニ稲荷神
現メ丸樂ヲ與ヘヱル
随從ハ道正庵主ナリ

FIGURE 2. Feeling ill during his trip to China, Dōgen receives help from the god Inari, in Zuikō Chingyū and Daiken Hōju, eds., *Teiho kenzeiki zue* (1806), in *SZ*, 17, *Shiden*, 2, rev. ed. (Tokyo: Sōtōshū shūmuchō, 1970–73).

He tells us that the troubles that occurred at Eiheiji were caused by the presence of troublesome deities. Were they also perhaps caused by Dōgen's lack of respect for these deities? But we must not exaggerate the contrast between Keizan and Dōgen on this point, as on so many others, because its principal cause may be the differences in the literary genres through which their thought has come down to us. After all, while Dōgen hardly mentioned the *kami* in the *Shōbōgenzō*, Keizan is almost as silent on this matter in his *Denkōroku*, and without texts like the *Record of Tōkoku* we might believe that he, too, attached no great importance to them.

Yet, as we have noted, Keizan was convinced that in a previous existence he had been a tree spirit and, thanks to his karmic affinities with the northern continent of Uttarakuru, could be reborn as an *ujiko* of the deity of Hakusan, in northeastern Japan. According to the *Record of Tōkoku*, the tutelary god of Tōkokusan was Inari, and the Yōkōji monastery founded by Keizan was placed under the protection of Shōhō Shichirō and the *kami* of the Keta shrine (Daichinju ichinomiya). The fact that Shōhō Shichirō has to be *named* god of the mountain and god of the earth is meaningful: this shows that he acts in terms of functions attributed to him by human agents and not from any natural right. We have here a paradoxical case in which a foreign god becomes an autochthonous figure alongside a local *kami*. Keizan also calls on Buddhist (or rather, Buddhicized) deities of Indian origin, Bishamon (Vaiśravana, or Kubera), and Karaten (Mahākāla, that is, Daikoku under his Indian form, another aspect of Kubera). He tells us that these gods came down personally to offer their services and ask for worship. According to the *Sōjiji chūkō engi* [History of the restoration of Sōjiji], compiled by Keizan toward the end of his life, the three "avatars" (*gongen*) that protected Sōjiji in northern Noto peninsula were Hakusan Gongen, Sannō (the tutelary god of Mount Hiei), and, in an unexpected fashion, the "Bodhisattva" Gyōki, an eighth-century monk famous for his social activities.[43]

As we have seen, Keizan presents himself as an *ujiko* of Hakusan, thus as a being bound to the soil, to the place, to the tutelary deity. At the same time he connects this idea with the Buddhist *imaginaire* (Himalayas, Uttarakuru). In the contrast between the *ujigami* (tutelary god) and the cosmic Buddha, two models are opposed and articulated: that of the agnatic line and that of transmigration. Chan/Zen monks always had rather complicated relationships to local cults, and Keizan is no exception in this. As we have already seen, in spite of the denial of the intermediary world required in principle by the dogma of emptiness, this world had a troubling reality for Keizan. The gods, spirits, and other beings of the invisible world were for him an undeniable presence that had to be taken into account in everyday life. Still the spirits or gods had a largely positive nature for Keizan, while for Dōgen and the clerical elite they were "pagan," falling outside the Buddhist spiritual realm. *Gedō*, "non-Buddhist," means literally "outside the Way" or "outside the [Buddhist] Dharma," outside religion. As Jacques Le Goff points out, folk

---

[43] On the Sannō cult, see Grapard 1987.

culture may be rejected by destruction, obliteration, and adulteration.[44] We should note, however, that in reported cases of Buddhist "victory over local spirits" there is rarely any mention of killing, only of subjugation.[45] In all these cases we seem to have a rite concerned with foundation and improvement of a piece of territory.

What role did these gods from the popular pantheon play in the liturgy of the Chan/Zen monasteries they came to protect? We must obviously distinguish between gods that are strictly tutelary deities (*chinju*), of local origin, and protective gods at the monasteries who have lost their local connections and can be found in Chan/Zen monasteries everywhere. In Japan the institution of the *chinju* reached its apogee, and the growing importance of these tutelary gods brought with it their redefinition as "provisional manifestations" or "avatars" (*gongen*) within esoteric Buddhism.

The distinction between tutelary deities (*chinju*) and deities protecting monasteries (*garanjin*) is not always clear, but the two categories seem to be opposed structurally to the class of "deities protecting the Dharma" (*gohōjin*). Thus most Zen monasteries have at least two separate sanctuaries, one consecrated to the tutelary god and the other to the god protecting the Dharma, or, to put it otherwise, to the protection of Zen in its local and nonlocal aspects. Shōkokuji in Kyoto, for instance, maintains two shrines, one consecrated to Hachiman in his aspect of tutelary god, and the other to Benzaiten in her aspect as protector of the Dharma.[46] The two categories sometimes seem to blend, but at least in Zen the tension persists between tutelary deity (*chinju*) and monastery god (*garanjin*) on the one side (both marked by their local character) and the god protecting the Dharma (*gohōshin*—with its universalist tendency) on the other. The "rationalist" tendency of Zen, wanting to lower the status of the god and get around his individual identity, tended to interpret the avatar (*gongen*) as a simple tutelary god or monastery protector, or even better (or worse, depending on the point of view), as a protector of the Dharma. Inversely, the tendency that we may call "hieratic" sought to promote the tutelary god to the status of a Buddhist avatar.

We must admit that the theoretically "pure" teaching of Chan/Zen Buddhism was from the outset two-sided, at the same time philosophical and mythological.[47] The transformation of the cosmic hierarchy into a psychological hierarchy, characteristic of Indian Buddhism, is repre-

---

[44] See Le Goff 1980: 157.

[45] As a comparison, see Le Goff's study of the cult of Saint Marcellus and the dragon in "Ecclesiastical Culture and Folklore in the Middle Ages," in ibid.: 159–88.

[46] Yōkōji also has a shrine devoted to Benzaiten, but there is no evidence that this shrine existed in Keizan's time.

[47] For more details, see Faure 1991: 258–83.

sented by a partial integration of the Indian gods into the Buddhist pantheon, but also by their domestication, even emasculation. Despite its growing pantheon, Mahāyāna Buddhism was fundamentally atheistic in that it did not recognize the ultimate reality of the gods. The universe is ruled by the law of karmic causality, and the one who has recognized its principle, that is, the Buddha, is superior to all the gods. Furthermore, the concept of emptiness took all the content out of any symbolic hierarchy, both that of Hinduism and that of early Buddhism, and later Chinese religion. However, as we shall see, in the case of Japan at least the gods were sometimes able to hold onto or retrieve the power they had lost to Buddhism.

We have a talisman allegedly drawn up by Keizan himself on which are written the two words *Dragon-king* and *Hakusan*.[48] It seems thus that the tradition making the dragon-king (Shōhō Shichirō) and the deity of Hakusan into the protectors of the Sōtō school goes back to the period of Keizan or of his successors. It subsequently gave birth to a lineage of widespread talismans. Various *kirigami* present the deity of Hakusan as a form of Izanagi, of Kannon, or of a dragon-king. When it comes to the significance of dragons (*nāga*) in the Sōtō school, several of these documents tell the story of the meeting between a ninth-century Chan master, Juzhi, and a dragon protector of the Law and stress that Juzhi transmitted "Dragon Zen."[49] We also find stories of dragons going back to the Indian Buddhist tradition, a tradition that includes eight assemblies of heavenly dragons. We may mention the episode in which the Buddha converted a "dragon" after having asked him to appear in his original form, in this case a cloud. The dragon hands his mountain over to Śākyamuni, and this mountain becomes the Vulture Peak, the famous site where the Buddha preached. The *kirigami* that tells of this episode follows it with a whole stream of stories in which Chan/Zen masters convert local spirits, ending with the example of Dōgen's relationship with the dragon-king Shōhō Shichirō.[50]

Shōhō Shichirō is often confused with another deity of Chinese origin, Daigenshuri. Like the latter, Shōhō Shichirō protects sailors, and he is the tutelary deity of Mount Ayuwang (the Mountain of King Aśoka) in Zhejiang. In the Sōtō tradition he is none other than the dragon-king who escorted Dōgen on his return from China. Dōgen brought him in, in the form of a white snake, inside his *kāṣāya* bag. Daigenshuri for his part is often represented in Sōtō monasteries along with Bodhidharma. He is dressed in Chinese style and shades his eyes with one of his hands, as if he

[48] See Ishikawa 1983–94 (6): 128–29.
[49] Ibid., 138–39.
[50] Ibid., 139–40.

were studying the horizon. Some legends make him a double of Mahendra, the older son of King Aśoka, but this attempt to connect him with India seems to derive from his role as the tutelary god of Mount Ayuwang. According to a widespread legend, he helped Dōgen to copy a famous collection of *kōan*, the *Biyan lu* (Emerald Cliff Record), on the eve of Dōgen's return to Japan. But he was later eclipsed in this role by Hakusan Gongen, the "avatar" of Hakusan. Although his ritual function is not very clear, his importance is obvious from the symmetrical position he occupies opposite Bodhidharma in Sōtō temples and is probably explained by his role in the ideological context of the transmission of Zen in the "three countries" (India, China, Japan). Just as Bodhidharma is seen as transmitting Zen from India to China, Daigenshuri symbolizes the transmission from China to Japan. In this sense he functions as a symbolic or mythological double of Dōgen. The important role played by this obscure tutelary god can be attributed to the fact that, while the transmission of Zen to Japan cannot (as in the case of Bodhidharma) be attributed to a single individual, most of the Chinese and Japanese masters who contributed to this transmission had, at some time, studied in the monasteries of Zhejiang and had doubtless sought the protection of Daigenshūri as tutelary god and protector of navigation. He was thus well qualified to become a symbol of the transmission of Zen to Japan.[51]

The monks' attitude toward tutelary deities was usually one of respect and devotion. But the ambiguous and somewhat secondary position of the monastery god in the Chan/Zen tradition is revealed in various episodes in which he is badly treated by a monk for not having correctly carried out his role as a protector. Thus the "mad monk" Shide, later deified himself along with his fellow Hanshan as "gods of union;" let loose a deluge of blows from his staff on a monastery god who did not prevent birds from stealing the offerings made to him, arguing from this fact that "you cannot protect your own food, so how can you protect the monastery?"[52] In the same vein, in the medieval Zen tradition Kyōō Unryō is well-known for having thrown into the water a statue of the local god, Hakusan Gongen himself, whom he reproached for not having known how to protect the monks from an epidemic.[53] In certain cases the violence of the monk toward the god is euphemized, reduced to the

---

[51] See Durt 1983: 608–9.

[52] See *Jingde chuandeng lu*, in *T.* 51, 2076: 434a.

[53] See Hanuki 1962: 46; Hirose 1988: 415–21; Bodiford 1993–94. According to Hirose, there are no less than forty-nine biographies referring to the conversion of local gods by monks in the *Sōtōshū zensho*. See Hirose, ibid.: 233. The most common ones are foundation stories, telling how a monk is allowed by a local god to build a monastery on the god's territory. These stories shed light on the land-clearing activities of Sōtō monks around the fifteenth century.

merest allusion. Sometimes it is completely absent, for example when we are told that a god moves away to make way for a monastery. Typical in this respect is the way in which the Chan master Yangshan Huiji (807–883), surnamed the "little Śākyamuni," set up his community at Mount Dayang on the advice of the local god: "One night the mountain god's temple shifted a distance of thirty *li* from its original site in order to make room [for Huiji's monastery]."[54]

These stories go back to one particular hagiographic genre: tales of the conversion of non-Buddhist deities—a genre well attested in early Chan and later in medieval Zen.[55] As we have seen from the episode involving Yuangui, the ascendancy of the Chan masters over local gods derived not only from "powers" acquired by meditation, and in particular from their understanding of the ultimate emptiness of everything, but also from their ability to confer the Bodhisattva Precepts on both humans and non-human creatures. Originally a sign of conversion, the Bodhisattva Precepts soon came to be considered as efficacious in themselves, and magically saving.[56] In some cases the Zen monk simply received help from a god who, favorably disposed toward him, indicated the propitious placing for the erection of a new monastery. Thus the site for the future Yōkōji was revealed to Keizan by a fox, clearly a divine messenger. In the same way, Saijōji (in Kanagawa prefecture) was founded by Ryōan Emyō (1337–1411) in 1394 after a god had shown him where to put it. Subsequently, his disciples discovered that their master was giving instruction every night to two strangers who turned out to be the *kami* of the place. In other cases the contacts were less cordial and ended in exorcism and the monk's expropriating the site.[57]

This kind of story was obviously intended to fire the imagination of the

---

[54] *Fozu tongji*, quoted in Jan 1966: 109.

[55] See Faure 1987c; Ishikawa 1984; Hirose 1983; Hanuki 1962; Suzuki 1987. One locus classicus is the story, quoted above, of the Northern Chan monk Pozao Duo, "Duo the Stove-Breaker," in *Song gaoseng zhuan*, T. 50, 2061: 828b.

[56] See Bodiford 1993: 173–79. In his *Denkōroku*, Keizan tells us that Dōgen had divine visitors twice, at Kōshōji and at Eiheiji, who asked to receive the Precepts. Keizan concludes: "Until then this is something that had not happened. This is because, for the first time since Buddhism spread in Japan, the master [Dōgen] promoted the True Dharma." See T. 82, 2585: 407c.

[57] Another well-known case in the Sōtō tradition is that of Tsūgen Jakurei's disciple Ikkei Eishū (died in 1403). Ikkei had noticed that when Tsūgen was teaching at Yōtakuji, a woman habitually mingled with the crowd to listen to the master's sermons. Ikkei confronted her and asked what she wanted. She replied that because of her karma she had been reborn in the shape of a snake and she was seeking deliverance. Ikkei told her that she could stay if she could answer this question: "Since retribution is ultimately empty, what do you want to free yourself from?" She did not understand. He nevertheless administered the Precepts to her. See Meikyoku Sokushō, *Yōtakuji Tsūgen zenji gyōjō* [1571], in *SZ* 17, *Shiden* 2: 270b; quoted in Bodiford 1993: 176–78; and Bodiford 1993–94.

local people by showing that the monks, through the practice of meditation, the doctrine of emptiness, and the ritual or ordination, had a symbolic capital superior to that of the autochthonous gods. In the absence
of contemplative practice and philosophical achievement, reserved for
the monastic elite, the Precepts were perceived as adequate to achieve the
salvation of laypeople and their spiritual counterparts, the *kami*. Between
the fourteenth and sixteenth centuries, scarcely a single god escaped being enrolled willy-nilly into Sōtō Zen (not to mention other Japanese
Buddhist schools).

In comparison with some of the examples given above, Keizan's relations with local gods were apparently free of violence, euphemized, since
the gods themselves came to him one by one to offer their protection
(there again, in the expectation of a "return" in the form of worship or
pure offerings). In contrast, the Buddha Śākyamuni and the Bodhisattva
Maitreya, along with Bodhidharma, appeared to Keizan to authenticate
not his monastery but his awakening.

The question of the validity of the *kami* cult is taken up in dialogue
form in a Sōtō *kirigami*:

> The master says, "If we understand Zen correctly, we enter into the lineage of
> the Buddha-patriarchs. Why then should we worship the *kami*?" He continues:
> "Why should monks who observe the Buddhist Law worship the *kami*?" Re-
> ply: "In India they worship the Buddhas, in China the patriarchs, and in Japan
> [we worship] the *kami*: this is conforming [to customs]." The master: "[Why
> does] one speak of the seven upper, middle, and lower shrines?" Reply: "The
> seven upper shrines protect the Buddha Dharma, the seven middle shrines are
> for the prosperity of one's descendants, the seven lower ones are for the com-
> pletion of this receptacle."[58]

The *Genkō shakusho* contains, in the section on "gods and immortals"
(*shinsen*), information about five great Japanese *kami*: Amaterasu, Hakusan Myōjin, Nyū Myōjin, Shiragi Myōjin, and Tenman Daijizai Tenjin.
Its author, Kokan Shiren (1278–1346), was well versed in the Buddhist
esoteric tradition, and his work reflects the influence of the *honji suijaku*
theory, according to which the Buddhas are the "original state" (*honji*) of
the *kami*, who are their "manifestations" in this world, their "traces"
(*suijaku*).[59] All the *kami* mentioned above play an important role in esoteric Buddhism. They are not simply, as in the earlier Chan tradition,
protectors of the Dharma, but more fundamentally they are themselves

---

[58] See *Bukke ichidaiji yawa* 43, in Ishikawa 1983–94 (2): 148.

[59] As Mujū Ichien puts it: "In our country, as the land of the gods, the provisional
manifestations of the Buddha leave their traces. Moreover, we are all their descendants; and
it is no trivial fate to share with them a common spirit." See Morrell 1985: 78. See also
Matsunaga 1969.

manifestations of the Buddha. This ennobling of the *kami*, although originally only a tactical maneuver intended to overcome local resistance to
Buddhism, came to have important consequences. The "militant syncretism" of Shiren shows up clearly in his account of the sun goddess Amaterasu. He first tells how Emperor Shōmu asked the holy monk Gyōki to
offer a relic of the Buddha at Ise Shrine. On the seventh day after the
offering, the sanctuary opened and the voice of Amaterasu was heard
saying that she had just achieved salvation thanks to that offering. Subsequently the emperor had a dream that Amaterasu was in reality none
other than the Buddha Vairocana (J. Dainichi, literally "Great Sun").
Shiren used this story and others of the same type to prove that Amaterasu was not fundamentally hostile to Buddhism, as Shintō sectarians
have claimed.

The deity of Hakusan also played an important role in medieval Buddhism, and it was one of the key elements in the territorial expansion of
the Sōtō sect. Shiren explains that this deity is in fact one of the manifestations of Izanagi, the male protagonist in the primordial divine couple
of Japanese mythology. As such, he should have had priority over his
daughter Amaterasu, but, when asked about this by one of his worshipers, he himself explained that this was not the case because he had
revealed himself only much later than Amaterasu.[60] In various other accounts, the deity of Hakusan is a goddess, Shirayamahime or Kukurihime
(see figure 3).[61] When the holy man Taichō first climbed the mountain
at the beginning of the eighth century, the deity appeared to him in the
form of a nine-headed dragon—a god of water and fertility. In the Sōtō
kirigami, the deity of Hakusan is often associated with the dragon or
nāga (*ryūten*).

Nyū (var. Nibu) Myōjin is the tutelary deity (*jinushigami*) of Mount
Kōya, the headquarters of Shingon Buddhism;[62] Shinra (var. Shiragi)

[60] Shiren follows the tradition of the *Taichō oshō den* [957], according to which the
deity who appeared to Taichō was Izanami. But this seems to be a later interpolation,
representing the viewpoint of Heisenji, a Tendai monastery at the southern entrance of
Hakusan, in opposition to the main shrine (*hongū*) at the top of the mountain: in this
shrine, called Shirayama *jinja*, Kukurihime is worshiped as the main deity, flanked by
Izanami and Izanagi.

[61] According to the *Nihonshoki*, Kukurihime appeared to Izanagi at Yomotsuhirasaka,
at the limit of the underworld (Yomotsu), after he escaped the wrath of his wife and sister
Izanami. The role of this deity is not very clear, but she seems to have helped Izanagi to
purify himself from the pollution of death. She is also apparently related to childbirth, a
characteristic that may explain her identification with Kannon. See for instance the "Hakusan Myōri no zu," in Ishikawa 1983–94 (6): 133. Various scholars, from Yanagita Kunio
and Orikuchi Shinobu to Gorai Shigeru and Miyata Noboru, have emphasized the connection between Hakusan and rebirth. On this question see Ōwa 1989: 100–120.

[62] This deity, also called Nibutsuhime-no-kami or Wakahirume-no-kami, is said to be
the daughter of Izanagi and the sister of Amaterasu.

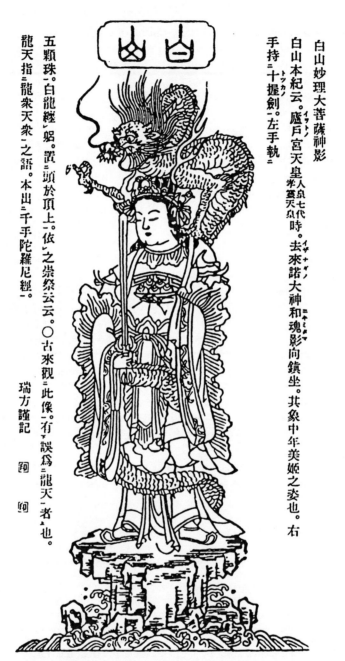

白山妙理大菩薩神影

白山本紀云。應戶宮天皇孝靈天皇時。去來諸大神和魂影向鎮坐。其象中年美姫之姿也。右手持二十握劍一左手執二

五顆珠一白龍經一躬。置二頭於頂上一依一之崇祭云云。○古來觀二此像一有下誤爲二龍天一者上也。

龍天指二龍衆天衆一之語一。本出二千手陀羅尼經一。

瑞方謹記

FIGURE 3. The goddess of Hakusan (Hakusan Myōri Daibosatsu), in Zuikō Chingyū and Daiken Hōju, eds., *Teiho kenzeiki zue* (1806), in *SZ*, 17, *Shiden*, 2, rev. ed. (Tokyo: Sōtōshū shūmuchō, 1970–73).

Myōjin is the protector of Miidera, a well-known Tendai temple on the southern shore of Biwa Lake. Tenman Daijizai Tenjin is the honorific name of Sugawara no Michizane (845–903), a famous scholar of the Heian period. After his death in exile, Michizane became a powerful evil spirit (*goryō*). To appease him, the emperor promoted him to the status of a god. His learned nature meant that he would become the god of literature. This mythological figure is an interesting combination of elements borrowed from Hinduism, Confucianism, and various local cults.[63] The growth of his legend in medieval Zen plays a strategic role and serves several purposes. In particular, the story according to which the Chan master Wuzhun Shifan (1177–1249) transmitted the patriarchal robe to Michizane seems to have been widely disseminated in Zen circles. At the time that this school started its territorial expansion, such a legend offered the advantage of associating Zen with the cult of Michizane. At the capital, where the "five mountains" (*gozan*), official Zen monasteries, had become centers of neo-Confucianism and literature, it reinforced the claims of the Zen masters who preached the harmony of the three teachings (Buddhism, Confucianism, and Daoism, with the last being later replaced by Shintō), or the harmony of Zen and poetry.[64]

Another example of transmission of the Dharma to a *kami* brings onto the stage Amaterasu herself and the Zen monks Shinchi Kakushin (1207–1298) and Beppō Daiju (1321–1402). When the latter, a monk in the lineage of Enni Ben'en, visited Ise Shrine, he had a vision of Amaterasu, who told him that she had formerly received the patriarchal robe from Kakushin.[65] The biography of the latter tells us that he had received this robe himself from Tiantong at Mount Tiantai before passing it on to Amaterasu.[66] Elsewhere we learn that the god Hachiman appeared to Enni Ben'en when the latter was returning to China, and it was also supposedly Hachiman who invited to Japan the Chinese master (and presumed Arhat) Wuxue Zuyuan (Mugaku Sogen), a disciple of Wuzhun Shifan.

The main difference between Chan and Zen when it comes to the role of the popular pantheon is perhaps that while the Song Chan masters addressed a Confucianist elite, the Zen masters of the Kamakura and Muromachi eras, and especially those of the Sōtō persuasion, were trying to convert rural populations. In this context, where the *kami* had never been threatened by Confucianist or Daoist ideology, the situation was radically different. Although they had been to a large degree manipulated by the monks, the *kami* remained unpredictable and their oracles could

---

[63] See Iyanaga 1983.
[64] See Harada Masatoshi 1987.
[65] See *Amaterasu taishi sōden kesa ki* [1382], in *Tōfukuji monjo*, quoted in ibid., 383.
[66] Ibid.

bring the best plans into question. In the eighth century, the monk Dōkyō had already seen his attempt to seize power blocked because of one of Hachiman's oracles, while at the beginning of the Kamakura period the Kegon master Myōe had to abandon his plan to go on pilgrimage to India because of an oracle from the Kasuga deity.[67]

The monks generally considered the *kami* either as subordinate protectors of Buddhism or as avatars of the Buddhas or Bodhisattvas. These two categories reflect the fact that we find in Zen a few very important gods and a large number of less significant, strictly functional ones. These latter played a purely ritual role and were not as individualized as the former. Among the important gods for the Sōtō sect, apart from Hakusan Myōri Daigongen, we should also mention Sumiyoshi Myōjin and Kōjin. Sumiyoshi Myōjin was a god of navigation and poetry. His native character is well reflected in Zeami's *Hakurakuten*, where the god is presented as protecting the people from the deleterious influence of Chinese literature (symbolized by the Chinese poet Bai Juyi).[68] He is often mentioned in Sōtō *kirigami*, mostly in connection with an oracle allegedly given to Dōgen just after the latter's return to Japan.[69] The figure of Kōjin borrows many elements from esoteric Buddhism. He was an object of worship at Sōjiji in Noto under the name Sanbō Daikōjin, a title that refers to his role as protector of the "Three Jewels" (*sanbō*, Skt. *triratna*, i.e., the Buddha, the Dharma, and the *saṃgha*). He is a Tantric deity usually considered as an evil god whom it is better to leave in peace. At the same time legend tells that he appeared from a pond at Sōjiji to Taigen Sōshin (d. 1371), one of Keizan's second-generation disciples, and vowed to protect the monastery.

If, taking as our point of departure the distinction drawn by Lévi-Strauss between "implicit" and "explicit" mythology, we try to situate Zen mythology along the spectrum between two poles, one predominantly mythological and the other ritual, Chan/Zen is clearly closer to the ritual pole. To put it another way, we have here examples of "implicit mythology" in which the mythological element subordinates itself to the ritual and the gods do not have any strong individual nature. The gods who are the object of worship in Zen monasteries have a primarily ritual function: they protect the monastery, or one of its parts (the meditation hall, the Dharma hall, the kitchens, the bathroom, the latrines).

All these figures are conceived of only as symbols of ultimate reality, relative manifestations of an absolute moving forward, masked, on the human stage. These conceptions contrast with the one that the *kami* are

---

[67] See Morrell 1982; Tyler 1993: 145–48, 159–60.

[68] See Arthur Waley, *The Nō Plays of Japan* (Rutland, VT: Charles E. Tuttle, 1981), 207–15. On the question of "Chineseness" vs. "Japaneseness," see Pollack 1986.

[69] See Ishikawa 1983–94 (20): 118, 121.

themselves not simple, kaleidoscopic reflections of reality but so many ultimate realities, even if local ones, not subservient to any higher principle. This true, agonistic, plural polytheism, which would find its ideological form in the "pure" Shintō that emerged in the fourteenth century, sought to be something more than a disguise of monism and challenged the pantheism (or rather pan-Buddhism) that emerged from the theories of the *honji suijaku* or the "preaching of the inanimate" (*mujō seppō*).

The ritualization of Chan/Zen reflects the growing importance of the gods and of the sacred sphere in monastic life. At the same time a certain rationalism, which, as Max Weber has shown so well, is inherent in the monastic mentality, tended toward a demythologization of the tradition and a "routinization" of ritual. One example that we have already mentioned is that of the reinterpretation of the cult of the god of Hakusan within Sōtō during the Tokugawa era. We may see here another attempt at domesticating the *kami* after the relative defeat of the *honji suijaku* theory. It is characterized by a movement from what was essentially a purification rite against the defilement brought by death to a redefinition of the Hakusan god as a "guardian of the place," or even, in a more abstract fashion, as a "protector of the Dharma." Another attack, a more subtle one, lay in "abstracting" the gods. This was the case especially with the *nāga* or "dragons" (*ryūten*), protective gods often described as abstract symbols rather than as real (or imaginary) beings. This demythologization is obvious in one *kirigami* entitled "Dialogue of the Dragon,"[70] which reinterprets dragons as personifications of the fundamental spirit of all beings, manifestations that fade away when one recognizes this fundamental spirit.[71]

This reductionist syncretism has behind it a long history of symbolic and ideological attacks on local gods and cults. The tension is sometimes apparent in stories where we see gods gaining the upper hand for a time and making monks pay for their presumption. But more often they are reduced to silence, willy nilly, by their new masters. Still, certain *kami* like Amaterasu, Hachiman, and the god of Kasuga, were generally treated by the monks as interlocutors worthy of respect. The Japanese pantheon was not organized along the hierarchical lines of the Chinese "celestial bureaucracy," and the Japanese gods could not be treated as simple officials. The "functional" nature of the *kami* is not as obvious as that of their Chinese homologues. Japanese mythology, or at least its accounts of the gods, was more developed than Chinese mythology, with the latter consisting mostly of stories of saints promoted to the rank of

[70] See "Ryūten no san," in *Bukke ichi daiji sanwa*, in Ishikawa Rikizan 1983–94 (2): 148.

[71] Likewise, the *kami* are reinterpreted as metaphor for the mind by Zen masters like Shidō Bunan. See Pedersen 1975: 101.

heavenly bureaucrats. In Japan the imperial lineage was of divine origin, and the divine thus transcended the bureaucracy, even if the latter was celestial. We know of many aristocratic families, like the Fujiwaras, who sought to extend their own lineage back to a *kami*, so imitating the imperial family.[72]

Although it goes back to esoteric Buddhism, this invocation of the *kami* at the consecration of the Yōkōji is representative of Zen ritual invocations, both Sōtō and Rinzai:

> The vast merits that have been accumulated, we offer them respectfully to the great deity Amaterasu who created this country, to the seven generations of heavenly *kami*, to the five generations of earthly *kami*, to the ninety-six generations of human emperors, to the primordial star that governs the ultimate fate of the present emperor, to the seven luminaries, to the nine luminaries and twenty-eight mansions of the year in its round, to the various *daimyōjin* who protect the imperial capital, to the great and small divinities of the five [provinces of] Ki[nai] and of the seven districts, to the great ridgepole of the Dharma, Hakusan Myōri Daigongen, to the past and future protectors of this district, to the great Bodhisattvas of the two sanctuaries, the various shrines of this county and community, to the tutelary god of this mountain, to the dragon-king of this mountain, . . . to the god Katoku of the south, to the group of stars in the fire section, to the eighteen gods who protect this monastery, to the members of the category of the great Bodhisattva Kita of Ichinomiya in this province, to the members of the category of the great Bodhisattva Shohō Shichirō Daigenshuri, Tamonten, Karaten, the Acolyte with the Blue Face [Shōmen Dōji], . . . to the various celestial emissaries robed in white, to the ancient tutelary god Inari Daimyōjin, and to the great Bodhisattva Hachiman who gave his protection [during the conquest of] Silla.[73]

As we see, it is within the context of a ritual dedication or the "deflection" (*ekō*) of the merits accumulated for the welfare of all beings, that the gods are invoked, Buddhist and non-Buddhist alike, usually along with the Buddhas and Bodhisattvas. The list is open and varies according to circumstances. The traditional dedication of merits ends with the following formula: "We also make offerings to the tutelary god of this monastery and to all the gods who protect the Dharma, with prayers that the Dharma may prosper, that all nations may live in peace and harmony, that the precincts of this monastery may be peaceful, and that all karmic conditions may be happy."[74]

---

[72] These cases recall that of Mélusine and the Lusignan family in France. See Le Goff 1980: 205–22.

[73] *Keizan shingi*, T. 82, 2589: 437b.

[74] Ibid.

As a phenomenon of belief, this dedication constitutes a sort of contractual relationship with the gods, implying a certain give-and-take. According to Michel de Certeau, belief makes up part of a contractual practice of debt and the expectation of a return on it.[75] As needed, the repayment of the debt may be demanded violently. In the case in question, the dedication is not to a single god but to the entire pantheon who will guarantee the debt. This example underscores the extent to which the phenomenon of belief, far from being purely mental, is part of a well-established juridical/ritual practice.

But the monks held no monopoly on violence. The *Shasekishū* ("Collection of *Sand and Pebbles*"), a collection of edifying stories put together by the Zen master Mūjū Ichien (1226–1312), shows not only the blessings bestowed by the *kami* on their worshipers but also their revenge against those who do not believe in them or do not treat them correctly. The author addressed particularly those adepts of the Pure Land school who held themselves, because of their direct relationship with the Buddha Amida, free from any obligation to worship other spiritual intercessors.[76] The will of the *kami* had to be taken into account even by monks as eminent as Myōe or Jōkei (Gedatsu shōnin), described by the *Shasekishū* as "beloved children of the god" [of Kasuga], his "Jirō and Tarō."[77] We can doubtless read the *Shasekishū* as a propaganda work in favor of traditional Buddhism, even if the author is a Zen monk. But his attitude toward the *kami*, or rather more generally that of the monks of the time, cannot be reduced to a purely utilitarian strategy. The gods were present in the everyday life of Buddhists of the Kamakura period, and their curses or oracles retained their full force. Although one can find unbelieving spirits in every epoch, there are periods when social and ideological pressures make agnosticism difficult to practice.

The erection of a national ideology in the period of the Mongol invasions led to the belief that Japan was the "land of the gods" (*shinkoku*). We know that the Mongol fleets were twice destroyed by providential typhoons or "divine winds" (*kamikaze*), sent, it was believed, in reply to prayers by Japanese Buddhists. On this occasion the Zen monks vied in patriotism and joined their incantations to those of the other Buddhist and Shintō sects. They tried at the same time to respond to the criticisms from the new Shintō sectarianism and other "nativist" movements, and to speak the language of the social classes whom they wanted to win to

[75] See de Certeau 1985.

[76] See Morrell 1985: 97–103. Note in passing that one of the most vindictive *kami* is Hakusan Gongen: not only does he give a fatal curse to a man who had commited an offence, but he also refuses to forgive his mother, a nun, on the grounds that, despite her attempt to amend her son's behavior, she had remained too partial to him.

[77] Ibid.: 84.

their cause, especially of the *bushi*, or warriors. This attempt at pros-elytizing perhaps explains in part the frequent references to the *kami* in *kōan*, as well as in the rituals of esoteric transmission of the Sōtō and Rinzai schools.

The spirits of the dead, and more especially that category of spirits regarded as particularly powerful and capable of evil, the *goryō*, have always played a major role in the Japanese imagination. As we have seen, the most prestigious among them, the spirit of Sugawara no Michizane, inherited the Dharma from a Chinese Chan master, Wuzhun Shifan. We also see that, on the pattern of the *goryō*, particularly charismatic Zen monks were sometimes "deified," doubtless in order to channel their po-tentially dangerous energy. Sociologists have often discussed the way in which societies try to protect themselves against anything that could question the established order. In a sense, awakening, or *satori*, consti-tutes one such challenge. Meditation, considered to result in the experi-ence of transcendence, transformed Zen monks into eccentrics, or "energumens" in the etymological sense, that is, into individuals who were no longer "agents" in control of themselves but were "acted on," carried along and moved by an unpredictable energy. This is perhaps one of the reasons why, after their death, Chan patriarchs become the object of an ancestor cult that seems intended to reintegrate them into some kind of family structure. This impression is reinforced by their icono-graphic "representation" (*chinsō*), which is related to the cult of relics (particularly of mummies). Yet, in these majestic representations, they seem completely in command of themselves. This may not be paradoxical since, according to Dōgen, it is only by losing oneself that one finds one-self.[78] However, the ideals of self-mastery and spontaneity seem to have been perceived often as antithetical.

We should also mention in this context the phenomenon of the "living gods," humans deified during their lifetime or shortly after their death. We noted earlier the case of Dōryō, who had vowed to protect his monas-tery, Saijōji, and later became, in the popular imagination, a powerful *tengu*, god of the mountain. His case is not without analogy to that of the Tendai monk Ryōgen, who survived in a demonic form in the popular imagination under the name of Tsuno daishi (Great horned master), a terrifying figure intended to put evil spirits to flight.[79]

---

[78] See *Shōbōgenzō*, "Genjō kōan," T. 82, 2582: 23c.

[79] According to Mujū's *Shasekishū* (above, note 13): "Perhaps it was during the reign of Emperor Murakami [926–67] that a Five-Pedestal Ceremony was held at the palace with bishop Jie [Ryōgen, 912–85] acting as Esoteric Master at the central platform. The emperor secretly observed the performance, during which he saw Jie assume the form of Fudō, so that there was not the slightest difference between him and the object of worship." See Morrell 1985: 80. Tsuno Daishi is still dispelling demons every year during Setsubun (in

The success of Buddhism in Japan may be explained in large part by its apotropaic function, and the Zen monks in particular often played the role of exorcists. From this fact they showed certain affinities to the practitioners of Shugendō and were sometimes confused with them. Dōryō was actually an adept of the Miidera branch of Shugendō, who took part in several princely pilgrimages to Kumano (in 1384, 1390, and 1393).[80] Sometimes it is the Zen monk himself who turns into a vengeful spirit. Thus one tradition tells that Ejō, the successor to Dōgen, returned to take his revenge on a monk who had converted to the Rinzai school. Sectarian disputes continue in the other world.

Even if, as many scholars think who are influenced by an elitist conception of Zen, the Zen masters made use of the *kami* for utilitarian purposes, as skillful means (*upāya*), it is likely that, in many cases, the means came to predominate over the ends. Certain preachers, perhaps caught in their own trap, ended up losing the interior distance that allowed them to believe they were "masters over the gods." If we see them only as agnostics, the reason is that we have forgotten the role of ritual in the establishment of belief. As we have known since Augustine and Pascal, ritual performance tends to produce or strengthen belief. To understand the resurgence of sacrality alongside (or in reaction against) the routinization of the sacred within Chan/Zen, we must examine the function of ritual more closely. Given a Mahāyāna theology that tends to deprive the gods of their transcendence and make them only accessories to ritual, there developed within Japanese religion, most notably with the emergence of Shintō nativism, a radical "remythologization" that would affect all the schools of Buddhism, including Zen.

February) at Rozanji in Kyoto: people wait patiently in line to be exorcized by the fierce deity, impersonated by a priest holding a sword in his hand. On the historical Ryōgen, see McMullin 1987: 161–84.

[80] See Nihon bukkō kenkyūkai 1991: 160–61.

Chapter Five

DREAMING

A S WE NOTED earlier, the *Record of Tōkoku* is not only a narrative of the origins of Yōkōji but also an oneirical autobiography. Keizan dreamed of making the monastic community of Yōkōji into a dream community, in every sense of the word. When he spent his first night at Tōkoku, in the home of his patrons, Keizan saw in a dream a magnificent monastery prefiguring the future Yōkōji:

> It also happened that the night after the donors' decision and gift I was staying at their home and I saw in a dream the halls of a wonderful monastery. When I reached the great *enoki* tree on which people hung their straw sandals, the one standing in front of the gate, I realized that this was a special site, where wandering monks could reimburse the cost of their straw sandals. Having received [this mountain] as a gift, I wanted to make it into a place of retreat for the rest of my life. [*JDZ*, 392]

In a collective instruction dated 1320, that is, eight years later, Keizan returns in more detail to that founding event:

> The original owner of this mountain, the lady Taira *no uji*, wanted to invite me and make me a gift of it. At first, I went with [her husband] Unno Nobunao to look for a site on the mountain for my hermitage. I then took possession of this hollow and made it my meditation place. Then, during the night that I spent in the home of my benefactors, I dreamed that I went to squat on the summit of the mountain and looked way down to the base. Between the high peak and the deep valley, the interval [was that which separates] heaven from earth. In a court in the hollow, a monastery suddenly appeared. Many buildings, their rooftops aligned, filled the whole valley. On the right, in front of the monastery gate, was a great *enoki* tree with burgeoning branches. Pilgrims came from all quarters and hung their straw sandals on it. When I interpreted this dream, it became clear to me that, if I settled in this place, monks would come from the four cardinal directions to repay here the price of their sandals. This is the sign that it was an extraordinary site.
>
> Furthermore, the next year when I saw the slope that had appeared in my dream, I noted that there actually was an *enoki* tree there, one whose branches, as they grew, were becoming luxuriant. Thus the monastery would prosper, just as the clouds mass together, swell up, and finally conceal the valley, or streams in flood flow down and fill the rivers and lakes. Strange, truly strange!

See how wakefulness and sleep merge together, dream and waking harmonize. [*JDZ*, 397]

Thus, this dream revealed to Keizan that this site, of no very distinguished appearance, was in reality one of the focal spots of the invisible world, a place peopled by extraordinary beings whose secret presence would protect present and future monks.[1] Two universes, and two monasteries (visible and invisible) are superimposed on the axis formed by the great tree that Keizan dreamed of and whose real existence he had subsequently uncovered. Fortified by this proof, he was thenceforth convinced of his mission. He knew then for sure that Yōkōji, the Monastery of the Eternal Light, would become the center from which the Buddhist Law would radiate out over Japan. The center had moved from Eiheiji to Yōkōji (to be understood as from Dōgen to Keizan), as the Arhat Vajraputra would confirm in the course of another dream that was to rule over the destinies of Yōkōji and its monastic community. This dream, recorded in the *Record of Tōkoku* just after the one quoted above, actually took place one year later [1313], when Keizan began to build at Tōkoku a thatched cabin that would serve as a provisional refectory for the monks.

Keizan was an inveterate dreamer who made dreams into a veritable way of life: they supplied a criterion for truth, but also an instrument of power. His visions gave him privileges to which the ordinary dreamers could not hope to aspire. But Keizan did not lose himself in his dreams. To a certain extent he controlled them, manipulated them. As he dreamed, he found himself. He stood on the dangerous boundary between the real and the oneiric, on the threshold of an invisible world that called him ceaselessly without causing him to lose his sense of reality. Keizan remained a realistic dreamer, one who found in dreams the foundation of his adaptation to real life. Although he seems at times to have preferred his visions to the prosaic reality of the external world, he did not reject the latter. He acquired through his dreams and visions a feeling that he had a supernatural mission and then set to work to transfigure everyday events, which he turned into so many "Buddha affairs."[2]

---

[1] On the basis of a similar dream, Kohō Kakumyō, one of Keizan's disciples, named his monastery Unjuji, "Monastery of the Cloud Tree." The water/fertility symbolism in Keizan's dream is particularly striking in light of William LaFleur's remark that early Buddhism rejected precisely this kind of symbolism. See William R. LaFleur, *Liquid Life: Abortion and Buddhism in Japan* (Princeton: Princeton University Press, 1992), 18.

[2] Significantly, Keizan has nothing to say about bad dreams or nightmares, which were, however, an important object of Buddhist discourse, particularly in esoteric Buddhism. On this question see Strickmann 1996: 291–336. Likewise, evil states of mind likely to occur during meditation were an important concern of the Tiantai/Tendai tradition, as can be seen in Zhiyi's description of these phenomena as "demoniac dhyāna" or "dhyāna sick-

The *Record of Tōkoku* belongs to the literary genre of "foundation chronicles" (*engi*) but also has many of the features of another fairly widespread genre, that of the "record of dreams" (*yume no ki*), of which the most renowned example is by Myōe.[3] Nevertheless, this does not seem to have been its primary function. In a "record of dreams," the dreams are usually set down in writing soon after the dreamer awakes and they are saved as basic materials for a psychological or spiritual hermeneutic. In the *Record of Tōkoku*, the dreams are often recorded long after the fact and only insofar as they cast light on the foundation of Yōkōji. Keizan does not give us all his dreams. Far from it. But neither, doubtless, do the compilers of "records of dreams." This is not important, however, since all these works (whatever may have been their ulterior motives) give us a privileged and invaluable access to the *imaginaire* of the medieval monk.

At the outset we should note that for Buddhists there is no clear distinction between dreams that come during sleep and visions achieved in a waking state, or more precisely during meditation, in a state (*samādhi*) that, like trance, is often defined as being "neither sleeping nor waking." As Keizan himself notes: "In the first Genkō year [1321], *kanenoto tori*, on the night of the beginning of spring, while I was seated in meditation, [in a state that was] neither dreaming nor waking, I expressed by myself the confirmation [of awakening]" [*JDZ*, 399]. This different conception of the boundary between sleep and waking sometimes makes it difficult to tell whether we are dealing with visions or dreams, with modes of waking or of sleeping, with lucid or deluded consciousness. The border dividing the visible from the invisible does not follow the line we think of as obvious. As in ancient Greece, where a single term, *opsis*, meant "sight (objective or subjective), presence, but also a dream," dreams in Buddhism constitute part of the visible and "they function like an 'autopsy' [*auto-opsis*, "self-vision"] for the person who receives them."[4] Dreams and visions establish a quasi-hallucinatory connection with reality, which in turn brings up the question of their truth: are we dealing with a

---

ness." See also the *Zhi chanbing biyaofa* ("Secret Essentials for Curing the Dhyāna Sickness"), quoted in Strickmann 1996: 320; and the discussion of the Vināyakas in the *Binaiye jing* (Book of Vinaya), ibid.: 316–20.

[3] Although the genre was not fully developed in China, Xuanzang already recorded his dreams during his travel to India (629–645), while Daoxuan noted his oneirical encounters with the god Weituo. In Japan we know that Jōjin kept a record of his dreams before and during his trip to China; we also have the dream diaries of Shungi (*Musō nikki*, ca. 1219, preserved at Kōzanji), and of the abbot of Kōfukuji Jinson (1430–1508). On Jōjin see Arthur Waley, "Some Far Eastern Dreams," in Morris 1970: 364–71; on Myōe, see Girard 1990a, 1990b; Tanabe 1992; Kawai 1992. On the question of dreams, see Strickmann 1988 and 1996; Saigo 1993.

[4] See Hartog 1980: 278.

connection—a privileged connection even— or a nonconnection? When Keizan sees in his dream a wonderful monastery on the site of the future Yōkōji and later discovers in the real world certain elements of his dream, he is fusing two levels: not so much the antagonistic ones of waking and illusion, as Mahāyāna doctrine would have it, but rather those of the real and the imaginary. In this case dreams are perceived as the highest expression of reality. Far from being one who, in Balzac's words, "dreams and does not think, . . . stirs and does not create," Keizan is one of those for whom to dream is both to think and to create. Thus dreaming his life is not better than living it because it is precisely living it, and one lives it fully only as one dreams it. Dreams do not make up a "parallel" and illusory reality, since they tend to blend with the waking state: they make up this life, the only true one. Yet, in the end, the separation betwen waking and dreaming must be maintained: dreaming defines a particular, sacred time and space. Although Keizan keeps these two spheres of reality separate, he allows a regulated overflowing from the one into the other. Standing on the threshold between the two realms, he acts as a mediator, a "keeper of the gate."

DREAM AS METAPHOR

To understand the importance of dreams in a monastic community at the end of the Kamakura period, we really should retrace in some detail the beliefs about the oneiric realm in the Buddhist tradition and in the communities where it became established. This would lead us far afield, however, for now we must be satisfied with some generalities, accompanied by a few remarks about the immediate predecessors of Keizan.[5] Buddhist hagiography has retained a number of premonitory dreams that punctuated the life of the Buddha (dreams of Śākyamuni himself, but also of his father, of his disciple Ānanda, etc.). Early Buddhist dreams had nothing very specific.[6] Because dreams constituted a potential challenge for the "planified" practice of the monastery, they had to be carefully assessed with regard to monastic discipline.[7] On the theoretical level, whereas in Hinduism the *Upaniṣads* attach more value to dreams than to the ordi-

[5] See Gotelind Müller, "Zum Begriff des Traumes und seiner Funktion in Chinesischen buddhistischen Kanon," *Zeitschrift der Deutschen Morgenländischen Gesellschaft* 142, 2 (1992): 343–77; Strickmann 1988; Ong 1985; Saigō 1993; and Faure 1991: 209–30.

[6] As Michel Strickmann points out: "Just as the syntax of ritual is virtually identical in medieval Śaivist and Buddhist sources, the semiotic of dreams is equally identical in its very substance. Buddhists and Śaivists agree in their interpretation of oneirical signs." See Strickmann 1996: 305. On the Indian and early Buddhist oneirical tradition, see O'Flaherty 1984.

[7] See Strickmann 1996: 294.

nary waking state, dreams in Mahāyāna Buddhism play essentially the role of a negative metaphor, serving to reveal the lack of reality of this world. As Stephan Beyer points out, "The metaphysics of the *Mahā-prajñāpāramitā* is in fact the metaphysics of the vision and the dream: a universe of glittering and quicksilver change is precisely one that can only be described as empty. The vision and the dream become the tools to dismantle the hard categories we impose on reality, to reveal the eternal flowing possibility in which the Buddha lives."[8] In the idealistic tendency of the Yogācāra movement in particular, dreams and reality, insofar as they are mental creations, are both stripped of any ontological status. Even the "absolutization" of dreams, as formulated by certain Mahāyāna thinkers, does not lead to its revalorization. Dōgen, for example, in the section of the *Shōbōgenzō* entitled "Muchū setsumu" ("Explaining dreams within dreams"), insists that dreams are more real than reality: "Just as the profound Dharma of all the Buddhas is transmitted only from one Buddha to another, everything in dreams and the waking world derives from ultimate reality. In waking as in dreams we find the initial thought of the awakening, practice, awakening itself, and Nirvāṇa. Dreams and waking are ultimate reality. One is not better or worse than the other."[9]

Still we may wonder whether we are not dealing here with a theoretical position, one that is to a large extent rhetorical, deriving from the principle of nonduality. Until we have more information on the subject, we must resist the temptation to read such statements as the last word on the revelatory nature of dreams. Dōgen is apparently only taking up a position opposed to that of his predecessors, most prominently that of Dahui Zonggao who claimed, in line with Mahāyāna orthodoxy, that dreams were nothing but the product of false ideas and that the entire universe is only a dream that must be categorically rejected.[10] Influenced as he was by Yogācāra idealism, Dahui saw everything as a dream; only the dreamer is real. Despite his opposition on the basis of principle, it would be easy to guess that Dōgen agreed with him on this point. This did not, however, prevent these two rivals from being very realistic in practice.

During his travels in China, however, Dōgen had met several Chan masters who greatly valued premonitory dreams.[11] Although he mentions his own dreams from time to time, it seems that he uses them very selectively. According to his biography, he attached some importance to a dream in which he received the branch of a plum tree from Mount Damei, suggesting that he received the transmission from Damei Fachang

---

[8] See Beyer 1977: 340.
[9] *T.* 82, 2582: 162c.
[10] See *T.* 47, 1998(a): 897a.
[11] See *Shōbōgenzō* "Shisho," *T.* 82, 2582: 67c–72a.

(751–839) in this dream (see figure 4). On the other hand, he refused to accept the transmission from another master whose choice had landed on Dōgen as the result of an auspicious dream.[12] Ironically, it is on the basis of a dream that Dōgen was accepted as a disciple by the Chan master Rujing (1163–1228): the night before, Dongshan Liangjie had appeared in Rujing's dream and foretold to him Dōgen's coming.[13] Dōgen does report as worthy of belief a vision, apparently a collective one, of the Sixteen Arhats that occurred at Eiheiji in 1249 during a ceremony in their honor.

Dōgen's attitude toward dreams is fairly typical of Chan. On the whole their status as images led Chan/Zen masters to reject dreams, and along with dreams a whole series of meditative practices based on the visualization of Buddhas and Bodhisattvas. Insofar as this type of meditation was seen as typical of other schools (like esoteric Buddhism and the Pure Land school), we may see in the denial of the validity of dreams a purely tactical maneuver on the part of Chan/Zen, a way for this school to mark itself off from rival sects. In addition, the prejudice against dreams also derived naturally from Chan subitism and its suspicion of all forms of mediation.[14] On the other hand, the considerable importance of dreams in the actual life of Chan/Zen monks suggests that their daily practice was still ruled by gradualist views since "there must be a recognized continuity between dreams and life if dreams are to influence life."[15]

Dōgen often cites the maxim that "one should never tell one's dreams to a fool," but he is doubtless also not far from treating as fools those who assign too much importance to their dreams. Quite different is the position of a master like Chewu Jixing (1741–1810), a representative of the Pure Land tradition strongly influenced by Chan, in whom we can detect a return to the hierarchy of dreams and a cosmological conception of awakening. As has been the case in the West since the time of Homer, Buddhists have always distinguished "true" dreams from misleading ones.[16] For Chewu, the ambiguity of dreams is ontologically founded and plays a crucial soteriological role: while dreams based on illusion lead to further ignorance and suffering, some dreams constitute an outburst of reality into one's consciousness. Thus dreams of ascent to heaven

[12] See *Kenzei ki*, in *SZ*, 17: 77.
[13] See Bielefeldt 1988: 24.
[14] For more details on this, see Faure 1991: 209–30.
[15] See J. Poirier, ed., *Histoire des moeurs* (Paris: Gallimard, 1990–91), vol. 2, 1165.
[16] According to Homer, "All the obscure and unfathomable dreams do not foretell the future of men; because there are two gates for uncertain dreams, one of ivory, the other of horn. Those that emerge from the ivory gate are misleading, but those that come through polished horn will come true for the mortal who has seen them." Quoted in *Histoire des moeurs* (above, note 15), vol. 2, 1164.

大梅山ノ
且過ニテ
靈夢ヲ
感シ玉フ

FIGURE 4. Dōgen receives the transmission of Damei in a dream, in Zuikō Chingyū and Daiken Hōju, eds., *Teiho Kenzeiki zue* (1806), in *SZ*, 17, *Shiden*, 2, rev. ed. (Tokyo: Sōtōshū shūmuchō, 1970-73).

lead in actuality to a place/state of purity from which one can progressively advance toward ultimate awakening: "Although [both kinds of] dreams exist, their cause is totally different."[17] Elsewhere in various Chinese Buddhist masters, most notably Daoyin (tenth century),

[17] See *Chanwu chanshi yulu*, in ZZ 2, 14, 4: 386d.

we find criticisms, apparently directed at Chan, of those who do not understand that oneiric images are part of the fundamental nature of things.[18]

Dreams, as an incomplete state of awareness, thus do not differ fundamentally from ordinary thought. Like it, they are connected with karmic retribution. But they may, even better than thought, let us grasp this process. As Roland Barthes has stressed in another context: "Dreams permit, support, hold, illuminate an extreme delicacy of moral, sometimes even metaphysical, feelings, the most subtle understanding of human relations, precise distinctions, a highly civilized knowledge, in brief, a *conscious* logic, articulated with unexpected delicacy, that would seem to be obtainable only as the result of intense waking activity."[19] It remains to be determined whether dreams can also affect karma: we know that in their councils Indian Buddhists passionately discussed the question of knowing not only whether the Arhats, these eminent, puritan disciples of the Buddha, were still subject to nocturnal emissions but also, more precisely, whether the ejaculation of semen during dreams constitutes a transgression of the Buddhist rule.[20] In his masterful study of Chinese Tantrism, Michel Strickmann mentions the case of an evil *yakṣa* named Bhūti, Demon of Dreams, who causes monks to have wet dreams.[21]

THE PRACTICE OF DREAMS

In the *Zazen yōjinki*, a short treatise on meditation, Keizan seems to deny all soteriological value to visions achieved through meditation.[22] But Keizan was still a person who lived his dreams, or dreamed his life. The *Record of Tōkoku* alone mentions about twenty separate dreams, and other texts by Keizan report his oneiric experiences. Despite his enunciation of the Buddhist principle of emptiness, Keizan lived in a world permeated with very "real" dreams. He shared this worldview with many Buddhists of the period, for whom dreams provided a privileged access to the invisible world. On this point he was very close to Myōe, for whom "dreams should be feared," because they eventually come true.[23] Like Myōe, Keizan cultivated the gift of dreaming and having visions, and during these episodes he frequently communicated with transcendent beings. The *Record of Tōkoku* can thus be read as the account of a quest after visions.

18 See *T.* 46, 1955: 998b; quoted in Girard 1990a: xxvii.
19 See Barthes 1975: 59–60.
20 See Faure 1994: 77–80.
21 See Strickmann 1996: 320–21.
22 See Keizan, *Zazen yōjinki*, in *T.* 82, 2586: 413a.
23 See Girard 1990a: 121.

Actually Buddhist dream practice was not entirely passive. It was possible to induce auspicious visions, and various methods existed to achieve this. Thus the *Great Dhāraṇī Sūtra* (*Da fangdeng tuoluoni jing*) includes a discussion of "dream practice" in which are described a dozen typical dreams, corresponding to the twelve demon-kings converted by the Bodhisattva hero of this text. Also described is the so-called "seven-day" method, the period during which visions come that must be kept secret.[24] This method was taken up again by the founder of the Tiantai school, Zhiyi (538–597). According to his disciple Ryūben, Myōe cultivated an esoteric method, implying the use of mantras and *mudrās*, to encourage "true dreams" (*masa yume*). Such methods had long been practiced in China, as is attested by a document from Dunhuang.[25] The monk-painter Guanxiu (832–912), celebrated for his Arhat "portraits," explains their genesis thus: "Each time I paint one Arhat, I positively pray for a dream. Thus I obtain the real shape of the saints and I paint them quite differently from the ordinary Arhat figures."[26] Likewise, it is a *kami* who explains to Keizan in a dream how to make an icon of the Buddhist guardian Bishamon. On every important occasions, Keizan tried to obtain auspicious dreams. As he notes after recording the two solemn vows he made at the end of his life, "If one accords with the will of the Buddhas, one will certainly have auspicious dreams." Having gone to sleep with this thought, he effectively had at dawn a dream that he considered to be auspicious.

DREAMS AS SIGNS

On the level of practice, dreams and visions played an essential role in marking and authenticating the steps on the Buddhist way. It was through them that "auspicious signs" were received, which provided the only way to verify the spiritual progress of the practitioner. In the sensitive case of "self-ordination," for example, it was during a true period of incubation before a statue of the Buddha that the postulant, in the absence of any human master, obtained confirmation of his new status.[27] Thus, Eizon (1201–1290) obtained an auspicious dream before ordaining himself at Tōdaiji in 1236. The ordination was authenticated much later, in 1245, by another vision during which the Bodhisattva Mañjuśrī transmitted to him the Tantric unction ritual (*abhiṣeka*). The same was

---

[24] *T.* 21, 1339: 652a; quoted in Kuo Li-ying, 1994: 101–4.

[25] These methods were based on texts such as the Yuqi jing, *T.* 18, 867. See Girard 1990 (above, note 18): xliii.

[26] Quoted in de Visser 1923: 105–6.

[27] See Kuo 1994.

true for this ritual: in the dream journal of Shungi, for instance, we find dreams recorded in 1129 during exercises preliminary to the unction ritual.[28]

Various canonical sources specify that beings, according to their faculties, receive different kinds of visions and that, among these, dreams actually are reserved for the least gifted practitioners.[29] One of these sources goes so far as to insist that the best practitioners do not see signs but simply achieve serenity. We obviously have here yet another veiled criticism—of the kind that inspired Chan—of the meditative practice of visualization.

But on the whole dreams and visions appear to be one way among others, not only of achieving conversion, but also of deepening religious practice.[30] They offer auspicious signs that can, for example, guarantee the repentance that is a necessary preliminary to ordination or any other important ritual. In certain cases these signs can even provide an authentification of awakening through dreams. They furnish a criterion of choice for what one could call a "hermeneutic of practice," which, a little like the Yi jing, reveals to the practitioner his place on the "Chutes and Ladders" game of the Buddhist Way and lets him constantly advance or correct himself. As such, these oneiric signs play an essential role in the life of the community. During Keizan's time the Zen community itself made great use of "self-ordination." In spite (or because) of its purely individual ethic and its theoretical rejection of all external moral laws, it depended heavily on dreams as a means of checking collective morality. Furthermore, dreams provided the place and means of communication with superhuman entities. An absolute refusal to recognize the value of oneiric visions and give these entities their "dream dues" (le denier du rêve) would have constituted too blunt a denial of the sacred. No Buddhist community could have allowed itself such a refusal to communicate with the beyond without falling at the same time "outside the Law." This is why dreams, banished from Chan discourse, come back to haunt the Buddhist imagination by the rear entrance of ritual—not only by incubation, a technique based on an anxious waiting for dream signs that can ensure not so much a physical cure as a spiritual one, but also by deliberate dream practice, or rather practice within dreams.

[28] See Girard 1990: xlii.

[29] See for instance T. 24, 1484: 1008c.

[30] Dreams were instrumental in the conversion of various eminent Chinese and Japanese monks such as Yongming Yanshou, Hōnen, Shinran, and Ippen. The Tendai monk Ennin, stranded in China during the anti-Buddhist repression of 845, vowed that he would built a "dhyāna court" if he returned safely to Japan. He subsequently dreamed that eight worthies (Bodhidharma, Baozhi, Huisi, Zhiyi, Huineng, Shōtoku Taishi, Gyōki, and his master Saichō himself) came to protect him. See Reischauer 1955a: 293.

MYŌE AND HIS DREAM DIARY

Whereas Keizan notes in his *Record of Tōkoku* only the auspicious dreams that have accompanied the foundation of Yōkōji, there is another elite dreamer we cannot neglect when we approach the subject of dreams among Japanese Buddhists, and who can serve as a counterpoint. It is Myōe, whose *Dream Diary* extends over a period of thirty-five years.[31] During sleep or in periods of meditation, this master of the Kegon school had all sorts of dreams and visions, which he noted (apparently) at random. Many of these dreams are rather ordinary and some of them have a decidedly sexual bent. In one of the most detailed of these dreams, he found a Chinese doll representing a young woman who told him of her sorrow at having left her native land. When Myōe promised to help her, right in his hands she turned into a living young woman. After accompanying Myōe to a ritual, she was accused by another priest of having mated with a serpent. Refusing to believe these accusations, Myōe decided that the young woman perhaps also had a reptilian form. Interpreting this dream, he concluded that she was none other than the *nāga*-maiden Zenmyō (Ch. Shanmiao). According to legend, Shanmiao was a beautiful young Chinese woman who had fallen in love with the Korean monk Ŭisang, during the latter's visit to China. When Ŭisang had to return to Korea, she assumed an animal form—she is represented in the iconography as a dragon—and escorted his vessel until it reached port. Then, changing into a rock, she became the protective deity of the monastery founded by this monk. This fine Platonic love apparently made a big impression on Myōe because he often refers to it. The sexual connotations of his dream have been noted by various commentators, but Frédéric Girard, in his study on Myōe, rejects them and sees the dream as fundamentally didactic.[32] The two hypotheses are not mutually

[31] This journal has been translated into English by Tanabe 1992; and in French by Girard 1990a. I do not share Tanabe's assumption that the imagery of light in Mahāyāna literature, or other such literary "visions," originate in dreams and visionary experience. Tanabe thinks that "the literary treatment of the Hua-yen visions reached beyond mere reporting to codification, conceptualization, and interpretation without, however, sacrificing the visionary character of the sūtra" (p. 26). For him, "the line of tradition thus runs from original visions to sūtra to interpretative dogma to further visions of a man whose life itself was envisioned in legends" (p. 13). I am doubtful, however, that a scripture like the *Avataṃsaka-sūtra* is merely a literarily or philosophically amplified form of some "*Ur*-dream diary," and that its "visions" ever were true, "visionary" experiences. These experiences found their main expression in hagiography, not in doctrinal literature. Even if at times they resurface in the Mahāyāna sūtras, they are foreign elements in the mythic plots of the latter.

[32] See Girard 1990a: 329; 1990b: 185.

exclusive, however, since sublimation and elaboration are among the motivational causes of dreams.

Women often appear in Myōe's dreams. In many cases they are explicitly sexual relations with an upper-class woman. Myōe is seen as "the purest monk in Japan," and it is clear that, in spite (or perhaps because) of his nocturnal outlets, purity remained his main concern. One of the basic reasons why he recorded his dreams was to find in them indications of his progress toward complete purification. In many cases he gives a religious interpretation to dreams of a strongly sexual connotation: thus in one dream a court lady wanted to embrace him and he saw in her an emanation of the Buddha Vairocana.[33] Doubtless the most striking example in this respect is the dream in which he met a physically attractive noblewoman whose appearance "was truly in conformity [with Buddhist doctrine]." "Everything about her revealed the Dharma. . . . I spent the night with her and we had sexual relations. Everyone said that this ceremonial act would certainly become a cause of awakening. We embraced each other, full of compassion." Myōe adds in a note: "The emotional atmosphere of this ceremonial act was in accord with the Commentary on the *Avataṃsaka-sūtra* authored by the Chinese Huayan Patriarch Fazang."

Myōe also records dreams whose religious quality is less ambiguous. In certain cases he had visions in which appeared an Arhat (Piṇḍola, Mahā-kāśyapa), a Bodhisattva, or various deities. He also describes several dream flights that stood out in his memory: usually dreams that carried him to Tuṣita Heaven, the palace of the future Buddha Maitreya. In one case he notes: "In front of Maitreya I took up a golden tub and filled it with incense. A Bodhisattva was there and he made me take a bath." During a meditation session, after having asked the Buddha for a sign attesting to his spiritual progress, he obtained a vision in which his body and his spirit had fused. He then saw coming down from the sky a pole carved of beryl; he grasped the end of it and was lifted up into Tuṣita Heaven. There he was purified by the water that poured out of the pole and his body changed into a clear mirror, then became round, a crystal gem. A voice told him that all the Buddhas had entered into him, and that he had obtained purity. The dream was accompanied by revelations about the fifty-two stages in the career of the Bodhisattva.[34] In another dream of the same type, Myōe climbed to the top of a cosmic pagoda from which he could look out over the entire universe: "The sun, the moon, the stars, and the heavenly mansions were far below me, and I felt that I had gone beyond the Akaniṣṭha Heaven. Then I returned to earth."

[33] Ibid.
[34] See Girard 1990a: 151; Tanabe 1992: 182.

Just as Myōe's body and soul fused in his dream, dream and reality tended to blend in his life. The significance of dreams in his daily practice led his disciples to attribute to him visionary talents. One of them tells that when Myōe was forty he often slept during the day and thus learned to read the thoughts of others. It is also reported that, on various occasions, he woke up to tell his acolytes to run outside the monastery to save a wounded insect or sparrow that he had seen in his dream. All these examples suggest a practice of "directed dreams" reminiscent of that in Tibetan Buddhism.[35] It is very likely that such practices would have been rejected by orthodox Chan masters as deriving from "demonic *dhyāna*": from the intransigent point of view of "subitism," Myōe had clearly fallen into the "Dark Cave of Demons." However, he did not see anything wrong with his visions, considering them to be the natural outcome of his religious practice.

KEIZAN'S DREAMS

The *Record of Tōkoku*, Keizan's "dream diary," is less well known and not as extensive as that of Myōe, but it does contain many interesting dreams. Like Myōe, Keizan noted down his premonitory dreams and especially those that were connected to the monasteries he founded. As we have seen, he had an oneirical revelation of the future prosperity of Yōkōji: "I saw in a dream the halls of a wonderful monastery. When I reached the great *enoki* tree on which people hung their straw sandals, the one standing in front of the gate, I realized that this was a special site, where wandering monks could reimburse the cost of their straw sandals" [*JDZ*, 392]. This vision was confirmed by the prediction made in 1312 by the Arhat Vajraputra, again during a dream. Keizan remembered this dream ten years later and noted that the prediction had come true since his teaching had prospered since his move to Tōkoku. The dream here justifies after the event the schism between Gikai and Keizan and shows that, in spite of appearances, Keizan's community in the Noto peninsula was just as orthodox as, if not more so than, that of the successors of Dōgen at Eiheiji. Even more meaningful is the dream in which Keizan received the transmission of the Buddhist Law, successively from Bodhidharma, Maitreya, and Śākyamuni. The latter appears to him in a specific context, at the time of his preaching the *Ratnakūṭa-sūtra*, and more precisely the teaching of the "Three Deliverances"—from time, mind, and phenomena. This sūtra seems to play an important role in Keizan's dream world, as it appears at least in another dream. At any rate

[35] On dreams in Tibetan Buddhism, see below, note 76.

the denial of the phenomenal world is paradoxically based on the ultimate assumption of this world within a dream. It is during an experience that includes time, mind, and phenomena that Keizan must deliver himself from these three aspects of reality. Just as in the esoteric rituals so well known to him, the denial of images in the name of emptiness is permitted through a manifestation that is itself eidetic.

Keizan's dream (if it is truly a single dream) corresponds quite closely to that in which Myōe went up to Tuṣita Heaven.[36] Bodhidharma takes the place of Mañjuśrī, but we seem to have here some kind of oneiric tradition. The dreams experienced by Myōe and Keizan, while they fit into the Buddhist framework, have all kinds of connotations that would lead us to call them, for want of a better term, shamanistic. The symbolism of ascent that characterizes some of them is also found in many other Chan/Zen dreams, usually in connection with Maitreya's Palace. We know, for example, that Dainichi Nōnin, the founder of the Darumashū, also went up into Tuṣita Heaven. These shamanistic elements are even more striking in the case of the dreams of the Chan master Hanshan Deqing (1546–1623). In one of these in particular, Hanshan was invited by the Bodhisattva Mañjuśrī to take a bath on the northern terrace of Mount Wutai. Just as he was about to get into the bath, he realized that there was already someone in it, a young woman. Overcome by disgust [sic], he refused to get into the bath. But when the person in question turned out to be a man, Hanshan did not wait any longer. The man washed him from head to toe and what is more cleaned his five visceral organs "as one washes a basket of meat." Hanshan soon had, literally, no more than skin over his bones, and his body became as transparent as a crystal cage. A little later an Indian monk brought him something to drink in a skullcap filled with bloody bone marrow and brain tissue: an especially disgusting mixture, but one whose taste, going against all expectations, was that of sweet dew. The draught gave Hanshan the impression of being purified in every pore of his skin. After having rubbed his back, the Indian monk suddenly clapped his hands and Hanshan woke up. Although he was covered with sweat, he felt himself "very clean and relaxed."[37]

THE DOUBLE KEY TO DREAMS

As we can see, beyond the Tantric and shamanistic (even homosexual) connotations of this dream, the resemblance with Keizan's dream is striking. We may see in it only the expression of certain ideas and practices

---

[36] See Girard 1990: 179.
[37] Quoted in Hsü 1979: 73.

from esoteric Buddhism. But even though they appear as more or less cryptic messages or as expressions of a stereotypical *imaginaire* (with the ascent to Tuṣita Heaven), the dreams of Keizan, Myōe, and Hanshan are all equally events that "impressed" the dreamer, marked him with the seal of (sur)reality, and transformed him in the depths of his being. A paradigmatic example, even if hagiographical, is the dream of Guṇa-bhadra. This Indian translator, who came to China to spread Mahāyāna Buddhism, was in despair because he did not know Chinese. One night he dreamed that a man, with a single stroke of his sword, cut off his head and replaced it with another. When he awoke he could express himself in perfect Chinese.[38]

While acknowledging the symbolic or doctrinal content of these dreams, we should not lose sight of their performative nature and must avoid reducing them to some kind of psycho-hagiographical interpretation that gives too much importance to methodological individualism.[39] Tuṣita Heaven became a necessary representation that was part of heavenly voyages of more or less shamanistic origin.[40] Still, as we have seen them in the three cases given above, these voyages have more than simply an allegorical or a literary value. This is revealed by the dream of the modern Chan master Xu Yun who, emerging peacefully from the apparent coma he had fallen into during beatings by the Red Guards, brought back a dazzling vision of Tuṣita Heaven. Moreover, such dreams are supposed to lead to an "actual" rebirth in Tuṣita. Some interpreters, adopting a Corbinian perspective, see these visions as retaining an element of authenticity and so constituting evidence for the existence of the intermediary world. Others do just the opposite and see in them only signs of confirmation or prefiguration of practice, in all cases oneiric doublings of events that have happened or are on the point of happening on a real-world level. We have thus two models for dreams: the hermeneutic model that leads to "keys to dreams" and to oneirology; and the "per-

---

[38] See *Lengqie shizi ji*, T. 85, 2837: 1283c.

[39] As Michel Strickmann points out, even the lists provided by the traditional "Keys of Dreams," far from being simply descriptive or explanatory, are resolutely prescriptive: "They seem to say: here are the best dreams; dream them!" See Strickmann 1996: 307.

[40] In Japan Tuṣita Heaven was associated with Amaterasu's Rock-Cave of Heaven, which points to the practice of incubatory reclusion. Likewise, Bodhidharma's nine years of sitting "facing the wall" in a cave on Song shan is sometimes associated in esoteric Zen texts with Amaterasu's withdrawal into her cave. All these stories draw on the symbolism of the womb-cave, on which see Stein 1988; and Saigō 1993. One can thus argue that the ascent to Heaven and the descent into the underworld are structurally similar. In T. 1418 (quoted by Strickmann), the Bodhisattva in Tuṣita is compared to Śākyamuni in the maternal bosom, and to the compassion in the temple icon. As a paradise opened to women, Tuṣita is also a place of rebirth for mothers like Māya or Dongshan's mother. See *Denkōroku*, T. 82, 2585: 388c.

formative" model that tries to recognize the higher truth of an "imaginal" (but not purely imaginary) event like the transmission of the Dharma, as it figures in the dreams of Keizan and Hanshan.[41] Buddhist masters thus appear as "elite dreamers," established at the summit of the oneiric hierarchy.

If we admit that the "performative" dreams of Keizan, those, for example in which he receives the transmission, are the oneiric replica and confirmation of a transmission ritual taking place in the framework of the monastery itself, should the confirmation of his awakening be taken as a "sign" or as a performative act? The notion of a sign should not lead us into error. Favorable signs have the effect of actually wiping away faults and so can lead to spiritual progress. Dreams and visions are "vectors of action," because in a way they "find their place in the transmigratory cycle, as in a single system, which is ruled by the law of causality and action."[42] Finally, we must take into consideration the sectarian strategy in these dreams of ascension, which, by legitimizing with the seal of the otherworldly a transmission that may at times be problematic, permits an end run around established hierarchies. Thus a document dated 1460 reports that Dainichi Nōnin, who had never been to China and so had difficulty in gaining recognition for his new Darumashū, went up in a dream to Tuṣita Heaven where he received from Maitreya a relic of the Buddha.

If we wanted to establish a typology of dreams for Keizan, we could distinguish between hermeneutic, performative, and premonitory dreams (although these last constitute a category of the hermeneutic type). To the last category belongs the dream in which Keizan sees a majestic monastery stretched out over the entire Tōkoku valley, the dream featuring a huge tree with luxuriant foliage, or the vision of clouds and flooding waters. Keizan himself gives a quasi-psychoanalytic interpretation of the latter when he sees in it an oneiric transposition of the term unsui, "clouds and waters," used metaphorically to designate Zen adepts. And he concludes, "Strange, truly strange! See how wakefulness and sleep merge together, dream and waking harmonize" [JDZ, 397]. As another premonitory dream, we have already cited the prediction of the Arhat Vajraputra concerning Yōkōji. The Arhat based his predication on the geomantic excellence of the Tōkoku site. This dream would later actually permit Keizan to go against geomantic norms. When he planned to construct the Gorōhō funerary mound on a hill behind the monastery, a disciple informed him that this was contrary to the normal rule: "When

---

[41] Myōe himself gives a theoretical interpretation of his ascension-dream, which shows clearly these two aspects—doctrinal and performative. See Girard 1990: 338.

[42] Ibid.: xxxv.

the site of the stūpa is higher than that of the monastery, the lineage will be interrupted. How was this [error] possible?" Keizan then thought, "From the outset all my decisions concerning this monastery have been based on revelations [received] in dreams. Thus, when I began to build my hermitage, the Venerable [Vajraputra] announced to me, 'Nothing will stand in the way of the numberless activities of this monastery, and you will be able to spread the Buddhist Law there as you will.' As a result, the site of this stūpa will remain for all eternity, because it was in a dream that I learned it and understood it" [*JDZ*, 409].

Keizan then decided to trust his next vision in order to determine the placing of Gorōhō. In a similar vein, when he explained why he decided to rename the mountain Tōkoku, Keizan referred to the tradition of Dongshan Liangjie (J. Tōzan Ryōkai), but also to his own oneiric universe. "In distant matters, I aspired to emulate Tōzan; for matters near at hand, I valued dreaming. It was thus that, combining the two [approaches], I baptized [this monastery] "Magnificent Hall of Eternal Light of the Peak of the Great Enoki Tree on Mount Tōkoku" [*JDZ*, 398]. A dream is thus not only a "memory palace" in that it permits one to know about past lives, but it is also an instrument of divination that permits one to foretell the future. Dreams thus constitute a beginning of transcendence when it comes to time, a harbinger of awakening.

Keizan also records dreams with a doctrinal tendency. It really seems that, like Myōe, he expected from dreams not only predictions but also a gnosis. During a discussion with his disciples, he mentioned that he had been able, during meditation, to "meet the men within the mirror" and, entering into the form of concentration known as "*samādhi* of illusion" (*nyogen zanmai*, Skt. *māyopamasamādhi*), "perform Buddha work within a dream." The *samādhi* to which he refers seems to have played a certain role in Mahāyāna before being itself rejected as illusory in the general movement of disapproval of the imagination and the intermediary world.[43] Still, as we have seen, it retained its full value with masters like Myōe and Keizan. In one of these "doctrinal" dreams, Keizan read a passage from the *Ratnakūṭa-sūtra*, a sūtra that often recurs in his dreams. As soon as he woke up, he checked the original and found that the two versions (oneiric and "real") of the passage reflected each other, were mutually explanatory.

> On the fourth day of the second month [of the year 1321] I read the *Ratnakūṭa-sūtra*. Then, having fallen asleep sitting up, I saw in a dream a passage of the sūtra that said, "Do not reject vain thoughts; do not desire wisdom." On my awakening, [I realized that] this passage was really saying,

[43] See *Nyogen sanmaji muryō inhōmon gyō*, T. 12, 372; and *Kanzeon bosatsu juki kyō*, T. 12, 371.

"After having purified and cultivated the vision of the Buddha, one makes manifest and ascertains all things." With these words, I obtained awakening. As I have already explained, in the Dharma there is nothing that can be revealed, and nothing that can be denigrated, for all things are like space. This is why I have supplied these explanations [*JDZ*, 399].

In another dream, Keizan continued a dialogue with two of his disciples that he had begun while awake. In a meaningful fashion, the dream itself resolves the problem of levels of reality. Keizan explains to Koan Shikan that these different types of awareness do not imply any duality:

On the twentieth of the twelfth month [of the year 1321], towards midnight, I was explaining to the *shuso* [Shi]kan the words of Jiashan to Luofu, "When there is no one in the whole empire whose tongue has not been cut out, how can one make men without tongues understand what words are?" [. . .]

After this conversation, when I had fallen asleep, I had a dream in which I saw Shikan and Sōin discussing the story in question. Shikan was saying, "It is precisely the man who has lost his tongue who [best] understands words." To which [Sō]in replied, "A man without a tongue and the understanding of words are completely unrelated items." I [then] said, "There is the man without a tongue, the man who understands words, and the man who understands how to understand words." Shikan said, "Since [this latter] understands the man without a tongue, it is he [who grasps] the ultimate truth. But if one distinguishes between the person who understands words and the one who understands the understanding of words, are there then degrees within the ultimate truth?" I said, "Although the ultimate truth admits of no degrees, it is as though, in speaking about the eye, one could distinguish three different things: the white of the eye, the dark of the iris, and, within the iris, the pupil. This does not imply that one has two pairs of eyes. The men who achieve awakening within the ultimate truth are also of three types. You must understand this in detail." I made a note of this as an example for future generations. [*JDZ*, 400]

The dream functions here as a "supplement" to the dialogue that has just taken place, whereas in the former case, the opposite occurred: Keizan started from the textual passage seen in the dream, then found a supplement of meaning in the "real" text, and this supplement produced his insight. As Georges Didi-Huberman points out, "There is no awakening without the dream from which one awakens. The dream at the moment of waking up becomes then like the 'rubbish' of conscious activity. . . . The awakening as forgetting of the dream must not be conceived of on the model of a pure negativity or deprivation: as forgetting itself leaves its traces, like 'nocturnal remainders' that will continue to work—to bend, to transform, to 'shape'—conscious life itself."[44] The logic of the dream seems here to be that of the "symbol" (in the etymological sense) or of the tallies—a logic to which we return in Chapter 9.

DREAMS AS CRYPTOGRAMS

In that they are signs requiring decipherment, dreams involve a hermeneutic; but at the same time, like all oracles, they are also self-sufficient. An especially strange dream, one that for this reason is seen as a form of "divine response," tends in spite (or because) of its semantic obscurity to be taken as a happy portent and may thus be considered as performative. Dreams are often divine responses to a religious act, and they are invoked by the practitioner as an indication that the act is meritorious. They form part of the cycle of gift and counter-gift, as a token of indebtedness. Keizan records, for example, a dream that he had about a year before his death, one about the Dharma robe. He had earlier made two vows and felt that if these were in line with the Dharma he should be granted an auspicious dream. That night, at dawn, he had the following dream:

> I owned an old robe that I had not put on for a long time. I now wanted to wear it, but when I found it, rats had made their nest in it and it was spotted with filth that looked like cow and horse excrement, hairs from horses' tails, and human hairs. I brushed it off, and then, after I had cleaned it, I put it on. It was truly a strange dream, an auspicious dream. It was the sign that my fundamental vows would be accomplished. The Buddhas and patriarchs had replied to me and confirmed my two vows. [JDZ, 433]

Keizan's interpretation may seem strange to the outside observer. Perhaps we should see here an allusion to the etymology of one of the words used for *kāṣāya*, *funzōe* (litt. "robe to sweep excrements," Skt., *pāṃsukūla*).[45] It could thus be an attestation that Keizan's practice is in conformity with the traditional Buddhist ideal of austerity (*dhūtaguṇa*).

Dreams can be explicitly oracular, particularly when they emanate from native gods. After mentioning the explicit predictions made by the Arhat Vajraputra and by the gods Ichinomiya and Inari, Keizan records two oracles that seem to come from the *kami* Hachiman:[46]

---

[44] Didi-Huberman 1992: 145.
[45] On this question, see Faure 1995.
[46] See *JDZ* 405, 409.

On the twenty-seventh of the first month of the second Genkō year [1322] I saw in a dream the following oracle:

"It has now been a year since	*kotoshi yori*
The god of Yahata	*yahata no kami no*
Appeared to me	*arawarete*
And made himself the guardian	*wagatatsu soma no*
Of the wooded mountain where I reside."	*mahoto naru kana*

On the fourth day of the sixth month of the same year, on the *kinoe ne* day [first in the cycle], at the hour of the tiger, I saw the following oracle in a dream:

"At the foot of Mount Nasaka	*ware sumeru*
Where my house stands	*nasaka no yama mo*
The moss is churned up	*bumi naraji*
So much is the soil beaten down by the steps	*koke no shita kaherite*
Of those who come to see me."	*hito zo tohikuru*

Both oracles are given in the form of poems and apparently read (or in any case are recorded) in the syllabary using Chinese characters (*man'yō-gana*).[47] Keizan remarks on this point that the use of "unconventional characters" is itself a happy portent. We may note in passing that the use of this archaic (and therefore numinous) form of writing—composed of Chinese characters used for their strictly phonetic value—to transcribe a Japanese poem constitutes a paradoxical rejection of Chinese and Buddhist poetry (on the part of someone who writes in Chinese) and the emergence of a "purely" Japanese version of the sacred.[48] Oracular dreams of Hachiman, which in earlier times had a purely public and political character, now seem to have a more private nature.

Here is another example of decipherment. It is the last dream reported in the *Record of Tōkoku*, one month before Keizan's death—which, despite his premonitory talents, he does not seem to have anticipated in a more precise fashion:

On the sixteenth of the seventh month [of the year 1324] I had this auspicious dream: Someone had a container about a foot deep in which there was some clear water. On the surface of the water floated letters that looked like golden

[47] As Mujū points out in the *Shasekishū*, "Such instances of poems being revealed in dreams are known from antiquity." See Morrell 1985: 171.

[48] See for instance how Mujū describes the identity of *waka* poetry and Buddhist *dhāraṇī* in his *Shasekishū*: "The god Susano-o initiated composition in thirty-one syllables with the 'many-layered fence at Izumo'" (Morrel 1985: 163). Mujū argues that Japanese poems do not differ from the words of the Buddha (as expressed in Sanskrit *dhāraṇī*), but the point is that *waka* are the words of the native *kami*. The distinction will remain operative in the Japanese *imaginaire*.

hooks and spelled out *"shitsu ganden tōkoku,* the same pure stream." After waking up I understood their significance: *shitsu* is Shōshitsu [Shaoshi, i.e., Bodhidharma]; *ganden* is Sekitō [Shitou]; *tōkoku* is Tōkoku [Keizan]. The knowledge of these three men [Bodhidharma, Shitou Xiqian, and Keizan] is not separate because they all belong to the same pure stream [i.e., school]. This was a very auspicious sign. [*JDZ,* 433–434]

This dream, an almost Freudian rebus, indicates according to Keizan that among these three individuals there is a perfect harmony. It has the same structure as the set of portraits of the patriarchs, which usually represent Bodhidharma (the founder of Chan), the founding father of a specific lineage (here Shitou, patriarch of the Caodong/Sōtō line), and the most recently deceased master. It is thus perhaps, after all, a veiled prediction of Keizan's death. Another example of glyphomancy, this time inverted: the way in which Keizan interprets the dream in which he sees a flourishing monastery:

Furthermore, the next year when I saw the slope that had appeared in my dream, I noted that there actually was an *enoki* tree of that kind there, one whose branches, as they grew, were becoming luxuriant. Thus the monastery would prosper, just as the clouds mass together, swell up, and finally conceal the valley, or streams in flood flow down and fill the rivers and lakes. Strange, truly strange! See how wakefulness and sleep merge together, dreaming and waking harmonize. Indeed, is it not true that wandering monks are called "clouds and waters"? Seeking a master to consult regarding the Way, they cross mountains and seas; wandering with no fixed abode, they go towards east and west, towards south and north. Far from beaten tracks, they ascend suddenly, and slowly go back down. Like clouds, like water, they explore all the mountains and travel all the seas. They wear straw sandals and sling a staff over their shoulder. If, by chance, they meet a worthy friend, he will immediately open the True Dharma eye of these pilgrims. Paying back the price of one's straw sandals and breaking one's [pilgrim] staff, this is the common rule for monks. [*JDZ,* 397]

INCUBATION

Dream images are "animated" images in the same sense as icons in that they reveal a presence, channel a "force." Buddhas, Bodhisattvas, and gods appear in dreams. Dreams make up a kind of ritual area where the invisible takes form, the framework for a hierophany. The mental space of dreams provides a counterpart to the physical space of the temple, the oneiric image of the god is the double of the icon. Thus it is no coincidence that incubatory dreams are conjured up in the presence of a statue of the Buddha—or perhaps we should say rather that dreams allow precisely a kind of coincidence of the profane and the sacred, of the consciousness of the dreamer and the super-consciousness of the Awakened Ones, the Buddhas. In the case of initiatory dreams preceding and making possible ordinations, we are dealing with a form of incubation that requires sleeping in a sacred place, in the presence of icons.[49] In a more general fashion, we may say that initiation is a dream lived in a waking state, a dream wished for and put into effect by an entire society in its rites of passage.

In some cases the anthropomorphic presence of the Buddha or god is not necessary; an oracular pronouncement may take his place, because just like the icon, although in a different form, it is a "substitute body" of the god. Thus when Keizan talks of poetic oracles received from the god Hachiman, he does not mention the actual appearance of this god. As the monk-poet Saigyō stressed, "A poem is the true external body of the Tathāgata. Thus when one composes [or receives it], one has the feeling of erecting the statue of a figure from the Buddhist pantheon, and when one forms a vow, it is as though one were reciting an incantatory formula pregnant with mystery."[50]

The point, however, is that dreams are taking place on the "other scene"—the stage where the other manifests itself in "response" to a prayer or an expectation. Dreams in this sense are never casual; they are elements of an incubatory ritual. Incubatory dreams were a very significant element of the medieval imaginary landscape. Clerics and laypeople alike went into retreat in shrines and temples to receive dream revelations from the gods and the Buddhas. Keizan was no exception, and it is worth recalling at this point his interest in Kannon. Kannon was popular, not only as a child-giver but also as a dream-giver. The three main temples dedicated to her—Ishiyamadera, Hasedera, and Kiyomizudera—were all famous places for incubation.[51] It is at Ishiyamadera, for instance, that Murasaki Shikibu is said to have received the inspiration for the plot of the *Genji monogatari*, after a one-week retreat. Likewise, the female authors of the *Kagerō nikki* and the *Sarashina nikki* were granted divine

---

[49] In the Western context, incubation traditionally had to do with healing, for instance in the Greek cult of Asclepios. Although healing is also important in the Buddhist context, it was only one of the "benefits" (*riyaku*) hoped for. A method of incubation is already given in *T.* 20, 1191, which decribes the "dreams of the four watches": only the dreams of the fourth watch will come true; the others are ominous signs. Other oneirical sūtras include the *Sūtra of the Seven Dreams of Ānanda* (*T.* 12, 393), and the *Sūtra of the Ten Dreams of King Prasenajit* (*T.* 2, 146). On the role of Guanyin (Kannon) in Chinese Tantric incubation, see Strickmann 1996: 127–163, "Sous le charme de Kouan-yin."

[50] Quoted in Girard 1990a: 252.

[51] See for instance Dykstra 1976; Komatsu Shigemi, ed., *Ishiyamadera engi*, in *Nihon no emaki*, vol. 16 (Tokyo: Chūō kōronsha, 1988); Saigō 1993: 73–112.

responses from Kannon at the temple.[52] The first author, commonly referred to as "the mother of Michitsuna," feeling abandoned by her husband, went repeatedly to Ishiyamadera between 968 and 971 in search of signs about her future and that of her son. On one occasion, after spending the night weeping and praying at the temple, she dozed off and had the following dream: "A priest, the manager of the temple's affairs, it appeared, came up with a pitcher of water and poured it on my right knee. It must have been a sign from the Buddha, an unhappy one, no doubt."[53] In 971, after a retreat of some twenty days, she dreamed that her hair was cut and her forehead bared like a nun. Seven or eight days later, she dreamed again that a viper was crawling among her entrails and gnawing at her liver, and that the proper remedy for the difficulty was to pour water over her face.[54] One year later she received a letter from the priest who had performed the services for her at Ishiyamadera, and whom she had asked to pray on her behalf. He now reported a recent dream he had had, in which she held the sun and the moon in her two hands: "The moon you trampled underfoot, but the sun you held to your breast. Perhaps you had better question someone who knows about such things." She remained unconvinced by the dream and even suspected the monk of having invented it, but she nevertheless consulted an interpreter of dreams, who saw the dream as very auspicious, showing that "her house will be close to the Emperor and will be able to run the country as it chooses." She remained skeptical, however, until she received further dreams that seemed indeed auspicious for her son's future.[55]

Lady Sarashina, the author of the *Sarashina nikki*, reports in her "diary" a number of dreams that marked her retreats at Kiyomizudera and Hasedera, from youth to maturity. At first she had many auspicious dreams. In one of them, for instance, was the revelation that she had been in a former life the priest who had carved one of the icons of Kiyomizu. In another dream during a retreat at Hasedera, she received a token from the god Inari. However, the most important sign, actually an ominous one, was perceived not in one of her dreams but in one that a priest had on her behalf: her mother had ordered a one-foot mirror to be made for Hasedera, and, being unable to take it there herself, had sent a priest in

[52] See *Kagerō Nikki*, trans. Seidensticker 1964: 65–66, 88–90; *Sarashina nikki*, trans. Morris 1971: 49, 69–72, 90–99, 106–7.

[53] Seidensticker 1964: 90. This dream is also recorded in *Ishiyamadera engi emaki*. Seidensticker notes that the caption on the scroll, "no doubt for propaganda purposes," says that because of this benevolent sign from the Bodhisattva the author and her husband Kaneie were reconciled. See ibid.: 185.

[54] Ibid.: 98.

[55] Ibid.: 125.

her place. She instructed him to stay in retreat for three days and to pray for a dream about her daughter's future. On his return the priest reported that, after performing all his observances, he was granted a dream in which a most beautiful and noble-looking lady appeared behind the curtain, dressed in splendid robes. Raising the mirror that had been dedicated to the temple, she asked if a Statement of Dedication had been presented with the mirror. When the priest answered negatively, the lady seemed surprised. Then she pointed to the mirror, and began crying bitterly. In the mirror the priest saw a figure rolling on the floor in weeping and lamentation. "Very sad, is it not?" said the lady. Then she showed him the other side: there was a beautiful room, with many colorful robes, and beyond it one could see a blossoming garden with birds singing and flying from tree to tree. "This makes one happy, does it not?" said the lady. At this point the priest's dream came to an end.[56] However, Lady Sarashina paid no attention to this dream at the time. It is only much later, after the death of her husband, that she realized its meaning: "The priest had dreamt about a weeping figure rolling on the floor. Such was my present state. There had been no happy person in the priest's dream; nor could I expect any happiness in my own life."[57] She has become disillusioned about life and her unfulfilled dreams: "Alas, the only thing that had turned out exactly as predicted was the sad image in the mirror."[58] Yet, as she is now concerned with her rebirth, she still hopes that one of them at least will come true. In this dream she had seen the Buddha Amida standing in the far end of her garden, in the mist, invisible to everyone but her. She had been greatly impressed but at the same time frightened and did not dare to move closer. He had told her that he had to leave but would later return to fetch her. It was on this dream alone that she set her hopes for salvation.[59]

It is also at Kiyomizudera that Keizan's mother was told about her mother's whereabouts, after performing a weeklong retreat. Although in that case the answer did not come in the form of a dream, we can infer that her retreat was of an incubatory nature. Later on she did receive a dream that allegedly caused her pregnancy after she performed another round of ritual observances dedicated to Kannon. This Bodhisattva not only appears to women, however. As is well known, Kannon appeared in

[56] See Morris 1971: 70–72.

[57] Ibid.: 106.

[58] Ibid.: 106–7.

[59] Ibid.: 107. For other examples of incubation, see Kyōkai, "On the Appearance of Good and Evil Omens which were later Followed by Their Results," in *Nihon ryōiki*, trans. Nakamura 1973: 279–83; *Shasekishū*, in Morrell 1985: 87, 90. In one case a believer obtains relics during an incubatory retreat in the tomb of Shōtoku Taishi (ibid.: 103–4).

a dream to Shinran while he was secluded at Rokkakudō, and solved Shinran's anxieties.[60] Keizan himself received several auspicious dreams from Kannon, some of which he describes in his *Sōjiji chūkō engi.* Saigō Nobutsuna has argued that Kannon, in her oneiric function, inherited many characteristics from the pre-Buddhist earth goddesses.[61] One of these characteristics is the womb symbolism: the dark place into which one has to descend, to remain in reclusion (*komori*) in order to be reborn to a world of light.[62] As noted earlier, the Hakusan cult, centered on Kukurihime/Kannon, was permeated (impregnated?) with the symbolism of pregnancy or incubation (in both senses of the term).[63] The same can be said of Keizan's *Record of Tōkoku.* In the Buddhist context, incubation was at first opposed to the more orthodox *samādhi*: but *samādhi* itself was eventually redefined as a kind of incubation, *komori*.[64]

THE IDEOLOGY OF THE DREAM

If we are to take Keizan seriously when he tells us that he takes dreams seriously, we should also examine the ideological function of these dreams and statements. Even if dreams should, according to Myōe, "be feared," this does not prevent dreamers and others from manipulating them, for all sorts of down-to-earth reasons. The dreams are also ambiguous in that they are at the same time collective and individual. If they usually serve the interests of tradition, they can also threaten them, inasmuch as they reflect "the power of a personal religion in which dreams were a means of contact with divinity."[65] Sometimes they tend to impose themselves to the detriment of "pure" Buddhist values. In the words of Georges Duby, "The mark left by a dream is as real as a footprint." It is thus that priestly marriage, a major structural change in the history of Japanese Buddhism, and flagrantly contradictory to the Scriptures, was supported by the oneiric revelation that Shinran received from the

[60] According to some versions, Kannon appeared to Shinran as Shōtoku Taishi, the traditional founder of Rokkakudō. Shōtoku is himself famous for his practice of incubation at the "Palace of Dreams" (Yumedono). We are told that, during his incubatory trance, his soul flew to China to fetch the *Lotus Sūtra*. On Shōtoku and Yumedono, see Dykstra 1983: 25–26.

[61] Saigō 1993: 92–98.

[62] On this question, see Stein 1988.

[63] The name of the goddess of Hakusan, Kukurihime, seems to point to the notion of *tainai no kuguri*, "dwelling in the womb."

[64] In India the term *samādhi* designates the grave into which the candidate for self-mummification locks himself, in the hope of an ultimate rebirth.

[65] Le Goff 1988: 200.

Bodhisattva Kannon. In this famous dream Kannon addressed the future reformer of the Pure Land movement in these terms: "If you should happen, due to your karma, to succumb to sexual desire,/ I shall take the body of a 'jade woman' to be ravished by you./ I shall be the ornament of your entire life,/ and on your death I shall lead you to paradise."[66] Although the case of Shinran is "exemplary," the representation of Kannon as a woman ready to prostitute herself in order to save men was popular in Buddhist circles long before Shinran's dream.[67]

The soteriological value of dreams sometimes remains problematic, even in the eyes of those who champion it.[68] Insofar as their uncertain origins make them fundamentally ambivalent, dreams may always constitute an obstacle on the path to awakening. They are thus truly the "guardians of sleep" Freud speaks of. They are also two-edged swords for the community since they can just as well provide arguments both for or against change and either increase communal control over the individual or undermine it. On the whole, reliance on dreams seems to have developed in medieval Chan/Zen, and especially in the Sōtō tradition, in the context of a "return of the sacred," of a resurgence of local cults. This resurgence of dreams and the sacred went along with the geographical expansion of Zen during the fourteenth to sixteenth centuries.[69]

One of the essential functions of the dreams in the Record of Tōkoku is to legitimize Keizan and his teachings. If dreams are "guardians of sleep," they are also, according to Freud, "the realization of a desire." Thus, Myōe, when he ascends in a dream to Tuṣita Heaven, feels as if he is walking on the roads of India, realizing a deep desire that had been denied by the deity of Kasuga.[70] This wish-fullfilling aspect is also clear

[66] See Shinran yume no ki ["Record of Shinran's Dream"], in Shinran Shōnin zenshū kankōkai, ed., Teihon Shinran Shōnin zenshū (Kyoto: Hōzōkan 1969–70), vol. 3, 640. This revelation—also mentioned by Shinran's wife, Eshinni, in a letter to her daughter—has received many different interpretations, both within and outside Jōdo Shinshū. See for instance Nishiguchi 1993: 20–38.

[67] See R. Stein 1986. See also the story of the man who makes love to the goddess Kichijō, in Nihon ryōiki, trans. Nakamura 1973: 178.

[68] The female author of the Kagerō nikki, for instance, after dreaming that her hair had been cut like that of a nun, or, a few days later, that a snake was crawling among her entrails and gnawing at her liver, writes: "I do not know whether these dreams were good or bad, but I write them down so that those who hear of my fate will know what trust to put in dreams and signs from the Buddha." See Seidensticker 1964: 98.

[69] Saigō Nobutsuna thinks that the belief in dreams declined toward the end of the Heian period, and he sees the above comment of the author of the Kagerō nikki as an indication of this. However, this might have been a temporary eclipse, and as he himself makes the point that dreams were intimately connected with the native gods, the "return of the gods" described earlier would manifest itself as a "return of the dreams."

[70] See Meikanden, in DNBZ 74: 109.

from the dream, already quoted, in which Keizan receives the approval of Gien, the former superior of Eiheiji, whom he had left in order to follow Gikai at the time of the controversy between the two factions represented by these two masters.[71]

Keizan may be a dreamer, but he is a realistic dreamer whose dreams (at least those that he writes down in the *Record of Tōkoku*) usually have useful outcomes. We have noted that the foundation of Yōkōji, and later that of Sōjiji, had been encouraged by various deities of Buddhist and non-Buddhist origins. A dream also influenced Keizan to undertake new constructions like that of the Gorōhō memorial or the Dharma hall of Yōkōji. After the closing of Gorōhō, Keizan notes, among other auspicious signs, the dream of one of his disciples: "The same night the supervisory officer [*kansu*] Keidō dreamed that he was putting a silver sword into a water-colored raw silk bag and putting it upright on the west bank. Alongside there was a box fastened crosswise. In addition, crystals as white as rice were placed into a provisions chest standing there" (*JDZ* 409–10]. Unfortunately he does not attempt to elucidate the dream.

The construction of the Dharma hall was undertaken less than four months after Keizan had the following dream:

> In the third Genkō year [1323], on the twenty-fourth of the tenth month, at night, at the hour of the tiger, I dreamed that at the very spot where I was right then a new Dharma hall was being inaugurated. In front of the Dharma seat there were three steps. I went up to the seat and preached the Law. Unthinkingly I descended from the highest step and stood on the ground. Then Mugai [Chikō] of Jōjū[ji], the *shuso* Meihō [Sotetsu], and others came to bow before me. I clasped my hands and preached as follows: "The eye of the True Dharma is open and bright, the Dharma hall is wide open. For whoever can understand, [this means] that men should not be arranged in hierarchies." (*JDZ* 420)

Keizan was not the only person at Yōkōji to benefit from oneiric oracles and other auspicious signs, and he attached almost as much importance to his disciples' dreams as to his own—at least insofar as they agree. Thus he reports the dream in which the god Inari appeared to his disciples Shikan and Genka as the ancient protector of the mountain, or that in which the dragon-king Shōhō Shichirō told another disciple named Kōei, "I have received from your superior the order to reward or punish the monks and to keep the gates of this monastery." As Keizan notes, "The protection of the Dharma was therefore received in a dream." In the same way, when Keizan fell heir to the temple that would become Sōjiji, it was under the dream auspices of Kannon. At the begin-

---

[71] See *JDZ* 401, quoted above, Chapter 2.

ning of 1321, this Bodhisattva appeared in a dream to the Vinaya master Jōken and told him: "Now, a great good friend in the fifty-fourth generation of transmission from Śākyamuni has appeared in this province, at Mount Tōkoku in Sakai, and he has set in motion the wheel of the Dharma . . . He has received [the Law] transmitted at the Vulture Peak. You should immediately give your temple to this holy man so that he may turn it into a 'place of awakening' [*bodhimaṇḍa*] where the Law of the Buddha may prosper through eternity."

If we are to believe him, Keizan had also received a similar dream. He was not surprised, therefore, when Jōken asked him to succeed him as the abbot, or more precisely as guardian (*ushiromi*), of Morookadera.[72] Various indications may lead us to believe that things may actually have happened rather differently in reality, and we are justified in wondering to what extent Keizan was sincere, and to what extent he was manipulating his dreams—if he really had them.[73]

Keizan also used his dreams to legitimize his predecessors. In the *Denkōroku*, he reports a dream of the Chan master Shitou Xiqian (700–790), who we shall see shortly, along with the sixth patriarch Huineng, immersed in the eternal dream of mummies. After having read a treatise on the identity of the self and the other, Shitou fell asleep. He dreamed that he was riding on the back of a tortoise along with Huineng, in the middle of a deep lake. On waking up, he understood the meaning of the dream: the miraculous tortoise symbolized knowledge, and the lake was the ocean of essence. Later, Keizan tells us, Shitou put together a "Treatise on the Fusion of Difference and Identity," which was very highly regarded. This dream indicated that his spiritual knowledge was already the equal of that of the sixth patriarch and was identical to that of his master Qingyuan [Xingsi].[74]

It would be oversimplifying things to make Keizan out to be a cynic who took advantage of his followers by having recourse to the unanswerable argument of dreams. There certainly are cases in which Keizan settled matters by referring to dreams. But the imagination does not submit servilely to sectarian or material interests. Rather than an "easy way out," dreams for Keizan provided a touchstone to the real. From all the evidence, Keizan attributed to these various "provinces of meaning" provided by dreams a quality of reality beside which the reality of the waking state seems secondary, impoverished. In addition, it may be rather

---

[72] On this question, see Bodiford 1993: 97–98.

[73] Keizan reports other dreams that he had regarding Sōjiji: in one of them, for instance, he has a vision of two magnificent geese, symbol of fire (i.e., of the south, and therefore of the monastery gate).

[74] See *Denkōroku*; T. 82, 2585: 385b. We have seen above that one of Keizan's dream put him on a par with Shitou and Bodhidharma.

that meditation, or more exactly *samādhi*, the place of visions, should be termed "reality," since our ordinary waking state is, according to Buddhist doctrine, no more than a state of torpor. Finally, dreams and reality for Keizan are not mutually exclusive. They form a kind of braid that is difficult for us to imagine, let alone describe, given that the dichotomy between dream and reality, and the downplaying of the former, are the very foundations of our whole culture. It is not easy to do justice to dreams in a work like this one since, as Georges Bataille has said, "Analysis introduces an unusual work into a framework that makes it null and void, and substitutes for awakening a sleepy heaviness."[75] It is this dull-wittedness that runs the risk of seeing ideological contradictions in what was initially perhaps a form of original fusion between the *imaginaire* and the real. Conversely, the preference for dreams can never be entirely free of ideology. Oneiric imagination is doubtless destined to remain an arena where conflicting interpretations constantly arise. Between dreams and the writing down of dreams, there is a "spacing," a "travail de l'écriture" that modifies radically for us—condemned as we are to written "traces"—its content and meaning. It is in the last analysis as impossible to retrieve the original experience that left this trace, or even to affirm the existence of such experience, as to deny it.

It is true that the use of dreams, as we have seen it in Myōe and Keizan, seems a little backward in relation to Mahāyāna doctrine. If there is an oneiric tradition, it is not the same as that of Tibetan Buddhism, which is judged to be more orthodox.[76] It is one that has to do with the practice of incubation, which, according to Saigō Nobutsuna, can be traced back to pre-Buddhist Japan. However, it can also be found in Chinese Buddhism—whether or not it represents in that case a shamanistic influence. At any rate, whereas Tibetan Buddhists try to concretely realize the emptiness of dreams, the oneiric realm remains for Myōe and Keizan more an "enchanted garden," to which one must remain in submission. Despite the startling realism of some of their dreams or visions, there does not seem to have been any kind of awareness of working toward a practice of "lucid dreaming," as is preached by Tibetan Buddhism in particular. In Tibetan Buddhism the dream becomes obscured or at any

[75] Georges Bataille, *La Littérature et le mal* (Paris: Gallimard, 1957), 102.

[76] For instance the Tibetan practice called *rMilam*, (litt. "dream"), a kind of "dream yoga" aimed at modifying consciously the oneirical content. It is one of the "six teachings" that Naropa inherited from Tilopa: 1. Production of "inner heat" (*gTum-mo*); 2. Experiencing that "the body is an illusion" (*sGyu lus*); 3. The state of "dream" proper (*rMilam*); 4. The perception of the "clear light" (*'Od-gsel*); 5. Theory of the intermediate state (*Bardo*); 6. Practice of thought transmission (*'Pho-ba*, litt. "change of place"). See Anne Chayet, *La Femme au temps des Dalaï-lamas* (Stock-Laurence Pernoud, 1993).

rate loses its symbolic importance to the act of dreaming, a dreaming in which what matters is the state of consciousness, lucid or not, of the dreamer. While they insist on the ultimate emptiness of the world of the imagination, Myōe and Keizan both chose to follow quite passively the thread of their dreams rather than seek to control and eventually dissolve them. In this sense they are not so different from lay believers like the authors of the *Kagerō nikki* and the *Sarashina nikki*, who traveled to Kannon temples in search of dreams. Unlike the idealist thinkers among whom they are counted in theory, thinkers for whom the dreamer, isolated in himself, does nothing more than take his desires for realities, dreams for Myōe and Keizan are an "arena of awakening" in which a truly real presence manifests itself. The dream opens onto the divine Other or Others. It belongs to the realm of the "other power" (*tariki*), not to that of "self-power" (*jiriki*).[77]

[77] Buddhists were divided on the question whether dreams are produced by the gods or by the dreamer. In Chinese esoteric conceptions, for instance, the spirits that appear in oracular dreams are manifestations of the seven *po* souls. The two approaches need not be entirely at odds: as Saigō Nobutsuna points out, the soul is itself a kind of "other" that appears as deity. However, in the case of dreams induced by gods like Hachiman, we are dealing with an entirely Other (*totaliter aliter*).

Chapter Six

IMAGES OF DEATH

KEIZAN DIED on the fifteenth of the eighth month of the year 1325, two weeks after recording in the *Record of Tōkoku* his Dharma transmission to Kohō Kakumyō, who was later to make his career in the Rinzai school. A passage inserted in the *Record of Tōkoku* reports Keizan's death as follows:

> On the fifteenth of the eighth month of the second year of Shōchū, at midnight, he gathered his disciples and told them: "The arising of thought is a sickness; not to pursue it is the remedy. Avoid thinking of anything good or evil. As soon as one has done with thinking, white clouds extend over ten thousand *li*." He then composed the following verse: "This peaceful rice-field that one has cultivated by oneself, however often one has gone to sell or buy [rice], is as a virgin land. Young sprouts and spiritual seeds, infinitely, ripen and shed [their leaves]. Ascending the Dharma Hall, I see men holding a hoe in their hands." Then, throwing away his brush, he passed away. After the cremation, *śarīra* were collected, and a stūpa was built in the northwest corner of the monastery. The site of this stūpa was named Dentōin. [Our master] had inspected the world during fifty-eight years, and had been through forty-six summer retreats. He received the posthumous title of Butsuji Zenji ["Dhyāna Master Compassion of the Buddha"]. (*JDZ*, 435)

Keizan's death is in many respects typical of the "good death" according to Chan/Zen: his awakening allowed a Zen master to foretell the moment of his death, and he would leave one last poem encapsulating his thinking or experience. His body, when cremated, yielded numerous relics (Skt. *śarīra*, J. *shari*) that were deposited in a reliquary stūpa.[1] To fathom the exemplary nature of Keizan's death, we need to step back and examine the attitudes adopted by Chinese and Japanese throughout the centuries toward death. Followers of Chan subscribed in theory to the nonexistence of death as a subjective experience, since in good Buddhist orthodoxy the self does not exist. But in actuality Chan practitioners were embedded in the ancestor cult and by the fourteenth century came to specialize in funerary rites—all of which reintroduced the related beliefs about death into the heart of ritual practice.[2]

---

[1] See *Nichiiki Tōjō shosoden*, in *DNBZ* 110: 12a.
[2] On that question, see Tamamuro 1963.

THE OTHER WORLD

Imaginings about hells and heavens seem to have had much less importance in Zen than in other Japanese Buddhist schools. However, we can detect a strong influence from the cult of ancestors and the ideology of presence that underlies it. Zen had little interest in the other world, already a preoccupation of other Buddhist schools like that of the Pure Land, or of popular Buddhism. The Zen school took as its bailiwick the world around us but did insist that they ruled it as its sole masters, denying or eliminating all enclaves or intrusions of the invisible world (that of ghosts, local spirits, etc.). The Zen monks are for instance rarely described as traveling into the subterranean world of demon spirits, and tales about "descents into hell" developed outside Zen.[3] The only wanderings they seem to indulge in are celestial, visionary, or oneiric wanderings to the paradise of those who meditate, the Tuṣita Heaven of Maitreya, leaving the Pure Land of Amida to other, well-(re)born souls.[4] A rare exception is found in a work attributed to Dainichi Nōnin, the founder of the Darumashū. Nōnin actually cites a Chinese text about the descent into hell of a certain Wang. When he was on the point of coming face-to-face with the infernal judge, King Yama (J. Enma), Wang met the Bodhisattva Dizang (J. Jizō), who taught him a poem implying that all hells are only the product of the mind. Ironically it was not by understanding the truth of this poem that Wang obtained deliverance, but by citing it before Yama as his only meritorious act. Another story of descent into hell that was known in Chinese Chan circles reports how the minister Pei Xiu, having gone into a kind of coma, succeeded in returning to life, thanks to the intercession of an old monk.[5] In Japanese Buddhism the paradigmatic story is that of Nichizō Shōnin (d. 985), who, while practicing incubation, fell into a cataleptic state while his spirit visited the other world. The description he gave of his encounter with the vengeful

---

[3] Despite this theoretical rejection, the importance of hell in Chan/Zen monasteries is well documented. An examination of Chan popular predications during the Song shows that stories related to karmic retribution were more popular than discourses on the essential teaching of Chan. One may note in particular the importance of the *shuilu* ("Water and Land") Assemblies, ritual offerings to *preta* (hungry ghosts) that combined the theory of karma and the notion of filial piety. See Nagai 1985: 292.

[4] As noted earlier, these two types of shamanistic experience have structural similarities. However, they define different otherworldly spaces. On the "spatialization" of the other world, see Grapard 1991.

[5] See Demiéville 1976.

spirit of Sugawara no Michizane in hell contributed significantly to the spread of the belief in malevolent ghosts (goryō).[6]

In several Sōtō kirigami we see an esoteric interpretation of the "Thirteen Buddhas" in the form of kōan.[7] The cult of these thirteen Buddhas and Bodhisattvas (Fudō, Shaka, Monju, Fugen, Jizō, Miroku, Yakushi, Kannon, Seishi, Amida, Ashuku, Dainichi, Kokūzō), along with that of the Ten Kings of Hell, developed in Zen along with the belief in hells and funerary rites centered on the intermediary period of death.[8] But the Zen attitude remains ambiguous. While some of these documents constitute contributions to the cult of the Thirteen Buddhas, others deny the reality of hells and punishment and call for the deliverance of the dead at the moment of the funeral by preaching to them the emptiness of all things. We should thus linger over the Chan/Zen funerary ritual since it reveals the ideology and *imaginaire* underlying other forms of ritual.

RITUALIZED DEATH

When Dōgen died in Kyoto in 1253, his coffin was placed in Kenninji before transfer to the cremation site. The funeral ritual seems to have been quite simple, perhaps because of the special circumstances surrounding his death, which happened far from Eiheiji. At the time of his cremation, Dōgen's successor, Ejō, recited a short text about relics (*Shari raimon*). Gikai's funeral in 1309, one of the first to be well documented, was much more elaborate and the ceremonies lasted seven days, requiring the use of a great deal of ritual material (banners, lanterns, censers, paper money, flower vases, etc.). The opening ceremony was led by one of Keizan's disciples, Meihō Sotetsu, and the later ones by the main dignitaries of Daijōji. Keizan himself had the honor of lighting the funeral pyre of his master and confirmed by this act his status as legitimate successor, following the model set by Kāśyapa at the Buddha's funeral.[9] The complexity and lavishness of the ritual are revealed by the need to auction off

---

[6] Here is for instance the *Shasekishū*'s account:

After the Emperor Daigo (885–930) died, Nichizō Shōnin (d. 985) went into seclusion at Shō no Iwaya in Shōhei 14 (944). At noon on the first day of the eighth month he suddenly dropped dead, but later revived to tell of his experiences in the land of darkness. He said that he saw Daigo living in a thatched hut surrounded by four iron mountains, each fifty to sixty feet high. The Emperor told Nichizō that during his lifetime he had commited the Five Serious Offences, and now he was suffering retribution—especially for having unjustly exiled Sugawara Michizane.

See Morrell 1985: 229.

[7] See *Bukke ichi daiji yawa*, in Ishikawa 1983–94 (2): 152–55.

[8] See Ishikawa 1983–94 (7): 263.

[9] See *Gikai sōki*, in SZ 2, *Shingi*: 1–7; quoted in Bodiford 1993: 192.

Gikai's possessions in order to cover the expenses occasioned by these elaborate ceremonies, which would become the norm in Zen.

Already in China the tendency to glorify the dead and to wander from Indian Buddhist traditions had become more marked from the Tang onward, as Zanning points out in his commentary, in the *Song gaoseng zhuan*, on the sumptuary funerals of the Indian translator Bodhiruci: "Are not the funerary ceremonies of the Western regions too simple? Even in the case of a ruler or a great headman, the most emotional and solemn [officiants] never do more than carry the body to the cremation ground. To carry a monk in a funerary chariot and to escort him according to imperial ceremonial, as is done in China, is something unheard in these regions."[10] In Japan, however, funerary rituals become more specifically Buddhist. We cannot understand the significance of these rituals if we do not grasp their complex symbolism.

Important in this regard is Keizan's reply to one of the ten written questions that were allegedly sent to him by Emperor Go-Daigo. The emperor, arguing from the fact that offerings to the dead are not consumed, questioned the existence of an intermediary state after death. Keizan replied thus: "These things work in much the same way as for bees gathering nectar from flowers and taking only the taste away with them. The flowers do not lose their color or their perfume, so how can we know that feeding has gone on? It is said . . . in the *Abhidharmakośa-śāstra*, "Intermediary beings feed on odors; this is why they are called *gandharva*. Those who have only a few merits consume only bad odors; those who have many delight in subtle aromas."[11]

The documents give the impression of a kind of ritualization and, we may even say, a growing collectivization of death in Zen. As a form of mediation, funeral rites at the same time hide death and reveal it. The ritual marks the apotheosis of death, but simultaneously it deadens death's impact by transforming the corpse or its substitutes into pure signifiers. These signifiers reflect a form of ancestral, collective transcendence rather than the individual, experiential transcendence so often considered the trademark of Chan. Thus Dongshan Liangjie, after his mother's death, took the rice that she had with her and mixed it into the gruel eaten in the monastic community, so marking, as in the Indian funeral ritual in which the deceased is symbolized by balls of rice, her reintegration into the community.[12] Just like the ancestors in Chinese cults, Chan patriarchs survive only in their line of descent. If they concern themselves about the worship to be offered to them by their successors,

---

[10] *Song gaoseng zhuan*, T. 50, 2061: 720c.

[11] SZ, *Shūgen* 2: 496a.

[12] See *Denkōroku*, T. 82, 2585: 388a–b; and Jonathan Parry, "Sacrificial Death and the Necrophagous Ascetic," in Bloch and Parry 1982: 74–110.

the reason is that they know, as Marc Augé has said of an African context, "that there is only one alternative: to live in the plural or die alone."[13]

In the case of Chan masters, ritualization affects all the stages of the tripartite process described by Arnold van Gennep in his classic study, *The Rites of Passage*. At the preliminary stage, ritual is marked by three significant events: prediction of the time of death, the last words, and the "entry into *samādhi*." The death of a Chan/Zen master was dramatized as a ritual "representation" of the Buddha's *parinirvāṇa*. The first duty of a master, and the proof that he had truly reached awakening, was to predict the day of his own death. These predictions were very popular: among the twenty marvels of Song China, the Japanese pilgrim Yōsai listed the fact that "many monks know the moment they will die."[14]

The death of a master—the very act of dying—constitutes an apotheosis of his deeds and gestures, a ritualized and collective event, determined in its slightest details by the *imaginaire* of the community. It is not simply, as it has often been presented, a final act of defiance on the part of a preeminently individualist thinker. The deceased was apparently considered to be a collective property, a fact evidenced by the auctioning of the dead man's possessions to cover the growing costs of funerals.

The critical phase in the funeral ritual is the liminal period of forty-nine days during which the deceased is considered to be transiting the Buddhist limbo before being reborn into the world or achieving the final Nirvāṇa. This ritual is one of an ideal sequence of rites carried out during the funeral of an abbot: the placing of the body in the coffin, the transfer of the coffin to the cell of the abbot in the Dharma hall, the closing of the coffin, the setting up of a portrait of the abbot over the altar, the wake in the form of a consultation between master and disciple, the transfer of the coffin to the crematorium, the offering of libations of tea and hot water, the lighting of the funeral pyre.[15]

In Japan the ritual came to be played out mostly within a symbolic structure built on the site of the cremation. This temporary structure was divided into two spaces: the coffin room (*gandō*) and the cremation ground proper (*hiya*), connected by a passageway bordered with hedges. This Zen symbolism was adopted, with some minor changes, by other Japanese Buddhist schools.

An important rite was that of hanging the portrait of the late master (*shin*) near the coffin. According to the *Pure Rule of Chan Monasteries*

[13] Augé 1988: 145.

[14] See Ichikawa et al. 1972: 88. See also Mujū, "Felicitous Final Moments Among Followers of the Kenninji," in Morrell, 1985: 262–65.

[15] The *Keizan shingi* (*Tōkoku shingi*, T. 82, 430c) describes a sequence of sixteen rites, which were later reduced to nine. See Matsuura 1985: 156–66.

(*Chanyuan qinggui*), a disciplinary code dated 1103, three days after the death of an abbot his body is to be put into a coffin and placed to the west of the Dharma hall. To the east various contact relics (robe etc.) are laid out; in the center of the hall, his funerary portrait is hung on a "Dharma seat," and the ceremony is carried out in front of this portrait.[16] The portrait is later carried to the cremation site where, set up on an altar, it is still the center of the ceremony. On the return to the monastery, it is hung in the Dharma hall for other rituals, and then in the cell of the abbot, where offerings of food are made to it twice a day. After the installation of the new abbot, the portrait is moved to the temple's memorial hall. During its stay in the Dharma hall, it holds the spirit of the deceased and the monks come to consult it ritually, as they used to consult their master when he was alive. There is therefore a functional equivalence between the portrait and the funerary tablet. As Mujaku Dōchū points out, "According to the ancient worthies, if the portrait has an inscription in which appears the name [of the deceased], then there is no need for a funerary tablet."[17] The portrait of the deceased thus constitutes in a way his "body of glory." It denies death in two ways: ritually, by becoming a substitute body, and psychologically, by representing the deceased as he was when he was alive. A mummy, on the other hand, reveals death, or rather life under the paradoxical traits of death, making up a funerary oxymoron, the living dead.

CREMATION SYMBOLISM

The cremation hall (*hiya*) is usually a building with four gates symbolizing the four stages of Buddhist practice: 1) production of the initial thought of awakening (*hosshinmon*), to the east; 2) cultivation (*shūgyōmon*), to the south; 3) awakening (*bodaimon*), to the west; and 4) Nirvāṇa (*nehanmon*), to the north. The coffin is carried three times in circle, in a clockwise direction, around the hall, passing through all the doors, thus symbolically taking shortcuts from the world of illusion to the final Nirvāṇa. These circumambulations correspond to the three (or seven) circumambulations that the faithful make around the stūpa of the Buddha. Traditionally, as Paul Mus has shown, circumambulation of the four cardinal points signifies also mastery of the fifth, the center (or the zenith). It implies (and at the same time produces) the presence of a Buddha (in the form of the deceased) at the center of the cremation site.[18]

According to the *Kirigami of the Four Gates*, "By opening the four doors, one transcends the three times [past, present, and future]. All the

[16] See Kagamishima 1972: 259.

[17] See Yanagida 1979: 484.

[18] For a more detailed account, see Faure 1991: 191–203.

receptacle worlds [hells etc.] have the same circular form. This is what one calls leaving a circle to enter a circle." The three circumambulations represent the "three points"—otherwise termed the three aspects—of the mind: dharma body, wisdom body, and deliverance body. These three points, which are found also in the ceremony of eye-opening for an icon, a tomb, or a funerary tablet when the priest visualizes three times the character "mind/heart" (shin), correspond to the ritual creation of a Buddha, an immortal double of oneself or of the deceased.[19] After completing the three turns to the right, one sometimes makes three further turns to the left, to signify the unity of life and death, and the freedom the deceased now has, as a new Buddha, to leave the world or return to it as he wishes. The turns to the right ("with the flow," jun) symbolize an upward movement, from saṃsāra to Nirvāṇa; those to the left ("against the flow," gyaku) a downward movement, from Nirvāṇa to saṃsāra. The to and fro thus signal the identity of saṃsāra and Nirvāṇa.[20] Another kirigami, supposedly transmitted by Keizan's disciple Meihō Sotetsu (1277–1350), describes the procession from the coffin room to the cremation site:

> One must circle the room to the left. . . . This means that one goes against the flow, towards death. The left-turning swastika symbolizes the four stages: birth, old age, sickness, and death. Those who transcend all the stages are called Buddha. The subtle mark is perfect and clear; it transcends all names and marks. Having circled the hall, one goes directly to the cremation site to circle it three or seven times. In Buddhism, to go with the flow (jun) means to go from the first to the tenth stage [of the career of the Bodhisattva], to obtain all the fruits of deep awakening, and to reach Nirvāṇa without remainder. Such is the meaning of the cremation of saints. Buddhism holds that dying is going with the flow while Confucianism considers it to be going against the flow (gyaku).[21]

The same document indicates that the procedure for circling the cremation site is different for saints and ordinary people. Saints go round three or seven times to the right, because they consider that to die is in the order of things and that to live is to go against that order. Ordinary

[19] A Sōtō kirigami describes as follows the "pointing" of the funerary tablet (sotoba). After having written on it the name of the deceased, one draws a circle while holding it in one's hand—a circle that symbolizes that the three bodies of the Buddha (body of Law, of retribution, and of metamorphosis) form only one mind. One then recites the name of the deceased, burns incense, and recites three times the word shin (mind). Hands joined, one utters three times an incantation (dhāraṇī). Eyes closed, one contemplates emptiness. Finally, one shakes one's sleeves to mark the end of the ritual. See Bukke ichi daiji yawa 49, in Ishikawa 1983–94 (2): 149.

[20] See Sugimoto 1982: 132.

[21] See Ishikawa 1983–94 (8): 205.

people go around to the left, because life is for them natural and death goes against nature.

This exegetical overkill should not lead us to lose sight of the fact that in other funerary contexts the circumambulation of the coffin is intended to prevent the deceased from finding his/her way back to the living. Even though the ambivalence that characterizes funerary rituals of the liminal stage does not characterize Chan/Zen funerals, we should not conclude that it is totally absent. The redundancy of positive symbolism itself should alert us to the contrary.

The ritual of the "lowering of the torch" (ako), carried out, like all the rites marking the end of the liminal stage, at the "Nirvāṇa gate," is based on the legend of the Buddha's funeral. According to tradition, the Buddha's disciples tried in vain, for a whole week, to light his funeral pyre. However, when Kāśyapa—who was absent when the Buddha died—returned and could lead the ceremony, he was greeted by auspicious signs (like that of the feet of the Buddha emerging from their shroud) and the pyre caught fire by itself.[22] Here the important thing is that the cremation rite (that it to say, the reincorporation of the deceased) had to be carried out by the successor, or rather that the rite itself established or confirmed the successor.

It is highly suggestive that the detailed descriptions of the ritual of lighting the pyre—just like many funeral sermons for Chan/Zen masters—hardly mention the actual cremation process. The fiery metamorphosis of the Buddhist body—unlike that of ordinary corpses in Indian Buddhism—seems to be a taboo subject for Zen discourse and meditation. The negative symbolism of the cremation process (as a dissolution) has been replaced by a lenitive ideology of reincorporation, through the stress placed on the transformation into a Buddha. This idea is well expressed in a Chinese literary text strongly inspired from Chan, the fictitious "Recorded Sayings" of the "mad monk" Daoji, alias Jigong (d. 1209). When Jigong lights up the funerary pyre of his master, Xia Tang, he concludes his funerary eulogy with these verses:

The torch in the hand, [manifesting] the kingly law without attachment,
What is, you will ask, the kingly law without attachment?
Yi! To shed through fire your stinking skin bag to exchange it against the indestructible Diamond Body.

Jigong lifted his torch and lighted the fire: the venerable's ashes fell like rain, and suddenly the Elder Xia Tang appeared in their midst and said: "Take good care of yourselves!" Then he changed into a pure wind and disappeared.[23]

[22] See Fujii 1977: 3.
[23] See *Jidian yulu*, ed. Lu Gong, *Guben pinghua xiaoshuo ji*, vol. 1 (Beijing: Renmin wenxue, 1984).

We find this torch symbolism over and over again in the *kirigami*. Several of these documents stress the connection between the cremation rite and the rite of transmission of the Dharma between Śākyamuni and Mahākāśyapa. The story of this transmission is well known. The Buddha showed a flower to the assembly of his disciples. All were puzzled, with the exception of Mahākāśyapa, whose face lit up with a wide smile. The Buddha then said that he possessed the Treasure of the Eye of the True Law (*shōbōgenzō*), the profound mind of Nirvāṇa (*nehan myōshin*), and that he was transmitting it to Mahākāśyapa. In a document titled *Kirigami of the Torch*, we find the following interpretation: the Buddha corresponds to the officiating priest, while his smiling disciple corresponds to the deceased. The flower, symbol of the spirit, is represented by the circle drawn in the air. The presentation of the flower, thus of the mind—fiery in nature—to the assembly stands for the lighting of the pyre and thus the integration of the deceased into the Dharma lineage, the equivalent of a posthumous ordination, which in some *kirigami* is interpreted as an emergence from the circle of beings and an entry into that of the disciples of the Buddha. The officiating priest, being delivered from illusion, is like the living fire of the sun, the devouring fire of the mind; the deceased, who has not yet achieved awakening, is like a dead moon, like a smoldering fire. The lighting of the pyre is the union of these two fires—symbolized by red and black tipped sticks—the transmission of the flame between master and disciples, the fusion of the absolute and the relative.[24]

Around Keizan's time, and largely at his instigation, the ritual sequence described above, originally reserved for monks and nuns, was gradually extended to laymen and laywomen—not without resistance, it seems: Dōgen was still of the opinion that lay funerals were a matter for laypeople to take care of, and that the best way a monk could show his filial piety toward his dead parents was to concentrate on his practice of the Buddhist Way, not to celebrate funeral services for them. In the same way, in the Pure Land school, Shinran (1173–1262) insisted on the uselessness of funerary rituals. This position would recur, even more strictly, with his disciple Kakunyo (1270–1351), who even fought with his son over this point and disinherited him. We have here the tragic paradox of a son, Zonkaku (1290–1373), who quarreled with his father to defend the principle of filial piety.[25]

Unlike Zen masters who had in theory reached awakening while alive, the ordinary dead—whether monks, nuns, or laypeople—were the object of specific rites aimed at ensuring their deliverance in and beyond

---

[24] See Ishikawa 1983–94 (10): 172; and Nara 1990: 108–9.
[25] See Nara 1990: 80.

death.[26] In the case of laypeople, a post mortem ordination took place, which gave them the benefits of a ritual initially reserved for monks. After proclaiming, as is proper, the inexistence of the self, the officiating priest, for each precept administered, asks the deceased three times if he intends to observe this precept. The silence of the deceased is interpreted as a positive answer, or as a manifestation of his "silent" understanding of the ineffable truth—after the model of the mythic layman Vimalakīrti, because, as a *kirigami* puts it, it is precisely by saying "neither yes nor no" that one can become a monk.[27] At the end of the ceremony, the deceased receives an alm bowl, a robe, and a lineage that are proof, beyond the grave, of his kinship (quasi-physical, and not purely spiritual) with the Buddha. He or she is henceforward treated as a full-fledged monk or nun, a son or daughter of the Buddha.[28] As noted earlier in reference to succession documents, the lineage of transmission of the Bodhisattva precepts—whether we are dealing with a normal or a post-mortem ordination—was considered a talisman whose efficacy owed nothing to the spiritual achievement of the postulant. In other words, it mattered little whether the latter was alive or dead.

Thus, before benefiting from the power of the Zen ritual, lay followers still had to go through a preliminary postmortem tonsuring and ordination. When it was possible, ordination took place just before death, functioning thus as a kind of extreme unction. Thus the regent Hōjō Tokimune (1251–1284) was tonsured on his deathbed by the Chinese master Mugaku Sogen (Ch. Wuxue Zuyuan, 1226–1286).[29] Post-humous ordinations became the occasion for collective sermons, which ended up by constituting a large part of the Chan/Zen literature of "Recorded Sayings" from the thirteenth century on. Funerals for laypeople were accompanied by a sermon to fit the occasion. Toward the fourteenth century, this sermon more and more took the dialogue form of the *mondō*. It usually contains four parts: a setting of the scene, an initial question, a pause—often indicated in gesture by the torch being waved

---

[26] According to the *Keizan shingi*, on the eve of the funeral, the priest explains to the deceased monk the meaning of impermanence. Then he asks the monastic community to recite the sūtras for the Buddhas of the Three Bodies [*dharma-*, *saṃbhoga-*, and *nirmāṇa-kāya*, i.e., Vairocana, Rushana, and Śākyamuni), for all the Buddhas in the ten directions and the three periods, the *Lotus Sūtra*, the Bodhisattvas Monju [Mañjuśrī], Fugen [Samantabhadra], Kannon, all the other Bodhisattvas and Mahāsattvas, and the *Prajñāpāramitā*. The merits thus obtained are dedicated to the "awakened spirit" [*kakurei*] of the deceased, to ornament the Retribution Land where he will be reborn and to lead him to the final awakening. See *SZ* 2: 449.

[27] See *Bukke ichi daiji yawa*, in Ishikawa 1983–94 (2):148.

[28] See Bodiford 1993: 194–96.

[29] See Collcutt 1981: 70–73.

around in the air before being thrown onto the pyre—and a final remark by the master.[30]

Yōkōji was first and foremost a *bodaiji*, a temple that specialized in ceremonies for the salvation ("awakening," *bodai*) of the souls of lay donors. The *Record of Tōkoku* mentions the ceremonies that marked the thirteenth anniversary of the death of a donor. These rituals were obviously important in the monastic routine, and in the material support of the monastery. Later, this status was emphasized by the erection of a stūpa "for the benefit of all beings (*rishōtō*)." The *Record of Tōkoku* clearly shows the importance of lay funerals in the life of the monastery. The main consecrations of Buddhist statues or buildings took place on the anniversary of the death of the parents of the lay patrons who paid for them. Thus the monastic liturgy supported the collective life, according to a rhythm marked by funerary anniversaries (one, three, ten, thirteen years). The consolidation of the lineage matches the important occasions in this funerary liturgy, the time of the dead thus structuring the time of the living.

The center of gravity of Zen monasteries consists not so much of the meditation hall as of tombs and stūpas. A fusion of the two results when a monastery becomes a *bodaiji*, as happened not only with Yōkōji but also most Zen monasteries. Tenryūji, for example, one of the main Rinzai monasteries in Kyoto, was founded to pacify the tormented spirit of Emperor Go-Daigo (reigned 1319–1338), who had been dethroned by the shōgun Ashikaga Takauji (ruled 1305–1358). The selection of Yōkōji as the site for the erection of a "Stūpa for the benefit of all beings" also meant that it became a temple where prayers were to be offered for the spirits of warriors who had fallen in the war between the partisans of the Ashikaga shōgun and those of Go-Daigo.[31]

HAKUSAN FUNERARY CULT

Because of its social and territorial expansion throughout feudal Japan, Chan/Zen, originally a contemplative movement in theory opposed to the ritualism of official Buddhism, became one of the main forms of what has been called funerary Buddhism. One solution that the Zen monks tried, to resolve the problem of pollution from their contacts with death, was the development of the cult of the god of Hakusan in the Sōtō tradition.[32] The function of this cult in Sōtō Zen seems to be connected with the purification rituals for participants after a funeral. The *Kirigami of the Tutelary God (Chinju kirigami)*, a document that seems to have been

[30] See Bodiford 1993: 194–204.
[31] See Collcutt 1981: 106–9.
[32] See Ishikawa 1983–94 (6): 128.

widespread in the Sōtō sect around the fourteenth to sixteenth centuries, explains how one may be purified after a funeral service by reciting two poems while facing from a distance the sanctuary of the god.[33] There is also in Japanese folklore another Hakusan (Shirayama) that shows certain similarities to the deity of the *kirigami*. Japanese scholars, beginning with Yanagita Kunio, have pointed out that the term *Shira* ("white") in Shirayama ("White Mountain") did not merely refer to the fact that Hakusan is covered with snow a good part of the time. Drawing a connection with Oshirasama, an agricultural deity, Yanagita argued that Shirayama symbolized the "death" of the rice seed and its rebirth as rice plant, and consequently human birth in the "parturition hut." We noted earlier the relations of Hakusan with incubation (*komori*), childbirth, and rebirth.[34] The term *shirayama* also designated a bamboo building, covered with white fabric. According to Gorai Shigeru, this recalls not the parturition hut, but rather the edifice within which the body was placed during the *mogari* ritual that marked the liminal period after death in archaic Japan.[35] There is also a Shugendō rite, carried out at the Flower Festival (*Hanamatsuri*), during which young men and women are closed up in a square hut called Hakusan. To go into this Hakusan signifies death, and emerging from it equals a rebirth in the Pure Land.[36] The white light, symbol of enlightenment, presupposes the darkness of the liminal, incubatory stage. The semiotics of black and white is operative in a document entitled *Chōri yūrai no ki*, describing the origin of the *chōri*, a category of outcasts (*hinin*) in charge of funerals. Their name is analyzed as meaning "black" (*chō*) and "white" (*ri*), because these descendants of Hakusan Gongen, like Shirayama, had the power to unify the black and the white, death and life.[37] In the Hakusan of Shugendō as in the Shirayama of folklore, ritual achieves an inversion of signs that permits the transformation of death into life, pollution into purity.

This inversion and purification were also essential to the cult of Hakusan as it was practiced in the Sōtō school at the end of the Muromachi period. Later tradition would move on to a radical reinterpretation of this symbolism. In some late *kirigami* Hakusan is interpreted in terms of the specifically Sōtō dialectic of the "Five Ranks" (*wuwei*) of the absolute and the relative, and the purificative aspects of the ritual were passed over in silence.[38] Insofar as the Sōtō tradition became established in the provinces, the god of Hakusan came to be considered as a protector (one

[33] See Satō 1986–87; Ishikawa 1983–94 (6): 129–32.
[34] See for instance "Hakusan Myōri no zu," in Ishikawa 1983–94 (6): 133.
[35] See Miyata 1972: 126–34; 1994: 56–60.
[36] See Gorai 1983: 153–76.
[37] See Ōwa 1989: 117.
[38] See Ishikawa 1983–94 (6); Satō 1986–87; Hirose 1993: 613–16.

among many) of monastic communities. Once it became one of the pillars of the Tokugawa politico-religious system, the Sōtō school no longer had such great need of funeral income to survive. At the same stroke, connections between Hakusan and funerary rites were clouded over, and the very name of Hakusan, too closely tied to the Sōtō school, was cleansed of any impure associations. Once again it was time, as it is today, for the promotion of Dōgen's "pure Zen."

THE BUDDHIST CULT OF THE ANCESTORS

On an ideological level, funerary rites can be seen as an attempt to speed up the process of death. They incorporate the deceased into a cyclical process, skirting around the embarrassment of death by introducing it into a symbolic structure that seems to permit the perpetuation, on another level, of a certain individual quality. If, as Robert Hertz has noted, the fate of the cadaver seems to be an index to that of the soul, the speeding up of the process that ends in incorruptible ashes or relics (and sometimes a mummy) symbolizes and accompanies the reintegration of the spirit into the eternal world of truth.[39]

In contrast to the Indian ascetics who, already ritually dead to the world, have no need of funerals, Chan/Zen adepts were deeply involved in funerary ritual. Despite their awakening and the spiritual autonomy it bestows on them, the assumption of the Chan masters into the status of patriarchs makes them into citizens, or rather "hostages," of this world. For them and for their disciples, ancestral transcendence tends to supersede experiential transcendence. In theory, Buddhism recognizes only two levels: the absolute, characterized by the absence of individual nature, and the relative, the world of egocentric illusion. But an attachment to a lineage, as it is revealed in the theory of patriarchal transmission and in funerary ideology, constitutes an intermediate level, which transcends the individual and subordinates him to the collective cult of the ancestors. The patriarchal lineage is simply another kind of ancestral lineage, which depends on the cult of the ancestors carried on by their descendants. Mystically identified with the lineage, with the entire collective grouping of his predecessors and successors, or even with a double or an effigy transcending death, the Chan master tended to lose his individuality and could thus become a source of renewal for the group.[40] The fact, for example, that Huineng's mummy was carried through the countryside during times of drought confirms that it was associated with rain and fertility. This relationship between death and procreation, to which we shall return, was also described clearly in some of the *kirigami*.

[39] See Hertz 1960: 83.
[40] See Bloch and Parry 1982: 35.

Around the eighth century, death seems to have become for the Japanese a phenomenon whose impurity was no longer accepted as before.[41] This impurity was handled more and more by the Buddhists and by certain groups of outcasts. However, Zen can be seen as having contributed to a partial rehabilitation of death, by reversing its signs, interpreting it no longer as a purely negative event but as a unique occasion to obtain instant awakening. The power wielded by Zen priests over the popular imagination came from their assumed power over death. This ascendancy resulted from a cluster of factors: Chan practice, which constitutes a perpetual *memento mori*, a quasi-Stoic preparation for death; extension to the funeral ritual of the enigmatic, hieratic language of the *kōan*, which indicates transcendence over death; the theory of "fundamental awakening" (*hongaku*), which denies the ultimate reality of death. The Chan/Zen adept is a "being for death," but death cannot occur to him since it concerns only an illusory entity—the self—with which he refuses to identify himself. Ironically, this denial of and apparent mastery over death, source of the liturgical prestige that made Zen funerals so imposing in the eyes of laypeople, also fostered a fascination in Chan for signs of death (relics etc.). The emergence of a Chan/Zen discourse on death, while doubtless reflecting a strategic adaptation to the needs of the faithful, also reflects an inner Chan dynamic. During Keizan's time, the implicit agreement limiting the theoretical excesses of subitism, the twofold truth of practical logic, now had to be explained in "black and white," quintessentially funerary colors, a drastic change from the Chan of Tang times.

The rhetorical denial of death may be explained in part by the fear of death, omnipresent in a country ravaged by wars. This was the sepulchral, funerary, nocturnal side of Buddhism, which Zen monasteries would try in vain to reject, as did the Shintō sanctuaries, in their desire for purity. Death is at first glance absent from these stone and moss gardens, "dry landscapes," from which all change seems to be excluded (except the aestheticized and euphemized evanescence of plum and cherry blossoms). [42] Domesticated nature is essentially a "domesticated death." R. A. Stein has shown that miniature gardens functioned as a ritual artifact in the individual search for longevity.[43] We have here an apotropaic negation of death, recognized even as it is being denied, or to put it differently, misunderstood. But death is at the same time really present, even in

---

[41] Macé 1986.

[42] And yet, even the spirits of cherry-blossoms, symbols of a premature death, were believed to turn into *goryō* and were placated during the Chinkasai (Blossom-Appeasing Festival). The famous cherry-tree in the garden of Tenryūji, for instance, was a symbol of Yoshino and of Emperor Go-Daigo, the most powerful *goryō* of the fourteenth century. See Plutschow 1990: 214.

[43] See Stein 1990.

those places of out-of-time serenity, monasteries like Tenryūji or Myō-shinji, that remain *bodaiji,* "funerary temples."[44] It returns in the shape of the "uncanny." In one corner of the garden, inevitably, a mausoleum is hidden.[45] As we shall see soon, a great part of Zen ritual activity consists of practices intended to produce a double, to anticipate death, to prevent it, or rather to rehearse it, to give oneself to it in advance. And the first and foremost of these doubles are the relics.

THE CULT OF RELICS

Undoubtedly one of the high points in Keizan's career, a kind of echo of his awakening, was the moment when he deposited in the funerary mound that he had just erected on a hill behind Yōkōji the relics of the "Five Elders" (among whom, as we have seen, he counted himself, creating in this way "preposthumous" relics). The importance of this event emerges from various documents, especially one text entitled "*Okibumi* of Mount Tōkoku for Centuries to Come," in which Keizan says:

> This place is that of the stūpa where, in the future, my relics will be kept. This is why I have deposited my own documents of succession, those of my late master, the sūtra [copied by Ejō in his own blood], the sacred bones of Dōgen, and the *Recorded Sayings* of Rujing on this mountain, [in a place] that I have called the Peak of the Five Elders. Thus, the abbot of this monastery will be the guardian of the stūpa of the Five Elders. My disciples should observe the order of succession of the Dharma and revive the abbatial function. This is why the remains of this mountain monk [Keizan] will be venerated in all the monasteries. . . . Even if the transmission of the Dharma is interrupted, the disciples and secondary masters should reconcile their criticisms and decisions, and foster the abbatial function. For, whatever happens, the other sects must respect the Five Elders. This is why all those who have inherited from my Dharma, whether they be tonsured disciples, disciples who have come to study or who have received complete ordination, monks, or lay people, all must, united by a single spirit, revere none but the Peak of the Five Elders and promote the style of our school. Such is the wish I make for future generations. [*JDZ*, 487–88]

[44] It is perhaps no coincidence that both monasteries remained outside of the Gozan system, a system, established for political reasons, which kept Zen monasteries isolated from the people.

[45] A good example is that of Tōjiin, a monastery whose famous "heart-shaped" garden is attributed to the alleged founder of Zen gardens, Musō Soseki, and which contains the mausoleum of the Ashikaga family, with statues of all successive generations of Ashikaga shōguns.

Obviously, Keizan was trying to organize during his lifetime the cult of his own memory and to associate closely the fate of his relics with that of his school. We cannot but be struck by the importance attached to these relics, and by their composite nature: documents of succession, sūtras copied by hand (or even in blood, in the case of Ejō), *Recorded Sayings*, and finally relics proper, *śarīra*, or ashes and fragments of bone left by cremation (in the case of Dōgen (see figure 5)). Among these relics Keizan omits any mention of the *śarīra* grain he received from his master Gikai that had earlier been transmitted in the Darumashū. In the biography of Gikai that Keizan inserts in the *Record of Tōkoku*, he notes, "I now respectfully deposit on this mountain the documents of succession that he [Gikai] had kept during his life, as well as the relics of Samantabhadra preserved by the six patriarchs and transmitted in the school of Nanyue [Huairang], the frontal bone of my late master and the scriptures of the Five Mahāyāna sections copied in my own hand. Let these [relics] guard the gates of the monastery and sustain the Dharma lineage" [*JDZ*, 416].

Despite the differences between these two lists, we can form two clearly separate groups: relics in the broad sense or "contact relics," everything that has been touched by the deceased; and relics in the strict sense, or *śarīra*, produced by cremation (or, we shall see, by mummification) of the body. Among the regalia that patriarchs transmitted to one another, we have already mentioned the Dharma robe (*kāṣāya*) and the major role it played in Zen imagination since its—probably fictitious—transmission to the sixth patriarch Huineng. If that robe, or various other "contact relics," could legitimize the transmission ritual, the reason is that it constituted a substitute of the *śarīra*, a substitution body of the Buddha. Keizan tells us in his *Denkōroku* about the encounter of the patriarch Basiasita with an Indian king, who objects to him that since Siṃhabhikṣu, Basiasita's predecessor, had been executed, Basiasita could not have received his transmission. Basiasita replies that Siṃhabhikṣu had transmitted the robe and a poem to him before dying. When the king wants to test the robe by burning it, it suddenly emits—like a *śarīra*—a multicolored light and remains intact within the flames. Seeing this, the king is finally converted to Buddhism.[46]

---

[46] See *Denkōroku*, T. 82, 2585: 374b. The episode is actually inserted in the notice on Puṇyamitra. Earlier Keizan said that this robe with golden sleeves [*sic*] is the same that was transmitted by the seven Buddhas who preceded Śākyamuni; then he gives three different accounts of its origins: according to the first, the Buddha wore this robe while he was still in the womb; according to the second, he received it from celestial beings; according to the third, the robe was given to him by a hunter. Keizan mentions various kinds of robes: the one transmitted from Bodhidharma to the six Chan patriarchs was made from a blue-black mousseline, to which a blue-green edge was added. Keizan continues his notice with a

Keizan's attitude toward relics was not new in Zen. In the first text that he drew up on his return from China, the *Record of the Transmission of Śarīra* (*Shari sōdenki*), an epitaph to his master and friend Myōzen (1184–1225) whose relics he had brought back, Dōgen tells how, when Myōzen was cremated, the flames became multicolored. Witnesses to this phenomenon saw in it a sign of the presence of relics. Sure enough, when the ashes were inspected, three white *śarīra* grains were discovered. Then, when the ashes were collected, more than three hundred sixty grains were found. The fame of Myōzen then spread among monks and laypeople, and a stele was raised to him in the monastery in memory of this event. Dōgen ends by saying that such a phenomenon had never been heard of in the six centuries since Buddhism had been introduced into Japan. This was a proof that the transmission from Yōsai to Myōzen was in the direct, authentic line from the Buddha.[47] We know that later, as his awareness of representing Sōtō tradition became stronger, he would change his opinion on this point. Thus it is not surprising that his opinions on the matter of relics should also change.[48]

The cult of relics is one of the basic components of Buddhism, in India as in the rest of Buddhist Asia. A priori, we should not expect to find it in as theoretically "iconoclastic" a school as Zen. But practice often tends to belie theory, and all the Chan or Zen masters seem to have attached a certain importance to the fate of their remains.[49]

What in fact were these relics (*śarīra*) that played such a role in Zen imagination and politics? To understand this, we must review briefly the history of their cult in Buddhism. The most famous relics are naturally those of the Buddha himself, whose distribution between kings of neighbouring kingdoms prevented in extremis a "war of the relics." Their cult in China grew out of the legend that King Aśoka had founded eighty-four thousand reliquaries, of which several were in China. One of them was located in a place called for that reason Ayuwang shan (King Aśoka Mountain), where Japanese monks, come to shore not far away, always went in pilgrimage, some of them to study Chan. This was the case with Dōgen and the adepts from the Darumashū.[50]

---

strange anachronism, saying that it is Basiasita's robe that must be transmitted to Maitreya—while the tradition speaks of a direct transmission from the first Indian patriarch Mahākāśyapa to Maitreya (ibid., 347b–c).

[47] Dōgen, *Shari sōdenki*, in DZ 2: 395.

[48] In the *Shōbōgenzō zuimonki*, for instance, Dōgen argues that, although relics such as the tooth of the Buddha may be venerable, to believe that they may lead one to awakening is deluded thinking. See DZZ 2: 428.

[49] For more details, see Faure, 1991: 132–47; and forthcoming.

[50] See for instance the case of Giin (1217–1300), the founder of Daijiji in Higo (Kyushu), who is said to have gone to Ayuwang shan and Tiantai shan during his second trip to China. At Ayuwang shan, he prostrated eighty-three thousand times in front of the

Philological discussions do not consider the full richness of the semantic, ritual, and mythological field covered by the notion of relics. To illustrate this we must bring in not only the cult of stūpas and the legend of King Aśoka but also phenomena as apparently diverse as the cult of images and of the book, cremation rituals and double burial rites, mummification, or even the transmission of the patriarchal robe, of the portrait or last poem of the Chan/Zen master. By what might be called a "logic of metonymy" (and synecdoche) which takes the part for the whole and considers as a "part" everything that is in a metonymical relationship with the "original," it is not always possible to distinguish the cult of "reliquaries"—whether they be funerary stūpas or statues holding śarīra—from that of relics proper. It is also not possible to say that they are identical, for each of the cults possesses its own symbolism and dynamic.

Bodily (physical) relics of the Buddha include fragments of his body preserved intact (teeth, hair clippings), as well as ashes and crystalline fragments produced by cremation. The power of relics, like that of images, also depends on the faith and karma of the faithful, along with their reactivation by appropriate ritual. Considered as the supreme field of merit, these relics could also appear miraculously in response to the prayers of the faithful. Benefits to laypeople from the worship of relics were just like those coming from adoration of the Buddha. They made possible rebirth into the Pure Land or Tuṣita Heaven. This belief explains the custom of burial *ad sanctos*, whose importance for Indian Buddhism we are just starting to understand;[51] the best-known Japanese example is the cemetery of Mount Kōya, which grew up around the tomb of the Shingon master Kūkai (774–835). The custom is still alive in Japan, as witnessed by the success, in Shin Buddhism, of the Higashiyama columbarium in Kyoto, justified by the existence on this hill of the mausoleum of Shinran. A fourteenth-century document gives a list of the ten virtues of venerating relics: among others, modification of karma, increase of good fortune, protection by good deities, easy childbirth for women, and, finally, assurance that one would become a Buddha. The benefits are also collective: protection of the country, rich harvests, etc.[52] A Japanese chronicle reports that in 827, during a ritual to bring rain, those prayers addressed to relics were crowned with success. In the *Denkōroku* Keizan compares śarīra grains to grains of rice: "When the Dharma disappears, the relics of the Tathāgata will become gems that

---

reliquary-stūpa. See *Nihon Tōjō rentōroku*, in *DNBZ* 111: 225b. On Giin, see Bodiford 1993: 37–43.

[51] See Schopen 1987.

[52] See *T.* 76, 2410: 544a.

grant all wishes, and they will fall everywhere like rain; they will also become grains of rice to help the people."[53]

Relics are also associated with meditation in various ways. On the one hand, the ritual of circumambulation around the stūpa forms, as Paul Mus has shown for Borobuḍur, part of a sort of cosmological meditation.[54] On the other hand, meditation can produce relics. According to a tradition reported by Keizan in his *Denkōroku*, the tenth patriarch, Pārśva, saw thirty-seven *śarīra* grains appear in front of him in response to his meditative practice.[55] Other exploits of the same type are noted in the biographies of those who practice *dhyāna*. Finally, as we shall see later, relics are at the same time the effect and the proof of supernatural powers, and fluctuations in the cult of relics reflect changes in the attitudes of Buddhists toward these powers.

The Chinese prided themselves on possessing several of the Buddha's teeth. According to the Japanese monk Ennin, there were in the Chinese capital, around the middle of the ninth century, four teeth of the Buddha, of which one, kept in the Chongshengsi, was the "heavenly" tooth given by Nazha (son of the heavenly king Virūpākṣa) to the Vinaya master Daoxuan. According to another tradition it was from the god Weituo that Daoxuan received the "heavenly" tooth. The biography of Daoxuan indicates simply that in 767 an edict of the Emperor Daizong declared that in this temple the *bhadanta* Daoxuan had transmitted the tooth of the Buddha Śākyamuni and "fleshly *śarīra* "; he demanded that they be sent to the palace.[56] In 893 the relic was transferred by the Emperor Taizu to Xiangguosi in Chang'an. His successor, Taizong, having some doubts about the nature of the relic, had it tested by fire, and when it emerged untouched by the test, converted and composed a eulogy in its honor. Such eulogies were also composed by Zhenzong (in 998) and Renzong (in 1043). This relic was admired by the Japanese pilgrim Jōjin during his visit to Xiangguosi in 1072, and he described it in his travel journal. According to some sources, it was brought to Japan during the reign of Emperor Saga, at the beginning of the ninth century. But other Japanese sources indicate that it was still at Nengrensi (J. Nōninji) toward the end of the Song, and it was transferred from there to Japan.[57]

Another famous relic was the Buddha's finger, preserved at Famensi in Fengxiang (near Chang'an, present-day Xi'an). This relic, which at-

---

[53] *Denkōroku*, notice on Nāgārjuna, in *T*. 82, 2585: 361c.

[54] See Mus 1935.

[55] *T*. 82, 2585: 356c.

[56] See *Song gaoseng zhuan*, *T*. 50, 2061: 791b.

[57] This does not seem to be the Chinese version, since in 1961 the "heavenly" tooth was sent to Sri Lanka by the Chinese government, through the skies, as is only proper.

tracted crowds, was used on various occasions by Chinese emperors trying to divert to their own profit this source of legitimacy and spiritual power. In 819 the right-thinking Confucianist Han Yu was exiled, after a stunning memorandum submitted to the emperor expressing his indignation at what he considered to be a vulgar superstition on the part of the emperor.[58]

But alongside these relics of the Buddha are also those of the Buddhist saints, obtained at their cremation. People believed that the powers obtained by meditation produced certain physiological changes that translated, at the time of cremation, into the formation of indestructible pearly balls, śarīra proper. Chronicles report how, on various occasions, an incredulous emperor submitted a śarīra to tests by hammer blows without being able to destroy it. Between the fourth and the tenth centuries, we see a constant growth in the numbers of śarīra: while the first cremations produced only a few, toward the end of the Tang they were collected by the hundred. Śarīra became a less numinous product, the object of trade, as was the case with relics in the West. They no longer appeared only on the occasion of cremations but could appear miraculously after any act carried out in a spirit of authentic faith. This is how we may be able to explain the śarīra of the Bodhisattva Samantabhadra transmitted in the Darumashū. We have here a sort of "hemorrhage of the sacred," which could not be curbed by the protests of outraged Confucianists as well as "rationalist" Buddhists, among them some Chan masters.

In Japan there were already many reliquaries in the monasteries of Nara, but the first mentions of relics are earlier than the eighth century. In Japan as in China, it was to the power of these relics that the first successes of Buddhism were attributed.[59] In 584, under the reign of the Emperor Bidatsu, a relic was discovered and presented to Soga no Umako, who put to it the test of hammer and water, and who converted when presented with the results of this experiment. In 588, under the reign of the Emperor Sujun, two priests from the Korean kingdom of Paekche offered relics to the court. In 593 relics of the Buddha were placed in the foundation stone of the pillar of the pagoda of Hōkōji. Toward the middle of the seventh century, the Chinese monk Jianzhen (J. Ganjin, 688–763), founder of Tōshōdaiji in Nara, brought to Japan thirty śarīra grains.

The cult grew during the Heian period (794–1192) with the legend of Shōtoku Taishi. According to this legend, a tiny reliquary containing a śarīra of the Buddha had appeared in the joined palms of the child Shōtoku, aged two, when, turned to the east, he recited the name of the Bud-

[58] See Dubs 1946.
[59] On this period see Kidder 1992.

dha.[60] The interest in relics of the Buddha seems also to have grown with the development of the theory of the "final Dharma," which involved a certain nostalgia for the past and a renewal of devotion to the Buddha Śākyamuni.

Group worship of relics took place during the second half of the ninth century on Mount Hiei, around the relics brought back from China by Ennin (793–864). Because women were forbidden on the mountain, similar ceremonies were held for them at the foot of the mountain.[61] During the Kamakura period, other mass meetings focused on the relics brought back by Yōsai. It is reported that Taira no Kiyomori and Minamoto no Yoritomo, the two clan chiefs whose rivalry would precipitate the eclipse of imperial power and the end of the Heian period, secretly worshiped relics from Mount Ayuwang. Śarīra were also distributed to fifty sanctuaries at the beginning of each new reign. According to the *Chronicle of the Relic of the Tooth of the Buddha* (*Butsuge shariki*), the third shōgun Minamoto no Sanetomo (1193–1219) received a tooth of the Buddha from Nengrensi (Nōninji), which he deposited in a monastery, Daijiji, built for the occasion, and for which he ordered the celebration of an annual ceremony. This story merits closer attention: it was as the result of a dream that Sanetomo came to take a great interest in this relic. In the dream he had gone to China, to a Chinese monastery that turned out to be Nengrensi, and heard there a sermon from a priest who, he was told, was the Vinaya master Daoxuan (596–667). When he expressed surprise that Daoxuan had already been dead a long time, he heard the reply that holy men transcend time and space. This is how Daoxuan had been able to be reborn in Japan under the name of Sanetomo. When he woke up, the shōgun's puzzlement grew all the greater when he learned that two prominent Kamakura monks had had the same dream. He then decided to send an envoy to China to ask Nengrensi for the tooth. The monks of this monastery, apparently convinced by his dream (and by the substantial gifts offered by the Japanese delegation) finally agreed to be separated (temporarily, as they believed) from their relic. First deposited at Daijiji, it was later transferred, in 1285, to Engakuji in Kamakura, where it would contribute to the prosperity of the State. Then in 1396 it was moved to Shōkokuji (the Kyoto monastery that is the homonym, in Japanese reading, of Xiangguosi, the former shelter of the relic), before disappearing during the Ōnin war (1467–1477). Sennyūji, founded by the Vinaya master Shunjō (1166–1227), also claimed to possess the Buddha's tooth, transmitted by the Vinaya master Daoxuan. An assembly took place each year in this monastery, on the eighth of the ninth lunar

---

[60] See *Shōtoku Taishi denryaku*, in DNBZ 71: 126–40.
[61] See *Sanbōekotoba*, in Kamens 1988: 303–4.

month.[62] Finally, a document entitled *Nyorai hashari denrai* (The transmission of the relic of the tooth of the Tathāgata), dated 1367, reports how a tooth of the Buddha brought from India in 645 by Xuanzang was carried into Japan by the Tendai master Gishin, and then, after passing into the hands of the Fujiwara clan, continued to be transmitted in the monasteries of Kamakura.[63]

Outside clerical and political spheres, the impact of the cult of relics on the Japanese imagination is revealed by a Nō play entitled *Shari* (The Relic). A monk travels from Izumo to the capital, where he visits Sennyūji to worship the sixteen Arhats and relics brought from China. While he is weeping tears of emotion, a villager appears and the two men discuss the Buddhist Law and the virtues of relics. But suddenly the sky darkens and a strange light appears. Before the astonished monk the villager changes into a demon, grabs the relics, and flies off into the sky. At that moment the god Idaten (Ch. Weituo) appears, takes off in pursuit, tackles the demon, and brings back the relics.[64]

According to the biography of Shunjō, when he returned to Japan in 1209, after a stay of twelve years in China, he brought back three relic grains of the Buddha, a relic grain of the Bodhisattva Samantabhadra, and three relic grains of a holy man named Ruan. These relics were obtained by pilgrims who went to Mount Emei (in Szechwan), the home of Samantabhadra. Shunjō obtained one *śarīra* grain from one of these pilgrims, who claimed to have found several multicolored grains between his joined hands after twelve days of prayer.[65] Relics of Samantabhadra seem to have been fairly widespread. Under the Tang, the Chan master Yuangui had also found seven of these grains after seeing in a dream a young man in a blue robe.[66] During the time of Shunjō, relics of Samantabhadra were transmitted in the Darumashū, and it was, as we have seen, one of them that Keizan inherited.

The evolution of the cult of relics after the Tang, especially within Chan/Zen, tended to reduce the importance of the distinction, which had been observed until that time, between relics of the Buddha and relics of saints. In Chan we see that little by little the holy man (or patriarch) comes to replace the Buddha and take on some of his traits. Especially significant is the fact that prominent representatives of Song Chan—like Dahui Zonggao and his successor Zhuoan Deguang—were abbots of the monastery at Mount Ayuwang. This monastery became one of the five great official monasteries of Chan, and Yōsai, Dōgen, and most of the

---

[62] On the Sennyūji relic, see Strong and Strong 1995.

[63] See *Gunsho ruijū*, 716: 19.

[64] See Strong and Strong 1995.

[65] See Ishida 1972: 240.

[66] See *Shike shiliao xinbian* (Taibei: Xinwenfeng, 1982), vol. 7, 4849b.

Japanese monks who went to China at the beginning of the Kamakura era stayed there. It was actually from Deguang that Nōnin, the founder of the Darumashū and one of the first propagators of Zen in Japan, received his confirmation, along with a certain number of sacred objects. In spite of his violent criticism of Nōnin, Yōsai shared with him a profound respect for relics and the Mount Ayuwang tradition. In his *Kōzen gokoku ron*, he mentions miracles caused by the relic from the monastery at Mount Ayuwang.[67] We have seen that Yōsai transmitted three grains to the shōgun, and that these were the object of worship in various Kamakura monasteries. In this context it should also be noted that Daigenshuri, the local god who would play an important role in Japanese Sōtō, was also originally considered to be the guardian of the reliquary of Mount Ayuwang. However, relics could be obtained even by those who could not go to China: we are told for instance that Jōkei also gave relics of a *kami* [sic] to his friend Myōe.[68]

To judge from the *Keizan shingi* and various other sources, relics were also part of the cult of the Arhats. Beyond their ritual role, they had in Chan/Zen a hagiographic function. In Japan the cult of relics seems to have been especially popular within the Darumashū, as is confirmed by the recent discovery of a document that, in seventeen chronological entries, traces the transmission of the *śarīra* of the Six Patriarchs of Chan and of the Bodhisattva Fugen Kōmyō (Samantabhadra) in Sanbōji (in Naniwa, present-day Osaka).[69] This transmission apparently went on until the fifteenth century when it was interrupted during the Ōnin war (1467–77). Originally the number of grains transmitted seems to have been eight, but later the number varies and an entry dated 1218 mentions thirty-seven grains and indicates that these relics had been brought from China during the time of Dainichi Nōnin. We may remember that Gikai transmitted one of these grains to Keizan, who deposited it along with other relics in the Gorōhō. Another entry, dated 1405, tells us that each grain had been broken up into dozens of tiny pieces ("rice grains"). We may also note the entry, dated 1460, according to which Nōnin, having gone to Tuṣita Heaven in a dream, received from the Bodhisattva Maitreya a relic of the Buddha. The final entries describe the circumstances around the transmission of the robe of the master Dahui Zonggao, which Nōnin inherited, along with *śarīra*, through the intermediary of Zhuoan Deguang. The document ends with an account of the evacuation of the Sanbōji, threatened by war.

It is interesting to note that the relics, in a way "metaphysical," of the Bodhisattva Samantabhadra, and those, postmortem, of the Zen masters,

---

[67] See *T.* 80, 2543: 15c.
[68] See Tyler 1992: 158–63.
[69] On this question, see Ishii 1974; Faure 1987b.

御舎利ヲ
吉祥山へ
送ル

FIGURE 5. The transfer of Dōgen's relics, in Zuikō Chingyū and Daiken Hōju, eds., *Teiho Kenzeiki zue* (1806), in *SZ*, 17, *Shiden*, 2, rev. ed. (Tokyo: Sōtōshū shūmuchō, 1970–73).

are here blended together. If the distinction has lost any significance, the reason is the growth of Sino-Japanese Tantrism and the growing popularity of the mummification of Buddhist masters who thus become fully fledged Buddhas, and their relics tend as a result to be identified with those of the Buddha.

SACRIFICIAL RELICS

In many cases renunciants have burned themselves or mutilated themselves before relics of the Buddha, or before a stūpa containing them or symbolizing them. Sometimes the symbolic or material gain compensates in part for the physical loss. Thus a monk named Xichen achieved the much-desired post as chaplain to the palace thanks to the reputation he gained for having burned his own fingers. Later, having heard of the relic at Famensi, he went to that monastery and burned his three remaining fingers before the reliquary. Another monk, Yuanhui, sacrificed his arm to the reliquary holding the Buddha's tooth at Mount Baoen and then went to Mount Tiantai and managed to cross the famous rock bridge of the five hundred Arhats, an exploit testifying to his extreme purity. Finally, in homage to the bone of the Buddha at Fengxiang, he burned one of his fingers, which was restored miraculously.[70]

These monks were all following examples or instructions given in the *Lotus Sūtra* or in the *Fanwang jing*; but they seem to have obeyed as well a certain logic of transubstantiation.[71] According to the critical account given by Han Yu of the events of 819, practitioners "burned holes in their skins and boasted of having within themselves the bones of the Buddha." Apparently, "self-mutilation before relics of the Buddha was not just a sacrifice; it was an appropriation. By burning himself, the adept drew on the power of the Buddha's body, purifying his own body and transforming himself into a holy, living relic."[72]

Among other aspects of the cult, we should include the introduction of relics into icons and "ash icons." Although relatively rare, the case of "ash icons" is nonetheless significant because it constitutes an intermediate stage between the practice of cremation and that of mummification. However, this practice was generally replaced by the custom of inserting ashes or various other relics and objects into a cavity hollowed out for this purpose in the trunk of Buddhist statues, or sometimes between the eyes. Relics are felt to be living—or even better, they are "life" itself, the vital spark that animates the iconic body (or architectural body, in the case of a stūpa), conceived of as a womb. The term used to refer to this cavity, *tainai*, is written with two characters that mean both "inside the body" and "in the womb": it thus seems that we have here a gestation as much as an animation. We recall here that Keizan had put several personal relics, including his own umbilical cord, into a statue of the

---

[70] T. 50: 857–58.
[71] See Gernet 1959; Jan 1964; Kieschnick 1995: 71–78.
[72] Kieschnick 1995: 75.

Bodhisattva Kannon. This example will come up again later in our discussion.

A special way to produce relics is the practice that consists of copying the Scriptures with one's own blood. A well-known example is that of Hanshan Deqing (1546–1623), who spent two years (1579–81) recopying with his own blood the *Avataṃsaka-sūtra*.[73] The fact that the copy of the sūtra made by Hanshan was widely regarded as a *śarīra* becomes clear from the ceremony, under imperial auspices, during which it was placed inside a stūpa. We know that Hanshan, imitating the sixth Patriarch Huineng, also succeeded in immortalizing his "flesh body" by mummification.

THE "FLESH BODY"

The two series of *śarīra*, those of the Buddha and those of the Buddhist saints, come together in the mummy, the *śarīra* par excellence. A Buddhist chronicler of the tenth century has left us this statement: although the Bodhisattvas leave a varying number of relics, in the case of the Buddha it is his whole body that makes up the *śarīra*.[74] Putting it another way, the body of a Buddha does not decay; it mummifies naturally. This suggests that any body naturally mummified might be that of a Buddha. It is around this time that, especially within Chan, the number of "natural" mummies starts to multiply. The scenario usually goes like this: after the burial of a Chan master "in the odor of sanctity," most often at the end of three years at the time of the traditional second burial, but sometimes earlier or later, according to circumstances (sometimes as the result of a dream in which the deceased appears), the tomb is opened and the corpse is found to be "as if it were alive": the hair and nails have continued to grow, the flesh is still soft. It is a kind of "living corpse," and this spectacle is said to be sufficiently impressive to discourage future profaners.

Yet mummies were often profaned. The most famous case is surely that of the mummy of the sixth Chan patriarch, Huineng, believed to be still at Nanhuasi near Canton. In the eighth century a Korean supposedly tried to steal its head. His attempt, if we are to believe the Chinese tradition, was abortive. But the Korean tradition, as one might expect, presents us with another version, and even today one can see, in a Korean monastery, the Ssanggye-sa, a mausoleum that supposedly holds the head of Huineng.[75] At any rate the significance of mummies in Chinese Chan

---

[73] See *T.* 53: 989c–997c; and Hsü 1979: 72.

[74] See Zanning, *Song gaoseng zhuan*, *T.* 50, 2061: 830a.

[75] For more details, see Faure 1991: 162–64; Fontein 1993; and *Nihon miira kenkyū gurūpu* 1993, vol. 2, 259–76.

during the Tang leads us to the question of their disappearance in Japanese Zen. True, the discovery of Buddhist mummies dating from the seventeenth century made a sensation a few decades ago in Japanese scholarly circles, but these were mummies of Shugendō ascetics, not of Zen monks—even if, as we have seen, the distinction is not always clear.

The desire to conquer physical death by means of mummification seems at first sight to be out of line with the spirit of Buddhism. As Suzuki Bokushi pointed out, when he listed among the "marvels" of the northern province of Echigo in 1838 the most ancient known Japanese mummy, that of a Shingon master of the fourteenth century, Kōchi Hōin: "The very idea [of mummification] goes against the doctrine of the impermanence of all composed things, as Śākyamuni preached it, and we should not praise it."[76]

It seems, however, that very early on it was thought that the fate of bodily relics provided an indication of the spiritual fate of the departed: thus, the state of incorruptibility achieved after death, whether by the decay of the flesh in the (most common) case of double burial or by cremation or mummification, seems to indicate metaphorically that the spirit of the departed has reached the unchangeable state, Nirvāṇa. This is how we should interpret the desire that constantly recurs, even within a doctrine based entirely on impermanence, to obtain from this world some proof of otherworldly permanence. The very image of Śākyamuni seated in meditation "so motionless that he had spider webs in his eyelashes, a bird's nest on his head, and reeds grew through his meditation mat,"[77] emaciated to a point where, according to tradition, he retained only a minute part of his vital energy, could easily be seen as a meditating mummy. This imagery is taken up again in the legend of Mahākāśyapa, who survived his master only to fall indefinitely into *samādhi* as he awaited the future Buddha Maitreya. Referring to this legend, Keizan writes: "This is why Kāśyapa is still alive. . . . Do not look for him in the distant past. If you negotiate the Way today, he will appear in this world without any need to go and look for him on Mount Kukkuṭpāda. Thus, the flesh of Śākyamuni's body will become warm again, and the smile will reappear on the lips of Kāśyapa."[78]

Moreover, the power attributed to relics and mummies permitted all the emerging schools to affirm their orthodoxy, on the basis of the triumphant Buddhahood of their leader in the flesh. As one might expect, most of the mummies recorded in Chan chronicles are those of founders of

[76] Suzuki 1986: 283.

[77] *Denkōroku*, T. 82, 2585: 344b.

[78] *Denkōroku*, ibid., 346a. Note, however, that, according to another version of that legend, Mahākāśyapa, immersed in *nirodhasamāpatti*, is reduced to the state of a skeleton.

new branches, beginning with Huineng, the putative founder of the Southern school.

Given this, how can we explain the disappearance of mummies in Japanese Zen?[79] Certainly not by any rejection of sectarianism; on the contrary. Masters like Dōgen and Shinran were just as marginal as Huineng was, although certainly less determined to remain so. Why, then, did their disciples not try to "produce" a mummy that would have instantly raised their stock? Are we even sure that they didn't make the effort? Even if they did, the reasons for the change are probably to be sought in the area of technical and artistic innovations. To understand this evolution, we should return to Huineng. Once the apotheosis of their master had been achieved, his disciples coated his mummy in dry lacquer, according to a procedure recently developed in the field of sculpture.[80] A contemporary of Huineng, a wonder-working monk from Central Asia named Sengqie who died in 709, is one of the first attested cases of a lacquered mummy.[81] Although known in China before the beginning of the Christian era, mummification was rarely, as in the Buddhist case, the result of a natural process, and recourse was made to all sorts of chemical procedures to achieve it. The use of dry lacquer constitutes a new phenomenon. This technical innovation changed profoundly the status of the deceased, into a sort of icon, sometimes difficult to distinguish from a simple statue. From that time on, fear of the corpse became less intense, and the lacquered mummies gradually emerged from their crypts to take their place in the "icon hall," alongside their statues or portraits, in an orgy of representation (or more exactly, of presence). Still, lacquering did not resolve the fundamental problem for the disciples, that of knowing how they could be sure that their master would mummify correctly. In most cases natural mummification failed. Thus the statue came to take the place of the mummy, and ashes of the departed along with other relics were put inside it. As noted earlier, an intermediate solution, and one that did not spread very far, was that of "ash icons": they consisted of modeling with ashes and clay one or more statues that looked like the deceased.

Thus, as the mummy became an icon, the associations with death fell into the background and nothing prevented its being replaced by a real icon as an object of worship. This is what seems to have happened in Japan. But just as the mummy, once lacquered, achieved the features of an icon, this in turn took on certain characteristics of the mummy. A mummification of the icon resulted from the iconization of the mummy.

[79] Among the few exceptions, let us mention simply the mummy of the Sōtō Zen master Anzan Kichidō, who "entered *samādhi*" in 1677. See his biography in *Nihon Tōjō rentōroku, DNBZ* 110: 517a.

[80] See Kosugi 1937; Demiéville 1965; Croissant 1990; Sharf 1992.

[81] See *Fozu tongji, T.* 49, 2035: 372c.

Hair from the head and the beard were inserted into the head of statues of Ikkyū Sōjun (1394–1481) to "animate" them. In this case as in others, glass eyes are inserted into the face. Shining in the half-darkness of the altar, they give the statue a "living" appearance, and the observer has the macabre impression of standing before a mummy. Historians of art have often noted this realism of Zen portraits (chinsō). But actually they are not portraits in the Western sense of the word, but rather doubles. The statues are perceived as animated, holding strange powers, and these powers result from the ceremonial "opening of the eyes," as well as from the presence within them of ashes of the deceased, an inextinguishable store of the life that animated the master when alive. Thus the statue of Dōgen, kept at Kōshōji (in the town of Uji, south of Kyoto), is said to contain his ashes, and it receives each day offerings of food as if it were alive. It is significant that Ejō, Dōgen's successor as head of Eiheiji, left his post as abbot to dedicate himself to the worship of the ashes of his late master. Also to be noted is that before rejoining Dōgen at Kōshōji, Ejō and his codisciples of the Darumashū had gone to study at Tōnomine, a Tendai center located near Nara. It was at just this place that a Tendai master named Zōga (917–1003) had died and been mummified two centuries earlier. Zōga's mummy, the first documented in the history of Japanese Buddhism, must still have been at Tōnomine when the adepts from the Darumashū came there, and it is not impossible that it constituted one of the poles of attraction for these devotees of relics. As impressive as they may appear, mummies were only one of the modalities of the presence of the dead. Ancestral tablets and icons played an analogous role, and this is doubtless why the latter ended up replacing them as objects of worship. In one sense, the statues at Dentōin in Yōkōji are substitutes for the mummies of Keizan and his predecessors.

There are many mentions of the fact that a true master leaves behind no "traces," or relics, not even a "death poem." Such criticism is often expressed by an allegorical interpretation of the cult of stūpas and śarīra. In the Guanxin lun of the Chan master Shenxiu (606–706), for example, the stūpa stands for the human body. We find the same hermeneutic strategy among the Japanese Zen masters like Bassui Tokushō (1327–1387), who says: "There is no one, among the Buddhas and ordinary beings, who is not in possession of sacred bones. The body is what we call the temple, and its intrinsic nature makes up the bones. . . . Thus he who has eyes to see will not take the physical bones of the Buddha for true sacred bones."[82]

Despite its central importance in the history and doctrine of Buddhism,

[82] See Braverman 1989: 34–35.

the cult of relics has remained until recently largely ignored.[83] Yet this cult did not constitute merely some kind of doctrinal aberration or a concession to vulgar superstitions. On the contrary, as in the West it is the product of a monastic elite and forms a powerful instrument of monastic and imperial legitimacy. Beyond strictly sectarian interests, characterized by the wish to provide a given group a monopoly over the sacred, the development of a Buddhist cult of relics seems to testify to a change in relations with death quite analogous to that analyzed by Peter Brown in the case of the Christian West.[84] It shows the same kind of humanization of sites, insofar as the new mediators, the saints or the patriarchs, are now human and no longer vaguely defined cosmic entities.

The funerary aspect should perhaps be subordinated, in the case of many of the stūpas, to the commemorative aspect, but the stūpa, even without any relic, already implies, in its nature as an "architectural body," the *presence* of the Buddha or the saint. In the case of reliquaries, on the other hand, the funerary aspect is not always obvious. As André Bareau has noted, the cult offered to relics of the Buddha or the universal monarch (*cakravartin*) differs as much from the cult of ordinary dead as it does from that of the gods.[85] To sum things up, the opposition between a funerary cult and a commemorative cult seems to lead, in the case of relics, to a false dilemma and to mask the logic of a "transcendent immanence" that works through these substitute bodies.

Through the cult of relics, we witness a transition from individual to dynastic (or sometimes only professional) charisma. Unlike Saint Louis who ceased to be a sacred king in order to become a holy king, the Chan/Zen masters ceased to be holy men in order to become sacred individuals.[86] We have here, parallel to a monastic rationalization, a sacralization of Chan/Zen. Through the cult of relics, the Chan/Zen masters became, in actuality, ancestors, and at the same time they remained in this world as protectors of the community, divine mediators.

GHOSTS

The existence of funerary rites requires that the dead survives as a spirit that can benefit from them. In the various Asian cultures that Buddhism entered, the deep-seated belief in the survival of an individuating essence

[83] The situation is rapidly changing in the U.S., with the AAR Seminar on Buddhist Relic Veneration; and in Japan with the publication of *Nihon, Chūgoku miira shinkō no kenkyū* (1993) by the Group for Research of Japanese Mummies (Nihon miira kenkyū gurūpu).

[84] See Brown 1981.

[85] Bareau 1975: 179.

[86] See Le Goff 1982.

ran counter to the fundamental Buddhist dogma of the unreality of the self (*anātman*). A compromise seems to have been reached in the Buddhist notion of an "intermediary being" (*anantarabhava*), the remnant of earlier actions who, after a longer or shorter stay in a sort of limbo, comes down again to be reincarnated, in the best cases, in a human womb.

Given this, did the Buddhist monks believe in their own funeral rites, and if so, to what extent? Some of them apparently saw in them nothing but "skillful means" intended not so much for the dead person as for the living. The survivors needed to know that the dead person had reached a peaceful haven and would not return to haunt them, and they themselves needed guidance toward the doctrine of salvation. The ritual often implied or ended up by inspiring belief. The tension between the agnosticism of some and the faith of others appears in many dialogues. We may recall how Keizan attempted to quell the doubts of Emperor Go-Daigo regarding the actual consumption of funerary offerings: the "intermediary beings" are also called *gandharva* because they feed on the odors, not on the substance, of the food offerings.[87]

Despite the efficacy of its funeral rites, Zen Buddhism could not dispose of ghosts in quite so easy a fashion. Ghosts are actually major figures in Buddhist thinking about death, and they return in the memory and dreams of the living, "even when these latter try by means of rites and prayer to separate themselves from the ghost, trying to make him into a truly dead person, completely apart from the living and doomed to gradual oblivion."[88]

Often, as has already been noted, ghosts and other "spirits of the place" validate Zen masters who exorcise them by converting them to Buddhism or by returning them to the fold. We have already seen how Gennō Shinshō exorcised the spirit of the "killing stone" by reciting a sort of Zen incantation. We have also noted earlier how Ikkei Eishū once confronted a woman who mingled with the audience in order to listen to his master speak. She told him that because of her karma she had been reborn in the form of a snake and she was seeking deliverance. Ikkei eventually administered the Precepts to her, by this gesture delivering her from her current destiny.[89] This story is a lot like that of the fox who came to hear the sermons of the Chan master Baizhang. Keizan must have been thinking about the latter when he mentioned the fox who chose to die on the grounds of Yōkōji. These were cases of well-intentioned ghosts, sometimes even domesticated ones, like the Yōkōji ox who tempo-

[87] *SZ, Shūgen* 2: 496a. Ironically, Go-Daigo will himself become one of the most feared ghosts of the period.

[88] Schmitt 1994: 248.

[89] See *Meikyoku Sokushō, Yōtakuji Tsūgen zenji gyōjō* [1571], in *SZ* 17, *Shiden* 2: 270b; quoted in Bodiford 1993a: 176.

rarily took human shape. But good intentions are not always the case, especially when the dead person returns in the shape of an animal.[90] Rebirth, however, in animal form is not in itself an inevitable sign of dangerous wildness. The animal form may be a spiritual step, as can be seen from certain past lives of the Buddha, or Keizan himself. If snakes and foxes, as forms taken by ghosts, are dangerous because they are powerful, they can also, thanks to those powers that let them take temporary human form, escape the limitations of their destiny and benefit from Buddhist teaching.

There are other, more disturbing ghosts, like the "hungry ghosts," spiritual counterparts of those who suffer during times of famine and of stray dogs. They wander invisible among human beings, unable to satisfy the hunger that devours them. These "little brothers"—a euphemism by which they are sometimes designated—had already been a concern in Chinese Buddhism, in ceremonies like the "rite for the Burning Mouths" (an allusion to the fact that all the food they tried to eat burst into flame), but it was in Japan, around the Kamakura period, that their representation became truly hallucinatory, with the iconographic fashion for *gaki-emaki* (illustrated scrolls representing hungry ghosts) and other types of *memento mori*.[91] The horde of these hungry ghosts took on its full weight of culpability through its insidious presence among the living.[92]

Dangerous in a different way were those malicious ghosts—fortunately more exceptional—that are called respectfully *onryō* or *goryō* ("vengeful" or "august" spirits).[93] The most famous case in medieval Japan is with-

---

[90] The motif of rebirth in reptilian shape has a long history in Buddhism. Let us simply mention the well-known example of Chan master Puji's disciple, who had been reborn as a snake after dying in anger because one of his fellow monks had broken his alm-bowl. He came back to take revenge but was eventually pacified by Puji and obtained rebirth, not as an animal but as a human female—which indicated a small amount of progress. In a Japanese version of the same theme, the famous legend of Dōjōji, the monk who falls victim to the snake's hatred will not be saved, because the hatred of a woman disappointed in love is of the most violent kind.

[91] See for instance the *Gaki zōshi*, in Kobayashi Shigemi, ed., *Nihon no emaki* 7 (Tokyo: Chūō kōronsha, 1987). The appellation Burning Mouths is said to derive from the story of Ānanda's encounter with a demon bearing the name Burning Face. The demon announced to Ānanda his imminent death to be reborn among hungry ghosts. In order to escape this fate, Ānanda was told to make offerings to ghosts. The name Burning Face (Mianran) was transformed into Burning Mouth (Yankou) by the Tantric translator Amoghavajra. According to some versions, it is Guanyin who appeared to Ānanda as a hungry ghost. See Robert P. Weller, *Unities and Diversities in Chinese Religion* (New York: Macmillan, 1987), 119–21.

[92] On the *shuilu* ceremonies in Chan/Zen, see Mujaku 1963: 575–77.

[93] See Jien, *Gukanshō*, in Brown and Ishida 1979: 220–21. On this question, see also Shibata Minoru, *Goryō shinkō*, Minshū shūkyōshi sōsho 5 (Tokyo: Yūzankaku, 1984); and Plutschow 1990: 203–16.

out question that of Sugawara no Michizane, a statesman who died in exile at the beginning of the tenth century as the result of libel. The catastrophes that struck the capital shortly after his death were attributed to his desire for revenge, and a cult was hastily dedicated to his spirit in an effort to appease it. As a result Michizane was promoted to God of Literature and came to play a growing role in medieval culture. Other famous cases include the spirit of Sanemori, a warrior of the end of Heian who became a god of pestilence;[94] and that of Prince Sawara (d. 785), who died in exile after being accused of murdering Fujiwara no Tanetsugu. Emperor Kammu tried to placate him by elevating him posthumously to imperial status, under the name of Emperor Sudō.[95] A less obvious example is that of Prince Shōtoku, who was revered not only as an enlightened ruler, but to assuage his spirit, which had been angered by the destruction of his family by the Soga clan.[96] Finally, one of Keizan's contemporaries, Emperor Go-Daigo, became a goryō and appeared in a dream to the Rinzai priest Musō Soseki, in the form of a golden dragon.[97] The best way to appease such spirits was to dedicate to them a cult (in the form of ceremonies known as goryō-e) that would lead to their deification, or, in the case of less powerful spirits, to perform exorcisms (recitation of scriptures, mantras, nenbutsu). Several important festivals (Gion, Aoi, etc.) originated as goryō-e.

Among the less important ghosts (and thus those with least evil influence, but still able to hurt those close to them), we may mention victims of premature death—children, women dead in childbirth, virgins—and lower-class dead, outcasts by nature or by occupation. In certain of the Sōtō kirigami, fear of ghosts takes on its full force and this school owes a large part of its expansion to the ancestral fear toward those who had not been able to become ancestors.

All these ghosts are in a way prisoners of the intermediate world, either because a premature death deprived them of the appropriate rites or because death aroused such resentment in them that the rites lost their power. In their case, then, extra precautions had to be taken by means of

[94] Sanemori (1111–1183) is a warrior who was killed at the end of Heian when he tripped over a rice plant in a field. His vengeful spirit was believed to have become a crop-destroying pest. In certain villages one still burns today a straw man to repel this particular category of evil spirits. This ritual, widely known as mushi-okuri, is also sometimes called Sanemori-okuri, confirming that the scapegoat is none other than this pestilential spirit. There is also a Nō play Sanemori, in Yōkyoku taikan (Tokyo: Meiji shoin, 1930), vol. 2, 1250–51.

[95] Kami and Shimo Goryō Shrines in Kyoto were dedicated to this "Emperor," who nevertheless remained feared throughout the Heian period. See Plutschow 1990: 207–9.

[96] Ibid.: 207.

[97] This explains the name of the monastery founded by Musō, Tenryūji (Monastery of the Heavenly Dragon), to placate the spirit of Go-Daigo.

special rites that took on a growing importance in medieval Sōtō. Notable cases were the rites of sealing the tombs of women dead in childbirth and of outcasts (*hinin*).[98]

The case of women dead in childbirth is doubly revealing in this respect since, on the one hand they died, still too young, in the service of continuing their lineage, while on the other hand they were guilty of the pollution created by their blood, a crime that made them eligible for a particularly nasty hell, that of the "Blood Pond."[99] Although Keizan does not take up the subject directly, his emphasis on the beneficent powers of Kannon as an easer of the pains and protector against the risks of childbirth shows that he was well aware of the problem.[100]

There were finally the "normal" dead who languished in hell and who, from time to time, managed to return to the memory of the living in the hope that these latter would intercede in their favor. Although they only rarely had the power to appear before the eyes of the living, they were sometimes able to produce signs (especially sicknesses in those close to them) and thus enter into a tortured dialogue with them, a dialogue in which both parties were equally eager for an improvement in their infernal destiny. Although they did not always wish or know how to take the role of interlocutor in such dialogues, Buddhist monks did try to supervise them. It was in this way, for example, that Gennō Shinshō, during one of his journeys that took him to Hōki province, met the ghost of the wife of Shimazu Atsutada, lord of Kasuga Castle. Condemned to eternal tortures after a life of sin, she tried every night to escape and was terrorizing the people who lived around the castle. Gennō confronted her and obtained her repentance, and so was able to deliver her. Lord Atsutada received confirmation of his wife's salvation in a dream and naturally rewarded the brave monk.[101]

The mountains Tateyama and Osorezan, not too far from the Noto peninsula, were infernal places where one could communicate with the dead. Osorezan became during the medieval period a Sōtō center, still active today, although the monks only tolerate the presence, on the mar-

[98] See Ishikawa 1983–94 (9): 178–84.

[99] See ibid. (4): 165. On that question, see also Takemi 1983 and Faure 1994: 180–84. The fear of women who died in childbirth was apparently very strong in medieval Japan, judging from the number of *kirigami* dealing with that problem. See Ishikawa, ibid., (9): 178–82, 184. A similar evolution seems to have taken place in the West, if we are to believe Burchard of Worms when he denounces "bad Christians" who pierce with a spear the corpses of women who died in childbirth and of stillborn babies, in order to prevent them from returning as ghosts. See Schmitt 1994: 228.

[100] See *Sōjiji chūkō engi*, in *JDZ*, 489.

[101] See Bodiford 1993–94. See also the story of the ghost of a young girl who, having met an untimely death, appears to a Sōtō monk and is saved by the *Ketsubongyō* and the *kechimyaku*. Quoted in Bodiford 1993: 207.

gins of the monastic institution, of the blind medium-women, the *itako*, through whom the dead periodically return to the memory of the living.

Paradoxically, the adepts of Zen—a teaching that had attempted to exorcize certain mental attitudes judged incompatible with its theoretical subitism by projecting them outside of it and relegating them to the rank of popular superstitions—were in turn promoted to the rank of supreme exorcists in their relationships with popular culture. Even the awakening of Zen masters does not prevent them from returning as ghosts to haunt the living. This is at least what is suggested by the malicious story in which Ejō's ghost returns to take revenge on another disciple of Dōgen, Gijun (d. u.), who had had the bad idea to convert to Shingon after the death of their master and even founded a Shingon temple dedicated to Amida.[102]

Alongside these ghosts who are strongly "objectified" by a whole hagiographical tradition, we should say a few words about the "subjective" ghosts—those who appear, not in a corporeal form, but in the form of an oneirical image. Thus Keizan sees in a dream his late master Gien and concludes from this apparition that the benevolent spirit will accompany him his entire life. However, we are dealing here with an auspicious, wish-fulfilling dream, and not, as is so often the case with ghost dreams, a staging of the regrets and remorse of the living.

We examined earlier the strange case of the mummy, halfway between the ghost (*revenant*) and the recumbant statue (*gisant*—since it too is a "representation of the dead," a kind of "statuized dead," but it is also usually in a seated, not supine, position): on the one hand the natural preservation of the body indicates the entering into Nirvāṇa; on the other hand, it manifests the lingering presence of the dead, who has not entirely "gone to the other shore," who refuses to enter the collective anonymity of ancestors. This "corporeal ghost," who in a sense returns to the space of the living without having left it, is disturbing. It has the "beauty of the dead," but it also provokes the horror of the ghost. Although it is not a priori malevolent, it shares with those dead the refusal to disappear into the collective oblivion of common mortals, who submit to the common law of a "threefold progressive disappearance, that of their physical remains in the grave, of their soul outside of purgatory, and of their memory in the mind of the living."[103] However, mummies are only a particular case, within a circulation of *ling*, or "power," of a larger network (relics, icons, etc.). It is as a particular moment of this process, as a temporary crystallization, that they must be understood, inserted— without, for all that, losing sight of their specificity.

[102] See Ōkubo 1966: 245–46.
[103] Schmitt 1994: 228–29.

Chapter Seven

PLACES OF THE MIND

I
F, AS JACQUES LE GOFF STRESSES, every form of imagination, every *imaginaire*, seems to imply some kind of location, the *imaginaire* of place implies the existence of its opposite, a utopia, a nonplace, which still is the product of a certain spatial imagination.[1] The Japanese geographical imagination is therefore a hybrid, built on two different spatial orders. From the autochthonous framework derives a concrete, unique mythology that is essentially of a sacred history relating the divine origin of the emperors.[2] From the Buddhist and Chinese settings derives an abstract, theoretical, and symbolic space, that of the Buddhist cosmology or of the "Way of Yin and Yang" (Onmyōdō), all that would later be rejected by nativist scholars like Hirata Atsutane (1776–1863) as deriving from the "Chinese spirit" (*karagokoro*). The same cleavage operates within Zen thought, a thought that is simultaneously concrete, mythological, cosmological, and abstract, demythologizing (demythifying), and acosmological.

These two kinds of space coexist in Keizan, reflecting or encouraging the two types of imagination. In this he is the heir to a long tradition that we shall try to take up briefly. Chan monks have always had the secret desire to convert local deities, to wipe out the memory of places, to deconsecrate or reconvert spaces, to decode and reencode legends. We have here a confrontation between two incompatible worldviews (even though they do coexist in practice): the utopian, unlocalized, and universalist conception derived from Buddhism, and the "locative" and localized conception of local religion—two visions of space, two different anthropologies. Paradoxically, the utopian view is actualized spatially in architectural layouts, and temporally in the structure of ritual.

Even in classical Chinese cosmology, and to a much greater extent in local traditions, space was conceived of as a complex and unstable reality. Far from being always and everywhere the same, it was sometimes diluted, sometimes concentrated, and constituted a more or less hierarchical federation of heterogeneous, qualitative spaces. The adoption of Buddhism constituted a sort of epistemological revolution, imposing a new kind of homogeneous space that completely upset "the ancient het-

[1] See Le Goff 1986.
[2] On this question see Caillet 1991.

erogeneities of the various kinds of sacred space."[3] This homogenization of space is illustrated in the following passage, in which the fourth Chan patriarch, Daoxin (580–651), uses a visual metaphor to describe meditative practice: "When you are seated at meditation, it is as though you are seated at the top of a high, isolated mountain, looking far away in the four directions, without limit. Relax your body and your spirit so that they may fill the entire world, and fix yourself in the domain of the Buddha. The pure *dharmakāya* is without limits."[4] But, as David Eckel has underscored, "Emptiness lends itself inevitably to the language of place. And its localized character is what allows the existence of special points in space where emptiness is recognized or felt more powerfully or more fully than it would be otherwise."[5]

Paradoxically, while Chan monks worked to deconsecrate mountains and impose the abstract space of their monasteries, they were also busy building stūpas and putting relics inside them, so creating new sacred spaces protected by local gods, and eventually identified with them. This phenomenon, moreover, originated in sophisticated monastic circles and should not be interpreted simply as some kind of subversion of the "great tradition" by local cults. The building of stūpas reflected both the "humanizing" of cosmic sacred places and the "sacralizing" of Chan. Within Chan, myth gave way to hagiography, stories of the gods to those of the masters, who may have been prominent monks but were still human (with a very few exceptions). A superficial resemblance, namely the fact that these new cult places seemed to take over those of autochthonous cults, should not conceal their diametric opposition and the great change that had occurred in the minds of Chan adepts: the cult around a stūpa was not the same as that of a chthonian power, even if the two sometimes were confused. Analyzing this process in the case of Japan, Nakamatsu Yashū stressed that the semantic evolution by which the term *tera* came to replace the Sino-Japanese reading *ji* to refer to Buddhist temples may be related to the adaptation of Buddhism to local conditions. "*Tera* . . . was apparently originally used to refer to crypts used for human bones. . . . With time, the term *tera*, ditches containing bones, came to include any structure used for this purpose."[6]

But the direct vision of Chan/Zen did not simply give way to local cults; the process was more of a dialectic. On the one side, the cult of stūpas, relics, and mummies, while allowing for the popularization of Chan, implied a humanizing of the sacred, a sort of demythologizing that often went against beliefs in cosmic or divine mediators. Such mediators were re-

---

[3] See Jameson 1985: 374.
[4] *Lengqie shizi ji*, T. 85, 2837: 1289c.
[5] See Eckel 1990: 62.
[6] Quoted in Tada 1981: 22.

placed by idealized men, Chan masters whose power revealed itself through their relics. This evolution established a new "topography of the sacred" centered on sacred places like stūpas and monasteries. But at the same time Chan monasteries could not claim the "special purity" that characterizes the space in Shintō sanctuaries, "a purity free of any sign of death."[7] The emergence of Chan could thus be described as the appearance of a new system of "places," a new division of space, the creation of a new sacred geography centered on relics and funerary stūpas.

Japan was perceived at the beginning of the Kamakura as a small, barbarous archipelago on the fringes of the great civilization centers, India and China. As Dōgen put it, it is a country "very far across the seas, and the mind of people there is extremely dull."[8] The feeling of living in a peripheral country was reinforced by the desolation characteristic of the theory of the ages of the Dharma: in this time of the "final Law," Japan was far away not only geographically but also temporally from the India of the Buddha. Fortunately this pessimism was beaten back in various ways. Keizan, although he shared this perception, chose not to dwell on it. In his *Denkōroku*, he writes: "In this great matter, there is no separation between eras of truth, imitation and dereliction; and the various countries are no different. So don't lament that it is a sick society where Buddhism is degenerate. Don't regret that you are people of a remote country. So far as this matter is concerned, even if a thousand Buddhas came all at once and tried to give it to you, even the power of the Buddhas would not suffice."[9] Furthermore, by the sheer play of the imagination, and the strength of practice, the exotic world of India and China managed to overlay the real Japan and Japan became India, the central country, the land of the Buddhas, and not simply that of the gods. This view is found for instance in Myōe, the same person who, in his desire to get to India, had gone so far as to imagine the number of steps he would be required to take.[10] But eventually he was able to avoid this long march, which was in any case forbidden to him by the god of the Kasuga Shrine, and he recreated at Takao, to the west of the capital, the solitary contemplative pleasures of the Indian ascetics. For, thanks to the Mahāyāna equation between Nirvāṇa and *saṃsāra*, India, land of the Buddha and by extension of Nirvāṇa, ended up superposing itself on Japan, the land of gods, of *saṃsāra*, of this "floating world," certain aspects of which would later be popularized in prints.

[7] Ibid.: 24.

[8] See for instance *Shōbōgenzō*, "Keisei sanshoku," in *T.* 82, 2582: 40b.

[9] *Denkōroku, T.* 82, 2585: 394a.

[10] See for instance Myōe: "Thus it is quite clear that a vast distance separates ancient times from these Latter Days, and the great country (India) from this barbarous land. It is very sad to think of." Rasmus 1982: 91.

In this imagination of time and space, Japan is not only a peripheral nation, but it is also and above all the place of incarnate mystery: the imaginary superposition of India and Japan took place thanks to stories of flying mountains (Yoshino) or simply, in Keizan's case, through the symbolic equivalence between the mountains "of the north country," the Himalayas and Hakusan.[11] It also works through the discovery of a mental geography that locates hells and heavens in the mountain ranges of Japan: Hakusan, Tateyama, Yoshino, Kasuga, etc. High places in a spiritual geography, these mountains constitute so many stratified *imaginaires*.[12]

In Keizan we see an acute awareness of the "spirit of place," and at the same time a desire to "add to it," to impose a more abstract mythological grid (the "ten places"), a purely Buddhist local order, a Buddhist topology in which, as we have seen, Hakusan corresponds to the Himalayas, and the god of Hakusan is none other than the local manifestation (*suijaku*) of the universal, ultimate essence (*honji*), the Bodhisattva Kannon. There is thus a constant dialectic between these two concepts of sacred space: nonhuman and humanized, wild and ritualized. The copula that joins these two mythogeographical orders is none other than Keizan, who combines in his own person two types of space and two identities: that of an Indian nature spirit who has achieved the status of an Arhat, and that of a Japanese *ujiko*, a child of the tutelary deity of Hakusan.

Cosmological concepts bump up against each other in the imagined geography of Keizan: although Japan is only a little archipelago on the edge of Jambudvīpa, the southern continent of Buddhist cosmology, it constitutes at the same time a separate world insofar as its northern parts correspond to the northern continent, Uttarakuru. The cult of the Arhats (especially Piṇḍola), witnesses to the Buddha who are still alive, could be seen as an attempt to find again a direct contact with the historical past, but also as a ritual incarnation of the Buddha, a Buddhist *imitatio*. The ages telescope on each other: patriarchs and Buddhas are far away in time and space, even outside time-space, but they are also present here and now (through the awakening that actualizes them and by the direct connection furnished by the uninterrupted line of Chan). Thus Keizan in the *Denkōroku* mentions the Buddha and his disciple Mahākāśyapa as two living beings in this world, reincarnating themselves in the persons of the master and his disciple.[13] Likewise, in the *Record of Tōkoku*, he

[11] On "flying mountains" see Michel Soymié, "Le Lo-feou chan: Etude de géographie religieuse," *BEFEO* 48 (1956): 1–132; and Grapard 1982.

[12] Mounts Hakusan, Fuji, and Tateyama constitute the "three sacred mountains" of Japan. As noted earlier, Hakusan enshrines Shirayama-hime no Mikoto, whose *honji* is the Eleven-Faced Kannon.

[13] *Denkōroku*, T. 82, 2585: 345a-346b.

underscores on every solemn occasion the analogy between the present situation and that at the time of the Buddha. After transmitting the Dharma to Meihō Sotetsu, he notes: "On Vulture Peak and at Caoxi there were the *shuso* Kāśyapa and Qingyuan. At Daijōji and at Tōkoku there are the *shuso* [Keizan] Jōkin and [Meihō] Sotetsu" [*JDZ*, 410].

Moreover, the monastic existence at Yōkōji unfolds under the invisible protection of the Arhats, these eyewitnesses of Śākyamuni's predication, who are regularly invited to participate in the monastery's ritual. We already noted the etymology of Tōkoku, a reference to Dongshan Liangjie, the founder of the Sōtō school. On several occasions Keizan compares Tōkoku to the place of the Buddha's predication: "King Bimbīsara once offered the Bamboo Grove park to the Buddha. In the same way, when one enters this place with a pure faith, one sees one's desires lessen and one's pure acts increase" [*JDZ*, 394]. Keizan chooses the eighth day of the eighth month of the year 1322 to have the beams of Yōkōji's new Buddha hall installed, because this is a day of offering to the monasteries of the Three Countries: "Jetavana in India, Qinglongsi in China, Lord Sadanobu's Hōjōji and the Great Stūpa on Mount Kōya in Japan" [*JDZ*, 407]. When the construction of the Dharma hall begins, on March 3, 1324, Keizan notes: "On that day the Buddha, staying in the Deer Park, set for the first time into motion the Dharma Wheel. It is also on that auspicious day that the Buddha, having been reborn as heir apparent due to his karma, went to the palace of the dragon-king to fetch the wish-fulfilling jewel" [*JDZ*, 423].

THE SIGNIFICANCE OF PLACE

At the Tōkoku hermitage, it's as though one disliked the Bodhidharma style. In this remote retreat one is even far from the sun of wisdom that indicates the south. Like an idiot, like an imbecile, one tames badgers and foxes, finds companionship in hares and pheasants, and stays away from crows and dogs. The barrier of clouds is thick and solidly locked, the river and the reeds escort each other. On the pathways on the mountain the wind's drums sound loud, and when the armies of the rain begin to move, they turn into snow and hail. The eyes of the dragon throw down precious pearls, which fill the courtyard [of the monastery]; the teeth of the elk winnows the wild-growing rice, which fills the [monks'] bowls. The repeated teaching of the Buddha is especially received in this place, the correct practice of hermitage [living] is renewed on this mountain. Monks and cooks all observe restraint. The intrinsic mind and adventitious passions contribute equally to the work of the Buddha. Drawing water, carting wood—everything expresses the marvelous efficacy of spiritual powers; harvesting vegetables, gathering fruit—all this sets in motion the wheel of the profound Dharma. This place differs fundamentally from the world of men, and there are many things here that reveal indications of holiness. [*JDZ*, 401]

Despite the eloquent style of this "short preface" to Keizan's poetical description of the "Ten sites of Tōkoku," it is difficult to recreate the feel of the place where he founded his monastery. One can only evoke the solitude that must have embraced the monks as the evening fell over Tōkoku, the dense shade of the majestic Japanese cedars, the sound of the waterfalls. Higher up, emerging from the dark understory one reaches light and open space, the place where Keizan went to sit in meditation, a place whose memory is preserved in a "meditation rock" there. The view extends into the distance toward the coast and the Sea of Japan and, beyond, to Korea and China, lands of other mysteries, China above all, a land of fertile valleys, where nature was apparently kinder than in Japan, and gods less menacing because they are more "human-like." It was the land where Chan history unfolded, reassuring in its critical humanism, where dreams seemed to have less sway over everyday life. And yet farther away lay India, cradle of the Buddha and his doctrine and the setting for Keizan's own former existences, a place of every marvel, a land that fed the Buddhist imagination.

Keizan was heir to a doctrine that claimed to be a-topic, unlocalized, insofar as it was founded on the idea of emptiness. One of the basic metaphors of Chan/Zen is that of empty space. But even its mooring in a patriarchal tradition provides a kind of inscription in the place, a way of circumscribing the unlocalized by fitting it into more down-to-earth notions even if this place is not geographically defined. But above all, as he said himself, Keizan was proud of being an *ujiko* of Hakusan. He described himself in terms of his affiliation to a local community (*uji*) and his obedience to a tutelary deity (*ujigami*). He thus placed himself within a double system of reference, a double network of dependencies. And this is what creates, in his thought, that creative tension that we find expressed in various forms: a tension between rationalism and mysticism, between elitism and proselytizing, between a search for immediacy and a resorting to mediations.

In a significant manner, Keizan attributed his success not to the superiority of his teaching but to a matter of geomancy. When he took over the piece of land on which he planned to build Yōkōji, he received from an Arhat the revelation that this land, although not very impressive to look at, was in fact topographically superior to the site of Eiheiji, where the Sōtō community had grown up around Dōgen. Because it was located in a valley, a predominantly *yin* place and thus open to unhealthy influences, Eiheiji from its foundation had faced constant problems. Keizan, through the mouth of the Arhat, was apparently referring to the internal quarrels that split the Eiheiji community after the death of Dōgen and caused the eviction of his own master, Gikai. From his viewpoint, the renewal of the Sōtō sect at Yōkōji and then at Sōjiji is thus due in large part to the spirit of place, to a particularly successful choice of location—despite the fact that Yōkōji is also located in a valley—and not only to the abstract excellence of a doctrine.

Tōkoku

Keizan was thus acutely aware of the spirit of place, or rather "spirits." In Japan mountains are daunting places because they partake of the other world and anticipate the beyond. They are the home of the spirits of the dead, and of all sorts of strange deities designated collectively under the name of *kami*. Those who penetrate these haunted lands thus run the risk of becoming lost, of passing over to the other side of things. Hermits are dead to the world; by disappearing into the depths of mountains, they make a kind of return to the womb, often symbolized by the caves into which they go to meditate.[14] They thus become marginal beings, mediators between this world and the next, endowed with fabulous powers.

Often the mountain is one with the *kami*; it is the *kami* itself. As a mountain is a sacred place, those who enter it are purified naturally: it is to the influence of the mountain that Keizan attributed the filial piety that inspired the generous donors to participate in the upkeep of the monastic community by means of funeral services. The sacred nature of the place is revealed by all sorts of auspicious signs. The Arhat's prediction has already been mentioned. Other prodigies noted by Keizan when he settled down at Tōkoku are as follows:

> At the end of the summer of the same year [1318] a great rock was unearthed. When it was broken, a little snake emerged. In addition, there was at the foot of the mountain an ox customarily used for work around the monastery. It was used to transport food and vegetables for the monks, as well as wood and other burdens. A villager saw this ox change into a man who came and sat down in the Buddha hall. Finally, an old wild fox came to die at the monastery, under the awning on the reading room. All these events show that this site is a sacred place where one can be delivered from [the body,] this receptacle of suffering. [*JDZ*, 394]

[14] We have noted earlier the importance of incubation and of the Kannon cult for medieval Japanese Buddhism. Caves and rocks seem to have played a significant part in this phenomenon. See Saigō 1993 and Stein 1988.

When we realize that foxes are generally seen as spirits of the dead, it seems clear that this fox wished, by dying in this sacred place, to lay claim to karmic affinities with the monks and so to a better rebirth.[15] Or perhaps he had simply, thanks to the joint virtues of the sacred mountain and the monks, succeeded in transcending his karma. Another legend tells us how Keizan discovered the site of his future monastery guided by a white fox, probably a messenger of the god Inari, who turns out to be one of the protecting deities of the mountain.[16] In passing we may note an ambiguity of terminology: the Chinese character read *san*, designating a mountain, has come metonymically to designate a Buddhist monastery, which permits a transfer of sacredness between the mountain and the monastery. This sacred nature reveals itself through clues that cannot elude an attentive observer like Keizan—the little white snake or the ox that changed into a man. These were infallible signs of an invisible presence, a divine protection of all moments. Wonders recur at the time of the erection of the Peak of the Five Elders:

> The twenty-third of the sixth month [of the year 1323], a divine spring burst out in a corner [west/northwest] of the Peak of the Five Elders. Kakumyō, a Zen practitioner, said, "This mountain is truly a sacred place. The tea plant [which grows here] is a sacred bush. This water which appears naturally, on a plateau, is certainly sacred water." In all, this site has shown five times over the effects of its power [*ling*]. First when I was looking for a site for the stūpa, I found this platform. Second, I saw that the tea plant grew naturally here. Third, sacred water gushed forth spontaneously. Fourth, I deposited here the Mahāyāna Scriptures recopied by my efforts. Fifth, I deposited here the posthumous writings of the Five Elders. [*JDZ*, 409]

We should say a few more words about that spring, called Hakusan spring, whose water has been for centuries offered to the ancestors at the Founder's hall (Dentōin), at the Peak of the Five Elders, and at other stūpas. Buddhist hagiography is full of miraculous fountains, proofs that the monks' virtue could provoke a response from the local god or dragon (in China, after all, dragons are the lords of the water, and one of the criteria of sainthood is the gift of being able to divine water).[17] Springs and fountains were essential to the life of the monastery. Inversely, spiritual decadence translates into a drying up of the springs. In the case that concerns us, Keizan's virtues (or those of the Five Elders present in the

---

[15] In the *Hokekyō kenki*, for instance, priest Shunmyō has the revelation that he was formerly a fox living behind a temple and was reborn as a human through the merits obtained by hearing the *Lotus Sūtra*. See Dykstra 1983: 53–54.

[16] The fox, as symbol of Inari and Dakiniten, played an important role in the line of Giin (1217–1300), in particular at Myōgonji.

[17] See Soymié 1961.

form of their relics in Gorōhō) did bring a response from the deity of Hakusan. At least this seems to be indicated by the name given to the spring, and it seems that, in this case, the local god is effacing himself before a more powerful god to whom he is a vassal. We find, in the invisible world, the same hierarchical relationship as in Japanese feudalism. A similar Hakusan spring is found in the main Sōtō monasteries: Eiheiji, Daijōji, and Sōjiji.[18] At Eiheiji it is located right beside the memorial to Dōgen, and the water from this fountain is offered every day to the founder of the sect. From its geographical position, Mount Tōkoku (Tōkokuzan) is on the edge (and at the junction) of two mountain systems, Hakusan and Sekidōzan (Isurugiyama). We suggested earlier that the veneration at Yōkōji of the pair of Bodhisattvas Kannon and Kokūzō perhaps reflects an effort to reconcile two symbolic systems, one centered in Hakusan and the other in Sekidōzan. Furthermore, we may recall at this point that Kannon was said to inherit part of her symbolism from pre-Buddhist chthonic deities—in Hakusan's case, the goddess Kukurihime. Because many of these deities are associated with rocks, caves, springs, and waterfalls, the symbolism of rebirth through reclusion or incubation plays a central part in their cult. The same symbolism of regeneration of life seems at work in Gorōhō and the Hakusan spring.

SPATIAL PALIMPSESTS

If in some cases Chan/Zen monks attempted truly to create a tabula rasa, to impose a properly a-topic space over the ancient sacred places, to erase the memory of the places and its "places of memory" (*lieux de mémoire*), in most cases they were content to graft new symbols, to produce new places. However, these symbols can establish themselves only if they are resonating with the local *imaginaire* and profitably harness the native symbolism. This is what Keizan undertook to do at Tōkoku. While the text of the *Record of Tōkoku*, like Keizan's *imaginaire*, is localized (assigned to a place), this place is in turn imagined and *textualized*. In his desire to capture the source of "spiritual" energy (Ch. *ling*) of the mountain, Keizan undertook to organize its miraculous topography, and to achieve this he made an inventory of ten especially sacred places: the

[18] The origin of the Daijōji spring is explained as follows in the *Nihon Tōjō rentōroku*: One day, when Gikai was the abbot of this monastery, a strange man, of kingly countenance, appeared and said: "I am the god of Hakusan, and I would like to receive the Precepts." After Gikai had ordained him, the god asked him if there was anything he desired. Gikai replied that the place was fine, but that water was somewhat wanting. The god agreed and left. The next day a spring gushed forth in the south, and it was named Hakusan spring. See *DNBZ* 110: 221a.

Crouching Monkey Range (in the southwest), the Cloud Gathering Peak (in the northeast), the Whirling Water Peak, the Grain Growing Plain, the Peak of the Magnificent Lotuses, the Hillock of Abundant Rice, the Valley Where the Dead Are Buried, the Enoki Tree on Which One Hangs Sandals, the Crow Stone Valley, and the Plain of the Shamaness.[19] The choice of these ten places is, if we are to believe Keizan, a simple pastime, but this game is not as innocent as he makes it appear. If the poems about them were not added to the *Record of Tōkoku* by Keizan's disciples but really are by him, one may see them as reflecting his desire to make the site of Yōkōji the equal of that of Eiheiji.[20]

But the *mirabilia* of the mountain are not always natural phenomena. Some are the product of human effort. Thus the construction of the Peak of the Five Elders (Gorōhō) shows clearly Keizan's desire to "humanize" the mountain, to divert sacredness from the cosmic toward the human. The borderline is not always clear, and it is significant that the Peak of the Five Elders should have with time become practically indetectable in the landscape that surrounds it. Had not the man Keizan himself been, in a previous life, the spirit of a tree? It is perhaps this ancient personality that explains, beyond his affinities with the northern region of Hakusan, his interest for the great *enoki* that marked the site of his future monastery. In the dream where he saw it for the first time, it is to this tree with "luxuriant branches" that monks came, in great numbers, to hang up their straw sandals—in other words, renounced their wanderings to settle down at Tōkoku with Keizan. This omen of prosperity explains why Keizan made this tree into one of the ten "sites," going so far as to call Tōkoku the "Peak of the Great Enoki": this tree is the dwelling place of the genius loci who appeared in Keizan's dream to offer him his protection—Keizan who once had himself been a tree-spirit. The *Record of Tōkoku* contains the following poem on this subject:

[19] *JDZ*, 402–4. The ten places are disposed all around Yōkōji, in protective fashion: the Crouching Monkey Range in the southwest, the Cloud Gathering Peak in the northeast, etc. There names are in some cases self-explanatory. The Grain Growing Plain, because of its fertility, is also called Peak of Inari. The Peak of the Magnificent Lotuses owes its name to a former temple, Shōrenji (Temple of Magnificent Lotuses). The "Valley Where the Dead Are Buried" is another name for Gorōhō, the Peak of the Five Elders. According to the commentary, it is located south of the temple, although from my recollection it seems to be in the north. The Crow Stone Valley, located at the foot of the western hill, protects the temple from evil influences, and it is the location of the Stūpa of the Jewel-Box Seal (Hōkyōintō). The "Plain of the Shamaness," judging from the commentary ("Formerly there was a shamaness, now it is a strangely shaped stone"), seems to be an allusion to the legend, found on many sacred mountains, of a shamaness (often called *bikuni*, "nun") who was changed into stone after challenging the deity of the mountain. See Faure 1994, 186–87.

[20] One also finds lists of ten sites at Eiheiji and at Sōjiji in Noto, but they seem to have been created after the model of Yōkōji.

The god of the tree, entering into my dream, protects the monastery gate.
The monastery at Tōkoku is truly venerable.
Wandering monks, as soon as they arrive here,
Take off their straw sandals and strengthen their spiritual root.

[*JDZ*, 403]

This tree is also an item on a second list of *mirabilia*, the "Five Wonders" (Ch. *ling*, J. *rei*) that marked the completion of Gorōhō. Among these Keizan includes the Mahāyāna sūtras that he had copied by hand, and the posthumous writings of the Five Elders buried under the memorial tumulus. The progression is unconsciously one from the natural to the human. Let us mention, among other *mirabilia* symbolizing the place, the grafted plum tree standing in front of Dentōin. This tree was said to go back to Dōgen, who, during his stay in China, had dreamed that he received a branch of plum tree from the Chan master Damei Fachang (752–839). The Zen teaching is here compared to the Chinese plum-tree branch that Dōgen was to graft onto a Japanese stock to make it bloom. The episode, described at length by Keizan in his *Denkōroku*,[21] is illustrated in Dōgen's biography, the *Kenzei ki*, under the title "Passing at the Mount of the Great Plum Tree,[22] Dōgen experiences a numinous dream": he is shown sitting in meditation facing the wall of his cell and receiving in a dream/vision from master Damei a blossoming branch of plum tree.[23] The plum tree thus links symbolically Yōkōji to Mt. Damei and to the Zen "branch" of the above-mentioned Chan patriarch.[24]

Keizan's position is inevitably ambiguous in the sense that he is, as he says himself, a "land-clearer," one whose activities upset the natural order. The taming of wild nature was accompanied by a certain symbolic and physical violence toward the ancient holders of the land. The forces of the invisible world are themselves fundamentally ambivalent, and it is their reaction, positive or negative, to the invader that in most cases decides whether they will be regarded as beneficent gods or evil spirits. The Chan tradition reports many cases of assaults by Buddhist monks, land-clearers, or thaumaturges, against the local spirits. We should note that the monks, however, unlike their Christian counterparts, did not "slay the dragon" but were satisfied to tame and convert this paradigmatic symbol of autochtony. However, even if Keizan's settling at Tōkoku was not entirely free of symbolic violence, he redeemed himself by his sincere

[21] *Denkōroku*, T. 82, 2585: 407a-b.

[22] Damei shan, a mountain in Zhejiang famous for its plum trees, is the toponym of Fachang, a disciple of Mazu Daoyi. On Damei and "plum ripening," see Sonja Arntzen, *Ikkyū and the Crazy Cloud Anthology* (Tokyo: University of Tokyo Press, 1986), 45.

[23] *Kenzei ki*, 77.

[24] Incidentally, Fachang was in the line of Nanyue Huairang, the precursor of Rinzai, not Sōtō Zen.

love for this place. At the end of his life, Keizan, an ecologist before the term had been coined, worried about the pine trees of Tōkoku:

> On the first day of the fifth month of the same year [1325], [I issued] a prohibition concerning pine trees, saying, "Ever since I came to live on this mountain [. . .] I have particularly enjoyed the presence of the pine trees. [. . .] This is why, except on festival days [. . .], not a single branch [of these trees] must be broken off. Whether they are high on the mountain or in the bottom of the valley, whether they are large or small, they must be strictly protected. Let all administrative officers, all monks, and all those who work in this monastery hold this as said, and let none transgress this prohibition. [*JDZ*, 432]

FIGURES OF AUTOCHTHONY

On the threshold of the *Record of Tōkoku*, just as on that of Buddhist monasteries, stand the protecting gods. They are either the properly native deities, gods of the soil, of the mountain, of the province, or of the country (Ichinomiya, Inari, Hachiman), or ancient Indian and Chinese autochtonous gods (Bishamon, Karaten, Shōhō Shichirō) that have been "promoted" to the rank of transnational "Protectors of the Dharma."

The importance of the local context is also marked by the essential role of lay benefactors in the existence of the monastery. We have seen that Yōkōji, while remaining a place of meditative practice, was also a temple of prayer for the repose of the souls of these benefactors and their ancestors. The patrons were above all the two families Sakai and Sakawa, the families of territorial officers united by marriage. The most important patrons, because they were the "authors of the original vow," or those who made the decision to give a part of their land to Keizan, are Unno Saburō Shigeno Nobunao and his wife, for whom we have only the religious name Mokufu Sonin. As we have already noted, this woman played an especially large role in Keizan's life. Shigeno Nobunao was a distant descendant of the Emperor Seiwa (reigned 850–880) and he was in turn ordained by Keizan in 1321, two years after his wife, under the religious name of Myōjō.[25]

Keizan gave these patrons a place of honor in the community, which relied on them for a great part of its upkeep. In an *okibumi* intended to ensure definitively for Yōkōji its status as the main center of reformed Sōtō, Keizan exhorts his successors to revere the descendants of his pa-

---

[25] However, Shigeno Nobunao's name is conspicuously absent in the rest of the *Tōkoku ki*, contrary to that of Sonin, who continues to make donations to Yōkōji even after she has become a nun. Judging from the fact that a number of her female relatives joined her at Tōkoku, it seems that Keizan's support came mainly from her branch, rather than from that of her husband.

trons. He goes even farther, establishing a sort of two-part contract between his successors and the heirs of Sonin.[26] By this expedient, as by the establishment of a memorial, the Peak of the Five Elders, he tried to anchor the Sōtō tradition to a particular place, whose primary pagan sacredness is now raised to Buddhist saintliness. The efforts made by Keizan to ensure after his own death a harmony between the monks and the patrons of Yōkōji doubtless grew out of the lesson he had learned from the decline of Eiheiji and the changes that had taken place at Daijōji. With their incessant internal disputes, the monks of Eiheiji had progressively alienated the sympathies of the heirs to Hatano Yoshishige, and the monastery was abandoned by its patrons and fell into ruin. At Daijōji, on the other hand, the patrons seem to have set up a superior who did not belong to the Sōtō sect. Clearly the protection a monastery enjoyed could be a double-edged sword, and the emphasis placed by Keizan on harmony between monks and patrons can be best understood in the context of feudal relationships. We may note in passing that it was thanks to the support of powerful lay patrons and their firm regional establishment that Sōtō monasteries, unlike those of other Buddhist sects, could avoid having to arm themselves and becoming hideouts for so-called "warrior monks" (sōhei), that class of monks whose arrogance, and final submission by Oda Nobunaga at the end of the sixteenth century, would call into question the fate of Japanese Buddhism.[27] Thus Eiheiji could prosper at first, in spite of the proximity of two armed monasteries, belonging respectively to the Shingon and Tendai schools. The first, located on the bank opposite Eiheiji, was eventually razed during the peasant revolts (ikki) of the sixteenth century, and nothing remains of it among the rice fields that replaced it. The second, Heisenji, located at the Southern entrance of Hakusan, did survive, but only a few remnants testify to its former splendor. Having lost the support of its benefactors, Eiheiji would doubtless have met the same fate if it had not received timely help from the rival branch led by Keizan's successors at Sōjiji.

The autochthony of the monastery's patrons makes them, for Keizan, symbols of the place, of the genius loci. Thus one of the expressions he uses for his benefactor Sonin, "the fundamental overlord of this mountain," sounds almost like a term for a tutelary god, and it is possible that Keizan saw in her, beyond a reincarnation of his own grandmother, an emanation of the tutelary deity of the place. It is significant that he uses a similar expression to refer to the god Inari. This may explain in part the

[26] See "Tōzan jinmiraisai okibumi," in *Record of Tōkoku, JDZ*, 419–20.

[27] This was true even of the Rinzai sect of Zen, if we are to believe edicts aimed at disarming the monks of Shōkokuji and other official monasteries of the "Five Mountains" (gozan) system. See Tsuji Zennosuke, *Nihon bukkyōshi*, vol. 6. Tokyo: Iwanami Shoten, 1960.

importance he gives to Sonin and, more generally, his obvious idealization of lay benefactors. In a document on the future organization of the monastery, he writes:

> The Buddha has said, "when one wins [to one's cause] ardent benefactors, the Buddha Dharma will not disappear." . . . [Our] reverence towards our benefactors should be like that towards the Buddha because it is thanks to them that morality, concentration, and wisdom are achieved. So my practice of the Buddha Dharma in this life came about thanks to the spirit of faith of these benefactors. As a result, in generations to come, we must consider the heirs of the author of the fundamental vow [Sonin] as great protectors, as the source of the benefits enjoyed by this monastery. Thus, master and benefactors will live in harmony, becoming as close as water and fish.[28]

THE PREACHING OF THE NONSENTIENT

Keizan and his first disciples, living a life of reclusion, removed from the world of human beings, may have had the feeling of living in the midst of an enchanted nature—a feeling akin to that described by Baudelaire in "Correspondences": "Nature is a temple where living pillars/ At times allow confused words to come forth. . . ." In this magical environment, where "perfumes, colors, and sounds answer one another," the possibility to reach awakening without resorting to human mediation, and therefore the temptation of eremitism, must have become stronger. Had not the Buddha himself reached awakening alone, without a master, "when he saw the morning star"? The question of the status of the *pratyekabuddha*, that is, the one who awakens "due to conditions," had assumed a new importance during the Kamakura period: Dainichi Nōnin, the founder of the Darumashū, a rival of Yōsai and Dōgen but a master acknowledged by Keizan, claimed indeed to have awakened "without a master." Dōgen himself, who denied any value to this kind of awakening, was ironically labeled a *pratyekabuddha* by some of his detractors. It is within this context that we must place the theme of the "preaching of the non-sentient" (*mujō seppō*), which appears in a dialogue between Keizan

---

[28] *Tōkokuzan Yōkōji jinmiraisai okibumi*, in *JDZ*, 487–88. To show the crucial character of this document, dated 1319, Keizan makes two copies of it, one of which will be preserved at Yōkōji, while the other will be transmitted in Sonin's family, thus constituting "the ulterior mutual proof between master and patrons." The document, signed by the "land-clearer" Keizan, is co-signed by Sonin. Another *okibumi*, of almost similar content, and also co-signed by Sonin, is dated from 1318. Some Japanese scholars have questioned the authenticity of these documents. Whatever the case may be, these *okibumi* give us precious information on the state of mind of the abbots of Yōkōji.

and his disciple Koan Shikan—and which is actually a prologue to one of Keizan's dreams, already quoted:

> On the twentieth of the twelfth month [of the year 1321], towards midnight, I was explaining to the *shuso* [Shi]kan the words of Jiashan to Luofu, "When there is no one in the whole empire whose tongue has not been cut out, how can one make men without tongues understand what words are?" Shikan then said, "Even pillars can speak to people. Even if one can hear the language of him who does not speak, if one does not know how to speak the unspoken, what then? Pillars and lanterns are constantly talking, but only he who is familiar with their voices can hear them. Ordinary beings cannot do it: their abilities are inadequate, and thus their comprehension of what is said proves deficient." I said, "It isn't that pillars and lanterns are unable to speak to men: today as in the past there are many people who, having heard their discourse, obtain awakening. When it is said that Lingyun achieved awakening by seeing peach blossoms, it means that he had heard the speech of the speechless. If one person can hear it, a thousand or ten thousand people can also hear it."
>
> Shikan then said, "Whether one relies on a master or achieves awakening by looking at peach blossoms, this is all a matter of awakening thanks to the intervention of external aid. Is there nothing that one can produce oneself, all alone?" I said, "It is not impossible to awaken all by oneself, without a master. Those who achieve awakening in this way do not cast any doubt on the awakening of those who have awakened with the help of others. Similarly, those who have achieved awakening thanks to outside agencies in the same way should not cast doubt on the awakening of those who have achieved awakening by themselves, without a master. [*JDZ*, 400]

The "preaching of the non-sentient" is the theory according to which nature, once it is entirely Buddhist, is capable of preaching the Law to anyone who knows how to understand it. It had already played a significant role in the Sōtō tradition, most notably with Dongshan Liangjie (807–869), whose awakening verse became famous: "Strange, how strange!/ Inconceivable is the preaching of the Law by the non-sentient./ It cannot be perceived when the ears listen;/ Only when the eyes listen can it be known."[29] In his *Shōbōgenzō*, Dōgen rises up against those who, like Nōnin and his disciples, misunderstood this exemplum.[30] We also see in Shingon Buddhism, and especially in Kūkai, the related idea of the "preaching of the Dharma body" (*hosshin seppō*) of the cosmic Buddha Dainichi.

---

[29] This brings to mind Paul Claudel's expression, "L'oeil écoute."
[30] See *Shōbōgenzō*, "Keisei sanshoku," in *T.* 82, 2582: 39a.

Paradoxically, the Zen sacralizing of nature implies a demythologizing. Should one speak here of nature as miraculous or as demythologized? Or perhaps both at once? There is a fusion of nature and tradition: the universe, all of nature, is the voice of the cosmic Buddha.[31] As Dōgen says in the chapter "Sansuikyō" in the *Shōbōgenzō*, "Mountains and rivers are the realization of the Way [or words] of the ancient Buddhas."[32] From this evolves the possibility (not for Dōgen, but for the Darumashū and Keizan) of an awakening without a master, or at least without a human master. Still, Keizan, in order to remain true to Dōgen, insists on the importance of face-to-face transmission and, in the *Denkōroku*, he criticizes severely the *pratyekabuddha*, those who have awakened by themselves and who thereby interrupt the tradition.[33] For him the nonsentient in question should not be interpreted as the external world, "the walls, the pebbles, the lamps, and the pillars." It involves the nondualistic state of mind toward which the practitioner should move, a "nonsentient" awareness in the sense that, although perfectly lucid, it is stripped of all sentiment, all attachment, all discrimination.[34]

THE MONASTIC UTOPIA

The monastery, a total representation of the cosmos and the human microcosm, becomes by extension the sacred, ritual area to which descends the sacred, the divine. As an oriented building, facing south and not east, it makes up a kind of architectural circumambulation around the Buddha hall (itself set up so as to permit circumambulation around the statues of Śākyamuni and his acolytes). Its design thus reflects the internal dynamic of practice, but it is also definitely symbolic: by its division into four directions, a squaring of the circle is achieved. The master sits in *dhyāna* on a high chair, looking north, facing the Buddha: Buddha looks at Buddha, in a mirror effect. On each side, to the east and the west, the monks take their place in a highly hierarchized space.

A closed space, an enclave of the cosmos within the surrounding chaos, the monastery is also conceived of as a body (both temporal and spiritual) with the Buddha hall forming the head. The closure of monastic architecture reflects the Chan/Zen ideal of autarchy. It is also a living

---

[31] In his criticism of Zen meditation, a meditation that aims at erasing all thought content instead of producing visions, Kyōjō (1189–1268) attempts to rehabilitate images on the ground that the world itself is the "teaching of the nonsentient." Quoted in Girard 1990a: xxxvii.

[32] *T.* 82, 2582: 62c.

[33] *Denkōroku*, *T.* 82, 2585: 362a.

[34] Ibid.: 389b-c.

organism, a utopia, a microcosm sufficient unto itself. After the Tang we see the growth of a cosmic and human symbolism of the monastery, a symbolism that identifies each of the monastic buildings with a different part of the practitioner's body.[35] The monastery is actually an architectural body. It is finally a point of anchoring, fixing chthonic forces. This involves as much the harnessing of the source of power as an attempt to eradicate dangerous influences. To be noted first of all in this respect is the important role of the Buddha hall, manifesting in all his glory the presence of Śākyamuni, conqueror of local deities in Buddhist legend.

Fixing chthonic forces was also achieved by building stūpas or funeral mounds like Gorōhō (and later the "Stūpa of the Jewel-Box Seal," Hōkyōintō). Gorōhō, this "Peak of the Five Elders" built by Keizan, is also a "mesocosm," an oriented stūpa to which we may apply the analysis given by Paul Mus of the cosmology of the stūpa in his monumental study of Borobuḍur. Mus stresses that "the monument [stūpa] forms a middle term between the universal Law and the country: it is a mesocosm."[36] In spite of the difference of scale between Borobuḍur and Gorōhō, we have in both cases a "tomb-sanctuary," whose "funerary value and cosmological value are two simultaneous aspects of a single religious representation."[37]

Chan/Zen monasteries defined a new domain, a utopian space that, unlike the heterotopias of the local cults, was a non-place: a cultic center, of course, but one that refocuses or shifts the ancient spatial setting; a concrete place that, despite its ideal of self-reliance, depends on lay society for its subsistence but still claims to "represent the entire cosmos, including society."[38] Depending in principle on another order of reality, that of emptiness, it constituted a negation of the dense and pluralistic space of local religion.

The oneirical monastery described by Keizan serves as a preliminary

---

[35] This symbolism appears in many *kirigami*. See Ishikawa (1983–94) (5): 96–98. In the so-called "Seven halls monastery" (*shichidō garan*), the Dharma hall corresponds to the head, the Buddha hall to the torso, the refectory to the left arm, the bathhouse to the left leg, the main gate (*sanmon*) to the sexual organ, the latrines to the right leg, and the monk's hall to the right arm. The sequence is that of a circumambulation (*pradakṣinā*), and all the buildings are connected by a corridor. The *sanmon* ("mountain gate" or "triple gate") corresponds to the "three points" of the Sanskrit letter *i* or of the Chinese character "mind," that is, to the "three deliverances," and to the three cosmic levels (heaven, human, earth). It is the gate "through which all Buddhas and sentient beings enter and leave. This is why, when you circumambulate the seven halls, you worship this gate as a symbol of Maitreya's descent into this world to save sentient beings." See *Sanmon no kirigami*, in ibid. (7): 253; see also Collcutt 1981: 184–89.

[36] See Mus 1990: 253.

[37] Ibid.: 213.

[38] See Boon 1982: 202.

sign and model of the actual monastery. The special quality of Yōkōji lies not only in its layout in seven main buildings, but in the addition of two buildings (which actually form a whole), Gorōhō and Dentōin. Their construction would truly crown that of Yōkōji and give the monastery its real symbolic value. It would become, in Keizan's eyes, the guardian of his reliquary and thus the center of his posthumous cult as the founder (or reformer) of Sōtō. We have already looked at the instructions left by Keizan on this subject. It was in order to establish the institutional primacy of Yōkōji that Keizan tried to put into place a system of rotation of the position of abbot, a system that would become the norm in Sōtō monasteries. But the spiritual primacy of this monastery rested on the presence of the relics of the Five Elders in Gorōhō, and it was in order to confirm the supremacy of this reliquary over all other considerations that Keizan did not hesitate to break the rules of geomancy, which said that he should not erect the building at a level higher than that of the Dharma hall. The soundness of his enterprise would be revealed when, during work on Gorōhō, a "miraculous spring" suddenly spurted forth.

Dentōin is located behind the Dharma hall, halfway up the hill, between the latter and Gorōhō. It is reached via a stone stairway that leaves from the top of the left wing of the circular corridor. It is, properly speaking, a "founder's hall," and the same kind of building is found at Sōjiji in Noto, and in most Sōtō monasteries. But unlike the Dentōin at Sōjiji, where only Keizan is the object of a cult, the Dentōin at Yōkōji contains the statues and funerary tablets of the Five Elders (Rujing, Dōgen, Ejō, Gikai, and Keizan) as well as those of the main disciples, both monks and laymen, of Keizan. In addition this Founder's hall has the distinction of having been built by the founder himself. Its functional identity with Gorōhō is shown by the horizontal inscription on the facade, where the name of Gorōhō is carved.

Behind Dentōin is a "Hakusan spring," also found in all Sōtō monasteries, beginning with Eiheiji. Halfway up the stair that leads from Dentōin to Gorōhō, on the left, an esplanade holds the tomb of Keizan, surrounded by those of his successors. Later a stūpa said to be "for the benefit of all beings" (rishōtō) was built as an adjunct to the east of Gorōhō, perhaps correcting by its universal nature the slightly too sectarian and local nature of Gorōhō.[39] At the same time, while it raised the prestige of Yōkōji on the provincial level, it contributed to the recognition that this monastery had, during the fifteenth century, lost the unique

[39] These stūpas were erected throughout Japan after 1338 at the request of the Rinzai master Musō Soseki, together with official temples (Ankokuji), to console the spirits of warriors who had died in the dynastic troubles since the Genkō area (1331–33). After the death of the Shōgun Takauji, however, they lost political significance and were superseded by the Gozan system. See Akamatsu and Yampolsky 1977: 314–15.

place at the center of the monastic network that Keizan had given it. This stūpa, a symbol of the homogeneity of space and of an evenly distributed sacredness, was going to supplant Gorōhō, symbol of a qualitative, hierarchized space centered on the relics of Keizan. Still, Gorōhō survives today, even if covered by vegetation, while all that remains of the stūpa is its base. Gorōhō was popularly called "Mount Tiantong" (Tendōzan), from the name of the place where Dōgen received instruction from the Chinese master Rujing, the first of the Five Elders selected by Keizan. According to a well-established tradition, on the seventeenth of the seventh lunar month, the anniversary of the death of Rujing, monks from Eiheiji, Daijōji, and Sōjiji came to Yōkōji to make an offering of tea.[40]

Keizan's "unlocalized" discourse, as it unfolds in the *Denkōroku* and in some grafted sections of the *Record of Tōkoku*, was permitted by his anchoring in a specific site.[41] Or perhaps it is the other way around: after a long—discursive and meditative—practice of "emptiness," Keizan came to feel a need to settle down; Tōkoku offered itself to him as the place where he could at last hang his straw sandals and rest until the end, a place where his relics themselves would remain. For all his talk about emptiness, in his mind he still needed a place to be, even after death: hence the importance he attached to Gorōhō. We may see his attempt to anchor himself at Tōkoku as a reaction to his earlier peregrinations as a wandering monk (*unsui*), drifting like "clouds and water," like the unlocalized truth of Zen. This anchoring, this unacknowledged "localization," is what constrains and at the same time permits the bird's-eye vision, the "homelessness," of his Zen teaching. Keizan was able to live in a "China of the mind" because he also had a Japan of the "mind and body" to live in. Only in that condition was he able to "cast off mind and body."

[40] See Azuma 1974: 208.
[41] On that question see Eckel 1992.

Chapter Eight

THE RITUAL BODY

O N THE THRESHOLD between the inside and the outside, at the point of encounter between the real and the imaginary, we find the body—the biological body, but also the ritual body. This body has given rise in Buddhism to multiple and contradictory discourses. Keizan was heir to the traditional Buddhist idea that despised the body as a bag of excrement. At first glance his thinking belongs to Sōtō Zen idealism, which since Dōgen advocated "casting off body and mind" (*shinjin datsuraku*). Although "sudden" Chan is defined by the immediacy of awakening, this immediacy turns out to be mediate.[1] Is not the body precisely this "immediate mediation" that all idealisms vainly attempt to deny?

In the section of the *Denkōroku* dealing with the third Chan patriarch, Sengcan, Keizan tells the following story:

> The illness that afflicted [Sengcan] at the time of his first meeting [with the Chan master Huike] was leprosy. But after the meeting, this karmic illness disappeared. There is nothing strange about this: understanding that the nature of his offences was intangible, he realized that the mind and the dharmas are fundamentally pure. [. . .] Thus, the four great elements and the five aggregates do not exist, and we are fundamentally free from our skin, flesh, bones and marrow. This is why his illness disappeared and his innate mind manifested itself.[2]

We find in the whole Chan tradition a tension between these two tendencies, which one could term the *spiritualist* and the *somatic*. The school of the mind turns out to be at least as much a school of the body, and the body-mind nonduality put forward by Dōgen leads in fact to a reappreciation of the body as the "silent sentinel" without which spiritual awaking could not "take place." The eponymous activity of Chan/Zen, seated meditation, is after all primarily a physical technique. We cannot begin to understand the importance of ritual in Chan unless we take into account the essential role of the body in this school, which largely defines itself as a community of gesture. But to the extent that this community saw itself as an elite corps, the body whose reality it recognized remained a perfect body, a citadel from which sex and desire were

[1] See Faure 1991.
[2] *Denkōroku*, T. 82, 2585: 379a-b.

firmly banished. Moreover, it is through Zen that a new concern for the body emerged in medieval Japan—a trend that was to have a great influence on Japanese everyday life: vegetarian cooking; the introduction of tea, whose virtues as nourishment of body and mind are praised by Yōsai; development of the bath in monasteries; etc.

Total neglect of the body, characteristic of "Chan madmen" living among the animals or the dregs of society, also showed up in this "corporeal" register: a well-known case is that of the Northern Chan adept surnamed Lazy Can or Leftover Can, who used to sleep with the cattle and ate the leftovers of the monastery, and whose physical carelessness is emphasized by Chan chronicles. But while Chan "dialogues" assigned great value to spontaneity, harshness, wild clinches, various gesticulations, they were already becoming part of a carefully orchestrated ritual and survive as exceptions that prove the monastic "Rule."

In order to see a little more clearly among this profusion of discourses and techniques aimed at controlling or liberating the Buddhist body, and at the risk of oversimplifying, a rapid survey might be useful. There is first of all a realization of the ephemeral nature of the body, a realization that led to one of the Four Noble Truths (impermanence, Skt. *anitya*) expressed by the Buddha. From this follows the predication of the emptiness of the body. However, as the body becomes more diaphanous, its corporeality becomes less problematic. It is no longer seen as a real obstacle, but rather as an error of perspective, one that can be easily corrected by the Mahāyāna teaching.

These first two positions, unlike the following, imply a discontinuity, a mind/body dualism. Whereas the body disappears at death, the mind is often perceived—particularly in Chinese Buddhism—as an imperishable entity that transmigrates from one body to another, from one life to the next. The position specific to Chan/Zen, that body and mind are one, arises in reaction to that theory. With the notion of a symbolic body, a microcosm connected to the macrocosm, Buddhism remains, however, indebted to Chinese cosmology. This notion paves the ground for a progressive ritualization of the body in Sino-Japanese Buddhism. With the conception, whose importance becomes always greater, of a ritual body, a return to dualism is initiated. In a first phase, the body is revalorized as an instrument of ritual and of awakening: one goes from the divided body to the synesthetic body, in which all senses are fused—as in the case of Dongshan Liangjie's awakening.[3] In a second phase, the body is ritualized, produced by the ritual. This ritualization bridges the gap between reality (the perishable body) and the ideal (the perfect body of the Buddha, which could be reached only after many rebirths). One can now

---

[3] See above, chap. 7: 193.

"become a Buddha in this very body," because the body of the practitioner is ontologically and/or ritually double.

THE PERFECT BODY

The adept is supposed to direct all his aspirations toward the body of the Buddha, the Dharma body "born of innumerable good deeds."[4] This is the body to be reproduced, not only in the formal sense of an imitation of the meditative posture but in an interior rebirth. From the very first Mahāyāna sūtras, it has been the object of precise descriptions. It would be necessary to study the underlying symbolism of the thirty-two primary marks (Skt. *lakṣaṇa*) and the eighty secondary marks of the imaginary body of the Buddha. With all its markings, the body of the Buddha is a semiotic body, a sort of *maṇḍala* incarnating Buddhist doctrine. This nature is especially evident in the traditional representation of the soles of the Buddha's feet. While the Buddha's body, concealed or annihilated in Nirvāṇa, is no longer accessible except through iconic representations, we can still gaze on his footprints.[5] According to tradition he left his footprints in many places, not only on the ground of India, where he lived, but also in China, Korea, and Japan. These reveal symbolic motifs that marked the soles of his feet. Among these motifs the main ones are those of the Wheel of the Law and the swastika, but they include other, less "orthodox" symbols, some of them from Hindu astrology—like the double fish, the elephant tusk, the arm of Indra, the topknot of Brahma, or Viṣṇu's shell. The Buddha's feet, like all of his visible body, seem to have made up a "religious program," an illustration and mnemonic summary of Buddhist doctrine,[6] a physical "Dharma body," the counterpart of the metaphysical Dharma body, a kind of "table of the Law" or "memory place" (*lieu de mémoire*) in which was registered the Buddhist (and Hindu) *imaginaire*.[7]

One of the bodily signs, the "cranial protuberance" of the Buddha (Sanskrit *uṣṇīṣa*, Japanese *chōsō*, a term that, when read *chinsō*, came to mean the portrait of a Chan master), is especially paradoxical because it is held to be invisible. It constitutes a kind of vanishing point that, as it symbolizes that which cannot be symbolized, justifies the symbolic and sets into motion the entire semiotic system. As Mujaku Dōchū has pointed out, "The marks of the patriarchs are fundamentally 'without marks' [formless]. This is like the cranial protuberance [*chinsō*] of the

---

[4] See Lamotte 1962: 140.

[5] See Falk 1977.

[6] Admittedly, the tendency to hypostasize a Dharma body may have been a relatively late, Chinese and Japanese phenomenon. On this question see Harrison 1992.

[7] See "Bussokuseki," in *Hōbōgirin*, vols. 2 and 3, 187–90.

Tathāgata, which one cannot see. This is why [their portraits] are called *chinsō*."[8] Another mark considered invisible, because it cannot be represented visually as such, is the "Brahma voice," which is symbolized in the Nichiren sect by the name of the *Lotus Sūtra*. It is to give this final, phonic touch that the animation of a Buddhist icon (the "installation of the breaths" and at the same time the opening of the eyes) is done by means of the word, through the recitation of a *mantra*.

VERSATILE BODY

In contrast with this ideal body, how is the body of the ordinary practitioner defined? Various concepts seem to have been current. The most obvious, derived from Mahāyāna dogma, is that the body is illusory. This is the idea transmitted through the *Heart Sūtra* (Skt. *Hṛdaya-sūtra*, Japanese *Hannya shingyō*): not only is the empirical, corporeal self empty, but also the psychosomatic "series" or "aggregates" that make it up. Another locus classicus, *The Teaching of Vimalakīrti* [*Vimalakīrti-nirdeśa*], quotes a list of ten metaphors often associated with the body (foam or bubble, mirage, hollow banana-tree trunk, machine, magical illusion, dream reflection, echo, cloud, lightning.[9] Thus even when the body is conceded to exist minimally, it is considered under a very negative light. It is ephemeral, condemned to break down into its constituent parts; it makes us fall into illusion, succumb to the temptation of the senses, and ties us to *saṃsāra*, the eternal carousel of karmic retribution. This is why we should not hesitate to mortify it in order to achieve authentic ascesis. Of course, we must take rhetoric into account when Dōgen, for instance, encourages practitioners to "crush their bones and squeeze the marrow," but these formulas nevertheless reflect a fundamental contempt toward the body—an attitude that contradicts isolated passages where Dōgen seems to hold the body in high esteem.

THE NONDUAL BODY-MIND

In contrast to the qualitative, highly differentiated space of traditional Chinese thought, Mahāyāna put forward a conception of a homogeneous and empty space, a concept symbolized among others by the universality of the Bodhisattva Kokūzō (Ākāśagarbha, the one "who has space as a womb"). This perception of external space also applied to the interior

---

[8] *Zenrin shōkisen*, 163b.
[9] See Lamotte 1962: 132–38.

space of the body. Early Chan practice, as it is explained for example by Daoxin (580–651), consisted in realizing the emptiness of the body.

For Dōgen, for example, while awakening consisted of transcending body and mind, it remains understood that the body is an indispensable instrument in achieving awakening, since without the body, no practice could take place: "practice and realization are one" (*shūsshō ittō*). Already for some Indian Buddhist thinkers, the body had become the necessary organ for establishing contact with the absolute. However, parallel to that conception, and in reaction against it, another one emerges slowly, according to which the body makes up with the mind an indissociable whole.

We also see a rehabilitation of the body in Sōtō thanks to Dōgen's redefinition of seated meditation as *shikan taza*, "sitting only," a form of meditation allegedly stripped of all mental constructs. Dōgen himself, although hardly to be suspected of sympathies toward pleasures of the flesh (in spite of a certain sensuality that reveals itself in his portrait), put things this way: "Those who reject the body reject the Buddha."[10] However, Dōgen's statement is essentially strategic, aimed at condemning the "Senika heresy," that is, the trend represented by Dainichi Nōnin and the Darumashū. According to this trend, the Chan motto "This very mind is the Buddha" meant that the mind or Buddha nature is an indestructible entity that leaves the body at the time of death. In his *Shōbōgenzō*, Dōgen repeatedly attacks this interpretation, which he considers to be heretic.[11] Not to be left behind, Keizan, paraphrasing the formula, declares in the *Denkōroku* that "this very body is the Buddha."[12] Then, in a surge of Buddhist hylomorphism, he goes on: "The body and the mind, how can they be distinguished from each other?" Likewise, in the *Denkōroku* chapter consecrated to the patriarch Saṅghānandi, he writes: "The practice of Zen is in its essence the casting off of body and mind. What do you call body, what do you call mind?"[13] In another chapter consecrated to the patriarch Basiasita, the motivation of the previous remarks becomes clear: "At this point we should not say that 'The hundred bones may scatter, but there is one thing that remains composed: it is the eternal spirit.' What sort of thing would this eternal spirit be? . . . Therefore we must say that before and after are not two, past and present are not different. Thus this should not be called body, nor should it be called mind. If we do not distinguish mind and body, we should not distinguish

---

[10] See *Shōbōgenzō*, "Shōji," in *T.* 82, 2582: 305
[11] See for instance "Sokushin zebutsu," *T.* 82, 2582: 28b-29c; "Bendōwa," ibid., 19b; and Faure 1987a.
[12] *Denkōroku, T.* 82, 2585: 385b.
[13] Ibid., 364.

past and present. Therefore it is *thus*."[14] However, this psychosomatic unity, far from bringing life back to its corporeal reality, and consequently to the fatality of death, lifts human existence to a higher level of reality. In this sense it is still a form of idealism, in which corporeal reality is eluded.

THE BODY AS MICROCOSM

Another conception shows up in the traditional cosmological systems of India and China: there the body is seen as a microcosm through which one can come to understand the macrocosm and finally come to realize the principle underlying these two aspects of the universe. This conception, characteristic in Japan of the "Way of Yin and Yang" (*onmyōdō*), is also echoed by Yōsai. In his *Shutten taikō*, Yōsai inscribes the human body in a taxonomic schema that attempts to reconcile Buddhist cosmology and Chinese "correlative thinking." It is a quinary system of correspondances attributed to the Bodhisattva Nāgārjuna, which associates the five periods of the year (four seasons and an intercalary month, "center" of the year), the five Agents (wood, fire, metal, water, earth), the five phases of Buddhist practice (thought of awakening, cultivation, awakening, Nirvāṇa, and the "fusion of the four virtues"), the five Buddhas[15] and Bodhisattvas,[16] finally the five "wisdoms" of Buddhist esotericism[17] and the five sections of the Shingon *maṇḍala*.[18] Note in passing that this schema connects in a hierarchical fashion the two levels of conventional truth (Chinese cosmology) and ultimate truth (esoteric Buddhist cosmology). In a short treatise on the virtues of tea, the *Kissa yōjōki*, Yōsai returns to this schema and develops it. He adds the five corporeal organs, the five colors, the five tastes, the five types of mental activities, the five senses, the five "seals" (*mudrā*), and the five mystic formulas (*bīja*).[19] Likewise, in a Tendai ritual performed in 1198, Yōsai identified the Sanskrit letters of mantras with various parts of the body, a body he perceived as a stūpa or a cosmic system ruled by

[14] Ibid., 373c.

[15] These Buddhas are Ashuku (Amitāyus), Hōshō (Ratnasambhava), Amida (Amitābha), Shaka (Śākyamuni), and Dainichi (Vairocana).

[16] The five Bodhisattvas are Fugen (Samantabhadra), Kokūzō (Ākāśagarbha), Monju (Mañjuśrī), Kannon (Avalokiteśvara), and Miroku (Maitreya).

[17] The five wisdoms are: 1. wisdom of the intrinsic nature of the Dharma-realm; 2. wisdom of the great round mirror; 3. wisdom of the equal nature of all things; 4. wisdom of the profound insight; 5. wisdom productive of acts.

[18] The five sections are the following: Vajra, Jewel, Lotus, Karma, and Buddha.

[19] See Taga Munehaya, *Eisai* (Tokyo: Yoshikawa Kōbundō, 1965): 54–55 and 179.

the Five Agents of Chinese cosmology, and equivalent to the Five Wisdoms of esoteric Buddhism.[20]

RITUALIZATION OF THE BODY

The ritual, as it developed, would give to the body a consistency, a denseness, and a soteriological role that the idealist thinkers of the so-called school of the mind (Ch. *xinzong*) had a tendency to forget. It would also bring dualism back to the forefront: but it is no longer so much a body/mind dualism as a duality of bodies. Indeed, Buddhist funeral rituals imply the idea of a double body—one that is both mortal and immortal, individual and social. The ritual aims precisely at transmuting the former into the latter, or in some cases at transferring a vital principle from the former to the latter.

The body is essential to the two forms of ritual immortality: meditation and the funeral rite. In both cases there is a metamorphosis of the body, to obtain a kind of physical transmutation—whence the symbolic value of certain body parts that reveal this metamorphosis. We know the importance of the bones in the Daoist imagination: it is by their jointed, golden bones that we can recognize the Immortals, and this sign is sometimes also found in Chan "sublime corpses." But as we have seen, Sino-Japanese Buddhism has retained another feature: the production of *śarīra*, relics that result from the impregnation of the body by morality, concentration, and wisdom. Thus, despite its denial in principle, Buddhism also dreamed of a corporeal immortality.

Chan practice in a way involves first a body lost, and then a body recovered. The body that must be lost or transcended, even if it is necessary to mutilate or burn it, is the ordinary body, the common "bag of skin" or of "excrement," as is repeated ad nauseam by the master in collective meditation sessions that try first of all to overcome the physical pain caused by an extended sitting position. The body that one tries to rediscover at the end of these mortifications of the flesh is a glorious body, the body of a Buddha. This explains the hieratic position of seated meditation, one that is completely under control. Immobility, perfect sitting, interior distance: the practitioner adopts a posture that symbolizes and anticipates mastery. All the monk's acts and gestures are modeled on the idea of the four "majestic attitudes" of the Buddha. We see in Buddhism the same "ideological primacy of immobility" that Jean-Claude Schmitt has found in medieval Christianity:

[20] See *Mikkyō daijiten* (Tokyo: Naigai Shuppansha, 1931–33): 722–23.

In Christian ideology, the suspicions surrounding movement are related to those directed at the body, strengthening the a priori negative opinion about gestures. This has to be considered in order to reach a proper understanding of medieval rituals in which the adoption of immobility, hieratism, the "showing" of bodies and ritual objects, the slow, solemn processions are attributes of power and indications of the sacred. . . . More generally, the Middle Ages appreciated that part of gesture that derives from posture rather than from movement.[21]

The body of the practitioner is, or rather tries to be, a closed body, without "outflows" (a metaphorical reference to the passions). Significant in this respect is the story of the monk Wulou ("Without Outflows"), whose hagiography interprets his name literally and claims that he never urinated.[22] The metaphor of outflow-passion, as it was handled in "spiritual" Chan/Zen, draws our attention to the "truly" physical outflows, excrement. What the tradition does not like to mention—what might be termed its "soft underbelly"—appears to be expressed in its excremental imagery. Excrement, absent from Buddhist orthodoxy, makes its return in Chan discourse. This already appears in the ironic question addressed by a monk to his co-disciple who was explaining to him that the entire universe is the Buddha's Dharma body: "If that is the case, where can we find a place to shit?"[23] And Linji sets up against the Chan metaphysical ideal that of the "man with nothing to do" who is satisfied simply to "shit and piss" when he needs to. This is exactly what was done by the Tendai monk Zōga, a character who recalls the Chan "madmen." When he was called to court to tonsure a noble lady, he pretended to be overcome by bowel problems and defecated in public, so evading this religious drudgery.[24] The economic importance of human excrement as fertilizer in the horticulture of Zen monasteries and its ambivalence (execrable/precious) perhaps explain its "uncanniness" (or even familiarity) in Chan/Zen discourse and its ability, truly *unheimlich* as a "return of the repressed," to serve as a metaphor for the transcendent unity of opposites, a necessary feature of every religious experience worthy of the name. We see from then on a paradoxical valorization of the grotesque body: Budai, with his obese body; Ji the Madman (Jidian, *alias* Jigong), who "makes his excrement sacrament"; and the Arhats, whose weird faces and exaggerated postures betray their nature and marvelous powers. It is at the same time, at least with Linji and a few

[21] Schmitt 1990: 29.
[22] See *Song gaoseng zhuan, T.* 50, 2061: 845c.
[23] See *Chanlin sengbao zhuan,* in ZZ 137: 71.
[24] See Mills 1970: 362–63.

others, a return to the concrete, an attempt to go beyond (through an apparent return on this side that should not deceive us) the tendency to abstraction and idealism that periodically threatens to invade Chan (and Linji himself is not free from it). In this return to the concrete, which expresses actually the absolute nature of phenomenal reality, the body looms large, even if it is not yet a "body of glory." As Linji puts it, "Just be ordinary—put on your robes, eat your food, and pass the time doing nothing."[25]

Apart from meditation, the transmutation of the body can equally be achieved by other rituals such as partial or total immolation, cremation, mummification, and funery rituals in general. As noted earlier, what matters in relics is the creation of an immortal ritual body: a disseminated, open body in contrast to the apparently tightly closed-up body of the meditator. But this contrast should not conceal the fact that, in both cases, the goal is to obtain, or to rediscover under the dross of gross sensation, an "adamantine body."

The vogue of self-immolations through fire has been well studied in the Indian and Chinese contexts. For Japanese examples of self-immolation, we can look at the case of a monk named Ōshō who, imitating the Bodhisattva of the Lotus Sūtra, burned himself on a pyre near the Nachi waterfall after having followed a diet of abstaining from cereals. At the moment he set fire to the pyre, in the presence of many spectators, he turned to the west and left his body to religion, with these words:

> I give my heart to the *Sūtra of the Lotus of the Profound Law*, the top of my skull to all the Buddhas of the upper regions, my legs to all the Buddhas of the lower regions, my back to all the Buddhas of the east, my chest to all the Buddhas of the west, my two arms to all the Buddhas of the south, my five viscera to the Tathāgatas of the five wisdoms, my six receptacles to all the beings of the six ways. Having thus directed these roots of good towards the supreme path, may I obtain quickly my awakening![26]

As we can see, this orientation/dedication of his body transforms it into a body of glory, a perfect microcosm; it turns him, on the spot, into a cosmic Buddha. This case seems to be the first in Japan.[27] Other cases are recorded in the *Genkō shakusho* of Kokan Shiren, a contemporary of Keizan, and in the *Honchō kōsōden* of Shiban (1626–1710), a monk from Myōshinji. According to Shiban, these fiery self-immolations are

25 See Sasaki 1975: 26.
26 *Genkō Shakusho*, DNBZ 62 470: 134a; Dykstra 1983: 38–39.
27 This is what Yamaori Tetsuo calls *kajō zanmai*, "fire samādhi." See Yamaori 1973: 287.

completely different from a simple suicide; Kokan Shiren also classes them under the rubric *ningyō* ("practice of perseverance"). The burning of a living body is seen as analogous to the cremation of a corpse. In each case we have a purification by fire, which separates the perishable from the imperishable elements and results in the production of an incorruptible body, a Buddha body. In the same fashion, the ascesis of a practitioner who wishes to become a "Buddha in this body," or to put it differently a mummy, corresponds to a purification by desiccation.

Less dramatic, although it expresses the same logic of transsubstantiation, is the practice that consists in copying Scriptures in one's own blood. We may remember that, among the relics placed by Keizan in the funerary mound of Gorohō was a text that his master Gikai had copied in his own blood. This practice could doubtless be explained not only as an extreme act of devotion but also as a tentative attempt to become, by a sort of "blood transfusion," a Buddha and to create for oneself a scriptural immortal body. It is also an offering, prescribed in scriptures like the *Brahma Net Sūtra* (*Fanwang jing*). The forty-fourth rule of this treatise on Mahāyāna Precepts, relative to "offerings to sūtras," says: "With a constant mind, a son of the Buddha must always receive, keep, read and recite the sūtras and the vinaya of the Greater Vehicle. He must [be ready to] copy the Precepts of the Buddha by peeling off his skin to use it as paper, shedding his blood to use it as ink, extracting his marrow to use as liquid in the ink stone, splitting his bones to use as brushes."[28] As we can see, the metaphors of this "sūtra," whose references to Chinese calligraphy attest to its apocryphal nature, were sometimes taken literally. In China as in Japan, the custom of copying scriptures in this way became relatively widespread. During the Edo period, the monks of the Zen sect Ōbaku—a sect recently introduced from China, and one that clung to its Chinese character—were known for copying scriptures in their own blood.

Unlike the body "without outflows," closed in on itself in a majestic immobility, ritual carries the idea that the body of a Chan/Zen master is double, even plural, in that it breaks out of its own bounds to disseminate itself in other bodies or objects (relics etc.). As has been noted in the case of funeral rites, Chan masters, being as a result of their awakening "twice born," are also "mixed" individuals whose dual nature is revealed through a double body, or rather, whose bodies embody a "double truth." In the Kyoto National Museum, there is a magnificent wooden statue representing Baozhi (418–514), a wonder-working monk who was

---

[28] See *Fanwang jing*, T. 24; J.J.M. de Groot, *Le Code du Mahāyāna en Chine* (Amsterdam: J. Müller, 1893).

presumably contemporaneous with Bodhidharma. The sculptor has shown Baozhi's double nature by showing his face opening up, like an overripe fruit, to reveal another face, that of the Bodhisattva Dizang (J. Jizō), whose incarnation was claimed to be Baozhi.

This ideological conception dominates funerary rituals where everything is done to change from the single to the double, from the physical body to the "double body" of the Chan master. But this conception is undermined by the awareness that death inevitably returns the double to the single, to a simple body, or rather the "single body" of someone who remains "human, too human."

We noted earlier Keizan's criticism of those who advocated the superiority of mind over body. Perhaps these statements by Keizan reveal not only the influence of Buddhist esotericism but also that of the cult of relics. The significance of relics and funeral rites should be examined in the light of Buddhist embryology. Cremation and the ritual of double burial in general were clearly equivalent to a second birth (or perhaps even a third one, according to the Indian tradition, reported by Sylvain Lévi, which sees the Brahmanic ritual as a first rebirth).[29] There is a *kirigami* attributed to Keizan that explains the embryological ideas of the time. Even if, as is probable, it does not really go back to Keizan, we may suppose that the concepts in it were already widespread by his time and that he would not have rejected them. Without much fear of anachronism, we can file them under the Japanese medieval *imaginaire*. In vocabulary borrowed from Tantrism, this document expresses the Chinese belief that the decaying flesh is female and the bones male: "Human seed is formed by the union of two fluids, that of the father and that of the mother. The seed of the father is white and produces the bones [. . . .] The seed of the mother is red and produces the flesh."[30]

This notion of two kinds of seed, white and red, which appears in Dōgen's *Gakudō yōjinshū* and Keizan's *Denkōroku*, seems to have been current at the time.[31] Thus cremation, producing as it does the quintessential bones, may be interpreted as a reincorporation into the "patriarchal," i.e., male, lineage. The case of "flesh bodies" (Buddhist mummies) seems at first sight more ambiguous, but the flesh in question, transformed into incorruptible *śarīra*, may also be considered as male.[32] As Jonathan Parry has noticed, it is quite natural for beliefs and practices surrounding cremation to be impregnated with the symbolism of embryology. The theme of death as a parturition, studied by Parry in an Indian

[29] See Lévi 1966.

[30] See Ishikawa 1983–94 (8): 203.

[31] See *Gakudō yōshinshū*, T. 82, 2581: 2c; *Denkōroku*, ibid., 2585: 402c.

[32] On bones and flesh in Chinese religion, and their relation to gender, see James L. Watson, "Of Flesh and Bones," in Bloch and Parry 1982: 155–86.

context, is also well attested in Japanese Buddhism.[33] In the Sōtō tradition in particular, the parallelism between life and death is strengthened by beliefs about conception and embryology. The relationship between death and procreation is described well in some of the *kirigami*. According to these documents, the fetus is felt to develop in periods of seven days (like the funeral ritual), during which the Thirteen Buddhas, taking turns, produce the various parts of the body. If the child dies in utero, the parents should address their prayers to the Buddha of the period when the miscarriage took place. This periodization of pregnancy reproduces that of the liminal phase of the funeral ritual, the phase during which the spirit of the deceased, having achieved the status of "intermediary being," is moving toward his new rebirth, through the Ten Hells, helped by the Thirteen Buddhas.[34] Yet Keizan, in typical Zen fashion, rejects in the *Denkōroku* any conception of lineage and filiation: "There is a name (*shō*) that is not received from one's father, not received from one's ancestors, not inherited from the Buddhas, not inherited from the patriarchs; it is called the Buddha nature (*busshō*)."[35]

THE CORPOREAL TOMB

Paul Mus has pointed out that "the tomb becomes less the resting place of the deceased and rather a kind of artificial body substituted for his mortal remains, a funerary 'cosmic man' in which the magical entity that extends the dead person resides. . . . It is a new body that is, if you wish, the residence of the deceased, but only in the way his body was his residence during his lifetime."[36] If the stūpa is a kind of body, the body is also a stūpa, a tomb. This equation is strangely reminiscent of the old popular etymology *sôma = sêma*. Furthermore, the body and tomb are what Mus would call "mesocosms," instruments of ritual projection that permit the achievement of immortality.

This identification of the body with the stūpa makes possible a whole classificatory symbolism. As already noted, the esoteric symbolism of the "five-wheel" stūpa (*gorinnotō*), with its equation between the five elements of esoteric Buddhism and the five viscera of the body, along with various other Buddhist and non-Buddhist series (five Buddhas, five Confucian relationships, five points of the compass, etc.), allows the place-

[33] See Parry, "Sacrificial Death and the Necrophagous Ascetic," in Bloch and Parry 1982: 80.

[34] See Ishikawa 1983–94 (8): 201–4. See also the mentions of the cult of the "Ten Venerated Ones Protecting the Period of Pregnancy," in Frank, 1991: 140.

[35] T. 82, 2585: 380c.

[36] Mus 1935, Pt. 2: 213.

ment of the Buddhist body within the classification system elaborated by Chinese cosmologists and thus the perspective of the body as "oriented," like a microcosm.[37] By taking on organs, the body becomes thinkable, an object of thought. The symbolic (symbolized) body makes up a "total social phenomenon," inasmuch as it provides a support for various symbolic systems (body = stūpa = five elements of Chinese and Buddhist cosmology), systems that the initiate knows how to read through, seeing "one symbolic order shining through another one, for example, the social behind the psychological."[38]

Still, it is significant that yet another kind of stūpa developed in Zen (and thus another image of the body), the one called "seamless," "joint-less," or "ovoid." The ovoid form, characteristic in the West of the nursery rhyme character Humpty Dumpty, is in China that of Hundun, the primordial Chaos.[39] Pursuing the analogy between body and stūpa, we find in Chan/Zen the claim for the existence of a "body without organs" which is reminiscent of the "schizoid body" described by Gilles Deleuze and Félix Guattari, an ideal body "without outflows," undifferentiated, truly unthinkable, but the body of the ideal practitioner.[40] Let us keep in mind this contrast, or rather complementarity, between two types of stūpa or two types of body, the first allowing participation in a complex symbolic system and the second rejecting any symbolic accommodation in the name of a body without seam or outflow. The physical body, both as an object of thought and as a subject/instrument of perceptions, allows us to go from one symbolic system to another—or to a higher, nonsymbolic sphere (which still remains, actually, preeminently symbolic).

The ritualized body is also a socialized body, apparently the opposite of the spontaneous body of early Chan. We might, without forcing too much, apply to Chan/Zen the distinction that Jean-Claude Schmitt revealed as a motif in the evolution from Antiquity to the Middle Ages: the transition from a conception of the body (under the term *gestus*) that assumes an individual mastery and responsibility for one's gestures, to another (*gesta*) in which "the individual, submitted to the community, monastery, or lineage, is no longer the true master of his own gestures."[41] In Chan/Zen there was also a transition from the individual ethic of bodily spontaneity to a collective, completely ritualized choreography of body positions. We could also contrast this hieratic body of the meditator with the agitated, gesticulating body of the Chan "madmen," those "en-

[37] See Ishikawa 1983–94 (11): 142–44; and *Sho ekō shingi shiki, T.* 81, 2578: 668c.
[38] Augé 1988: 144.
[39] See Girardot 1983.
[40] See Gilles Deleuze and Felix Guattari, *Anti-Oedipus* (Paris: Minuit, 1972).
[41] Schmitt 1990: 133.

ergumens" no longer energized by communal ritual but by a return to their own nature, penetrated by desire, joy, a crazy wisdom that could not be comprehended except in total abandon.

Thus, a bodily attitude like seated meditation serves as a "common place" for various existential and ritual situations and allows us to entrust to the body the main part of a "hieratic" ideology. As Pierre Bourdieu notes, "By inducing an identity of reaction in a diversity of situations, impressing the same posture on the body in different contexts, the practical schemes can produce the equivalent of an act of generalization that cannot be accounted for without recourse to concepts."[42]

Perhaps we should consider the extreme forms of self-constraint (ascesis, mortification, self-immolation) that characterize medieval Buddhism to be the expression of a certain level of civilization—in Norbert Elias's sense. In these extreme manifestations of individuality, it is perhaps above all a certain state of society that is manifested. Ascesis, or sitting meditation, would not be that absolute foundation, that ultimate anchoring in an unchanging reality that they claim it to be. On the other hand, the shift to ritualism in Japanese Zen may correspond to a higher stage of civilization, one in which the control mechanisms of society have psychically modified the individual—"in the direction of a more continuous, stable and even regulation of drives and affects in all areas of conduct, in all sectors of his life."[43] Hence a disparition of strong personalities à la Linji (with one major exception, Ikkyū [1394–1481]), flourishing during the troubled times of the Ōnin war.

RITUAL IMAGINED

Ritual, centered on the practitioner's body, makes up one of the matrices of the Buddhist imagination. However, if ritual creates a ritual body, how is it treated in Chan/Zen, an allegedly antiritualist school? At first sight the primacy accorded by Chan/Zen to immediate, spontaneous experience implies a rejection of all ritual. But in fact, as we have already had occasion to note, exactly the opposite is true in the case of Sōtō Zen. Like their counterparts in the so-called old Buddhist sects, Zen monks like Keizan lived in an atmosphere saturated with ritual, and it is against this background that their radical, "spontaneous" stands can, and should, be understood. To grasp this paradoxical evolution, we must rid ourselves of the traditional view of Zen as it has been popularized in the West by D. T. Suzuki and others. According to this view, which we may almost term "protestant," Zen is a teaching entirely free from any formalism or

[42] Bourdieu 1990: 89.
[43] Elias 1982: 240.

ritual. But Suzuki himself on several occasions had to concede that this vision of an ideal Zen matches only very distantly the reality of life in the monasteries.[44] Even more, by the end of his life he denounced as a typically Western misunderstanding the antinomian interpretation of Zen. Still, forced to admit the importance of ritual in the maintenance of tradition, he nonetheless continued to insist that ritual was a mere excrescence, an "accident" that did not question the "essence" of Zen. In Suzuki and his fellows, we see a deep nostalgia, almost Daoist in nature, for an original spontaneity, and a pronounced disdain for all forms of ritualism.

Although most historians of Chan/Zen have ultimately admitted, somewhat reluctantly, the importance of ritual on an institutional level, they nonetheless retain their prejudice against ritualism. According to the dominant interpretation, the "scandal" of Zen ritual is in part redeemed by the intentions that give rise to it. Ritual is seen as a pious lie, a "skillful means" designed for the ignorant. All in all, it is a compromise with the spirit of the times, a way of responding to the needs of proselytizing and adapting to sociopolitical changes. This interpretation is found, in one form or another, in most of the recent studies on the question and may also prevail in various normative texts within the Chan/Zen tradition itself. But it is clear that one is dealing here with a normative discourse, consequently an ideological one, that should be examined closely and not simply repeated.

The functionalist conception of ritual considerably influenced the historiography of the Sōtō tradition. The evolution of this tradition after Dōgen has often been seen as a sort of degeneration, justified by the role of Buddhist ritual in the society of the time. With Gikai, and especially Keizan, rituals derived from Buddhist esotericism would have moved to the fore. It has, however, been established that Dōgen himself practiced a certain number of rites, like offerings to the Arhats, and we must perhaps be thinking about a broader continuity at the level of ritual than the partisans of Dōgen's "pure Zen" can imagine. According to all appearances, "original" Chan, far from being "pure," was "hybrid" and fairly ritualistic. The conflict between ritualism and antiritualism shows up in early Chan literature, sometimes within the same text.

Chan/Zen is usually presented as an effort to interiorize Buddhist practice and as a criticism of the formalism of traditional Buddhism. A typical example of interiorization is the "formless repentance" put forward by Daoxin and his successors. In his *Guanxin lun* (*Treatise on Mind Con-*

[44] See D. T. Suzuki, *The Training of the Zen Buddhist Monk* (New York: University Books, 1965).

templation), The Chan master Shenxiu (606–706) states that all ritual activities like making and consecrating icons, burning incense, offering flowers to the Buddha, circumambulating the altar, or holding vegetarian banquets, should be interpreted in their "spiritual" sense.[45] Shenxiu's criticism agrees with that of a Confucianist like Han Yu, who claimed that Buddhist rites are a total waste of material and human resources which cannot bring to awakening those who perform them.

In spite of this theoretical rejection, Shenxiu and his disciples did not stop performing rites, and, if we include meditation in ritual, we may even think that they spent most of their time at these activities. Other texts attributed to the same Shenxiu give ritual a central role. Nevertheless, on the basis of criticisms like Shenxiu's, Chan historians have tried to define this school as iconoclastic and antiritualist without reexamining statements that derive, in many cases, from a given rhetorical strategy. How can it be overlooked that this antiritualist position is itself transmitted in the most ritual fashion possible within a completely institutionalized orthodoxy? It is true that the sources provide arguments in favor of a rejection of ritual, which is most often presented as a "skillful means" but also as a "dangerous supplement," necessary, to be sure, in the interest of proselytizing but risking a certain vulgarizing of doctrine—in any case, definitely an activity inferior to meditation. Still, this spear waving suggests that ritual remained important in Chan/Zen and it actually inverts the image of concrete practice.

The repetitive, formal nature of ritual, its symbolic, magical efficacy, and thus its hold over the imagination are often rejected in the name of "spiritual interiority," spontaneity or, on the contrary, in the name of the intentionality of ideal practice. The *Guanxin lun*, for example, criticizes "empty" recitation of the name of the Buddha as somehow "magical" or "mantric," without necessarily rejecting the "commemoration" of the Buddha as a purely interior, mental activity. This attitude toward Pure Land doctrine and the cult of Amitābha Buddha (J. Amida) would be later radicalized. Here, for example, is how Dōgen disparages the practice of *nenbutsu*, recitation of the name of Amida: "If you think that by waggling your tongue and raising your voice you are doing the work of the Buddha and [getting] merit, this is completely futile. . . . To keep on raising your voice is to imitate the frogs who croak day and night in the rice paddies in springtime; it is just as useless."[46]

Once more the example of Dōgen reveals the gap between Zen theory and practice, discourse and experience. Because of their antiritualist prej-

---

[45] *Guanxin lun, T.* 85, 2833: 1271b.
[46] *Shōbōgenzō*, "Bendōwa," *T.* 82, 2582: 17b.

udices, many scholars of the Sōtō sect choose to dwell on passages like the following, which according to them express the essence of Dōgen's Zen: "From the beginning of your time of study with a wise master avoid offerings of incense and pious prostrations, the recitation of the name of the Buddha, repentance, or the reading of the sūtras: simply remain seated in meditation and achieve the dropping off of body and mind." This passage rejecting all forms of ritual, actually a borrowing from Dōgen's master Rujing, is often quoted.[47] But usually it is not mentioned that Dōgen is one of those who contributed most to the ritualization of Zen.[48] The opposite judgment has prevailed in the case of Keizan, who nonetheless wrote in the Denkōroku: "Until you reach this stage [of emptiness], even if you worship the Buddha throughout the twelve hours of the day and harmonize your body and mind in all your daily activities, this will only lead to excellence among men and deva; it is still a flawed karmic retribution. Just as the shadow follows the body: even though it does exist, it is not real. You should thus focus your energy on clarifying your intrinsic mind."[49]

Such selective reading, which emphasizes the gap between the two founders of Sōtō, still prevails, despite the central role of ritual in several doctrinal works by Dōgen, without speaking of the ritual treatise Eihei shingi, a work in which Dōgen tried to elaborate a purely Zen liturgy. A less cursory reading of the Shōbōgenzō shows that Dōgen undertook recitations of the Buddhist Scriptures on imperial anniversaries, or at the request of the lay patrons of Eiheiji. A document mentions a ceremony for the recitation of the Precepts, which took place in 1247 with the participation of about twenty laymen. This ceremony proved to be so efficient that auspicious signs appeared, making such a strong impression on these laymen that they wanted to leave their indisputable testimony for posterity. In Dōgen's Eihei kōroku there is also mention of "prayers for the return of good weather" offered up during the rainy season. In his disciplinary codes are also found recitations of sūtras dedicated to the Stove God and to the tutelary deity at the beginning and at the end of the summer retreat.[50] These few examples, which we could multiply, suffice to call into question the official Sōtō line that it was Keizan who altered and diluted by esoteric rituals and magical prayers and incantations the "pure Zen" of Dōgen. Dōgen's practice even included many religious

[47] One of the first to quote it is actually Keizan himself. See for instance Denkōroku, notices on Rujing and Dōgen, T. 82, 2585: 404c, 406b.

[48] See Hōkyōki, in DZZ 2: 377; see also Shōbōgenzō "Bendōwa," T. 82, 2582: 17a; "Sanmaiō zanmai," ibid.: 243c.

[49] Denkōroku, T. 82, 2585: 369b.

[50] Eihei kōroku, DZZ 2: 10.

ceremonies whose effectiveness is sometimes confirmed by the occurrence of supernatural events like the appearance of an Arhat or the materialization of heavenly flowers on the altar.[51]

In a conversation with Ejō, Gikai states:

> Although I had always heard that ritual is part of Buddhism, inwardly I felt that real Buddhism must lie elsewhere. However, I have recently changed my point of view. I now know that monastic ritual and deportment are true Buddhism. Even if, alongside these, there exists also the infinite Buddhism of the Buddhas and the patriarchs, it is still the same Buddhism. I now believe firmly in the deep principle that there is no separate reality apart from Buddhist actions like lifting the arm or taking a step.

Here Gikai seems to be alluding to the saying of the fourth patriarch Daoxin: "Lifting or putting down the foot, all this is [takes place in] the 'arena of awakening.'"[52] Along the same lines, in the *Platform Sūtra* it is the "direct thinking" of the practitioner that constitutes this arena of awakening (*bodhimaṇḍa*). Usually taken as a rejection of ritual, these statements can also be understood in quite the opposite sense: ritual can be extended to encompass all mental and physical actions. It is clearly in this sense, and not in that of some kind of radical spontaneity, that they are understood by Gikai; and Ejō, faithful preserver of Dōgen's thought, does nothing to contradict this interpretation.[53]

In Chinese Chan monastic codes, we also find various rituals dedicated to obtaining purely worldly benefits like a good harvest—for example, rites to ensure sunshine, rain, protection against insects and other agricultural banes, as well as protection against lunar and solar eclipses.[54] The merits produced by these rituals are offered to Buddhas and gods, and these in turn rain down celestial manna on the faithful, both monks and laypeople. But the monks' virtue and their power of concentration lie at the living source of these merits. The monks are thus the necessary intermediaries between the world of humans and that of the gods.

Yōkoji ritual, in other words the Yōkoji rule of life, is codified in the *Tōkoku shingi*, also known under the title *Keizan shingi*, a work drawn up by Keizan but one whose text was not compiled until 1423, or nearly a century later. This was a very detailed rule, a synthesis of the *Eihei shingi* of Dōgen and the various Rules compiled by Rujing, Yōsai, Ejō,

---

[51] See "Jūroku rakan genzuiki," in *DZZ* 2: 399; "Rakan kuyōshikimon," *DZZ* 2: 402–4; as well as Ejō, "Eiheiji sanko ryōzuiki," and "Ejō shōjōsha," 1267:9:22, in *Sōtōshū komonjo* #10, 1: 9.

[52] See Faure 1989: 140.

[53] *Goyuigon*, in *DZZ* 2: 503–4.

[54] See *Chixiu Baizhang qinggui*, dated 1338, in *T.* 48, 2025: 1115a.

and Gikai. It quickly became the reference handbook for all Sōtō ritual matters. The *Record of Tōkoku* also provides a simplified ordination ritual for monks who had moved over from other schools as well as for monks with children or lay disciples from all walks of life (domain stewards, *gokenin*, peasants, craftsmen, etc.).[55] However, the *Keizan shingi* differs from the *Eihei shingi* in that it is less centered on zazen and individual rules and concentrates more on local cults and group ritual. Yōkōji was not simply a monastery, a place of retreat for "religious virtuosos"; it was also, perhaps more importantly, a temple supported by offerings from lay donors and consecrated to prayers and rituals for the well-being of these people, both in this world and the world to come. The meditation of the monks was intended not only to ensure their own awakening but also to accumulate the energy and merits needed for these rituals to be efficacious.[56]

THE FIELD OF RITUAL

Every ritual begins with the plotting out of the sacred space (*bodhimaṇḍa*) into which the deity will be brought down. This definition also applies to meditation. Whether they involve visualization, confession, or whatever, all these rituals consist of "calling down" the Buddha or the Bodhisattva. The recitation of the names of the Buddha is an act of conjuring as well as invoking (*dhāraṇī*). In the same fashion, a kōan can be understood as being like a *dhāraṇī*, a conjuring of the ultimate reality into the ritual space established by the act of meditation. Thus, kōans are almost those "oracles of the Brahman" that the Jesuit Leon Wieger once talked about, only to decry them.[57]

The same may be said about the ritual of "ascending the hall" (*jōdō*). During his sermons, the Zen master takes the role of an incarnation of

---

[55] See *JDZ*, 450–51; see also Azuma 1982: 39.

[56] Meditation still played an important part in the daily routine. Here is the daily rule laid out in the *Keizan shingi*: Get up at five o'clock in the morning; meditation until eight o'clock, and then quick ablutions. From eight to ten, a breakfast of gruel, and then recitation of sūtras. From ten until noon, meditation. From noon to two in the afternoon, lunch, and then recitation of sūtras. From two to four o'clock, sermon by the abbot and study of "Recorded Sayings." From four to six, meditation. From six to eight, conclusion of the abbot's sermon, and then evening meal ("gruel") and recitation of sūtras. From eight to ten, meditation. Curfew at eleven. Midnight to two in the morning, well-earned rest. See *T.* 82, 2589: 424a–425c.

[57] See Léon Wieger, *A History of the Religious Beliefs and Philosophical Opinions in China from the Beginning to the Present Time* (New York: Paragon Book Reprint Corporation, 1969), 530.

the Buddha. He relives in the present Śākyamuni's preaching on the Vulture Peak *in illo tempore*. The ritual of the sermon encapsulates all the others in that it clearly indicates that there is, in meditation or the kōan, the creation of a sacred space, an "arena of awakening" (*bodhimaṇḍa*) onto which a transcendent power is felt to descend. The archetypical ritual of Buddhist "descent," one very popular in Sōtō Zen, is the invitation to the Arhat Piṇḍola issued during monastic meetings or the ritual bath. The presence of this Arhat during these ceremonies attests to the purity of the participants and the formal validity of the ceremony. "When Piṇḍola comes, then the imprint of a reclining figure can be seen on the cushions; in the bathroom one can see signs that someone has made use of the bath water."[58] This is the same kind of ritual authentification that we see in the appearance of the Arhats during a cermony carried out by Dōgen at Eiheiji.

Zen ritual did not limit itself to the performance of annual, monthly, and daily ceremonies. In the Sōtō sect in particular, ritualization ended up invading all aspects of monastic life, all sectors of private life. But at first it affected the highest form of spiritual practice, meditation. If one considers that it is the body or the mind that becomes the ritual area (or "arena of awakening," *bodhimaṇḍa*, Ch. *daochang*), seated meditation in fact constitutes a form of ritual activity, a sort of ritual of identification. Seated meditation in medieval Zen should probably be interpreted not as a form of introspection but rather as a ritual "re-presentation" of the original awakening of the Buddha. In this sense it is entirely mediated by tradition. The emphasis placed on "non-thinking" is perhaps an attempt to avoid defining the psychological content of meditation. The alternative is to keep concentrating on bodily posture and to force oneself to control this down to the very smallest details. This formalization of zazen reached an extreme degree in the Sōtō sect. Thus, the growing ritualization of Zen suggests the possibility of considering Chan/Zen as an extremely elaborate system of gesture (a *kata*) rather than as a doctrine, as a formalization, a production of bodily postures, the four "majestic attitudes" (walking, standing still, sitting, lying down). As Pierre Bourdieu has pointed out, "formalization" is always accompanied by ideological effects.[59] In any case we should remember that the apparent rejection of the Buddhist liturgy in favor of meditation should not be interpreted as a rejection by Zen of all ritual as such, but rather as a claim to possession of a "pure" ritual, an emblem of sectarian identity, as opposed to the "mixed," composite rituals of traditional Buddhism.

We also find in medieval Sōtō forms of Tantric meditation in which the

---

[58] See Lévi and Chavannes 1916: 216.
[59] Bourdieu 1990: 126.

psychic content assumes a great importance, even if it is not necessarily, as some have claimed, due to a Shingon influence. As Helen Brunner remarks in the Indian context, "The influence of Tantrism in ritual is revealed by the inner preparation of the officiant who, after having obtained a 'divine body,' draws to himself, then awakens in the image where it was supposedly asleep, the god that is the object of the cult."[60]

Where does Keizan stand in all this? The founder of Yōkōji is certainly more detailed than Dōgen when it comes to describing the concrete content of meditation; he is not content with poetic formulas or necessarily vague allusions to "non-thinking." This still does not prevent him from citing in turn the words attributed to Rujing about the uselessness of rites like burning incense, prostrating oneself, reciting the *nenbutsu*, repenting, or reciting the Scriptures.[61] Like Dōgen, he advocates the exclusive practice of seated meditation (*shikan taza*, lit. "sitting-only"), which he describes as keeping "the seated body free of any motion, the mouth free of any esoteric incantations, the mind free of any thought."[62] Yet this absence of thought does not imply for Keizan a denial of ritual since it should be achieved within ritual itself. More concretely, one can, according to him, use various "supports": one must, for example, concentrate one's attention on the palm of the left hand, or else on the soles of one's feet, when one is overcome by strange visions; on the top of the forehead when one is about to fall asleep; on the tip of the nose or the region below the navel (*tanden*) when one is distracted. One can also focus on one's breathing, or on a kōan.[63]

Kōans also play a major role in this ritual process. As Stanley Tambiah, in his study on the performative aspects of ritual, has noted:

> Whether literally meaningful or not . . . , the prime value of these repeated sayings is their therapeutic value as "focusing" mechanisms. . . . The repeated formulae as "supports of contemplation" or transporters into a trance state do so, not by a direct assault on the actor's senses and inflicting an immense psychic toll on him or her, but by a more indirect conventional illocutionary employment of them as instruments of passage and as triggering mechanisms.[64]

The importance in Chan/Zen maieutics of the direct meeting between master and disciple in very animated "dialogues" (Ch. *wenda*, J. *mondō*) has often been commented on. But we should also remind ourselves that, with the institutionalization of Chan, these encounters became largely

---

[60] See *Le Grand Atlas Universalis des Religions*, Charles Baladier, ed. (Paris: Encyclopédie Universalis, 1990), 302–5.

[61] See *Zazen yōjinki*, T. 82, 2586: 413b; see also *Denkōroku*, T. 82, 2585: 404c.

[62] *JDZ*, 247–48.

[63] *Zazen yōjinki*, T. 82, 2586: 414a.

[64] Tambiah 1981: 141.

fully rehearsed rituals. For Keizan, such dialogues continue to play a central role in the elucidation of his disciples' state of mind. The *Denkōroku* itself is basically a selection from the "Recorded Sayings" of Chan/Zen patriarchs. Various examples can also be found in the *Record of Tōkoku*, for instance the one in which his benefactor and disciple Sonin shows her realization to him. Likewise, when he asks the nun Meishō how she understands the story of "Linji raising his fly-whisk," she remains silent, a nonverbal answer approved by Keizan.[65]

While in official Zen monasteries belonging to the "five mountains" (*gozan*) system, kōans tended to become an object of bookish study, in other monasteries (collectively termed *rinka*) they were memorized and became the object of a kind of "fetishism." In fact, depending on how much money you had to spend, you could get ready-made answers to the main kōans. The initiation given by a master to his main disciples during private instruction sessions came to consist mostly of telling them the stereotyped responses to classic kōans in a Chinese language that very few understood.[66] The sale of such manuals to the profane was criticized severely by reformers like Ikkyū Sōjun, but these were apparently lonely voices crying in the wilderness of Zen forests. The esoteric language and dialogue form of the kōans ultimately invaded the sphere of meditation itself, but also all the other practices and rituals. We find a translation into kōans, a "dialogization" of all traditional Buddhist or "Shintō-Buddhist" discourse. Thus it becomes difficult to go on insisting that the only aim of the kōan is to promote an awakening. All the evidence indicates that it also played a semiotic and ritual role. Sōtō monks in particular used the hieratic style of the kōans to legitimize all monastic acts and rites, from initiation to funerals. The field of the kōans grew larger, going beyond the bounds of Zen monasticism to leave a larger role to laypeople, so relativizing more and more the ideal of seclusion advocated by Dōgen. Zen kōans may have been used originally in esoteric rituals of transmission, but they became the defining mark of postmortem ordinations performed on behalf of laypeople. The haughty style of these dialogues was in fact suited to the evocation of the transcendence of Chan masters with regard to death and provided those who aspired to succeed to their positions the necessary passwords and legitimacy.[67]

Making kōans into a matter of routine goes along with turning everyday acts into sacred matters. These acts turn into liturgical sequences that the monks must master, not only in their physical or technical aspect but

[65] See *JDZ*, 431.

[66] See Kabanoff 1993.

[67] See Bodiford 1993: 201–4; 1992; and Tamamura Takeji, "Nihon chūsei zenrin ni okeru Rinzai Sōtō ryōshū no idō: 'Rinka' no mondai ni tsuite," in *Nihon zenshūshi ronshū*, vol. 2, 981–1040.

also in their secret meaning. This meaning, which often resonates like a non-meaning to uninformed observers, is provided by formulas memorized during initiatory sessions or by the intermediary of *kirigami*. Such practices never take the place of traditional meditation and kōans but do echo them, thereby modifying their meaning very profoundly. We see the appearance, around the time of Keizan, of a new "art of speaking" that gives birth to new kinds of commentaries (*shōmono*) in spoken language. Inspired by classic Chan texts, these commentaries divert their meaning to the profit of ritual.[68]

In passing, we should stress the growing importance of secrecy within the Sōtō sect as well as in Japanese society as a whole. Texts of the masters became like "dynastic treasures," especially the works of Dōgen and Keizan. The great monasteries like Eiheiji and Shōbōji succeeded in monopolizing access to these works and so boosted their own prestige. Thus the *Shōbōgenzō* became a significant relic and token of transmission and disappeared from circulation until early modern times. This tendency already existed during the time of Dōgen, if we are to believe a passage in Ejō's *Eihei kaisan goyuigon kiroku*: "There are secret affairs and oral initiations. These matters that have never been spoken of to anyone else, concern the mental attitude of an abbot, temple rituals, the ceremony for conferring the succession certificate, and the procedure for bodhisattva-precept ordinations. [Dōgen had said:] 'These can be transmitted only to one's Dharma heir.' For this reason only I, Ejō, have received this instruction."[69]

Similarly Keizan notes the following in the *Record of Tōkoku* after a visit by Daichi (1290–1366):

On the twentieth of the fifth month [of the year 1325], the acolyte [Dai]chi of Chinzei [Kyushu] came from afar to seek my instruction. He brought with him [texts such as] *The Five Steps of the Absolute and the Relative, the Lord and the Vassal*, by Caoshan [in two fascicles], *The Recorded Sayings of Touzi* [Datong] (in one fascicle), and *The Final Words of Zhenxie* (in one fascicle). He gave me these and said, "The [Five Steps of] the Absolute and the Relative have not yet been spread through the great Song state. All the more reason why this is the first time they have been seen in Japan. They should therefore be kept secret. If someone is not worthy of them, they should not be shown to him. They constitute a precious treasure of our school. [On the other hand,] there is not reason why the *Sayings* of Touzi and Zhenxie should not be printed and put into circulation." [*JDZ*, 432]

We have already seen how this same process, which led to the kōan becoming sacralized, would lead to the same thing happening to ordination. The ritual of ordination originally simply marked one's entry into

---

[68] See Kaneda 1976; and Ishikawa 1983–94 (16) to (20).
[69] See *Goyuigon*, 1255:1:6, in DZZ 2:502, cited in Bodiford 1993: 55.

orders, but it came to take on a soteriological value. It indicated that as "sons" or "daughters" of the Buddha, the new monks and nuns, were assured of salvation. Even more, ordination charts, documents that established ritually and even magically this relationship with the primordial Buddha, acquired a talismanic or apotropaic quality. The power of conferring them gave the Sōtō monks a charisma that they did not hesitate to exploit. We see them converting one by one all sorts of supernatural beings, and then proceeding to collective ordinations of laypeople. Finally, the transmission to certain disciples of ordination manuals that authorized them in turn to ordain new monks and nuns came to be as significant a ritual of transmission as the transmission of the Dharma itself. "When I was twenty-five," reports Keizan, "I received from Master Gien of Eiheiji the ritual of ordination, and during the winter of the same year I began to administer the Precepts. I first of all ordained five people. When I was thirty-one, I had already ordained more than seventy people." Keizan became heir to Gien's lineage of the Precepts in 1292, three years before he received the Dharma transmission from Gikai. In 1324, on the occasion of the inauguration of Sōjiji, he once again ordained twenty-eight monks. He notes side by side in the *Record of Tōkoku* his transmissions of the Dharma and of the ordination ritual. Although the latter did retain a slightly inferior status, it justified the existence of a second hieratic lineage, more or less independent of the patriarchal tradition.

THE RITUALIZATION OF EVERYDAY ACTS

The doctrine of the Sōtō sect is characterized by an intense ritualizing of monastic life, the effort to redefine each everyday activity as sacred and to provide strict rules even (and above all) for the most trivial bodily functions. This is an extreme development of the Mahāyāna idea that the phenomenal world is no different from ultimate reality itself, an idea that is expressed in Chan formulas like "The ordinary mind is the Way" or "This very mind is the Buddha." All everyday acts are thus theoretically the expression of ultimate reality and so partake of the sacred.

The theory of the identity between practice and awakening, characteristic of Sōtō, results in the sanctification of traditional ritual forms and encouragement of their preservation. Ritual is interpreted as a manifestation of awakening, just as important as meditation, and not as a simple religious routine. This interpretation, which prevailed, for instance, with one of Keizan's successors, Kohō Kakumyō (1271–1361), would be severely criticized by the latter's disciple, Bassui Tokushō.[70] During the Edo

[70] See Bodiford 1993: 89.

period, the Rinzai master Tōrei Enji (1721–1792) would see in it only a variant of Hīnayāna practice.[71] At any rate it was a form of theological rationalization that masks the eminently pragmatic nature of ritual, whose goal is above all to obtain spiritual or temporal advantages in this life.

Ritual can be characterized as a formalization of the everyday, and this shaping consists first of all in the elaboration of a specific pattern of gestures. Ordinary gestures are performed in a gestural syntax that modifies their meaning. The "logic of gestures" (*raison des gestes*), to pick up the expression used by Jean-Claude Schmitt in connection with the medieval West, makes up a fundamental element of Zen doctrine, even if it is generally passed over in silence, being itself silent.[72] Keizan plays an important role in the codifying of gestures, as can be seen from a study of the *Pure Rule of Tōkoku* (*Tōkoku shingi*).

Monastery life, closed in on itself, constitutes a kind of echo chamber for the individual imagination. There the individual is in a way carried along by the collective *imaginaire*. The omnipresent ritual tends to wipe out the boundary between the real and the imaginary, the sacred and the profane, or at any rate to shift or blur it. At the same time it paradoxically creates and maintains the very difference that it is trying to wipe out. The practitioner is never entirely fooled, and no matter how immersed he or she may be in the world of awakening, he or she never completely loses sight of the reality of the objective world, the realm of conventional truth. The real constantly intrudes in connection with management problems that are hard to sublimate ritually, for example in relations with lay benefactors who must be handled carefully and whose language one must be able to speak. But, as we have seen with Keizan, even these are in return idealized and become, like the local deities, messengers from the absolute or, like Sonin, symbols and tokens of autochthony.

In all that has gone before, we have regrouped various sectors or significant moments of ritual, including under this rubric of ritual not only liturgy proper but also the master's sermons, seated meditation, "consultations," "dialogues," and kōans, right down to the most trivial acts of monastic life. According to this inclusive conception, a ritual area is no longer a sacred space, cut off from the rest of the world, but the field of every action. By thus taking over the private sphere, ritualization seems to wipe out any distinction between sacred and profane to the advantage of an imperialistic sacralization: instead of the classic dichotomy sa-

---

[71] See Tōrei Enji, *Shūmon mujintōron*, "Gyōji ron," T. 81, 2575: 604b.
[72] See Schmitt 1990.

cred/profane, we see various zones of lesser or greater sacredness, in a way differences of tension.

We may apply to ritual Octave Mannoni's statement about the theater and say that ritual is there "not to replace a life that is too narrow with a better or greater life . . . but to produce events of a totally different nature, different because they are produced only in the imaginary part of the Self. And it is not necessary that there be any confusion with reality. On the contrary, such confusion must be avoided."[73] Unlike Lévi-Strauss who sees in the redundancy of ritual an impossible attempt to reintegrate experience into its essential unity, a unity that has been broken down by dualistic thinking, Jonathan Z. Smith stresses the "differential" aspect of ritual.[74] Redundancy, for example the large number of prostrations, in groups of nine, during the ritual transmission of the Precepts, could rather indicate, as Pierre Bourdieu suggests, that one is here dealing with a "logic or practice" which "manages to extort what is essential while seeming to demand the insignificant."[75] The ideology in the ritual is, as a result, perhaps just as important as the symbolism proper in that it is a matter of an implicit *imaginaire*, carried by the body or enciphered in it.

[73] Mannoni 1969: 175.
[74] See Lévi-Strauss 1981: 668–75; and Smith 1987: 109.
[75] Bourdieu 1990: 69.

Chapter Nine

THE POWER OF SYMBOLS

IF WE ARE TO BELIEVE Roland Barthes, "the whole of Zen wages a war against the prevarication of meaning";[1] aiming above all at "the symbol as a semantic operation," it would constitute a breach, a jolt, a blockage, a "preemption of meaning" and would announce a "panic suspension of language," the end of the "reign of Codes," the "very fissure of the symbolic."[2] If it is true that Chan/Zen seeks to define itself by a kind of negation of symbols, in practice it is extremely symbolic, in more senses than one: not only does its ritual make great use of symbols (in the ordinary sense of the word: "that which represents another thing because of some correspondence between them"), but it is itself a symbol (in the etymological sense).[3] According to this second sense (which is also the primary meaning), the symbol does not simply represent "something else" (this "something" not necessarily being a thing), but it is an integral part of the reality it evokes. It has been noted, for example, that documents of transmission, or *kirigami*, while claiming to "describe" the lineage or transmission ritual in the Sōtō sect, actually constitute them. They have this power not only because of the performative nature of all language, but because they are perceived as qualitatively different from profane objects, as though they are part of a higher order of reality. Using Marc Augé's definition, we may here describe as symbolic the "reciprocal relationship between two beings, two objects, a being and an object, or let us say, in the broadest sense of the word, two realities of which one is not properly speaking the representative of the other since each of the two terms appears rather as the complement of the other, and vice versa."[4] A symbol is thus "any reality able to play simultaneously the double role of representing and putting into connection."[5] In the Sino-

---

[1] Barthes 1982: 73.

[2] Ibid.: 74–75.

[3] The Western tendency to see Zen and Japanese poetry (*haiku*) as places where "the symbol as semantic operation . . . is attacked" has been analyzed by Michel Beaujour, "Less is More," *New York Literary Forum: Intertextuality* (New York [1978]), vol. 2: 237–43. Beaujour shows that this interpretation served Westerners interested in what they took to be the "non-metaphysical, non-symbolic Orient," because they found what they had been looking for, namely, "muted signifiers that keep meaning in abeyance." See p. 240 of "Less is More," quoted by William LaFleur, "Too Easy a Simplicity: Watson's *Ryōkan*," *The Eastern Buddhist* 13, 1 (1980): 121.

[4] Augé 1988: 34.

[5] Ibid.: 43.

Japanese cultural setting, it is difficult to distinguish these roles clearly, and thus to separate these two meanings of the word, since they are themselves in a truly "symbolic" relationship in that they imply each other.

The primary sense of the *sumbolon*, "part of an object divided between two people to serve as a signal of recognition between them," strangely recalls the two-part signs used in China.[6] The term that refers to these juridico-religious objects, *fu*, is written with a logogram composed of the characters "bamboo" and "join"; it involves "joining bamboos."[7] In imperial China the word first had a juridical sense, that of a contractual document or insignia of power and referred to an object made of bamboo, jade, or metal divided into two parts, or tesserae. Each of the parties concerned held one of the tesserae (*qi*) and these had to be reunited, matching perfectly, in order to serve as proof (*faire foi*). Similarly, in feudal law it was a *fu* that established relations between vassal and overlord during gatherings at which "insignia were united": the "pledge" (*xin*) verified by the matching of the insignia was sanctioned by sacred powers.[8] The embrace of overlord and vassal, as found in Western feudalism, was in the Chinese context replaced, "symbolized," by the matching of their tallies (or tesserae).

These tallies, which served as a means of identification, or as tokens of

---

[6] This *sumbolon* is the symbol of the symbolic function itself, "the representation of unity and of the division of the opposites introduced by the operation of symbolic scission." See Jean-Joseph Goux, *Les Iconoclastes* (Paris: Seuil, 1978), 169.

[7] The *fu* (talisman) was originally a bamboo tab or tablet divided longitudinally into two halves to serve as testimony in a contract. As a verb, *fu* means "to concord, to adjust, to respond mutually, to fit." The compound *fuhao* means a symbol, a mark, a sign. Robert des Rotours notes that these insignia or contracts in two parts were of universal use. In France they were called "tailles" because of the incision made on the two juxtaposed sticks, and this is the origin of the English word *tally*. See des Rotours 1952: 3–4. According to the *Shuowen* dictionary, "The *fu* is what serves as testimony (*xin*). In the Han regulations, one divided a six inches long bamboo in order to join its two parts." The *Cihai* also defines *fuxin* as follows: "What is in the genre of insignia or tablets in two parts (*fuqi*) is also called *fuxin*," which means "insignia used as proof" (chap. *wei*, 6). The word *xin*, "faith, worthy of faith," also means "seal, tessera." These insignia were used in a lot of administrative and judicial functions from the Han onward. Before the Tang, they had the shape of a tiger; during the Tang, usually that of a fish, sometimes of a tortoise. Until the Tang, the inscription was written on the edge, before the insignia was slit; later it was written on each side of the fault line; finally, it was written inside the insignia, while the characters *hetong*, engraved on the edge, are split in the middle and must be reconstituted when the two parts of the insignia are reunited. In some cases, the inscription inside, *tong* (same), carved in relief (*yang*) on one side, must also fit together with the text carved *en creux* (*yin*) on the other side. See des Rotours, ibid., 123–24. A homonym is *qi*, a tablet used for a contract, generally divided into two and written. The etymology is "to incise," "to engrave," hence "an incision" (*taille*).

[8] See Kaltenmark 1960: 573. See also Robinet 1993: 24–37.

a contract or a promise, are closely related to the magic talismans that they seem to have preceded historically—even if it is not possible to establish any true logical filiation or to say which function (magical or juridical) preceded the other. We may, as did Kaltenmark, demonstrate how a particular class of *fu*, that of magical talismans in the Daoist tradition referred to as *lingbao*, derive from imperial *fu*, but that is not enough to demonstrate the "purely" contractual origin of these talismans. The compound *lingbao* is made up of two characters whose sense is more or less equivalent, and it refers to an object imbued with magical virtue, virtue that is *ling* (a term we shall come back to) in Heaven, *bao* on earth. A *bao* was a dynastic treasure that would gain or lose weight depending on the level of virtue in the ruling house. These *sacra* were thus perceived as a token of good fortune, a guarantee of life and power, a proof of the Celestial Mandate. Although they apparently originally consisted of precious stones, they came to include magical diagrams and sacred texts. The most ancient of these diagrams are the *Hetu* (River Chart) and the *Luoshu* (Book of the River Luo), talismans of supernatural origin, which led to the cosmological speculations of the *Yi jing* (Book of Changes). According to Kaltenmark, "between the sacred jewels (*pao*), dynastic or family talismans, and magical charms (*fu*) there was no difference in substance but maybe at the most a difference of degree, all in all proportional to the prestige of their owners—whether a king, noble, or simple magician."[9]

The same model operated in the Chan transmission ritual which, as we have seen, can be read as a "sworn fealty" from vassal to overlord. We can see to what point the symbolism of the Dharma robe, the robe that Huineng's rival could not lift when he tried to steal it, grows out of these ideas. It is no coincidence that, in the *Platform Sūtra*, this robe is said to be the token of the "pledge" (*gage de la foi*). The model finally worked when applied to the relationship of the believer to the divine powers. Awakening or transmission is characterized by the perfect matching of two parts, the fusion of two levels of consciousness. The words most often used to refer to this mystical union are actually *fu* and *qi*.[10]

In the case of eminent monks as in that of the ruler, spiritual harmony with Heaven is revealed by the appearance of an auspicious sign that has the value of an emblem, a "*bao* that serves as a guarantee." The model also works on the ritual level: the *bao* or *fu* is only one-half of a pair and

[9] Ibid.; on the use of talismans in Daoism, see also John Lagerwey, *Taoist Ritual in Chinese Society and History* (New York: Macmillan, 1987), 155–61.

[10] See, for instance, the biography of Keizan in *Nihon Tōjō rentōroku*: "The seal of the Buddhas is verified in a secret joining [*qi*], and cannot be searched through words. Only when minds attest [each other] and spirits are united [*qi*] does the life-blood circulate." See *DNBZ* 111: 58b.

was compared to a female pheasant who attracts the male, thus symbolizing a ritual hierogamy. As Kaltenmark points out, "the entire domain of the sacred [in China] is dominated by the idea of a hierogamy, or at least by a tendency towards dichotomy."[11] In this dichotomy *ling* refers to the deity and *bao* to its human receptacle, and the entire ritual can then be interpreted in terms of a sexual union, or like the attraction between iron and a magnet, if we may use the metaphor Keizan used to describe his intimate relationship with Sonin. Keizan further notes, on the occasion of the vows he made toward the end of his life, "If one is in harmony with the will of the Buddha, one will surely have auspicious dreams." Keizan's dreams, for example the one in which he was initiated in turn by Bodhidharma, Śākyamuni, and Maitreya, are *fu*, the right-hand tally that sanctions his union with the Buddha and Bodhisattvas. Similarly, after having transmitted his robe, his fly-whisk, and his staff to his disciple Gasan Jōseki, Keizan states that "auspicious events continued to happen throughout three days," a sign that the Buddhist Heaven had sanctioned the transmission. Much of Keizan's practice—and in this he is no exception—was an attempt to match omens or dreams with actual events.[12] Furthermore, as we have seen, there is a *kirigami* called the "Seal of the Joining of the *fu*," which describes the transmission from master to disciple in precisely this metaphorical strain.

Buddhist *kirigami*, made up mostly of diagrams, owe a great deal to this tradition. Like other insignia of transmission, individually or as elements in a series of *tradita* they make up a kind of talisman, or tessera. In fact, these sheets of paper are magical talismans as well as a token or "symbol" of transmission. Master and disciple, coming together at the moment of transmission like two matching parts or tallies, also form a "symbol," their relationship being, properly speaking, a symbolic relationship. The same can be said, mutatis mutandis, for the relationship between the Buddha and his icon, or that of the Chan master and his portrait.

Insofar as the symbolism of the *fu* is also juridical in nature, we are led to the idea of indebtedness and contract. The *bao*, moreover, have no ordinary exchange value; they are not goods that circulate, except occasionally in the form of gifts. Normally they remain shut away, stored with a single mystical purpose.[13] This difficulty has not prevented Marcel Mauss, perhaps a little too hastily, from deriving the idea of money from

[11] Kaltenmark 1960: 576.

[12] In the case of dreams, this practice was called *yume-awase* ("matching dreams" [with reality]). We may recall Keizan's delight upon discovering in reality the *enoki* tree that he had dreamed about: "Strange, truly stange! See how wakefulness and sleep merge together, dreams and waking harmonize" [*JDZ*, 397].

[13] Ibid.: 568.

that of the talisman. In the Chinese case, the use of *fu* in contracts helps to explain their transfer to the register of the debt.[14] Debt falls precisely into the class of the symbolic. In any case we have here two distinct but related concepts: on the one hand, the juridical idea of contract and guarantee, and on the other the idea of a hierogamy. Depending on the model adopted, the interpretation given to ritual may vary considerably. In the one case, ritual is a redemption of a debt, as Charles Malamoud has shown in an Indian context.[15] In the other, it is a mystical joining that permits a shift from one level to another, as is suggested by Paul Mus, also in an Indian (and Buddhist) context. In religious practice the two models do not seem to be exclusive, and we may detect signs of each of these attitudes in Keizan.

From all this we should keep in mind that, unlike the *sumbolon*, the *bao* is not simply a passive token but a "tessera," an active principle that tries to attract, even to trap, its "mate," just as the female pheasant attracts the male. Because it leads to the hoarding of virtue, the creation of a ritual area is in a way the creation of a *bao* to which the gods can descend.[16] Laozi said that by holding onto the feminine, one can open the gates of Heaven.[17] Similarly, if the Buddhist ascetic acquires powers, "spiritual penetrations" thanks to which he can communicate with Heaven and get a divine response, the only reason is that he himself has become a *bao*, a right-hand (female) tessera. He is the symbol, the mediator par excellence.

BUDDHIST COSMOLOGY

As we have seen, the Chan/Zen symbol is also valuable for its "representational" aspect, and especially for its cosmological connotations. In fact,

[14] See Mauss 1967: 69–76.

[15] See Malamoud 1980: 39–62.

[16] Rolf Stein has shown that the miniature landscape, perceived as microcosm, constitutes a kind of tally. It "calls" the powers of the macrocosm, which flow into it, fuse with it. Like the icon, the *bonsai* is a trap for power, and it was used by the Daoist adept to increase his longevity: another interesting, and quite radical, case of aestheticization. Originally, as Hubert Delahaye has shown, landscape painting had a talismanic value not so different from that of the Daoist "sacred maps." This explains why these paintings, despite secularization, have remained "compelling images" in the hands (and eyes) of the literati. See Stein 1990: 91–104; and Hubert Delahaye, *Les Premières Peintures de paysage en Chine: Aspects religieux* (Paris: Ecole Française d'Extrême-Orient), 1981.

[17] This passage seems to contradict another passage of the *Laozi*: "The Sage holds the left tally (the heavenly tessera), but demands nothing." In this case the Daoist sage seems indeed to be totally identified with Heaven, with the Yang, male principle. But if alternation is the very principle of the Dao, the sage would be he who, embracing the Dao, produces in himself the alternance of Yin and Yang and thus holds alternately the two tesserae.

if the *imaginaire* is indeed structured like a language, it would be surprising if, in spite of the theoretical Chan rejection of cosmology, this language were not in large part cosmological. Before we can, so to speak, join the two tesserae of tradition, we must turn to cosmological symbolism in Chan/Zen. Chan actually inherited two cosmological systems, that of Indian Buddhism and that of Chinese thought. Unlike Chinese cosmology, Buddhist cosmology is first of all a soteriology: the structure that it describes, copied mainly from Brahmanism, is oriented; it exists only "to be left." The dominant idea is clearly that of transmigration through the three worlds (of desire, absence of desire, and subtle matter) and the six destinies (the damned, animals, hungry ghosts, *aśura*, human beings, and *deva*). Beyond these six "ways" one enters the Buddhist path proper, structured according to the schema of the four levels of holiness or the Ten Stages (*bhūmi*) of the Bodhisattva career, at the end or summit of which one reaches the ineffable Nirvāṇa, at the same time the goal and the negation of all cosmological theorizing. The universe is also conceived of as a circle centered on a cosmic mountain, Mount Sumeru, surrounded by five concentric oceans and by five continents. The continent of humans, Jambudvīpa, lies to the south of Mount Sumeru, while that of Uttarakuru, where Keizan believed he had passed the most vividly remembered of his earlier lives, lies to the north. Mystical or contemplative ascension is described as an ascent of Mount Sumeru, at the summit of which is found the Heaven of the Thirty-three (*Trāyastriṃśa*), gods of Hindu origin ruled by Indra. This symbolism of the center and four directions is found again in the stūpa, another representation of the cosmic pillar or Mount Sumeru, all of whose implications Paul Mus has described in inspired pages. There is, in addition, the cosmological symbolism of the *maṇḍala* and that of the *dharmakāya*, the cosmic body of the Buddha (and at the same time his acosmic body, since the entire universe is reabsorbed into its emptiness).

An analogous spatio-temporal symbolism is found in Chinese cosmology, as it is revealed by the compass, the basic instrument for the study of "winds and waters" (*fengshui*), an expression that is translated usually, for lack of a better term, as "geomancy." Chinese cosmological thought, which was formalized during the Han, is dominated by the theories of Yin and Yang and the Five Agents. Marcel Granet was the first Western scholar to reveal all the complexity of this way of thinking, often called "correlative thinking" in contrast to the so-called "rational" thinking of the West—as if all thinking was not at the same time rational and correlative.[18] Michel Foucault has given in *The Order of Things* a superb description of the analogies that governed the prose of the world on the

---

[18] See Granet 1968.

eve of the classical age.[19] According to the Chinese version of this form of thinking, "things respond to each other on the basis of their affinities. Clouds appear in response to dragons, the wind rises in response to the tiger, water flows towards the wet, wood grows towards the dry: such is the law of nature." Thus, each level of reality, whether physical or social, is bound to all the others by a complex network of affinities, according to the flexible logic, the vague but nevertheless effective symbolism of everyday practice. And it is precisely the Chinese compass that allows us to read as superposed strata, and to make communicate with one another, all these orders of reality.

Transplanted to Japan under the name of Onmyōdō (Way of Yin and Yang), this Chinese cosmological theory came to dominate everyday life to the point where no one, not even Zen adepts, could avoid being influenced by it.[20] Chan/Zen rejection of cosmology itself takes its inspiration from Zhuangzi, the Daoist thinker for whom the emergence of cosmology marked the end of the golden age, the death of chaos—a death that he dramatizes in the myth of Hundun ("Chaos"), the (a)cosmic egg both destroyed and completed by the holes pierced in it by two well-intentioned friends. But there too, cosmos and chaos are in a relationship of reciprocal dependence and the Dao, which embraces and articulates them, could be defined as a "chaosmos," to use Norman Girardot's play on words.[21]

Here we cannot go too far into these cosmological theories. A few examples taken from the Zen medieval "esoteric" tradition must suffice. With very few exceptions, Indo-Buddhist cosmology does not seem to have played any important role in China outside strictly Buddhist circles, probably because of resistance from the native cosmology. In Japanese Buddhism we see a fusion of the two systems. Especially in Zen we find a cosmology inherited from neo-Confucianism alongside purely Indian star gods. The *Record of Tōkoku* gives us an idea of the liturgical calendar of Sōtō Zen. We learn, for example, that the erection of the various buildings that make up Yōkōji, and of the stūpa that crowned it symbolically (Gorōhō), was begun at certain significant times in the months: on the third, eighth, sixteenth, eighteenth, or the twenty-sixth day, particularly auspicious days. Keizan uses as his guide a calendrical sūtra translated by the Tantric master Amoghavajra, the *Xiuyao jing* (J. *Shukuyō gyō*), which specifies a total of fourteen auspicious days per month.[22] This is a reference to Indian astrology, not Chinese. But elsewhere he makes great use of the Chinese geomantic and calendrical system.

[19] See Michel Foucault, "The Prose of the World," in Foucault 1974: 17–45.
[20] For an analysis of this theory, see Frank 1958.
[21] See Girardot 1983.
[22] T. 21, 1299: 387–99.

The fusion of the two cosmological systems, especially evident in the *kirigami* of the Sōtō sect, was made easier by the presence, in the two cultures, of analogous generative schemata—especially the centered and oriented conception of space and time. Already with Yōsai we saw an attempt to match the Five Agents (wood, fire, metal, water, and earth) with the five Buddhist elements. According to him it was the Bodhisattva Nāgārjuna who established the connections between these five agents and the five seasons, the five Buddhist elements, and the quinary symbolism of esoteric Buddhism.[23] It is in the esoteric symbolism of the stūpa that the assimilation of the two theories seems to have reached its most elaborated form. This funerary monument, explicitly built to match the pattern of a human body, is made up of five parts symbolizing the five elements according to Japanese Tantrism. These five elements are in turn related to the five Buddhas, the five directions and seasons of Chinese cosmology, the five virtues of Confucianism, and so on. On the whole, the funerary symbolism is more Buddhist than Chinese. It would be well to examine Chan funerary or architectural symbolism. For now we shall be content to analyze the symbolism of a few obvious ritual objects.

THE SYMBOLISM OF RITUAL OBJECTS

Some ritual objects, permeated by a symbolism that is described at length in the *kirigami*, provide us with a more accurate notion of this syncretism of everyday practice. Among them we may note the Dharma robe (Skt. *kāṣāya*, J. *kesa*), the staff (*shujō* or *shakujō*), the fly-whisk (*hossu*), or the scepter (*shippei*).[24] The *shujō*, a ritual staff held by the master when he ascends in the hall, is the symbolic equivalent of Mount Sumeru or the cosmic pillar. To understand this symbolism, we must go back to the myth of the staff's origin. In an Indian country there lived a monster whose body filled all the space between earth and heaven, and who consumed innumerable victims. To come to the aid of beings, the Buddha, using his skillful means, converted him (by placing his hand on the top of his head as in the transmission ritual), baptized him *shujō*, and gave him the task of pacifying the world and converting all beings.[25] We have here a mythological theme that is common in Indian Buddhism. This monster, who could swallow earth and heaven, finally took the form of a staff. As his body was identified with the space between earth and heaven, each of the parts of the staff was said to correspond to, from top to bottom, the

[23] See *Shutten taikō*, quoted in Yanagida 1967: 33; and *Kissa yōjōki*, in Tsunoda et al., 1958: vol. 2, 238–40.
[24] See Ishikawa 1983–94 (6): 105–28.
[25] Ibid., 119–23.

twenty-eight constellations, the thirty-six stars, the seven and nine luminaries, the five agents, the four seasons, the two *maṇḍalas* of esoteric Buddhism, and all the creatures of the earth. This representation of the cosmic pillar that connects earth and heaven is said to be "mountain-shaped." The same symbolism is found in the *shippei* (variant, *chikuhei*), another emblem specific to Chan masters, which is a carved bamboo staff wrapped in raffia. Its name does not occur in canonical sources, although Sōtō tradition says that it originated in India. This time we have a lion, named Heiha, who lived on an Indian mountain called Bamboo Peak (J. *chikuhō*) and ravaged the local population. Having converted it, the Buddha pulled out one of its hairs to make a *chikuhei* (*shippei*), an object whose name comes from a combination of the initial characters in the names of the mountain and the monster (*chiku* + *hei*). This *shippei*, whose touch can turn all beings into Buddhas, at the same time symbolizes and actualizes the dharma body of the Buddha: the three knots of the bamboo it is made from represent the three bodies of the Buddha, the three dots of the Siddham letter *i* or the Chinese character "mind," the three vehicles, the three times (past, future, present); the four sections represent the four classes of beings, the four elements, the four gates of funerary ritual or religious practice (*hosshin, shugyō, bodai,* and *nehan*), the four stages of life, and so on.[26] The same symbolic efficacy is claimed for the *hossu,* or "fly-whisk," an instrument very close functionally to the *shippei* and the *shujō,* and made from a short wooden handle to which was originally attached a horse's or yak's tail.[27] But the practical usefulness of these objects is not nearly as great as their symbolic value, since they are at the same time scepters, symbols of authority that recall to a certain extent the tesserae (tallies) of Chinese officials. The *hossu* is not used only to chase away flies: like a witch's broom, it can sometimes even be a magical steed for the practitioner, to whom it gives the freedom to roam through imaginary lands and space. This is shown in a screen at Eiheiji with its picture of Arhats riding their *hossu* through the air. The fly-whisk thus becomes the symbol of that which transcends the symbolic, that which cannot be written, Keizan tells us, "with ink and paper." After having verified that the nun Meishō, by her silence, was in complete agreement with him and thus understood perfectly the "story of Linji raising his fly-whisk," Keizan granted her confirmation.[28]

Another object that is symbolic in more than one way is the Dharma

[26] Ibid., 125–26.

[27] Ibid., 126–27.

[28] The master and his *hossu* appear in several episodes of the *Linji lu.* See for instance the following: "A monk asked: 'What is the great idea of Buddhism?' The Master raised his whisk. The monk shouted. The master also shouted. The monk hesitated. The master struck him with his whisk." See Sasaki 1975: 4; See also Watson 1993: 15.

robe (*kāṣāya*), often compared to a "field of merits."[29] This metaphor of a field gives rise to all sorts of glosses concerning the five, seven, nine, or twenty-five strips of cloth that make it up. A kind of numerical exegesis also goes on: a robe made of five strips is said to be a robe of the "practice of the Way" because the number five represents the five Buddhas and the five wisdoms. This is why it can fend off the five desires, the five passions, and allow the obtaining of the five powers and the five knowledges. In the symbolic interpretation given in a *Kesamandara kirigami* (Kirigami of the Robe *Maṇḍala*), the robe is assimilated in its finest details to a *maṇḍala* and thus becomes the symbol (and mnemonic device) for the metaphysical universe. The four corners of the robe correspond to the four protective gods, the horizontal pieces to the Buddhas, Bodhisattvas, and two esoteric *maṇḍalas*, the vertical strips to the nine worlds, the horizontal strips to the fields of merit formed by the Arhats and the Bodhisattvas of the Ten Stages, and finally the outer borders correspond to the four oceans.[30] This spatial symbolism is supplemented by a temporal and embryological symbolism according to which the kāṣāya represents a process of biological and spiritual gestation. Another *kirigami*, dealing with the "Method for transmitting the robe, bowl, and lineage chart," indicates that the Dharma robe, and its transmission, symbolize the gestation of the fetus in the womb—itself a model for spiritual gestation: "After having spent ninety days in the paternal body, I spent nine more months in the maternal womb. The 'method for receiving the robe' represents the sequence of practice during this time."[31] According to other sources, the red robe of the patriarch Bodhidharma would represent the placenta, and the nine years spent by the Indian master absorbed in *samādhi* are said to signify the nine months of fetal gestation.[32]

We have considered in Chapter 2 the talismanic role that the lineage chart came to play in medieval Buddhism. The importance of this lineage chart was so great that its owner kept constant watch over it. To do this, he put it into a bag, one also permeated with symbolism: its four inches of width symbolized the four forms of birth, the four knowledges, the

---

[29] The robe was one of the objects that a monk was authorized to possess. Due to their extreme rarity, these objects very soon acquired a heavy symbolical meaning. The Indian tradition lists six, eight, or eighteen authorized objects. The Chan list is rather different, for it reflects local customs: it goes far beyond the traditional three robes and one bowl. Mujaku Dōchū lists ninety-six objects (including, it is true, collective properties such as chairs, etc.)—among which the most important are the three monastic robes.

[30] See Ishikawa 1983–94 (6): 108–9.

[31] Ibid.: 109.

[32] See *Sangai isshinki* (ca. 1649) by Zen master Dairyū. I am indebted to James Sanford for this reference. The embryological symbolism is already apparent in Dōgen's and Keizan's use of the legend of the patriarch Śaṇavāsa, who was born wrapped in a robe. On this question see Faure 1995: 352–66.

four sufferings; the five inches of depth corresponded to the five psycho-physical aggregates, to the five elements, to the five wisdoms. On the front a swastika and two foxes stand face to face, symbolizing the god Inari by whom Dōgen was cured on his return from China.[33] The monk was never separated from this bag, even to go to the latrine. So, to avoid polluting the chart, the bag was made of nine layers of fabric. This strengthened protection can also be explained by the talismanic role of the lineage chart. Indeed, one of the characteristics of the *bao* mentioned above was that it was kept in a box with multiple walls.

The begging bowl was equally important as a token of transmission. In many Chan chronicles, the robe and the bowl are mentioned together, as if they constituted another kind of bipartite symbol.[34] The bowl's spherical shape symbolizes the mind, the true form of the Buddha Śākyamuni. Like the robe, it is guarded by four protective gods and thus represents the center and the four cardinal points.[35] Last we may mention the vase that the monk used for drinking and for washing his hands. As may be expected, the symbolism of "communicating vases" evokes "mind to mind" transmission. "Water from the vase," says a *kirigami*, "corresponds to that called in Tendai 'water of the principle of the essence,' in Shingon 'water of the knowledge [flowing] from the letter "a",' in the Buddha-mind school [Chan/Zen], 'water of the essence of the original Self.' This precious vase is my body, and the water [it contains] is that of my mind."[36] In addition to this watery symbolism, a more complex classification system matches each part of the vase with a specific Buddha, transforming the vase into a Buddhist microcosm.[37]

By the constant material handling of ritual objects and the ideological manipulation of the symbols adhering to them, the Zen adept gradually learned how to read through the superposed symbolic systems, using the logic of the "two truths," and to move from one symbolic system to another. The truth of these systems lies in their relationship to each other, and the Zen master, who was supposed to reject all symbolic mediation, is himself above all a mediator, a symbolic shifter. Still, cosmological

---

[33] See "Kechimyakubukuro kirigami," in Ishikawa 1983–94 (6): 146–47.

[34] However, the complementarity seems to have been perceived as a hierarchy, as can be seen from the following dialogue in the *Keiran shūyōshū* at the point when a disciple asks about the meaning of the statement "The robe expresses the spiritual essence, while the bowl expresses the doctrinal method." The master replies that this statement expresses the difference between esoteric and exoteric Buddhism. See *T.* 76, 2410: 768b.

[35] See Ishikawa 1983–94: 114–15. See also *Shōbōgenzō*, "Hatsuu," in *DZZ* 1: 565.

[36] Ibid., 116. The importance of the bowl and vase, as symbols of the practitioner's body, was such that we have stories in which the destruction of the bowl means (or brings about) the death of the monk. See the case of Puji's disciple, in *Shenseng zhuan T.* 50, 2064: 990.

[37] See Ishikawa 1983–94 (6): 116.

symbolism, far from being the private property of Zen, forms the common basis of all Sino-Japanese culture, a sort of symbolic syntax that does not imply on the part of its users any deep faith but rather a kind of weak, generalized belief. In certain cases it is nothing more than a common cultural reference to which one should not attach much hermeneutic importance. Nevertheless, belief in the talismanic value of certain ritual objects seems, in its turn, sufficiently deeply rooted to hold in check or subvert any attempt to demythologize the tradition. As we decipher these symbols, the temptation sometimes arises to see them as expressing the unchanging anthropological structures of the Buddhist *imaginaire*.[38] Not only is the weight of these symbols very different, but such "anthropological" structures themselves are always historically determined.

This analysis of the underlying symbolic system of the *Record of Tōkoku* could appear at times to be pushed too far. Probably neither Keizan nor the anonymous authors of the *kirigami* were aware of all the implications of this system. But, as Le Goff has insisted, "a symbolic system can be fully effective without explicit awareness."[39] The *imaginaire* makes up a system, but not in the purely logical sense. The tradition reflects the pattern seen in the stūpa and in relics. These, like all icons, imply a presence; as with apparitions in dreams, they are doubles. Are we faced, as Le Goff insists, with a realm of mentalities "rife with distortions, psychic automatisms, survival and rejects, and obscure, incoherent thoughts erected into pseudo-logical systems"?[40] It seems that we are dealing more with a "practical logic," in the sense used by Bourdieu, and thus with an attitude that does not deserve to be discredited as "pseudo-logical," as happens too often.

Furthermore, if the *imaginaire* does consist above all of images, it can also use the aniconic or the schematic, especially the classification schemata that give rise to the *kirigami*: among these, we may consider the ternary Buddhist schema (three in one, three bodies of the Buddha, three dots of the Siddham letter *i*, three superposed circles), the symbolism of the swastika or the wheel (circumambulation of the four cardinal directions and emergence at the center), the oriented trigrams and hexagrams of the *Yi jing*, and the diagram of the "five ranks" (*wuwei*) of the Chan

---

[38] Obviously we must be careful to avoid the extremes denounced by Vladimir Nabokov in the case of the symbolism of the *maṇḍala*, "a term supposedly meaning (in Sanskrit) a magic ring, and applied by Dr. Jung and others to any doodle in the shape of a more or less fourfold spreading structure, such as a halved mangosteen, or a cross, or the wheel on which egos are broken like Morphos, or more exactly, the molecule of carbon, with its four valences—that main chemical component of the brain, automatically magnified and reflected on paper." See Nabokov, *Pnin* (Garden City, NY: Anchor/Doubleday, 1953), 92.

[39] Le Goff 1980: 269–70.

[40] Ibid.: 71.

master Dongshan Liangjie. We have already mentioned this generative symbolism in our discussion of funerary rituals and return to it in Chapter 10 when we examine the rites used to animate the Buddhist icon.

MEMORY AND IMAGINATION

The symbolism of ritual objects also acts as a mnemonic device. It provides an aid to memorizing doctrine or the holy history of Buddhism. The role of memory in the Buddhist imagination, and of imagination in Zen memory, must be taken into account. Awakening is sometimes conceived of as a kind of anamnesia, a recovery of the memory of past existences. *Dhāraṇī*, seen as mnemonic devices; the commemoration of the Buddha (*nenbutsu*); and *memento mori*, memories, or rather "keepsakes," "reminders" of heaven and hell—all are so many "memory palaces." The *Record of Tōkoku* itself is a kind of memorial. The importance that Keizan attaches to documents that are supposed to "serve as an example"— literally "as a mirror"—for future generations is also significant. And in the *kirigami* we see the elaboration of a semiotics of the kōan and the ritual object: each thing or rubric becomes a symbol or an allegory, the carrier of a deep meaning, a mnemonic device.

Another function of memory is illustrated by the ritual importance of holy history. Thus, for the start of construction of the Dharma hall of Yōkōji in 1324, Keizan chose the anniversary of the first sermon of the Buddha in the Deer Park of Sarnath. The inauguration of the Dharma hall took place on the Buddha's birthday, the eighth of the fourth month of the same year. The ridgepole of the Buddha hall was put into place on the anniversary of the offering of the "three *vihāra*": the Jetavana in India, Qinglongsi in China, Hōjōji and the great stūpa at Kōyasan in Japan. Examples from the past are constantly present and one sees oneself in their mirror. As Cornelius Castoriadis has said, "When [Marx] stressed the fact that the memory of generations past weighs heavy in the awareness of the living, he was still indicating the past mode of the *imaginaire*, the past lived as if it were the present, ghosts more powerful than men of flesh and blood, the dead taking hold of the living [*le mort qui saisit le vif*], as he liked to say."[41] Those who imitate constantly the examples of the ancients, and thus place the present under the aegis of the past, are still bringing into play the symbolic logic of the tessera.

[41] Cornelius Castoriadis, *L'Institution imaginaire de la société* (Paris: Seuil, 1975), 184–85.

Chapter Ten

ICONIC IMAGINATION

CHAN/ZEN is often described as having an iconoclastic spirit or a strong tendency to aniconism.[1] Here I am using the word *icon* to denote what the Indian Buddhists call *buddhapratimā* (literally "replica" or "copy" of the Buddha) or *mūrti* ("representation, memory aid"), and the Chinese and Japanese *foxiang/butsuzō* ("Buddha image"). Although the etymology of the Indian terms suggests something close to the Western notion of an "image," we have here something quite different from a simple representation.[2] For this reason I have chosen to use the term *icon*—suggesting, as it does, the embodiment of a presence. This term has, as is well known, been used by Charles S. Peirce to mean a sign whose signifier and signified are in a natural relationship, possibly one of resemblance or evocation. Peirce contrasts the icon with the index or the symbol. While the *index* exists in a metonymic relationship with the thing represented, of which it constitutes in some sense a fragment, a trace, and the *symbol* breaks with both resemblance and contiguity, the Peircean *icon* retains its element of resemblance but is no longer contiguous.[3]

By contrast, the kind of Buddhist icon under discussion here is a *vera icona*, with a presence that gives it life. As a "manifest trace" of the Buddha, it has the nature of an apparition and is not just a simulacrum. In this sense it is closer to the Peircean index. But one could say much the same thing of the *symbol*, a term I have used up to now in its etymological meaning of an efficacious sign, which shares in the thing being symbolized. Thus the Peircean reader should not be misled by my use of the terms *icon* and *symbol*: we are always in the realm of *indices*.

Historians of art, who have inherited the Platonic notion of mimesis, have tended to undervalue or overvalue these images as "artistic representations," more or less realistic in their nature and hence aesthetic—

---

[1] I argue in Chapter 11 that there is also an "aniconic" imagination, a form of imagination that goes beyond images.

[2] The Chinese term used for "image," *xiang*, "is more accurate in its polysemy. It derives from a homophon which designates, among other things, heavenly configurations that had iconic counterparts or "doubles" on earth, talismans (*fu*), or what we will call here "symbols" (in the etymological sense). As Edward Schafer puts it, "Celestial events are the 'counterparts' or 'simulacra' of terrestrial events; sky things have doppelgängers below, with which they are closely attuned." See Schafer 1977: 292n.11. For a more detailed terminological discussion, see Foulk and Sharf 1993–94: 158–60.

[3] See Hoopes 1991: 239–40.

icons in the Peircean sense. They have for this reason missed their "indexical" truth, creating a gulf between "the real and its double."[4] A Buddhist icon, as we shall see, can be conceived of as a double, just like the funerary tablets (J. *hai*, which are "dotted" just as one "opens the eyes" of statues), the portraits of Zen masters (*chinsō* or *shin*), and stūpas (especially the "seamless," or "ovoid" stūpas).

At first sight the metaphorical logic of Western representation, according to which a thing takes the place of another without in any way sharing in its nature, seems to describe pretty closely the two-level structure of Buddhist cosmology and the cleavage that this cosmology imposed between the levels of the absolute and the relative. This logic is expressed, for example, in the words of the Chinese master Huiyuan on the subject of the Buddha: "There [in Nirvāṇa] is his [real] body, here on earth is his shadow."[5] But it seems to have been replaced by a logic of synecdoche and metonymy, according to which the shadow or trace acquires the reality of the body and is no longer separate from it. Thus an icon of the Buddha came to be perceived no longer as a "body of metamorphosis" (*nirmāṇakāya*) standing for the dharma body (*dharmakāya*) but as this dharma body itself. Chan/Zen discourse, however, has continued to oscillate between metaphor and metonymy, between transcendence and immanence, constantly replaying the game of absence and presence.[6]

Of course there are plenty of Buddhist texts affirming that, since everything is ultimately empty, the same must be said of wooden or stone images: they cannot reveal the slightest sign of feeling, and so it is useless to make offerings to them.[7] Even if, since we cannot adore the Buddha in person, it is meritorious for us to venerate images of the Buddha, these latter are still, from an orthodox point of view, devoid of any soul.[8] This rejection of idolatry led to an iconoclastic tendency, hints of which exist in various early Buddhist texts. This tendency, however, developed in

[4] I will give only one representative example, concerning images of Arhats painted during the Edo period by Katō Nobukiyo with letters of the *Lotus Sūtra*. Noting that this was a new technique, de Visser remarks: "We cannot but congratulate those ages that had not known this childish and tasteless way of showing one's devoutness by degrading art to a kind of puzzle." De Visser has indeed no difficulty in quoting Japanese art historians who totally agree with him on this point. See de Visser 1923: 52.

[5] See Walter Liebenthal, "Shih Hui-yüan's Buddhism as Set Forth in His Writings," *JAOS* 70 (1950): 258.

[6] Admittedly, this logic of presence is a radical departure from orthodox Buddhism, for which the *dharmakāya* was perhaps not the metaphysical essence that later commentators have read into it. On this question see Harrison 1992. However, in Japanese cultic practice the metaphysical interpretation seems to have prevailed.

[7] See, for example, *T.* 39, 1796, ch. 20, quoted in *Hōbōgirin*, vol. 3: 213b.

[8] *T.* 8, 224, ch.10, quoted in *Hōbōgirin*, ibid: 214a.

Mahāyāna and especially in Chinese Chan, where, when images are not rejected outright they seem to be accepted unwillingly, tolerated simply as "skillful means" insofar as they allow neophytes to strengthen their faith and acquire merits. Nevertheless, Buddhist practice, as a whole, seems to militate against these normative statements. They cannot provide our point of departure; or rather, we should depart from them in order to measure the gap between a certain theory (which too often ends up being taken as the only possible way of seeing things) and the stubborn logic of concrete practice.

Despite orthodox protestations, icons clearly played an important role even in a supposedly aniconic or iconoclastic school like Chan/Zen. According to the Zen scholar Mujaku Dōchū, one can identify three kinds of "spiritual images" (Ch. *lingxiang*, J. *reizō*, literally "images [charged] with power," *ling/rei*): those that protect the Dharma, those that fulfill a function in monastic life, and those that protect the individual after death.[9] Icons constitute thus an integral part of the spiritual economy (or rather, "iconomy," both from the same root *oikonomia*) of the monastery. By the mediation that they establish in helping to "make the invisible visible," Buddhist icons, like their Christian counterparts, are at the same time seeable and seeing, passive and active. Their "realism" is only the obverse of their supernatural quality.

YŌKŌJI ICONOLOGY

In the *Record of Tōkoku*, Keizan describes the statues and sacred images of Yōkōji and gives details about the circumstances surrounding their manufacture and installation. Thus we learn that the *honzon*, Shaka (Skt. Śākyamuni), was carved in wood thanks to the gift of thirty strings of cash from a layman on the occasion of the thirteenth anniversary of his mother's death. The right-hand acolyte, Kannon (Skt. Avalokiteśvara), was commissioned by a layman from Kyoto, this time for the thirteenth anniversary of his father's death. The left-hand acolyte Kokūzō (Skt. Ākāśagarbha) was commissioned by another layman on his own account. At least in the two first cases, the making of a Buddhist statue formed part of a funeral ceremony and was intended to help ensure the final repose of the dead person. In the third case also, even though the act seems to be a case primarily of seeking "benefits in this world," the post-mortem fate of the donor also appears to have played a role. The presence of these two particular Bodhisattvas beside the Buddha is unusual. In most triads in the Buddha Hall of Zen monasteries, the acolytes of the

---

[9] See *Zenrin shōkisen*, 1963: 108–65.

Buddha are either the Bodhisattvas Monju (Skt. Mañjuśrī) and Fugen (Skt. Samantabhadra), or else the Arhats Mahākāśyapa and Ānanda. Actually, whatever its composition, the presence of a triad in a Zen monastery is at first glance not very orthodox. In these monasteries, the Dharma hall—where the abbot, ritually identified with the Buddha, officiates from his high chair—was supposed to have superseded the Buddha hall with its icons.[10]

Keizan describes the installation and inaugural ritual for this particular triad after the selection of propitious days by making use of onmyōdō calendrical techniques. Funerary rituals were obviously important in the day-to-day life of this monastery and contributed to its upkeep. As noted earlier, Yōkōji had the status of a temple "dedicated to awakening" (bodaiji)—a temple that specialized in the liturgy for the dead of lay families. Thus it seems likely that the statues in the Buddha hall were not only objects of the monastic cult but also filled, as seems clear from their origin, a mortuary function for both laypeople and monks. In the case of this particular triad, Keizan seems to have participated as more than simply the officiating priest acting on behalf of the layperson making the offering: he himself shared in the financing of the undertaking, furnishing the funds to decorate the statues. Perhaps the priest and the faithful, the master and the disciples, joining their efforts in the production of the icon, should be seen as becoming its metaphorical parents. We shall return to this question, taking our cues from studies of sacrifice in India carried out by Sylvain Lévi and Paul Mus, and more recently by Charles Malamoud.[11]

Alongside the material iconology of Yōkōji, one must consider the implicit or "imaginary" iconology constituted by the rituals and distinct from the visible statuary in the monastery. Rituals for transferring merits (ekō), just like the visualization techniques of esoteric ritual, people the monastery with a multitude of deities whose imaginary presence is no less "real" than that of the deities in their icons.[12] Thus we should add to the material icons like the triad in the Buddha Hall or the statues of the various protectors of Yōkōji (Idaten, Shōhō Shichirō, Ususama, the sixteen Arhats, the patriarch Bodhidharma, etc.) the "mental" icons whose invisible horde, gathered together by ritual invocations, periodically fills the monastery's imaginary space.

After having recounted the installation of the icons of Kannon and Kokūzō in the Buddha Hall, Keizan dwells on the story of another icon of Kannon, the one that forms the honzon of Enzūin. This was a "Kannon with eleven faces" (Jūichimen Kannon) that he had inherited from his

---

[10] See for instance Jingde Chuandenglu, in T. 51, 2076: 251a.
[11] Lévi 1966; Mus 1935; Malamoud 1989.
[12] See on this point Colas 1990: 28.

mother Ekan, a statue that was by chance preserved among the treasures of Yōkōji and rediscovered recently. Here is this story, as told at length by Keizan:

> Long ago my merciful mother, at the age of eighteen, was separated from her mother. Not knowing what had happened to her, she grieved over her for seven or eight years. Then she went to Kiyomizu Temple to pray that she might be told where her mother was. For seven days she went daily to the temple. On the sixth day she found on her way there a [carved] head of Eleven-Faced [Kannon]. She then made the following vow: "In the course of looking for my mother, I came daily to Kiyomizu and I have found a carved head of the Venerated One. Given these circumstances, if I have any karmic affinities with you, take pity on me. Help me to find my mother again, and I will have the rest of your body carved and I will venerate [this image] throughout my life." [*JDZ*, 405]

As we can see, Keizan's mother, resorting to spiritual blackmail, took a vow to have the statue completed if the Bodhisattva would help her to find her mother. Apparently her prayer was granted because the statue received a body as an ex-voto.[13] Apparently well pleased, Kannon subsequently granted many prayers of Ekan concerning her son. Thus it was the Bodhisattva who gave Ekan this child, destined for greatness. It was Kannon who watched over Keizan to be sure that he did not fall into evil paths because of his irritable nature. Ekan, with her dearest wishes satisfied, dedicated herself to the cult of this icon until her death. When Keizan inherited the icon, he set it up in the nunnery that he had just established and entrusted to Sonin.

> This is why, when she died at the age of eighty-seven, she left me this *honzon*. I received it and kept it carefully when I withdrew to this mountain. Having chosen one of the peaks of this mountain, which I called Peak of the Magnificent Lotuses, I built on it a temple that I named the Temple of [the Kannon of] Perfect Penetration [Enzūin]. I gave to the proprietor of this mountain [Sonin] the places called Whirling Water Peak and Grain Growing Plain. It was at this time that my birth hair and umbilical cord, which my mother had always kept with her, were respectfully put into this statue. As for Sonin, through her non-dual spirit of faith, she produced the pure thought [of awakening]. This is why, after having passed this *honzon* on to her, I placed my birth hair and my umbilical cord inside the base of the Kannon, on the righthand side. I placed them in a tin tube to ensure the eternal protection of this mountain. [Thus, Enzūin] was

[13] This is confirmed by a variant of the text: "The day after her vow, my mother sent for a woman. On the next day, when she went to Kiyomizu, she met on her way this woman who told her where to find her mother. This is why she went to ask a craftsman to carve the body of the Venerated One, and dedicated a cult to this statue throughout her lifetime."

to become a temple of prayers for the well-being of women, according to the universal wish of my merciful mother, and I, Keizan would be enabled to spread the law and come to the aid of beings. [*JDZ*, 406]

A meaningful detail reveals that Enzūin must have also served as a maternal mausoleum: Keizan placed in the base of the statue his umbilical cord and the hair cut off at his birth, both piously preserved by his mother. He was thereby consecrating the place "to ensure the eternal protection of this mountain." In the symbolic (and almost incestuous) logic of this act, the mother of Keizan, identified with the icon of Kannon, once again became pregnant, this time eternally, in a way regenerated after death by the embryo of her son and carrying a past and a future that transcend life and death.

Let us set out a few stepping stones, to which we shall return later: unlike the icons in the Buddha hall of Yōkōji, which are completely manmade and then ritually animated, that of Enzūin is partially self-made, and thus naturally animate, before any ritual is performed. Its body is, however, a "conditional" body, one obtained after the granting of a wish. Finally, to transfer this icon from a private to a collective cult, Keizan saw fit to "reanimate" its power by enclosing within it "relics" of his own birth, symbols or seeds of life. Of course it could be a matter of revitalizing Keizan himself, by metonymically identifying him with the Bodhisattva. These two interpretations are not mutually exclusive.

We could also consider the *honzon* of the Buddha hall, Śākyamuni, as a "fixed image," a permanent source of power, which corresponds to the "all-pervading" aspect of the god, while his acolytes Kannon and Kokūzō are cult images, although not movable as is the case in India.[14] The fact that at Enzūin it is Kannon, originally a transferable image, who becomes the *honzon*, and thus fixed image, is not contradictory since the nunnery is in the same kind of hierarchical relationship to Yōkōji as Kannon is to Śākyamuni.

To understand the significance of Keizan's action when he animates the statue of Kannon with his own "natal" relics, one must look further at the cult of images or icons in Buddhism and Hinduism—and more especially in so-called Tantrism. In India the cult of a deity implies a dialectical relationship between two kinds of images: a mental image, secret, made of pure energy and produced by the officiating priest's visualization efforts, and a material image, visible and adored by the faithful. If the material image is the projection into material form of a mental image, it also serves as a basis for the latter even if not any more essential to the meditation of the priest than the mental image is to the worship of the

[14] See Colas 1989.

faithful.[15] Nevertheless, the orthodox view is that it is the mental image, the essence of the god, that one is considered to worship—even if, as is ordinarily the case, the worshipers do not know how to visualize the god—and not the material image, seen as a simple epiphenomenon.

LIVING ART

This set of representations (which I describe as an "ideology of immanence") is not limited to India. In China too, even before the introduction of Buddhism, statues were considered to be alive, and the Japanese tradition also reports many examples of statues that sweat, weep, move, walk, or fly. Throughout Asia, bringing icons to life involves an "opening of the eyes." A similar "dotting" rite animated ancestral tablets or funerary steles, even if these latter (doubtless not anthropomorphic enough) never acquired the "imaginary" mobility of icons. In addition the Chan/Zen "portraits of the masters" (*chinsō* or *shin*) were, as noted above, functional equivalents of Chinese mortuary portraits, funerary tablets, and other "seats of the spirit" (Ch. *shenzuo*).[16] These portraits thus became the locus and the proof of the immortality of the ancestors. In Daoism, finally, by a kind of overkill, we come to an "opening of/to the light" not only of the eyes but of every part of the body of statues, ritual puppets, or talismans.[17] In all these cases we see the operation of a flexible logic combining metonymy and synecdoche, logic of the part-for-the-whole and of identity by association or resemblance; a logic reinforced in the case of Buddhist statues by the presence within them of "living" relics.

Icons constitute the visible body of the gods, their "traces" in this world—but these traces imply an invisible presence rather than an absence. True, according to the legend about the first representation of the Buddha, a wooden statue made on the orders of the king Udayana, it was carved to take the place of an absent Buddha. Śākyamuni had temporarily gone up into the Heaven of the Thirty-three Gods to preach the Law to his mother Māyā. The legend seems to indicate that this "image," soon to be copied by King Prasenajit, was seen only as a simple replica (*pratimā*) of an absent original. But this interpretation is belied by the end of the legend, which tells how the statue went to meet the Buddha on his return from

[15] See Padoux 1990: 6, 28.

[16] See J.J.M. de Groot, *The Religious System of China: Its Ancient Forms, Evolution, History and Present Aspects: Manners, Customs and Social Institutions Connected Therewith.* 6 vols. (Taibei: Southern Materials Center, 1982 [1910]), vol. 1, 113–14. On the "pointing" of the funerary tablet, see ibid., 214–17.

[17] See on that point Chu 1991: 155–57; and the additional note in Frank 1988: 86.

Heaven.[18] It was thus in a certain way a sort of substitute, a counterpart. Just as, according to William Blake, the body is only the visible part of the soul, so the icon is only the visible part of the mind (or of the dharma body) of the Buddha (or the Chan master). Thus Menzan, in a text that deals with the bronze statue of an Arhat, states, "I have heard that, when the Tathāgata Śākya[muni] was still in this world, [King] Prasenajit made the first image of him, and that this image, which resembled the living Buddha to the finest details, possessed all his virtues. Here now is an Arhat image: how does it differ from a true Arhat? Both of them have the same virtues."[19] The presence, whether latent or manifest, of gods or Buddhas in their icons is only an example of the belief in a kindly divine mediation that ensures the acquisition of benefits in this world and in the others.[20] Thus there is nothing startling in the fact that in Zen, offerings of tea and hot water are presented to the Buddhas and Bodhisattvas, to the Arhats and patriarchs. Comparable offerings were also made to the tablet and portrait of a dead master during funeral services and thereafter repeated daily, or at least on each anniversary of his death.[21]

The role of icons is not only religious but also has legal consequences. We know, for example, that an icon of the Buddha, like his stūpa or relics, could become the owner of a monastic estate. The presence of icons is needed to legitimize the various phases of Chan/Zen monastic life: the preaching of the Law takes place when the Chan master is seated face-to-face with Śākyamuni, in the Buddha hall, thus becoming in a way his reflection. Meditation goes on under the direction of an elder, but he also is only a substitute for the Bodhisattva Mañjuśrī whose icon, in his form as a "holy monk," watches over the Monks' hall. According to Guifeng Zongmi (780–841), the twice monthly confession of sins has to be made in a ritual space where images of the twenty-four worthies have been set up, on a high seat.[22]

---

[18] See T. 51, 2085: 860b.

[19] Quoted in Michihata 1983: 227.

[20] See for instance the famous "Mikaeri no Amida" at Zenrinji, a Kyoto temple popularly known as Eikandō, after the name of Eikan (1033–1111), a practitioner of *nenbutsu*. According to the legend, one morning in 1082, when Eikan was circumambulating the Amida altar, the *honzon* came down from his pedestal and began to walk ahead of him. As the dumbfounded Eikan stopped, Amida turned his head back and admonished: "Eikan, you are dawdling!" Eikan subsequently had a statue carved to commemorate his vision of Amida looking back over his shoulder.

[21] Tea, whose transplantation in Japan is usually traced back to the seeds brought from China by Yōsai in 1168, is held to be a stimulant for meditation, preventing drowsiness. Yōsai wrote an entire work to exalt its therapeutical and soteriological virtues. The tea ceremony soon became a quasi-sacramental rite leading to a kind of spiritual catharsis. See *Kissa yōjōki*, in Tsunoda et al. 1958: vol. 1, 237–40.

[22] ZZ 1, 15: 219a.

Similarly, the ritual of receiving Bodhisattva precepts, as it developed in China and especially Japan, no longer required taking a vow before "visible" masters (the ten officiating priests of Indian Buddhism) but before "invisible masters," the Buddhas and Bodhisattvas of the ten directions who were present either in the form of icons or simply through visualization.[23] According to some sources, the postulant knows that his confession has been effective only when he receives some auspicious signs, and this may require him to confess his sins over a fairly long period of time (from one or two weeks to a whole year).[24] One frequently mentioned sign of this kind consists of the practitioner seeing the Buddha approach him to put his hand on the top of his head—a gesture that we also see between master and disciple during the Sōtō transmission ritual. According to a canonical source, "while the adept is sleeping or meditating, Ākāśagarbha [i.e., Kokūzō, one of the two Bodhisattvas set up by Keizan in the Buddha hall of Yōkōji] marks his arm with a seal shaped like the "wish-granting jewel" on which is engraved *xucui*, "sin eliminated." If propitious signs do not appear, the adept must purify himself by cleaning the latrines for eight hundred days before he can receive the Precepts.[25] All of this simply shows that the major rituals of Chinese Buddhism—preaching, meditation, ordination, and confession—are closely bound up with the presence of icons and the visualization of Buddhas and Bodhisattvas. The importance of icons in these rituals has even led the Japanese art historian Nakano Genzō to say that Buddhist iconology derives from the need for images during confession rites.[26]

Icons had a visual power so great that during certain "eye-opening" ceremonies the priest had to beware of their gaze, deflecting it by use of a mirror.[27] Certain deities, such as Vināyaka (avatar of the Hindu Gaṇeśa, known in Japan under the name of Shōten or Kangiten), were considered to have the "evil eye," and even today their images are carefully concealed.[28]

---

[23] See *Yogācārabhūmi-śāstra*, T. 30, 1579: 514; *Pusa chanjie jing*, T. 30, 1583: 1014c; quoted in Kuo 1994: 39–43.

[24] T. 24, 1484, p. 1006c.

[25] T. 13, 409: 677c; quoted in Kuo 1994: 137.

[26] Nakano Genzō, *Keika no geijutsu*, quoted in Kuo 1994: 146. See also *Fanwang jing*, T. 24, 1484: 1006c.

[27] See Gombrich 1966.

[28] This is also done in part because of official prudishness, an inheritance from the Meiji period when classical representations of the elephant-headed god and his companion and conqueror Avalokiteśvara (Kannon) showed them coupled, making "the beast with two backs." We know that a statue of this paired god was offered to Sōjiji, the second monastery founded by Keizan, although there is no indication as to its origin and function. During the medieval period, Kangiten was worshiped mainly in the Tachikawa school of Shingon Buddhism, a school that was eventually forbidden because of its "heretical" (i.e., sexual)

Is a physical icon really nothing more than a *mūrti*, a representation and aide-mémoire, as one orthodox view has it? Obviously it is much more than that. Its polysemic and multifunctional quality is clearly affirmed in the following Chinese poem entitled "The Gateway to the Worship of Relics, Images, and Stūpas": "[An icon] expresses our feelings, helps us to concentrate our thought, will make it compassionate and loving;/ It brings down the spirit [of the Buddha] by painting him in his image, and casts light on all doubts."[29] The icon is a support for the deity and a means of concentration for the priest and the ordinary worshiper. In this way it is a trapper of energy, it draws the deity, providing a matrix for it, and gives it a support or receptacle. Sometimes it even becomes a perfect hypostasis and is identified completely with the god.

RITUAL ANIMATION

Gods are attracted into their icons by a ritual "animation" that gives them a specific "efficacy" or "power" (*ling*) and transforms them into "spiritual icons" (*lingxiang, reizō*).[30] But this animation, carried out by various rites such as the "opening of the eyes," leads to an almost paradoxical situation. In esoteric Buddhism in particular, the consecration of an icon is at the same time both a birth and a death.[31] The consecration is seen as putting the icon into a state of *samādhi*, a sort of suspended animation that recalls the *samādhi* of Buddhist mummies. Whether it is seen as a death (in the case of mummies) or a birth (in the case of icons), this suspended animation brings with it a concentration of power that serves to regenerate the community. Like mummies, icons mediate between life and death, between immanence and transcendence, between the visible and the invisible.

---

symbolism. On this deity see Strickmann 1996: 243–90; Sanford and Kabanoff 1994: 99–126; Duquenne (forthcoming). Is the presence of icons of Kangiten in Zen monasteries like Tōjiin in Kyoto (founded by Musō Soseki) or Keizan's Sōjiji a mere coincidence, due to their past relationships with Shingon, or does it point to a more important role played by this Tantric deity in the "esoteric" rituals of Zen? The second possibility cannot be excluded, particularly because we find various elements deriving from the Tachikawa "heresy" in the Sōtō *kirigami*.

[29] Richard Mather, "Hymns on the Devotee's Entrance into the Pure Life," *JAOS* 106, 1 (1986): 93.

[30] Michel Strickmann has noted the striking similarity between the animation of icons and Tantric procedures to invoke a spirit into a medium-child. See Strickmann 1996.

[31] For the Tantric elements in the following description, I am indebted to Michel Strickmann 1996: 165–211.

Buddhist icons are animated by means of a process that may take various forms but can ultimately be reduced to five ritual sequences: 1) the "transmission" of the efficacy of an established, powerful icon to one or more new icons—in Southeast Asia such a transmission, which amounts to the continuation of a spiritual line akin to the Chan patriarchal lineage, is achieved through a cord connecting the old icon to the new one; 2) a consecration corresponding to esoteric anointing—at once a rite of birth, royal consecration, and entry into monastic orders; 3) the "imparting of breaths," during which one or several monks, by incantation, exhort a Buddha to descend into the icon, or else transfer into the icon the energy that they have accumulated in the course of their own rituals and meditation, so endowing the icon with their own Buddhahood; 4) the placing of relics (*śarīra*) and various other cult objects into a cavity in the body or the base of the icon; 5) the actual "opening of the eyes." Here we should note that *mimesis* also plays a role insofar as the degree of resemblance to the human or divine model can sometimes contribute to the magic trapping of the forces that bring the icon to life. However, this is not always a necessary condition, and very rarely does it alone suffice.

Various authors have noted that in Southeast Asia the umbilical cord connecting a statue with its "mother statue" or with the monks is considered essential to its animation. This is not true in Japan except in certain cases. At Tōdaiji, for example, all the monks hold the cord, so participating in the creative act.[32] Because this rite does not seem to have played a significant role in Chan/Zen liturgy, we shall not dwell on it. But it will be worth our time to linger a moment over the rites for mantric imparting of breaths, the placing of relics, and the opening of the eyes.

"Mantric" Imparting of Breaths

A *kirigami* tells how statues were brought to life in the Sōtō school. Although this document dates from later than the time of Keizan, we may assume that his own thinking on this point was based on esoteric orthodoxy. The document in question describes a very important rite called the "three dots of the *i*." This rite is associated with animating icons and delivering the dead—another point confirming that the animation of an icon or funerary tablet also corresponds to the consecration and simul-

---

[32] The opposite ritual takes place in Chinese funerals, whose aim is above all to avoid the return of the dead. Thus, in Taiwan, the relatives of the dead hold a string attached to the coffin, and they cut it off one after the other, symbolically expressing that all ties that bound them to the deceased are thereby cut off. According to the funerary *kirigami* of Sōtō, the "cutting off of ties" is, if not materially represented as in the Chinese case, at least inscribed as an apotropaic formula at the four orients of the grave when the latter is sealed. See Ishikawa 1983–94 (4).

taneous entry of the iconized being (or, in the case of a tablet, the dead person) into Nirvāṇa. The "three dots" are those constituting the letter *i* in the Sanskrit script called Siddham—the vowel that is considered, in the esoteric tradition, as the "root-sound" and so symbolizes (or better, actualizes) the origin of all things: "Because of the mystical virtue of this Sanskrit vowel, when one writes, pronounces, or hears it one returns to the origin of all things, the formless state (*wuxiang*), otherwise called Nirvāṇa or Buddhahood."[33] The three dots also actualize the three circumambulations (*pradakṣiṇā*) that the believer makes around the Buddha or his stūpa, themselves felt to actualize the Buddha's dharma body (*dharmakāya*), wisdom (*prajñā*), and deliverance (*vimokṣa*). According to some commentaries, these three dots are those of the Sino-Japanese character for "heart" or "mind" (Ch. *xin*, J. *shin* or *kokoro*), a character chosen because of its resemblance, in cursive script, to the Sanskrit letter. They are also represented in the Sōtō tradition by three circles that symbolize/actualize the three aspects of ultimate reality: "The uppermost circle represents the true essence of the formless state, that is, the virtue of the dharma body [of the Buddha]. The circle in which is written the character *myō* ("subtle, mysterious") expresses the profound nature of the formless state, that is, the virtue of wisdom. The circle holding the character *shin* ("mind") expresses the mysterious function of the formless state, that is, deliverance."[34] This is why, we are told, the officiating priest at funeral rites strikes the coffin three times before tracing a circle in the air for good measure—in ritual matters redundancy is no sin. A comparable rite takes place during the "opening of the eyes" of an icon, or other rituals animating a "substitute body," all intended to ensure immortality for a double (substitute body) of oneself or for the dead person.[35] These rites would be rejected as nonorthodox during the Edo period by reformers like Menzan Zuihō, but they probably made up an essential part of the practice of Keizan and his contemporaries.[36]

The Placing of Relics

The custom of putting relics inside an icon derives from the belief that the presence of *śarīra* is necessary to animate a statue, and the statue is thenceforth considered as a replica of the Buddha. However, as Paul Mus

---

[33] See Sugimoto 1982: 89, 235.

[34] Ibid.

[35] See Ishikawa 1983–94 (20). See also *Bukke ichidaiji yawa* on the pointing of the eyes of a funerary tablet (*sotoba*), in ibid. (2): 149. Other *kirigami* describe how to point the eyes of specific icons: Kannon, En no Gyōja, the Ten Kings of Hell, etc. See ibid. (20): 119–23.

[36] See Menzan, *Tōjō shitsunai danshi kenpi shiki*, in SZ 15, *Shitsuchū*, 197–218.

has stressed in the case of the stūpa, "the placing of relics crowns the symbolism, but does not create it."[37] But with the growth of the cult of relics in China, the placing of the *śarīra* seems to have become a requirement. This is illustrated by the case of the Chan master Danxia Tianran (739–824), who burned an icon to keep warm, with the excuse that it did not contain any relics.[38] Despite its importance, the placing of relics could not take the place of the ritual opening of the icon's eyes. We know that, according to the Vinaya master Yijing (635–713), when one makes a statue or a sanctuary, one can place inside two kinds of *śarīra*: 1) bodily relics of the Buddha; 2) the canonical passage dealing with "codependent origination" (*pratītyasamutpāda*).[39] A Japanese document dated 1183 reports that, when Chōgen restored the Great Buddha of Tōdaiji, relics of the Buddha Śākyamuni were placed inside the statue of the Buddha Vairocana, thus fusing the two bodies of the Buddha—the bodies of metamorphosis (*nirmāṇakāya*) and retribution (*saṃbhogakāya*)—to the greatest benefit of all beings. Sometimes in these two kinds of ritually animated structures we also find "preposthumous" relics: the most famous case is certainly that of the icon of the Zen master Ikkyū Sōjun, on the head of which were implanted hair apparently from the head of Ikkyū himself. This category of relics also covers the placing of the umbilical cord and birth hair of Keizan into the base of the statue of Kannon at Enzūin.

The Opening of the Eyes

The rite of "opening the eyes" (*kaigen*) was already known in Indian Buddhism and even in Brahmanism. It appears in esoteric Buddhist texts translated into Chinese during the Tang, and in Japanese chronicles of the consecration of the Great Buddha of Tōdaiji in Nara, a ceremony conducted by the Indian monk Bodhisena in 753. No reference to this ritual has been found in more ancient Chinese documents, even though "dotting the eyes" seems to have been a characteristic of Chinese iconology very early on.[40]

Richard Gombrich, describing a contemporary performance of this rite in Sri Lanka, also mentions the parallel rite of "closing the eyes" of an icon to deconsecrate it or make it temporarily powerless. A similar case is noted by Bernard Frank in the context of Japanese Buddhism. According to a Sōtō *kirigami*, the parallelism between the two rituals is such that

---

[37] Mus 1935: 211.
[38] T. 50, 2061, p. 773b.
[39] See Lamotte 1949: vol. 2, 623; and Boucher 1990.
[40] See Delahaye 1983.

one cannot "send back" a god or a Buddha if one does not know the precise method used to open its eyes.[41]

In his pioneering study on the *kirigami*, Sugimoto Shunryū describes two sorts of "opening": one is termed "abstract" or "based on the principle," and the other "concrete," "factual," or "based on phenomena." Only the first is actually termed "opening the eyes," while the second is, strictly speaking, a "dotting in" of the eyes. While the "concrete" ceremony resembles closely the rite described by Gombrich, the "abstract" opening is carried out simply by means of mantras and *mudrā* ("seals," symbolic gestures with the hands). According to our erudite commentator, the essential difference is that, while during the "dotting" the priest projects into the icon his own power (*jiriki*), or his own Buddhahood, in "abstract" opening he invokes and introduces into the icon the power of "another" (*tariki*), that of the cosmic Buddha Dainichi or one of his specific hypostases, a Buddha or Bodhisattva. As a result, when he wants to "close the eyes" of the icon, the priest sends the spirit dwelling in the icon back to its original domain, the metaphysical sphere if he is dealing with an "abstract" ritual, or his own body if it is a "concrete" ritual. The latter is the ritual used most commonly in Sōtō Zen, while the rite "based on the principle" comes mostly from Shingon esotericism. On the other hand, in the Pure Land school the two rites were complementary and followed each other, but only the "abstract" rite was performed by the priest. According to Hōnen (1133–1212), "what we understand by 'opening of the eyes' is first of all the act by which the master painter opens the eyes by marking them, a rite called 'opening the eyes based on phenomena.' Then the monks, with the 'Eye of the Buddha formula,' open the eyes [in turn]; then, with the 'Dainichi formula,' all the merits of the Buddha are actuated [in the icon], and this is called 'opening of the eyes based on the principle.' "[42]

Another Sōtō *kirigami* gives directions for "installing" and "dotting the eyes" of an icon. It emphasizes the importance of the verbal element, which is no longer simply a mantra but a typically Chan "dialogue" between master and disciple. This dialogue is completely stereotypical, and I give here only the first section of it:

> The master asks: "What do we mean by 'installing [the Buddha] and dotting his eyes?' "—Responding for [the disciple]: "This contains all the virtues; when the compassionate gaze falls upon beings, the ocean of happiness is without bounds."—At the moment of dotting [the eyes], the brush and ink are prepared by grinding the [ink] stone; the master stands in front of the icon and puts the ink on his brush; dotting the left eye, he chants, "Majestic energy and

---

[41] See Gombrich 1966; Frank 1988.
[42] See Sugimoto 1982: 92; Frank 1988: 71.

loving thought: the compassionate gaze falls on beings, the ocean of happiness is without limit."—Then, dipping his brush once more into the ink, he guides it towards the space between the eyebrows [of the Buddha]; as he marks the right eye, he says, "A drop of water and ink, in two spots, makes a dragon. These two spots are the majestic energy and loving thought; the compassionate gaze falls on beings and the ocean of happiness is without bounds."—He repeats this three times. Then, without thinking, he chants: "In the past, the Tathāgata Majestic Sound King [Bhīṣmagarjitasvararāja] adorned the seat of the lion and there installed the golden body of retribution and metamorphosis [of the Buddha]. How did he do this? He offered one part to the Buddha Śākyamuni and another to the stūpa of the Buddha Prabhūtaratna, and then [he said], 'May a Buddha enter this Buddha body!'"—[The master] then sits in meditation and during the consultation says: To 'install [the Buddha] and dot his eyes' [means that] the universe and I myself have the same origin. My eyes open [to the truth according to which] all beings are of the same essence as I am."—The master asks: "The proof?"—Reply: "The immense earth and all living and non-living beings reach enlightenment at the same moment as I do."—The master asks [further]: "Show me the true marks of the Buddha."—Reply: "During the day, it is the jewel of the sun; at night, it is the pearl of the moon."—The master: "What is it that we call majestic energy?"—Reply: "The majestic light of the Buddha, the majestic wind of the Dharma."[43]

The fictitious dialogue goes on like this, with the master quizzing the disciple on each of the expressions used in the course of the opening recitation. We should note the central importance of ritual here, considered to contain "all the virtues," because it permits the opening of a kind of channel between the two levels of reality, a channel through which will flow an infinite surge of happiness. Not only the eyes, but also the spot between the eyes is marked, the "third eye." Equally meaningful is the reference to the Chinese tradition according to which dotting in the eye of a painted dragon brings it to life. The master twice returns during his "dialogical soliloquy" to the definition of the rite, on the second occasion stressing the cosmic nature of the Buddha and his fundamental identity with all beings. By marking the eyes of the Buddha, one is thus carrying out an essentially demiurgic operation, and one opens one's own eyes to this world where living beings are none other than the Buddha and thus fundamentally awakened. The ritual thus implies a procedure of identification, on the one hand between the officiating priest and the icon and on the other between the two of them and the cosmic Buddha, an

---

[43] Note the triple recitation, which corresponds once again to the three points of the *i*, the triple deliverance, etc. See "Anza tengen," in *Bukke ichi daiji yawa*, Ishikawa 1983–94 (2): 146–47 and (20): 115–26.

identification giving rise to awakening, both for the icon and for the practitioner.[44]

The rite of consecration by "opening the eyes" recalls the story of the apparition of the Arhat Piṇḍola to King Aśoka. As John Strong has pointed out:

> With his white eyebrows covering his eyes, Piṇḍola sat before Aśoka like an incomplete, "blind" Buddha image. It is thus a very important point in the text when, we are told, in front of King Aśoka prostrate at his feet, "the old man lifted up his eyebrows with both hands and looked directly at the king." The point is clear; in the cultic situation established by Aśoka and confirmed by his offerings, the flesh-and-blood Piṇḍola is consecrated, or, to put it otherwise, sanctified in essentially the same way as is an image of the Buddha. And, just like the image of the Buddha, at the moment of his consecration Piṇḍola represents, he "makes present," speaking in cult terms, the Buddha who is away in Nirvāṇa.[45]

As we have seen, the consecration rite for a Buddhist icon is overdetermined, compressing into a single event various rites of passage, originally distinct, although symbolically connected. The rite (re)enacts concurrently the birth of the Buddha, his passage into adolescence and monkhood, his consecration as universal monarch, his awakening, and his entry into Nirvāṇa. The structure of the rite is thus superimposed on that of a funerary rite. Just as in the case of funerary rites, intended to ensure post mortem entry into Nirvāṇa, the rite provides a symbolic shortcut to that state: it recapitulates the entire life of a Buddha, from his birth to eventual Nirvāṇa. In the same way as a person who dies a layman must be ordained a monk before being able to profit from the rites that will lead him to salvation, the icon must receive ordination before the eye-opening ceremony that constitutes its awakening.

But the icon has scarcely been "awakened" before the priest plunges it, by means of another mantra, into a state of *samādhi*, a quiet catalepsy. It is doomed to remain in this state of suspended animation, serving as a mediator between this world and that beyond. We thus see the following ritual sequence: birth of an icon, awakening, entry into permanent *samādhi*.[46] We can remember that candidates for self-mummification entered into *samādhi*, with the term *samādhi* here signifying at the same time the tomb into which they descend and the spiritual state whose power let them escape bodily decay. The icon is also a kind of stūpa or mausoleum, just as the stūpa is an architectural body, a (living) double of

[44] A Tantric text of the eighth century, *T.* 1199, prescribes pointing the eyes of the icon with the blood of the officiating priest. Quoted in Strickmann 1996: 449.

[45] Strong 1979: 85.

[46] See Strickmann 1996: 189–202.

the dead person. Like a mummy, a relic, or a devotee temporarily sunken into *samādhi*, it is alive, present, awake.

In esoteric rites the scenario is slightly different because the icon receives life thanks to the action of the officiating priest, who first of all must awaken within himself a vision (*sādhana*) of the Buddha in his dharma body and then project it ritually into the icon by implanting into it the three "seed-syllables" of the body, speech, and mind. The special rites dedicated to "charging" the icon (the umbilical cord, the insertion of relics, the opening of the eyes) move into the background. Here the imagination becomes iconic in the true sense. Even the "projection" of the Buddha onto the material support is not required as long as the spiritual support—the visual icon—has been created, and the "installation of breaths" has taken place in the officiating priest who thus becomes deified, energized, iconized. Still the goal of the ritual remains the same: to create a source of beneficent power that is easily usable.

The process is a dialectical one: although the material icon owes its life—and the essential part of its efficacy—to the ritual action of the priest, he in turn derives some of his charisma from the icon (whether this icon be material or simply mental). The identification of the priest and the Buddha results from this psychological give-and-take between the Buddha present in the temple and the Buddha present in the mind of the priest. This constant interchange between the officiant and the icon and this perception of a Buddha who is interior and exterior in turn, define an intermediary space, spiritual and surreal, imaginary or rather "imaginal," in which objective and subjective realities tend to fuse, and where an identification with the Buddha takes place, leading eventually to awakening. As André Padoux has pointed out, "The absence of any separation between the corporeal and the mental spheres . . . rendered more easy (perhaps inevitable?) this presence at the same time "internal" and "external" of the mental image, just as it facilitated resorting to the latter and its association, in the cult, with the material icon, whether the latter was anthropomorphic, theriomorphic, aniconic . . . , or diagrammatic."[47] This space is also not limited to the specific, localized relationship between one worshiper and one icon but extends to all the faithful and all the "reproductions" of the icon, thus transcending all spatial limitations. When he prays, for example, before a Zenkōji icon, an icon whose proliferation throughout Japan on the basis of a single prototype sets up a complete imaginal space, strongly structured and panoptic, the worshiper has access to the central (invisible) icon in its Nagano sanctuary.[48]

[47] See Padoux 1990: 3. We should emphasize here the importance of diagrams in Sōtō Zen, and the role (not too well known) that these diagrams, like traditional icons, played as devices to settle energy and to trigger awakening. See Ishikawa 1983–94.

[48] On this icon see McCallum 1994. The unlocalized aspect of the Zenkōji cult is coun-

Thus an identification is achieved between the Buddha and the officiating priest by the intermediary of the icon (or the mental image) which constitutes, to use the term that Mus applies to stūpas, a "mesocosm."

The icon forms at the same time a basis for meditation, a postmortem means of passage for the worshiper, a source of power and benefits in this world for all parties. There is a mental projection for the officiating priest, sanctification by contact for the worshiper (or sacrificer), and in certain cases the sanctification of objects belonging to the worshiper and placed inside the statue in preparation for the postmortem journey of the worshiper. In some rare cases the monk himself arranges to be enclosed in an icon at his death. The mummy of a Pure Land adept named Shungi was found inside a stone statue of the Buddha Amida. Are we to see this as a case of the icon becoming a stūpa, a mausoleum, a reliquary? Or has the reliquary become an icon, like the Christian reliquaries of southern Gaul that took the form of the relic that they contained? In any case it seems clear that the icon serves, to use again Mus's terminology, as a "magical copula." This hierogamy—the union of the Buddha and the officiant by means of the icon (or even of the Buddha and the sacrificer by the intermediary of the officiant and the icon)—can also be interpreted as a passage, a shift to another level: while the Buddha can descend into this world, the officiant (and, by extension, the sacrificer) may also ascend to the world of the divine. This is precisely the model of Vedic sacrifice as described by Sylvain Lévi and Paul Mus.[49]

This analysis of the cult of Buddhist icons also applies in a general way to that of amulets and talismans. Like the Thai monks studied by Stanley Tambiah, Yōkōji monks consecrated talismans against all kinds of misfortune, both for their own use and the use of the laity. New talismans against fire were thus produced each year, during the third lunar month.[50] We have, for example, a talisman on which are inscribed the names of two protective deities, the god of Hakusan and the dragon king, names that are believed to be in the handwriting of Keizan himself. Unlike their Thai equivalents, however, Yōkōji monks do not seem to have used an umbilical cord to "charge" their amulets.[51] The rite of opening the eyes (or rather of "dotting" them in) that was held for talismans, amulets, and other ritual or apotropaic objects, consisted of inscription

terbalanced by the "womb symbolism" of Zenkōji, the existence under the altar of an artificial cave through which one experiences a symbolic rebirth. See Stein 1988.

[49] Lévi 1966; Mus 1935.

[50] See Tōkoku shingi, in SZ 2, Shūgen 2: 672b; JDZ, 315.

[51] The Sanbōekotoba, however, mentions a rite of this kind for the consecration of an icon. See Kamens 1988: 313. A similar rite took place at Tōdaiji in 752.

on the object by a monk in a state of concentration. This rite was followed by a meditation session.

Like relics and icons, amulets are doubly symbolic in that they refer
symbolically to the Buddha or saint who produced them, but also make
him present, actualizing his apotropaic efficacy.[52] They function both as
signifiers and signified and finally take on as much, if not more, reality
than that of the saint or Buddha they are considered to signify, uniting the
two tesserae of the bipartite symbol, blending into a single reality the
essential form of the Venerated and his "representation."

A THEORY OF PROJECTION

We have just seen that the ritual practices of esoteric Buddhism, as taken
up by Sōtō Zen, implied a theory of mental projection. We also find in
early Chan the equivalent of a "theory of projection," but the approach
is diametrically opposite. In the *Damo lun* (*Treatise of Bodhidharma*),
for example, a Chan master makes fun of someone who had a Buddha
carved from a block of stone in his garden and then worshiped the stone
and considered as real the creations of his own mind: "This has all been
created by the paintbrush of your mind; it is nothing but a figment of
your own imagination."[53] According to Chan orthodoxy, every cult of
icons involves a "forgetting of the origins." The Chan masters, at least in
theory, do not admit to the possibility of any hierophany or hierogamy
and see in the mental projection that gives life to the icon only a form of
alienation. However, one could object that the form of worship under
consideration does not involve a denial, a forgetting of oneself, and of the
ritual process that, in esoteric Buddhism, animates the icon. Moreover,
the Buddhahood that is thus objectified, projected into the stone or the
wood, and mediated through the cult, is not for all that reified: it is simply seen as more accessible and capable of being reactivated than interior
Buddhahood, too elusive in its deep latency. The image in the mirror—
whether the mirror be an icon, a diagram, or a mantra—is more accessible that its original, and it does permit the believer to fix and catch an
otherwise elusive power. Although the icon can serve effectively as a psychological anchor for worship, only an excessively narrow functionalism
would see in this kind of cult nothing but a fetishistic adherence to mere
skillful means.

The icon also constitutes, as noted above, what Mus called a "meso-
cosom," a means to project oneself ritually onto another plane, to break

[52] According to Peirce's terminology, taken up by Tambiah, amulets are both symbols
and indices. See Tambiah 1985: 4–5, 69–70.

[53] See Yanagida Seizan, ed., *Daruma no goroku* (Tokyo: Chikuma shobō, 1969).

through levels. The close connection established between the icon and the person of the donor (whether by its size, likeness, or the placing of relics inside it) implies that—as is the case with the Vedic altar—it constitutes a "substitute body." In this sense, "the sacrifice is the man," and by offering an icon, one offers oneself.[54] In 744 an edict from the Emperor Xuanzong ordered the Buddhist clergy to cast gold or copper images of the Buddha the same size as the emperor himself in the official monastery (Kaiyuansi) of each province. Mus analyzes another case, this time in an Indian context, in which a Buddhist statue was made in the image of the ruler. He emphasizes that this is not so much an example of royal apotheosis as an act of devotion on the part of the king: we should see a double magical implication, in that the king gives himself to the Buddha, projects himself into the Buddha, at the same time as his mortal body, thus iconized and immortalized, becomes the terrestrial "trace" of its divine original.[55] In Japan we have the example of the two Buddhist triads at Hōryūji, representations or "projections" of Shōtoku Taishi flanked in one case by his parents and in the other by his wife and son.[56] Likewise, it is significant that Emperor Shōmu gave himself the religious name of Roshana when he had the massive Roshana image (the Daibutsu) erected at Tōdaiji.

Besides these rather special royal or princely examples, a parallel mechanism operates in most Buddhist icons, which are filled with relics of the Buddha or of Buddhist saints as well as various objects belonging to donors and "representing" the latter. The icons thus also function as "shifters," ensuring communication and movement in two directions: they allow Bodhisattvas to "descend" into this world, and the faithful to "go up" toward final salvation. This passage beyond, as described by Mus, implies a break of level, a leap. The passage is thus paradoxical since, as is suggested by the expression of Saint Paul *per visibilia ad invisibilia*, the cult of icons seems at first glance to derive from a gradualism that does not involve any break in level: if there is a break, the *visibilia* in principle stop at the threshold of the invisible. And yet it is precisely this break that the Hindu and Buddhist *visibilia* are felt to bring about.

Thus, contrary to the subitist theory, the Buddhist tradition and the gradualist practice of the Chan/Zen that derives from it see in the "fetishism" of the object exactly the opposite of an alienation. Maybe we should say rather that they consider alienation as a necessary detour through the other back to the self, as the best means of preserving the

---

[54] See Mus 1935: 636, 640.

[55] Ibid.: 92.

[56] The Guze Kannon of Yumedono, in particular, was worshiped as an image of Shōtoku Taishi in Bodhisattva form, and scholars have noted the similarity between its face and that of many portraits of Shōtoku. See Plutschow 1990: 207.

self. The discovery of the self can happen precisely through the mediation of the icon, or the sacred text, or of any other ritual and "symbolic" object. In order for this discovery to occur, a place outside the self is necessary. Thus Dōgen and Keizan considered that their true self, the cosmic body of the Buddha, was in some way enciphered in the exterior world. Attention to external reality, which was for early Buddhists a form of sensory attachment, now becomes for some a deciphering of the self, a bringer of deliverance. The ontological status of exterior reality is modified, and this evolution leads to the coexistence of two different concepts of the self: as concentrated, inalienable interiority or as diffuse, decentralized subjectivity that can be discovered not by introspection, but, as Dōgen puts it in a famous passage, when all things come forward to authenticate the self.[57] We are then in the world of the "Other power" (*tariki*), in which the individual, conscious of his finiteness and no longer calling on his own strengths (*jiriki*), chooses to entrust himself or herself to this power. It is in this universe, or rather on the fringes of these two mental universes, that Keizan operates. But far from being a "lonely captive of the threshold," held in a double bind, he actually finds his liberty in this liminal, interstitial position, in this play and free passage between opposed symbolic systems.

DEGREES OF PRESENCE

An image is not always fully effective, even when it has been "animated." In most cases, the presence that animates it is subject to fluctuation and may have to be revived ritually. Putting to one side the comparatively rare case of a self-revealing image, whose immanent presence is independent of any human action and whose power is thus permanent, most icons are to various degrees "asleep." Their mind, or rather their spirit, in the true sense of the word, is elsewhere; they are awaiting the ritual or devotional jump-start that will revive them, bring back into them the temporarily absent deity. Thus icons not only have to be animated; they have to be maintained alive by daily cult activity, without which any icon ends up gradually losing its efficacy. This is a vicious circle, since an icon with no efficacy rapidly loses its worshipers.

In the statue of Kannon left to Keizan by his mother, Ekan, we have a hybrid case since the head of the statue, even if we can conceive that it was crafted by a human, is nevertheless accepted as "self-revealed," appearing as if by a miracle in response to a vow. All that remained was to find it a body. By promising to have one made, Ekan sealed a contract

---

[57] See *Shōbōgenzō*, "Genjō kōan," T. 82, 2582: 23b.

and reestablished the exchange of services and counter-services with the deity. The two parts of the statue constitute in a way the two tesserae, the interlocking parts, of the contractual symbol. This may explain why there is no mention of any ritual consecration of this icon: a self-revealed image, even a partial one, possesses an intrinsic power. It is not necessary to call down the deity into its material body. The icon in question, object of a private cult, was in a way brought to life by the faith of Ekan and sanctified in its very existence as a bipartite symbol of the contract. After the death of Ekan, when the icon was "installed" as the *honzon* of En-zūin, becoming the object of a collective cult, it was duly revived by the deposit of the natal "relics" of Keizan, even if this depositing can also be interpreted as an effort to ensure the longevity of Keizan and his teaching.

In order to understand Keizan's position in all its complexity, we must abandon for a moment the priest's point of view and try to fathom that of the ordinary worshiper. Keizan was not simply a master familiar with esoteric rituals. He had also inherited from his mother a fervent faith in Kannon. While the priest by his rites installs and maintains the divine presence within the icon, the worshiper simply "consumes" this presence. One may see the worshiper as also bringing life to the statue, not ritually but by the intensity of his faith. There are plenty of examples of statues responding to the prayers of worshipers, in the absence of any reanimating ritual. At any rate, the "relational" element, as Bernard Frank stresses, is essential in both cases: the icon, whether mental or material, exists and reveals its efficacy only in response to the believer—whether priest or lay worshiper.[58] The devotional identification of the worshiper with the icon matches the ritual identification of the officiating priest. Even if the methods that permit identification with the Buddha or the deity differ, in both cases we end up with a bracketing of the world and the physical perception of the icon and a superimposition of two orders of reality, or, to put it otherwise, an "imaginary" relationship with the invisible made visible by the icon.[59] From this point of view, the heuristic distinction that anthropological thinkers set up between officiating priest and ordinary worshiper is perhaps not quite so clear as it may seem. The priest also takes part in popular beliefs, and he passes constantly from one "truth program" to another, to use the term coined by Paul Veyne.

For the worshiper as for the priest, simply looking at icons has a transforming effect. In his analysis of the gaze (*darśan*) in the Indian context, J. Gonda stresses that the onlooker is felt to benefit from gazing at a powerful being: by participating in its essence, he is purified and carried

---

[58] See Frank 1988: 63.
[59] See Colas 1990: 107–8.

to a higher level.[60] However, the power of Buddhist icons depends not only on their ritual reactivation but also, as in the case of relics, on faith and the karma of the worshiper. The latent power of the icon becomes manifest, active only when certain subjective and objective circumstances coincide. Such, for example, is the point of view of Myōe: "When you think about an object carved from wood or drawn in a picture as if it were a living being, then it is a living being."[61]

ICONS AND *CHINSŌ*

We have seen the important role played by the live portraits of dead masters (*chinsō*) in the funerary beliefs of Chan/Zen. They also have an iconic function. The *Record of Tōkoku* tells that about a year before his death Keizan transmitted his Dharma to his main disciples. But it was only to Gasan Jōseki that he seems to have given his portrait (*chinsō*).[62] Properly speaking, a *chinsō* is only a special kind of icon, and the logic or spiritual energy that animates these "portraits of the masters" is the same. From our point of view, there seems to be no essential difference between the funerary ritual in which the *chinsō* play their role and the consecration ritual of an icon. Both lead to a ritual oxymoron, a representative of a "living dead" who can become a source of beneficial energy for the community of monks and the entire local or regional community.

Just as the individual master had been during his life an embodiment of the Dharma, his *chinsō* becomes the same thing after his death. The *chinsō* comes to play, in the same way as do the *śarīra* and other relics, an important role in the transmission (or, to put it more exactly, the diffusion) of the Dharma. We know, for example, that in 1189, through the efforts of two of his disciples, Dainichi Nōnin received a portrait of Bodhidharma on which the Chan master Zhuoan Deguang had composed a eulogy. It was probably on this occasion that Nōnin inherited the robe of Dahui Zonggao, Deguang's master, and the already-mentioned *śarīra* of the six Chan patriarchs. In addition the two disciples of Nōnin, before returning to Japan, commissioned a portrait of Deguang on which they asked the latter to inscribe a poem. The fact of a Chan master inscribing a poem on a portrait—whether it is his own or that of one of his predecessors—may be seen as a variant of the "dotting in" of the eyes of an icon, a means of transmission "sealing the faith." When Dōgen returned to Japan in 1227, he also brought a portrait—duly

---

[60] See Gonda 1970: 55; see also Eck 1985.

[61] See Morrell 1987: 60; and Rasmus 1982: 99.

[62] We possess actually two *chinsō*, with two different eulogies, one (dated 1329) preserved at Sōjiji, the other at Tōryōji in Ishikawa prefecture.

autographed—of his master, Tiantong Rujing. Although he later criticized severely the proliferation of *chinsō*, which in his opinion (whether right or wrong) contributed to the decline of the rival Linji (Rinzai) school, he nevertheless shared with his contemporaries the belief in "thaumaturgic immanence" that gave birth to the vogue of icons. He was apparently simply unwilling to share its symbolic gains with other schools—especially the Darumashū whose popularity offended him.[63] Like the patriarchal robe, the *chinsō* was not only the token representing the transmission, as we usually tend to think, but was its very essence.

Doubtless the possession of a *chinsō* was insufficient (or in any case quickly became insufficient) to claim a spiritual transmission, "from mind to mind," following awakening. In this sense we may consider that the transmission was not the essential goal of the *chinsō*.[64] However, the *chinsō* was the artifact that made possible the ritual transmission of the charisma of the master and gave access to this charisma, so connecting magically the owner of the *chinsō* (or of a lineage chart) to the lineage represented and continued by the master. The *chinsō* and the other objects transmitted thus delimit the ritual and semantic field within which the rarefaction of legitimacy through documents of succession can occur. To understand fully the significance of the *chinsō*, we must put it into its funerary context. In this sense it goes beyond the framework of patriarchal transmission, but the latter in turn picks up strangely funerary connotations. As he receives the "seal" or the robe of his master, the disciple becomes his double and symbolically kills him, in line with a funerary logic reminiscent of the juridical expression "The dead seizes the living" (*Le mort saisit le vif*). The patriarchal robe was also never simply the a posteriori "proof" of a purely spiritual transmission; it functioned more like a relic, a talisman whose possession transformed the disciple into his master, or, to put it in other words, into a full-fledged Buddha. The metonymic logic of the dissemination of the charisma of the master and lineage is not brought into question by the multiplication of *chinsō*, nor by that, less common, of robes, succession documents, and lineage charts.

Paradoxically, the single transmission claimed by Shenhui (684–758) for his master Huineng—and by implication for himself—was made possible by the very logic of diffusion that would soon serve to deconstruct it. Later, rather than transmit the Law to a single successor, the master disseminated it, and himself by the same token, since the *chinsō*, his "body of Law," is at the same time his Law and his body. Just as was the case with relics and lineage charts, the multiplication of *chinsō* and their

---

[63] See *Shōbōgenzō*, "Shisho," in T. 82, 2582: 69b.
[64] On this question see Foulk and Sharf 1993–94: 196–202.

spread among monks and laypeople led inevitably to their devaluation. As little by little they lost their power to legitimize this or that lineage, they came to serve simply as tokens of ritual affiliation to the Chan/Zen "ancestral line," or even as talismans and amulets, forms of an "objectified charisma" akin to that of the effigies of Thai monks studied by Tambiah.

Functionally close to the *chinsō* is the *shin* (Ch. *zhen*), literally "truth" (in painting), or portrait of the late master, which is considered to be "the substantial image of the Dharma."[65] Here again ordinary practice seems to contradict official doctrine, according to which the true *chinsō* is not a *chinsō*, the "truth in painting" (*shin*) is not really true, because the true "characteristic," "form," or "aspect" (all possible translations of the Sino-Japanese character read *xiang* in Chinese, *sō* in Japanese) cannot be seen.[66] At any rate, a *shin* is in many ways comparable to the effigy used in traditional Chinese funerary rites and seems to function as a substitute body. It was seen as a figure of the double, as clearly revealed by the fact that it was the object (or rather the subject) of the ceremony even while the dead master was still physically present there in his coffin. The ritual is held for this effigy, just as in the funeral rites for the French king "the center of the ceremony moves away from the body in its coffin and is concentrated on a realistic representation of the deceased."[67] Like the bodies of Roman emperors or Christian kings, the Chan/Zen master's body seems to have been differentiated into *ossa* and *imago*, or into a physical body that decays and a social, metonymic body that is imperishable. In his work on royal funerals in France during the sixteenth and seventeenth centuries, Ralph Giesey describes the evolution that led to the separation between the "king's two bodies," the corpse of the king in the coffin and the royal image, to the point that, after the death of Henry IV in 1610, priests and magistrates fought over who was to walk alongside the effigy (the living king), leaving the coffin (the dead king) to professional pallbearers.[68] From this point of view, the Chan/Zen monks seem to have exhibited more restraint.

Thus a portrait serves to perpetuate the social body of the dead master until he is appropriately reincorporated, by cremation or mummification, into his purified body—*śarīra* or "flesh body."—thus becoming a "collective" ancestor and source of regeneration. The portrait anticipates this state of affairs and continues to function subsequently alongside relics. According to a document from Yōkōji entitled *Chinsō kirigami*, there are various ways of painting or carving a "portrait of a master":

[65] See *Sho ekō shingishiki, T.* 81, 2578: 661.
[66] This is for instance Mujaku Dōchū's opinion (1963: 163b).
[67] Huntington and Metcalf 1979: 168.
[68] See Giesey 1987: 38–47.

As for the image of a master, he must be depicted as a host when he is painted while still alive and as a guest when painted after his death. Actually, while he is still alive and practices [the Way], he is a source of benefit to himself and others. Having arrived at the last of the Ten Stages, he obtains the full measure of the fruits of deep awakening and thus occupies the rank of host. After his death, he achieves Supreme Awakening, according to the usual practice, which consists of appearing no more in this world: thus his position as a host. In this case why must we depict [the master] as a guest after his death? Because all the saints, returning to the status of fundamental awakening, appear in the *Sahā* world to convert beings, in accordance with the practice called "going back." Once they obtained deliverance from the body, the ancients attained the Pure Land, but they returned to the impure world in order to save men and *deva*. This is what one calls appearing in the world. Thus their rank of guests. The Bodhisattva Vimalakīrti, practicing the non-Way, made it into the Buddhist way. A commentary states: "When the saint has become a Buddha, he returns to contact with things to bring benefits to beings and hold out his hand to them. This is what is called the 'non-Way.' This non-Way is the spirit that gives life to painted images. In the case of a wooden image, the role of host or guest must be indicated in the eyes. If the image was made during the lifetime [of the master], one must be able to see his rank as a host in his eyes; after his death, one must be able to detect the rank of guest. This means that if the image was created during his lifetime, he looks upwards; after his death, downwards. This is essentially the same for painted and carved images."[69]

In the case of a painting, the master must be depicted as turned toward the right (as a host) when he is painted during his lifetime, and turned toward the left (as a guest) when he is painted after his death. The well-known portrait of Dōgen that shows him turned toward the left actually does date to a time after his death in 1253. The Zen encyclopedist Mujaku Dōchū confirms that this iconographic convention was widely followed and he notes that the type of eulogy appended to the portrait depended on the orientation of the face. But Mujaku seems to be critical of this idea and favors a different tradition according to which the master should always be shown as a host, turned toward the right.[70]

PIOUS MANIPULATIONS

While esoteric ritual works toward an identification between the officiating priest and the deities being invoked, it also implies a certain distance, a certain detachment toward these deities which must after all be brought

---

[69] See "Chinsō no daiji," in Ishikawa 1983–94 (6): 141.
[70] Mujaku 1963: 164a.

under control, even manipulated. It is only in the devotional movements that the identification changes into a mystical ecstasy in which love, the initial component of "rememoration" (*smṛti*) in the Vedic tradition, returns to a primary position.

The relations between believers and icons (or the gods that they put into material form) are not always free from symbolic violence, even a certain kind of moral blackmail. We know that statues of gods who do not respond to prayers were sometimes manhandled and insulted. More often it was a matter of painting in glowing terms for the gods the lure of rewards to be theirs, or of depriving them of offerings and thus their regular ration of energy. No longer supported by ritual, the gods risked wasting away if they did not accede to the requests. In the case of Buddhas and Bodhisattvas, objects of special veneration and endowed theoretically with an overabundance of power, the blackmail had to be approached a little more subtly. But even these "awakened beings," otherwise irreproachable, were not entirely spared attempts at seduction. We have seen that Keizan's mother had tried to get the help of the Bodhisattva Kannon by promising to add a body to the head of the statue that she had just found. In the same way Gikai, Keizan's spiritual father, had two statues of Kannon and Kokūzō carved in 1262, while in China, and promised to decorate them if the two Bodhisattvas would protect him on his return voyage to Japan. Undoubtedly the most popular case of conditional completion of icons is that of Daruma (Bodhidharma) dolls made of papier-mâché, in which the pupil of the second eye (thus a completed opening of the eyes) is not painted in until a particular wish has been granted or an enterprise completed successfully. This ritual has been vulgarized to the point of becoming a specific feature of election victories in modern Japan.[71]

[71] See McFarland 1987: 62–67.

Chapter Eleven

BEYOND ICONS

ICONOCLASM in China was first of all a political matter. The best-known case is that of the repression of Buddhism undertaken in 845.[1] But there are plenty of other iconoclastic edicts. Their spirit is well represented by these words from an imperial edict issued in 955: "The Buddha teaches the Way of Good. If people attain the Good, this means that they are true worshippers of the Buddha. As for copper images, how can we call them Buddhas?"[2] Above all the emperor and his Confucian ministers wanted to control the Buddhist church, judged to have too much power. Thus the ban on casting images of the Buddha, drawn up in 714 at the beginning of the reign of Emperor Xuanzong, was accompanied by a ban on ordinations. The two measures were clearly related from a political point of view, but their pairing also has a meaning on the symbolic level, since the creation of a Buddhist icon corresponds to a symbolic ordination. This symbolic equivalence seems to have gone unnoticed by the critics of Buddhism. Thus, in the instructions that he left to his family on his death in 721, the prime minister Yao Chong states: "Only fools seek for merit by copying scriptures or making images."[3] His Confucian rationalism did not equip him to understand that the same logic, that of creating a duplicate of oneself and of the Buddha, was the basis for the two actions. And yet this duplicating logic worked (or was felt to work) willy-nilly, even among the enemies of Buddhism, as the following story shows: Having learned that his order for the destruction of an image of the Great Compassionate One [Guanyin] had not been followed, the emperor himself broke the face and torso of the image with axe strokes. Shortly thereafter, during a military campaign, he was stricken by cancer of the chest and died on his return to the capital.[4]

After the debate that divided the Japanese court at the time of the official introduction of Buddhism in the sixth century, the only great flare-up of iconoclasm in Japan came in the aftermath of the Meiji Restoration, in an ideological break marked by xenophobia and a "return" to the largely imaginary purity of Shintō. In this case Shintō aniconism came to strengthen an iconoclastic tendency directed at images regarded as

[1] See Reischauer 1955b.
[2] Quoted in Jan 1966: 117.
[3] Ibid.: 56.
[4] Ibid.: 118.

foreign. Buddhist icons and relics were also seen as impure because of their relationship with death and mortuary rites. Even within Buddhism itself a critical current drew on a long aniconic tradition, represented by scriptures like the *Vajracchedikā-sūtra*, which has the Buddha saying, "Those who seek me in the world of forms are deluded." The cult of relics and icons seemed to contradict openly the "sudden" teaching of Chan.

In Chan we can clearly see something we might term basic iconoclasm, a sort of antipaganism: local religion was often characterized by worship of gods in the form of images. This violent rejection of an "id(e)ology of presence" can extend to purely Buddhist icons. We may recall that Danxia Tianran (739–826) was notorious in Buddhist chronicles for using a wooden icon to build a fire, arguing that it did not contain any relics. But the argument cuts both ways: if there had been icons in the image, as was customary, would Danxia have acted or reacted in the same way? Apparently this iconoclast had plenty of imitators. Chan iconoclasm is made clear, for example, in a criticism addressed to Cuiwei Wuxue (d.u.) by a monk: "Danxia burned wooden Buddhas. Why do you venerate Arhats?"[5] But this passage also shows the limits of iconoclasm: if we take into account that this Wuxue (whose name significantly means "Arhat") was one of the main disciples of Danxia, we have to admit that the cult of icons was deeply entrenched in Chan practice.

But on the whole, Chan iconoclasm retained a more "theological" bent, justified by Buddhist idealism and its *via negativa*, or by subitism. A representative example is that of Linji Yixuan. When he was asked, "What is meant by 'burning scriptures and images'?" he replied, "When you can see the emptiness of causes and conditions, the emptiness of the mind, the emptiness of all phenomena, when the mind is every instant completely calm, far removed, and doing nothing."[6] This theoretical iconoclasm, following the spirit and not the letter, is more tolerant but no less subversive than that basic iconoclasm whose negative tendencies it reinforces: it justifies a kind of political iconoclasm springing from vastly different motivations, intended in particular to weaken the Buddhist establishment. The quarrel over iconoclasm extends beyond the cult of icons proper to include the cult of relics, a cult whose strongest witness and critic is the Confucianist Han Yu. At the same time the line of division runs right through the heart of Chan itself, while it contributes to separating this school from traditional, iconophile Buddhism.

Paradoxical as it may seem, Chan iconoclasm is not concerned necessarily with icons, or we could say rather that it could also be equally

[5] T. 51, 2076: 313c.
[6] See Watson 1993: 75.

concerned with "aniconic" icons. This is the case with Pozao Duo breaking the altar of the stove god on Song shan, or his master Shenxiu destroying that of the war god Guan Di on Yuquan shan. This vandalism
was not directed at images but at "symbols" of the gods (whose existence
it recognized, at the same time that it tried to demonstrate their inferiority). Apart from these famous cases, Chan iconoclasm remained theoretical and rhetorical. Thus iconoclasm is distinct from aniconism, to
which we shall return later.

If an icon is polysemic, so is its criticism. Iconoclasm is first of all the
rejection of a certain kind of presence. In Christianity, for example, relics
and icons of Christ were denied the privilege of manifesting a presence,
which was reserved for the host alone. In addition, if the desecration of
an icon is seen as the opposite of its consecration, this act presupposes its
sacred nature and is still a ritual centered on the image. Between the two,
desecration and consecration, there is only a reversal of signs, no difference in nature. More serious is, therefore, a simple ignoring of icons,
which strips them of any efficacy, or their reduction to simply aesthetic
objects, an all-too-frequent practice of art historians.

The functionalist interpretation of an icon as simple representation, an
approach that is useful for ordinary worshipers but potentially dangerous to Buddhist practitioners, represents a relatively critical effort at
compromise. The characteristic Chan version, already seen in Linji, consists of revealing the objectification achieved through the ritual or psychological projection and exhorting the practitioner to find again the
essence of the icon, which is actually the real nature of the practitioner
himself. It is doubtless in this spirit that Keizan reports in the *Denkōroku*
the following episode: "One day when Cuiwei was making offerings to
the Arhats, someone asked him: 'You make offerings to the Arhats, but
will they come here?' Cuiwei replied: 'What do *you* eat every day?' "[7]
Cuiwei seems to consider that the Buddhist icon is only a sublimated
double of his disciple; or that the latter is only an inactive, dormant
Buddha.

In spite of some radical but theoretical stands and a few celebrated
cases of iconoclasm, the Chan attitude toward icons seems on the whole
to be definable as one of *nec adorare nec frangi*. In practice, however,
another ideology seems to have held sway, one characterized by a desire
to manage the sacred efficiently. Chan/Zen iconoclasm constitutes above
all an attempt to dam up the real or imagined overflowing of the sacred,
the proliferation of symbols, and to reserve for an elite the privilege of
ritual access to the source of power. Icons imply a kind of circulation of
power (*ling*), a sort of political economy (or "iconomy"). By rejecting

---

[7] *Denkōroku, T.* 82, 2585: 390a.

icons, the Chan masters tried to short-circuit a network of power, to take it over for their own profit. Indeed, if icons could not function as mediators between this world and the ultimate reality, no more could the Buddhist church function as a mediator between the Emperor and the Buddha. As Theodore of Studios wrote of Byzantine iconoclasm, "Those who reject the image reject the economy."[8] This theoretical position could certainly be profitable only as long as no one insisted on putting it into practice. The Chan antisymbolic position was doomed to remain symbolic. We have here, therefore, a purely relative iconoclasm, even though the most radical strain of this school has always seen fit to denounce, either tactically or on principle, any form of symbolic mediation. Nevertheless, even though this radicalism often did no more than provide a useful excuse for more conservative tendencies that claimed this belief without actually applying it, Chan/Zen iconology has always remained out of line with respect to the school's official ideology.

CHAN ANICONISM

Thus, by an ironic (or iconic) circle, the Chan school, adhering as it does to the idea of "immediate" experience, came back to mediating through images, to the *dhyāna* to which it owed its name and which, in an Indian context, means among other things a form of creative imagination through which the officiating priest visualizes the god before projecting it into a material form. For all that, the examples just mentioned suggest that the opposition between iconism and aniconism is perhaps not as significant as historians of Buddhist art have claimed. If the same economy of efficacious power (*ling*), the same ideology of immanence, works for both the icon and the aniconic "symbol," in what lies the further contribution of *mimesis*, the anthropomorphic likeness of the icon? Iconism and aniconism seem finally to be no more than two variant forms of a single metaphysics of presence and not contradictory realities. As François Chenet has said in the case of Hinduism, "This double formulation and this constant circulation from the pole of the *plenum formarum* to that of the 'supreme truth of the formless'" explains why iconoclastic exclusivism has never prevailed in Asia.[9]

The tension between iconism and aniconism, but also the relatively easy oscillation between the one and the other, characterizes even the

---

[8] Quoted in Marie-José Baudinet, "The Face of Christ. The Form of the Church," in *Fragments for a History of the Human Body*, ed. Michael Feher (New York: Urzone, 1989) Part 1: 154.

[9] Chenet 1990: 168.

earliest forms of Chan. This is suggested, for example, by the words put in the mouth of the fifth patriarch Hongren (601–674) in the *Platform Sūtra*. Hongren had summoned a painter to draw illustrations from the *Lankāvatāra-sūtra*. However, after seeing the verse that his disciple Shenxiu had written on the wall, he changed his mind and sent the painter away, telling him that after all there is no need for paintings because the *Vajracchedikā-sūtra* says, 'all forms are unreal and false.'"[10]

Hongren must be given credit for his aniconism, even if it did come a little late in the day. If in Indian religious ideology, and Buddhism that derives from it, the sacred is apprehended first of all through sight (*darśan*), Chan (like other similar movements) constitutes perhaps an attempt to reach beyond the sacred by means of non-seeing and non-thinking. However, the aniconism attributed to the school, on the basis of its theoretical subitist stance, must, in order to make sense, be seen in the framework of Indian (and Chinese) iconism. Paul Mus, for example, has suggested that the Hindu iconism and the Vedic aniconism that preceded it are only two expressions of the same line of thought, two complementary levels of reality. According to Mus, one thus sees the genesis of magical representations of the human person at first not in statues but solely by means of ritual or funerary effigies, which were initially altars and then became stūpas or temples, cosmic bodies of the god/Buddha or of the ruler, or perhaps of both of them, identified precisely by the intermediary of this architectural "body"—or in it.[11] In other words, the construction of a stūpa means ultimately the architectural construction of the Buddha, and the icon would do no more than provide at a proper time a more convenient basis for ritual transposition.

In Christianity iconoclasm is likewise only a specific form of iconology, not its negation pure and simple. Recently anthropologists and historians of art have been stressing the complementarity of iconic and aniconic representations of gods. In India, even when a god is shown figuratively, we can still distinguish the "stable" or "static" aspect, "formless" or "undivided," from the "mobile" aspect, "endowed with form" or "composite," "endowed with divisions." Furthermore, the more or less abstract degree of representation of a god is not necessarily bound up with the intellectual (clerical) nature of the believer, and a "minimal" representation of a god can equally well emerge from a "popular" cult.[12] In addition, as we have seen in the case of the Enzūin Kannon, a "cult" image (thus a "mobile" one) can become a "fixed" image, and its status can be changed by the same token. In Hinduism these complementary

---

[10] See Yampolsky 1967: 130.
[11] Mus 1935: 663.
[12] See Colas 1990: 108–10.

tendencies crystallized into sectarian positions, represented by devotional *bhakti* and Tantrism on the one hand and Vedantism on the other. In the same way, Chan ended up with a sterile dispute over subitism and gradualism, a position that was fortunately quickly left behind in practice.

Does the icon indicate (as Mus seems to think) a weakening of ritual thought, a defeat of the imaginary? Would aniconism not in turn represent an extension of the *imaginaire* beyond the image itself, a "moving through" images that retains their active principle while applying it to more abstract models? The iconic-aniconic opposition does not exhaust all possibilities of this kind: an aniconic cult object seems closer to lifelessness, and animation, although it can happen to a noniconic object, does seem to indicate a tendency toward iconization, even anthropomorphism. As Mus stresses, "The statue is consequently a *caitya* [sanctuary holding a stūpa], just as the *caitya* is already an image."[13] The same must then be true of such noniconic and nonfigurative representations of presence as mystic diagrams: *yantra* and *maṇḍala*, or talismanic figures from the *kirigami*.

It is true that there exists in China a line of thought seeing a resembling, lifelike form or mimetic representation as a sort of snare to catch the efficacy of a specific segment of the real. Such is the case with the fake money burned in local cults: its symbolic semblance captures the value of real money and transfers it to the invisible world on behalf of both the dead and the living. Here we run up against this paradox: the figurative icon (whether material or mental, but always "imaginary") attracts divine power and brings it down to the ritual area, but a comparable result can apparently be achieved by means of a nonfigurative symbol. In funerary ritual, for example, whether it involves a mummy or an aniconic relic, a portrait or a funerary tablet, the same effects can be achieved by means of the iconic or the aniconic. At this stage we really cannot interpret the ill-understood variations of the cult of doubles—iconic or aniconic—as reflecting any historic fluctuation in the status of images. Should we for all that consider the opposition of iconic and aniconic a nonissue?

We know the great importance attributed in popular Buddhism to seeing and touching an image imbued with beneficial power. In certain Japanese temples dedicated to Jizō, the god-object is a gigantic pair of pincers that symbolize the function of this Bodhisattva who removes physical and spiritual sufferings as if they were nails driven into the flesh and the spirit.[14] The faithful, "gripped" by the desire for well-being, touch the body-object of the god and then the painful spots on their own bodies—

---

[13] Mus 1935: 664.
[14] A representative temple is the Kuginuki Jizō Temple in Kyoto.

thus making the beneficent power circulate within them. This is obviously a symbol in both senses of the word, because the object symbolizes the metaphorical activity of Jizō and thus the Bodhisattva himself but also shares metonymically in his beneficent nature. The Bodhisattva's beneficial power for good stands in marked contrast to the ambiguous power of the *kami*, as shown by the cautious Japanese proverb "You won't get a curse from a *kami* you haven't touched" (*sawaranu kami ni tatari nashi*). But in both cases it is by contact that the transfer of power takes place.

The fact that the *kami* are usually "formless" while the Buddhas are "endowed with form" (and a human form at that) suggests a high value for the figurative, anthropomorphic icon. In Buddhism, unlike Shintō, the divine moves away from nature (from the formless) toward humans (and culture). This concept has to be nuanced, of course, since there are in Shintō all kinds of *kami*, individualized to varying degrees, from god-object to anthropomorphic deity, and various representations, more or less figurative, of the same god or goddess.[15] We may wonder whether the representation (symbolization) of Amaterasu, a goddess with a relatively individual nature, by a mirror may not have had a strong symbolic impact in a school like Zen in which the mirror and the circle, prominent symbols of the mind, were highly honored. In the Sōtō school, for example, the circle is the highest "representation" of the Buddha Śākyamuni.[16]

In giving form to ultimate reality, the attempt was made to trap it in images in order to better manipulate it, whereas the formless, the non-figurative, or the nonanthropomorphic figurative all represent the same power in its indefinite, potential aspect. As a result, the absence of form is still another "form" of (this) power. Just like iconoclasm, aniconism ends up being a special pattern of belief in the power of images. We may equally well say that there is a lot of aniconic magic in iconology, or a lot of iconology in aniconism. The iconic-aniconic opposition does not lose all meaning, but it is rendered more relative.

In the case of Zen masters, we certainly have iconization, not only in mummification but in the rituals of ascending the hall, in which the master becomes a Buddha on his predication seat.[17] It has often been noted

[15] See Kanda 1985; Kageyama Haruki and Christine Guth Kanda, eds., *Shintō Arts: Nature, Gods, and Man in Japan* (New York: Japan House Gallery, and Seattle: Seattle Art Museum, 1976).

[16] In Sōtō *kirigami* the Buddha is also often represented by a peculiar graphic, called "half-form of Śākyamuni" (Shaka *hankei*), and assimilated to a variant of the swastika. See Ishikawa 1983–94 (7): 254–57. Note in passing that the goddess Amaterasu is sometimes interpreted in Zen as a symbol of the mind.

[17] See Sharf 1992.

that stillness (lack of motion) had a hieratic quality that seems associated with the ideology of kingship. The Buddha, and the Zen master who imitates him, are seated like monarchs, supremely motionless, with this stillness indicating sovereignty. The words spoken in the ritual area, on the "throne of the Law," take on the value of an oracle, independent of the state of mind of the person who utters them.

Paradoxically, while the icon comes to life (at least in the imagination of the worshiper), the Zen master seated opposite the icon in the Buddha hall freezes into immobility. The impression given by this scene is much like the one projected on the *bunraku* stage when life seems to flow from the puppeteer into the marionettes. Just like the ruler who tends to "identify himself with the mineral motionlessness of the world," the Zen master, in his consummate hieraticism, seems to move back toward the inanimate. Between the icon and the meditator, we see that two-way, chiasmic movement "by which men tend to animate matter in order to recognize themselves in it . . . and to freeze their relations in order to confer on them the unthinkable, indestructible, and irreducible evidence of the thing. A two-way symbolizing, in the one direction towards the fetish and life, and the other towards the object and matter."[18] Pushed to an extreme, the meditation of the worshiper risks the result of lifelessness, a limit-state comparable to that of ashes, dead wood, or stone, and one that would end all dialectic and all circulation of power. Chan texts constantly warn of this. True, we also find in Chan, and even in the case of Keizan, a sort of fascination for the "predication of the nonsentient," but the inanimate here is not completely mute, completely unthinkable. It suggests a limit, a transcendence, but it remains in the realm of the senses and in the closure of meaning. Rather than aiming at a mystic experience from which would flow a realization of his intrinsic Buddhahood, the Zen practitioner now aims to achieve awakening by a sort of purely ritual assumption (worship, meditation, kōan), which implies the conviction of being a Buddha *ex opera operato*.

THE IDEOLOGY OF IMMANENCE

The icon, as we have seen, functions as a way of capturing and channeling divine efficacy (*ling*) and thus of transforming those who place themselves in the path [downhill] of this power—officiating priest, adept, or simple worshiper. But at the same time the individual plays an active role in the energizing of the icon. If the icon revivifies him, he in turn can revivify the icon. They are in a state of mutual dependence. Efficacy and

[18] Augé 1988: 131.

the "powers" derived from it are obtained in various ways by the religious practitioner: by meditation, visualization, confession, recitation of texts. All these practices are, in a way, iconic or "symbolic," insofar as they capture energy (that of his own Buddha nature or that of an exterior power) for the benefit of the adept.

Finally, the icon is only one modality of a wider phenomenon, which also includes ritual. Icon and ritual are indeed inseparable and in a dialectic relationship. This is true even of the least anthropomorphic icons, like the "dry landscapes" of Zen temples, a variant of the miniature gardens and other *bonsai* of the Sino-Japanese tradition: their power derives from their ritual context—whether meditation or search for longevity. But in every case the degree of resemblance to the model—whether divine or natural—contributes to the capture of its essence or its energy.[19]

The icon is thus not only a reflection of the invisible. It does more than make the invisible visible, because by manifesting it it activates it, brings it "into play," providing for it a hold on the world of forms—and the inverse is also true: in this sense we may say that the icon creates the invisible. Rites to animate icons, and all later rites that the icon in turn animates, have as their goal the harnessing of power, but also, above all else, its taming—the transformation of a neutral, potentially violent, energy into a gentle, beneficent power.

THE PROFUSION OF DOUBLES

Although in some ways they resemble the funeral portraits of Chan/Zen masters, the icons of Buddhist deities (or those appropriated into Buddhism) worshiped in Zen monasteries differ in their ritual function, which is to protect the monastery either in its entirety or in one or another of its parts: the meditation hall, the Dharma hall, the kitchens, the bathroom, or the latrines. Like relics, mummies, or dream apparitions, these divine icons also belong to the category of the "double." This category connects vastly disparate realities and lets us see how the spirits and gods "respond" in dreams, visions, or apparitions to requests addressed to their relics and icons: through revelations, oracles, predictions etc.: all these figures of the double are brought together in representations, at the level of the *imaginaire*. Insofar as all these replicas are connected functionally and/or psychologically, we cannot speak of any original but only of a dissemination. As in the case of transmission between master and disciple, "there is no reflection in the mirror." If the icon is the double of the monk, the inverse is also true.

At this stage we are led to wonder whether it is only distant observers

[19] See Stein 1990.

who are inclined to create false windows, carried away as they are by a passion for symmetry or by what Vladimir Jankélévich called the "myth of mantelpiece decoration." It is certainly difficult for me to decide. But insofar as I can judge, Buddhist ritual does seem to be a machine for producing doubles, and thus to redouble on the level of ritual the effects of the philosophical "double truth." On a theoretical level, it also appears that the Zen master "sees double." Is he not a double-faced being who plays a double game: a skeptic *and* a believer, an intellectual *and* a thaumaturge? We find the same duality on a ritual and mythological level. In this case the double is a true, autonomous alter ego, a sublimated or disparaged doppelgänger. Usually anthropomorphic or mimetic (an icon), it can be aniconic. A funerary tablet, for example, brings to mind that Greek *kolossos* so masterfully analyzed by Jean-Pierre Vernant as a representation of the "category of the double."[20] According to Vernant, the *kolossos* is not an image but a double of the deceased, "just as the dead himself is a double of the living."[21] A Chan icon itself can be at the same time a double of the living and of the dead, of the practitioner or officiating priest and of the god or Buddha.

The ritual animation of the icon is overdetermined and redundant (installation of relics, mantric installation of breaths, dotting in the eyes, similarity of the icon to his divine or human model, etc.). It seems to be driven by a constant *mise en abyme*, in which each sequence reconstitutes in brief the course of the entire ritual. Does the priest "lay it on thick," without realizing that there is such a thing as overkill, that supplement creates a void within the supposed completeness, because each of the constitutive elements (and the ritual as a whole) is seen as ontologically deficient? Or maybe there can be no overkill in an area where the "logic of practice" uses all possible means in its power? Here we are dealing with a "soft," practical logic in which only the unceasing, litanic aspect of presence in all its forms stands out, in an orgy of presence. It is only in the perspective of a "hard," overintellectualized logic, too detached from its object, that there is any contradiction or impoverishment. From the point of view of performative logic, everything runs on to a crescendo, like a leitmotif, an infinitely varied musical theme.

In spite of the radical difference of soteriological context, the Chinese "icon question" was a controversy over the position of the sacred in society, much like that in Christianity. The much-vaunted Chan iconoclasm was essentially directed against "superstitions" that threatened to bring about an inflation of the sacred sphere and at the same time a diminution of sectarian legitimacy. It represents a tactical desire to limit the proliferation of sacred symbols and to keep for itself the privilege of

[20] See Vernant 1965: vol. 2, 73.
[21] Ibid., 2: 67.

possessing icons or other chosen symbols. A rationalist or purely aesthetic interpretation of Chan iconology would thus be wrong-minded. It
is undeniable that certain iconoclasts, carried away by the dynamic of
what I have elsewhere termed the "rhetoric of immediacy," sometimes
sought to deny all forms of symbolic mediation. In so doing, they tended
to forget that the aniconism of early Chan—another expression of "sudden" ideology—constituted a ritual inversion. It signaled the final stage
of a process that lost all its meaning if it did not include a preliminary
gradualist, iconic phase. Even in their subitism, early Chan masters still
relied on the idea of a line of patriarchs who had realized, one after
another, the formless truth. This idea has validity only in the context of a
funerary ideology based on the ancestral cult—an ideology according to
which each patriarchal generation is only the embodiment of an eternal
Dharma, as a kind of *lex incarnata*. Each patriarch is thus himself already
an icon, an individual form of the formless, a metamorphosis of the
"primordial double," the Buddha. In the same way, each Chan/Zen master, seated on his high chair opposite the icon of Śākyamuni, is the double
of the Buddha and of his alter ego, the universal monarch. And he is in
turn replicated in his disciples, seated on each side of him. Turning things
around, the Buddha, as he is manifested in icons, can be seen as a mental
projection of the real monks, and as a ritual projection of their Buddha
nature. Thus the ritual logic of dissemination came to "supplement" and
displace the metaphysics of presence characteristic of early Chan. Between these reflections in a mirror, which had become so many sources of
potency, power circulated endlessly, from mind to mind, body to body.
On this point we can remember that, among the motifs likely to give rise
to the "uncanny," Freud included the motif of the double, or *doppelgänger*, among whose characteristics he counted telepathy, the immediate transmission of psychic processes between two people that involves
identification with the other, and split, division, and permutation of the
self.[22] Masters like Keizan seem to have made the uncanny their element.

We can see that, beginning from the *imaginaire* of a Japanese monk,
we have had to break through narrow cultural boundaries and go back,
through China, all the way to India (and even to find affinities with the
question of icons in the West). It is not within the limits of this study to
pose the question of influences: some are obvious (Tantrism), others are
problematic, probably unprovable—and perhaps after all useless. From
this meandering journey through images, we should retain for now the
impression of a strong symbolic coherence underlying the "ideology of
immanence."

[22] See Freud, "The Uncanny," in *Collected Papers* (London: Hogarth, 1924–50), vol. 4:
368–407.

EPILOGUE

IMAGINATION AND IDEOLOGY

> What I am trying to do is something like describing the
> function of a king. As I do this I must not fall into the error
> of explaining royal dignity by the usefulness of the king; and
> yet I must omit neither his usefulness nor his dignity.
>
> *Ludwig Wittgenstein*

THE ANALYSIS OF ICONS and other Buddhist ritual artifacts, by revealing the existence of an "ideology of presence," suggests the inadequacy of a narrowly functionalist point of view, which considers an image as a simple representation or mnemonic device and justifies it by its good psychological effects on the worshiper. Can we for all that confine ourselves to the phenomenological level and remain content to uncover the "ideology of presence," the system of ideas that underlie the cult of images? Do we not risk overestimating this ideo-logy by attributing too great a coherence to it? It was important first of all to show that such a system exists. Although the system whose contours we have outlined is never, from its very nature, fully actualized, even its partial actualizations are nonetheless important. The virtual existence of the system being accepted, two reservations nevertheless remain. On the one hand ideology is always being challenged by that which, in the system, tends toward otherness. On the other hand we should not privilege the immanent, innocent meaning of these "symbols" to the detriment of their social and political function, their "ideological" (in the Marxist sense) nature.

MANA AND SYMBOLIC EFFICACY

The ("phenomenological") description of this ideology of immanence rests on the ever-present idea of "efficacy" (Ch. *ling*) or the power (Skt. *śakti*) of icons and other ritual objects (or subjects). This idea, which corresponds in objects to that of the "power" (*abhijñā*) or charisma in "religious virtuosos," cannot but recall that of *mana*, made famous by the analyses of Emile Durkheim and Marcel Mauss and become one of the commonplaces of classical anthropology.

One of the criticisms directed at Mauss's theory of *mana* is that he was too quick to accept and generalize onto a theoretical level a native interpretive category. In his "Essai sur le don" (*The Gift*), Mauss himself indicates that one must move beyond the point of view of "local knowledge" in order to elaborate a theory of practice that can take into account both the autochthonous descriptions and their objective function, or what, to use one of Pierre Bourdieu's distinctions, one may call the phenomenological and ideological dimensions of experience. We have already started to tackle this problem from its psychological side in connection with the "twofold truth" of belief or beliefs.

For Mauss, *mana* is not simply a force, a being, but also an action, a quality, a state. In other terms "the word is at the same time a noun, an adjective, a verb. It achieves that confusion of agent, ritual, and things that appears to be fundamental in magic."[1] But, in anthropological discourse, *mana* quickly became a noun, according to a process much like that which led to the idea of the "sacred." However, far from restricting himself to a definition of *mana* as a real force that could circulate from one object to another, Mauss saw this idea as a structural effect, a "supplement of copula" that allowed magical logic to function. Like the idea of the sacred, that of *mana* is only, in the last analysis, a category of collective thought which "imposes a classification of things, separates some, joins others together, establishes lines of influence or limits of isolation."[2] From the time of the essay he wrote in collaboration with his uncle, Durkheim, Mauss had attributed great importance to the pattern of Chinese classificatory thought according to which things act on each other by virtue of their classificatory affinities.[3] Mauss, however, hesitated to attribute any reality other than an ideal one to some kind of circulation of forces. He seems to have envisaged the thought of such a circulation when he proposed to identify classification, "the relative place or respective value of things," with a "difference of potential" by virtue of which things would act on each other. However, he ended up by admitting that the "idea" of *mana* is no different from the "idea of these values, of these differences in potential." Thus this idea would function "like a category; it would make possible magical ideas just as categories make possible human ideas," with the one difference that this category is of collective thought, not a given of individual understanding, as are ideas of time and space.[4] At any rate "the idea of magical efficacy is always present, and it is this which, far from being simply an accessory factor, plays in a way the role played by a copula in a clause."[5] *Mana*

[1] Mauss 1950: 101–2.

[2] Ibid.: 114–15.

[3] See Emile Durkheim and Marcel Mauss, *Primitive Classification*, trans. Rodney Needham (Chicago: University of Chicago Press, 1963).

[4] Mauss 1950: 111–12.

[5] Ibid., 116.

thus becomes a classificatory principle and, as such, it belongs more to the epistemological than to the ontological sphere.

In his ambiguous praise of the "Essai sur le don," Lévi-Strauss pushes to its logical extreme the reflection initiated by Mauss, since he empties *mana* of all its substance to make it into an abstract operator present in all logical functions. According to him, *mana* represents "an indeterminate value of signification, in itself devoid of meaning and thus susceptible of receiving any meaning at all."[6] It is a linguistic category, of zero symbolic value, a "floating signifier" that, like the italics in a printed sentence, indicates significance without adding to the meaning.[7] This concept may appear seductive in its demystifying dynamic, but it reveals a weak empirical basis: doing violence to the pragmatic and nonsystematic nature of Mauss's notion, it tends to reduce everything to a single common denominator, to conceal differences between archaic and modern societies, and to deny finally any distinction between rational thought and magical thinking. In the last analysis, it is just as rationalizing as the Durkheimian interpretation of the sacred was mystical. Lévi-Strauss's purely logical interpretation of *mana* seems too abstract to take into account the local functioning of the notion.

Although it may be important to stand back from supposedly autochthonous interpretations, must we abandon them entirely, as structuralism has? Must we, as Lévi-Strauss did in his criticism of Mauss's "phenomenological" approach to the gift, reject completely indigenous experience and interpretation and assume, for example (as Mauss himself did to a certain extent), that the exchange as a constructed object constitutes the primary phenomenon? One could argue, on the contrary, that it may be just as important to let oneself become "taken in" by the game (sometimes a dangerous one) so as, if not to understand it, at least to give it a chance to reveal its agonistic and performative truth. This is what Jeanne Favret-Saada has done in her remarkable study on witchcraft in the French countryside.[8] We may in any case wonder, with Wittgenstein, whether the elimination of magic does not itself partake of a kind of magic. On this point, in spite of all their differences, Frazer and Lévi-Strauss meet. Mauss, on the other hand, is more cautious and less easily classified.

Mauss's work has also inspired an entire ideological criticism that tends to emphasize the sociopolitical aspect of the phenomenon. His sociological bent is well summed up in this passage: "We move from the

---

[6] Lévi-Strauss 1987: 55–56; see also Smith 1987: 108.

[7] Lévi-Strauss 1987: 63–64.

[8] Favret-Saada 1980.

observation of the mechanism of a rite to the study of the setting rites take place in, since it is only in the setting where magical rites take place that we can find the purposes behind the practices of the individual magician."[9] Stanley Tambiah also tried to understand religious phenomena such as *mana*, Brahman, or the charisma of the Buddha as social experiences.[10] According to him, the circulation of "power" that takes place through amulets is ultimately a circulation of social power, because it causes a sedimentation of charisma that reinforces (or changes) social stratification. This analysis seems to be valid for icons, and we have already noticed that an "iconomy" is always more or less political. We thus have to detach ourselves from theological conceptions of religious experience in order to try to understand the real effects of these conceptions on the individual and social level, and not simply the imaginary or symbolic effects. Mauss already concluded that "in magic, it is always basically a matter of respective values recognized by the society. These values do not apply, in reality, to intrinsic qualities of things or people, but to the place and rank attributed to them by the ruling public opinion and by prejudice."[11] Basing himself on Mauss, Tambiah considers *mana* and charisma as "functions" of social stratification and the cosmology of a society: "If, on the one hand, they represent the principle of immanent order in the cosmos that cuts across its constituent elements, they are also the expression of differential potencies and relations of power that emanate from the classified positions of the society."[12] According to him, the process of objectifying charisma, the charisma deposited like sediment in objects such as amulets and icons, transforms these objects into focal points and vehicles of social exchange.

In all cases sociological objectivation tends to consider real-life experience and the phenomenological interpretation of the subject as largely illusory. This disenchanted approach is summed up by Mauss himself when, at the end of his study of *mana*, he says, "When all is said and done, it is still society deluding itself with the counterfeit money of its dream."[13] A believer, citing the words of Saint Paul or of Laozi on the paradoxical nature of truth, might easily object that the divine or the supernatural intervenes precisely in the context of flashy superstition

[9] Mauss 1950: 140.
[10] See Tambiah 1985: 337–39.
[11] Mauss 1950: 114.
[12] Tambiah 1985: 339.
[13] "En définitive, c'est toujours la société qui se paie elle-même de la fausse monnaie de son rêve." See Mauss, "Esquisse d'une théorie générale de la magie," 1950: 119. The English translation of this passage by Robert Brain unfortunately loses the important monetary metaphor: "The whole society suffers from the false images of its dream." See Mauss 1972: 126.

since it is not limited, as the "objective" observer is, by categories of the likely or unlikely. Ultimately Mauss's much-touted "extended reason" seems incapable of penetrating the "irrationality of magic or of the gift" as long as it rests on the "objectivist" or positivist positions of Western rationalism. Derrida's criticism of the "Essai sur le don," that of seeing nothing but exchange, system, and economics where perhaps a free and irreversible expenditure reveals itself, applies to the entire Maussian oeuvre and that of his followers.[14] And we are doubtless condemned to repeat this circular error as long as we cannot, like Keizan, move from one way of thinking to another, let ourselves be caught up in the symbolic game and then stand back from it, and catch hold, simultaneously or alternatively "in an obscure economy" that is no longer completely economical, of tradition in its systematic and unsystematic, economic and noneconomic, disenchanted and reenchanted aspects. As we can see, the unveiling of tradition presupposes the demystification of anthropological discourse and its presuppositions.

SYMBOL AND MEDIATION

Another idea underlying our analysis is that of the mediation of the *imaginaire* between the real and the surreal. Here again we started from the Maussian schema of sacrifice, updated by Paul Mus, according to which an icon, like a stūpa, is perceived as a "mesocosm," an intermediary between the domains of the profane and the sacred. To be sure, we should ask ourselves what this concept of the sacred involves, deriving as it does from a spatial division between sacred and profane, and whether this conception, founded on Indo-European semantics, is pertinent for other cultures. It still remains true, however, that in Hindu and Buddhist ritual, spatialization plays an important role. The *imaginaire* is spatialized, and this "spacing" is what makes it thinkable (as "writing" in the Derridian sense).[15]

Mus may be correct in his analysis of the symbolic structure of ritual, but it is not enough to reveal the system of representation that underlies any ritual operation. As Bourdieu stresses, rites "of passage" are also rites of demarcation. One might object that, unlike Greek ritual, which seems to establish a line of communication between gods and humans only to better "reiterate their differences" and consolidate the gap between the spheres of the sacred and the profane, Hindu and Buddhist rituals are clearly intended to bring about a passage to the beyond, a breakthrough to another level. And yet it is undeniable that Vedic ritual,

[14] See Derrida 1992: 24ff. A similar analysis was already made by Bataille 1988.
[15] See Derrida 1984.

like Greek ritual, also aims to maintain a distance between humans and gods just as much and perhaps more than to reestablish a line of communication between them.[16] Should we then consider that stūpas, relics, and icons (to take only these examples) also contribute to perpetuate this distinction between divine and human planes, and thence between different levels of society?

The Buddhist solution seems to consist of bringing about not so much a mediation between the two spheres as a transposition: the creation of a double that is at the same time the same and different. Altars, icons, or tombs all serve as circuit breakers, focal points—but nothing or no one passes from one side to another, from this shore to the other, as Mahāyāna scriptures put it. The end of a series on this side of the mirror (or of the river of existence) is only the beginning of something completely different (although mysteriously identical) on the other side—without any kind of passage, properly speaking. The expression "rite of passage" thus becomes meaningless inasmuch as there is only mimesis.

The ideology of immanence reveals itself also to be an ideology of the difference between the spheres of the profane and the sacred, of the visible and the invisible: the icon refers to an ever-present but never easily accessible power, a power that is in a way panoptic in that it implies the presence of a divine subject who sees the worshiper without ever revealing himself completely to his/her view. As a result the icon makes the invisible only partially visible, while it adds a dimension of mystery, of invisibility, to visible objects.

THE MODAL *IMAGINAIRE*

It emerges from our analysis of icons that the presence of the god in a statue is not perceived as identical to that of a living human being, nor is it perceived as pure absence. Everything goes on in the fashion of "one might say that" (in the two senses of the expression: as a performative act, "let us say that," but also as an impression, "it seems that"). Does this mean that the relationship with the icon is one of simple misperception (*méconnaissance*), confusion of true and false; or partial knowledge (*semi-connaissance*), halfway between true knowledge and ignorance? Can we still talk about true knowledge, although on a different mode? "Counterfeit money" of dreams—and what if this spurious money, *pace* Mauss, was fundamentally more real than the true, since, as in the Chinese theory of money burned as an offering, on the other side of the real everything is inverted? Or else, what if, as in Baudelaire's anecdote cited

16 See Herrenschmidt 1982.

by Derrida,[17] this counterfeit money was reserved for "the poor," in this case anthropologists and other "dissociated" intellectuals?[18]

We can easily admit the need to go beyond the phenomenological level, but such a movement remains problematic in many respects. It is easy to deny any validity to native theories, and to see in them only specimens of false consciousness immediately spotted by the practiced eye of the anthropologist or philosopher. Indeed, how can we not share Wittgenstein's criticisms of Frazerian rationalism?[19] But it is too simple to brush off exactly that which one should most pay attention to: to deny that a problem exists is not the same as solving it. In the case at hand, a phenomenological analysis cannot be satisfied by simply describing Keizan's *imaginaire* or the "power" circulating between doubles; it must also include the subitist conception to which he is heir. Subitism can be understood both as a notch higher in the phenomenological (the true *ling* is formless; it goes beyond images), and as a disavowal of the phenomenological (there is no *ling*; nothing circulates; emptiness is not a higher form of fullness but abandonment of illusion, of the very desire for fullness or presence, a going beyond any metaphysics of presence). Nothing is simple: the phenomenological level is itself double—a twofold truth that prefigures the duality of levels, phenomenological and ideological, meaning and function.

The *imaginaire* can be conceived of as an intermediate modality between the true and the false. It thus becomes the attitude, the domain, or the modality that allows us to keep together, and to mediate between, these two levels: belief and nonbelief, subitism and gradualism, form and formlessness. Bourdieu's notion of *habitus*, i.e., a system that engenders practices and representation that can be adapted objectively to their goal without implying conscious strategies, perhaps lets us reconcile the sincerity of belief with self-interest, at the phenomenological and ideological levels (as in the case of Keizan's dreams). But it nevertheless privileges the objective pole of experience or belief.[20]

Imaginaire is not really nominal, but rather adverbial, adjectival, or modal (a way of existing, in an imaginary way). We must guard against a tendency to substantivize, as we often do with the unconscious or the sacred, that which is only a modality of belief or perception. Along the same line of thinking, when should we speak of a double, a notion that leads us to think in terms of substance, exchange of attributes, flux,

[17] See Derrida 1992: Appendix.
[18] It is Mauss himself who qualified the professional scholar as a person "dissociated" from everyday practice and therefore unable to understand what may be obvious to common people.
[19] See Wittgenstein 1979.
[20] See Bourdieu 1990: 53.

rather than of a simple symmetry of position, of differences of tension (of social level) that create the illusion of a circulation of power from one pole to another? Ideally, it is important to distinguish between various figures of the double—by duplication or twinning—and not to confuse symmetry of position with substantial identity, mirror images, and circulation of forces. Unfortunately, it is for now impossible to choose between these alternatives.

What is the point of this profusion of symbols, doubles, and fetishes that we have discovered within Buddhism? According to Marc Augé, the fetish or "object god" (*dieu objet*), whether it is anthropomorphic or not, is the "instance and the place through which one must pass in order to move from one individual to another, from one point to another, or from one symbolic order to another, but also from oneself to oneself, since in our heart of hearts we are plural. The symbolic and fetish object confirms and denies boundaries; more exactly, it confirms their reality at the same time as it opens up the possibility and makes explicit the need to cross them, eventually multiplying prohibitions to suggest the possibility and the need for the passage."[21] In the form of the ritual object, the Buddhist double really does seem to be, as Freud thought, a way of anticipating, of preventing death.

A Problematic Economy

Keizan's *imaginaire* "presents" us with a generalized economy of *ling*. The Sino-Japanese *imaginaire* seems to be underpinned by the notion of *ling*, a reality conceived a little like the Dao, a force that is the source of images without itself being an image, impossible to actualize by images alone. Just as this force circulates through various levels of the real, the notion that derives from it permits a passage—intellectual or imaginary—from one level of existence or consciousness to another. Whether it really does circulate or not, it is this force, power, *ling*—or rather the notion that expresses it—that serves as a shifter, as a copula, and allows us to connect, as I have done, the various levels of the *imaginaire*. The *imaginaire* tends (without really succeeding) to organize itself around this idea and is permeated by it. *Ling* connects all sorts of phenomena that at first sight seem to belong to very different spheres.[22] In an

---

[21] Augé 1988: 144.

[22] *Ling* means, among other "things," the "spirit of a being, which acts upon others"; "spiritual, divine, supernatural"; "efficient"; but also "ingenious, intelligent." In combination it gives *lingyan* (Japanese *reiken*), "supranormal powers" (synonymous with *shentong/jinzū*); *lingyin*, "efficient, able to produce the desired effect"; "virtue, energy"; *lingqi*, "subtle influence, force, supernatural power"; *lingshen*, epithet of a god who responds to

overall way, the term connotes the efficacy attributed to the spirits of the dead and to invisible forces. The polysemantic nature of *ling* has been enriched, through the agency of Buddhism, with Indian and Japanese additions, and it is thus difficult to grasp the term in all its nuances, let alone the nonsemantic surplus that circulates in this semantic field and takes it toward its beyond.[23]

This idea of a force that circulates, that one can harness or lose, poses the problem of magic, or of a "metaphysics of presence." The Chinese notion of *ling* is not one of great originality since it seems to correspond in certain ways to the Polynesian *mana* or other classical figures of symbolic efficacy. Still, its main interest for us is that it grew up surreptitiously within a doctrine—Chan/Zen subitism—that rejected it in advance.

In its fluidity, its "liquidity," *ling* may remind us of the fetishism of money. In consumption, or in hysterical conversion, desire is floating: such and such an object does not answer to any particular need, nor such and such a symptom to a specific organ.[24] In the same way, in the economy of *ling*, the cult of such and such a god does not meet only some precise need (although he may equally meet it); it is rather the global investment of desire in belief and its symbols that counts. Belief can thenceforth be displaced, transferred, manifested even by a localized rejection of some god/object or another and pass into purely Chan symbols (Arhat, Zen master).

The Weberian interpretation of charisma seems fairly close to that of *ling*, but it has the inconvenience of being limited to exceptional individuals, to personal charisma and does not consider the charisma of objects. Max Weber did distinguish between "charisma of lineage," which refers to the transfer of charisma through bloodlines, and "charisma of function," in which the charismatic power of an individual depends on an established social structure.[25] But, as Stanley Tambiah has pointed out, Weber, who was so aware of the routinization and objectivation of charisma in institutional structures, did not pay sufficient attention to the objectivization of charisma in amulets, charms, *regalia*, *palladia*, and other objects of this kind. And yet it is a constant of all religion that

---

prayers; *lingxiang*, "spiritual icon," "efficient image"; *lingwei*, a "tablet placed in front of the coffin"; *lingwu*, "paper house burned at funeral rituals." In Japanese, *rei/ryō* is found in compounds such as *goryō* (or *onryō*), "malevolent spirits of the victims of violent death" (*malemort*).

[23] A similar case is that of *shi*, an important notion in Chinese thought that has recently been analyzed by François Jullien. See Jullien 1992.

[24] See "Consumer Society," in Baudrillard 1988: 29–56.

[25] See Weber 1978: 1114.

charisma should become concrete and sedimented into objects that then become stores of power.[26]

Just like the icon and the aniconic object, speech and writing are receptacles of presence and power. In the same way as speech is already writing, the aniconic is already, in a sense, iconic: or rather, the icon functions above all ritually, like the aniconic object; the mimetic, aesthetic aspect comes on top of the ritual aspect, as a "dangerous supplement." We should therefore relativize the opposition between iconism and aniconism while maintaining it—like the opposition between speech and writing.

The image, like writing or text, is citable in other contexts. The comparison with a quotation without context, with what Derrida calls the iterability of writing, is not without interest. This interruption of meaning is perhaps, for the icon, an interruption of the circulation of meaning and of its effects (subsumed under the term *ling*). However, there is always the production of another meaning and other effects (aesthetic ones, for instance, in the case of the images in museums). Perhaps we could therefore, pursuing the textual metaphor, interpret *ling* according to the two axes of metaphor and metonymy and speak of a metaphorical (vertical) circulation produced by substitution and a metonymic (horizontal) circulation produced by contact.

The scandalous origin of Buddhism, the unthinkable absence of a Buddha occulted by the unfathomable secret of Nirvāṇa, has given way to a plural, differed presence, a presence spread over time and space, spaced as a symbolic writing, one that therefore returns to the realm of the thinkable.[27] Ritual is indeed that device that institutes differences; and the field of these differences, the space of these different planes connected by the logic of *ling*, shape the Buddhist *imaginaire*.

We need to conceive this imaginaire on the mode of the debt and the gift rather than that of belief, as act rather than thought; but also on the mode of gift-giving, as something that breaks the economic circle, moving beyond into pure loss or expenditure.[28] Belief itself can be lent, as is shown by language when we talk of giving faith or lending credence to something. In this sense the *Record of Tōkoku*, or even the entirety of Keizan's works, constitutes an example of "en-gaged" literature, a token or guarantee left by Keizan. In the perspective of the imaginary/debt, we must bring up the notion of "transfer of merits" (*ekō*), a diversion that singularly (or plurally) complicates the cycle of exchange: it is no longer just a transaction between a layperson and a god through the intermedi-

---

[26] Tambiah 1985: 335.

[27] On this question, see Eckel 1990, 1992; and Campany 1993.

[28] On this question, see Bataille 1988; and Rodolphe Gasché's criticism of Mauss: "L'Echange héliocentrique," in *L'Arc*: special issue on Marcel Mauss, ed. Denis Hollier (Paris: Duponchelle, 1990): 70–84.

ary of an officiating priest, but a diffusion of efficacy that redounds on all the gods, the clergy, and the ancestors of the lay donor and sets the entire system in motion.

The diffuse logic of dissemination, as difference and deferring of the full presence, seems at first sight to organize this presence into a system (a chain or network throughout which *ling* diffuses and is disseminated). It seems to end up in a differential, hierarchized presence that in this way becomes conceivable—or almost. In other terms, if it tends endlessly toward economy, toward the circle, toward an image of ritual as exchange or transaction, it does not really ever get there completely, because the terms are always "different." Thus the double, as mediator between self and other, does not "amount to the same thing"; it never comes full circle (*il ne revient pas au même*), because it is unavoidably "altered" by the ritual transaction. Dissemination is never just a simple regulated dispersal; it implies an uncontrollable loss and/or surplus, a break in the economic circle. Awakening is, like the gift according to Derrida, exactly that cleavage, *hybris*, disjunction that causes the system to leak and sometimes to explode or implode, that sets into motion and at the same time short-circuits the *imaginaire*, the magical, ruled by the law of indebtedness and immediate benefit, by economy. Like Keizan, every Zen monk, by "leaving his family," also intends to leave the "law of the household," of economic circularity.[29] Even if monastic enclosure seems to replace or strengthen domestic enclosure, the hope remains alive.

THE QUESTION OF IDEOLOGY

While the *imaginaire* constitutes a system insofar as each element is connected to others, along a semantic/ritual chain including the Dharma robe, relics, talismans, doubles, it is also a flexible symbolic system, derived from practical logic. Thus, the division adopted here is purely heuristic, since the different types of *imaginaire* described above overlap, involve, and are connected to each other.

[29] See Derrida's terminological remark (1992: 6):

What is economy? Among its irreducible predicates or semantic values, economy no doubt includes the values of law (*nomos*) and of home (*oikos*, home, property, family, the hearth, the fire indoors). *Nomos* does not only signify the law in general, but also the law of distribution (*nemein*), the law of sharing or partition [*partage*], the law as partition (*moira*), the given or assigned part, participation. . . . Besides the values of law and home, of distribution and partition, economy implies the idea of exchange, of circulation, of return. The figure of the circle is obviously *at the center*, if that can still be said of a circle.

We have attempted to disentangle three levels of analysis: 1) theoretical discourse; 2) practical logic, which contradicts it; and 3) seeing both theory and practice as ideological, an analysis that reveals their collusion beyond their very contradiction, but one that also takes into account its own contradictions and its unavoidably ideological and reductionist nature.

Belief in a sacred presence within a relic does not necessarily require holding to a conscious ideology of immanence. Clearly in many cases we are dealing only with remnants from some ancient system, dislocated by time, with patterns of discourse or practices whose theological or mythological foundations have long crumbled. But like all true relics, this belief, a metaphorical relic itself, still has a vital life of its own. And if the logical reconstruction by historians or anthropologists of the body or system to which it attests is only virtual, has value only as a model, this is not to say that the integral body (or system) is unable to (and sometimes actually does not) reconstitute itself on this basis. The historian working over *longue durée* trends is thus justified in his effort to put the ideal body back together, as long as he sees in it only a model, a virtual reality, and does not commit the anachronistic error of identifying, in the precise case under consideration, the relic and the body, the belief and the system from which it derives historically and whose existence it seems to require logically.

We have thus tried to describe the "oscillating," or rather "interstitial," thought of Keizan, a thought that develops on the threshold of, in the space between, two contradictory systems, and draws its vitality from connecting them in practice (a logical impossibility). But Keizan's thought also (and always) derives from "two distinct and irreconcilable anthropologies." Thus it is important not to cling to the obvious meaning (or even the hidden one, insofar as we succeed in unveiling it) of texts and rituals. The overall symbolism, ideological and imaginary, must be considered as deriving, with very few exceptions, from a "personality planning," an enterprise of an ideological nature intended to produce a semblance of presence, a social and ontological/metaphysical legitimization. Keizan, in this sense, remains an ideologue because he tries to promote a certain vision, double or ambiguous, of the world. Perhaps this ambiguity reflects a phenomenon of acculturation (scholarly culture/popular culture); however, we must not overlook the fact that ambiguity is in large part inherent in the Chan tradition, that we can find its doctrinal antecedents, and that acculturation would not have happened if it had not been in tune with the internal dynamic of this religious movement.

But how can we reveal the unspoken—that which, because it is either hidden or too obvious, remains beyond words: the interstitial imagination (which fills the ellipses in the discourse) or the marginal imagination (which provides its framework, the surreal foundation), the fuzziness, the poetic fringe on a practice that may seem quite down to earth? The texts—more practical than literary—are often too concise, and the imagination erupts in them only occasionally, for example in brief records of dreams. We have to try to ferret it out, even at the risk of imposing our own imagination on it. The interpretation will be worthwhile, not so much for its value as an explanation, but insofar as it can produce "the satisfaction of a certain need and the fulfillment of a certain desire," if not in the reader (too daring a hope!) then at least in the author.[30]

Finally we must relativize this work, noting that the workings of the various motifs gathered here under the name of Keizan have above all a heuristic value. Keizan himself is only the name given to a character, and by extension his mental universe, brought onto the scene as I glimpse him or try to reconstruct him on the basis of scanty documents. He is thus also a mental construct, a figment of my imagination. Yes, he does retain some "objective" reality, historical or anthropological truth, but this is, I fear, inextricably mingled with the personal mythology of me, the author. As an excuse I can only invoke Wittgenstein's opinion and say that it is not enough to simply draw lines connecting the components common to the various forms of the imagination that can be detected in Keizan. "Then there is still missing a part in our view of things, and it is that part that connects the picture to our own feelings and thoughts. This is the part that gives things their depth."[31] On this subject we must keep in mind the active role of the author in setting the scene, framing it, organizing the facts. The significance of Keizan's actions and beliefs thus appears completely different according to whether one places them against the backdrop of the Chan/Zen tradition, of local culture, or both.

Trying to capture Keizan's imagining in the netting of my discourse is like trying to square the circle. Despite the nostalgia for closure and centering still discernible in this metaphor of the circle, I never intended to use the notion of mental universe as a cultural totality, a completely closed "world system" that would still require a structural analysis—a totality free from tensions and change, reconciled with itself in the ideological harmony of some kind of "pure" Zen.[32] It is doubtless better to avoid concluding, if only to leave the door ajar for a possible intrusion of the other, for a flight of meaning, for something finally that would not be only a mask of the social; to let us see that there are not just dead, pale, or obscure moons in the firmament of the Buddhist *imaginaire*.[33]

[30] See Jacques Bouveresse, in Wittgenstein 1982: 102.
[31] Wittgenstein, ibid.: 28.
[32] For a compelling analysis of this predicament, see Derrida 1970.
[33] This in in reference to Mauss's famous passage: "Then it will be seen that in the firmament of reason there have been, and there still are, many moons that are dead, pale, or obscure." See Marcel Mauss, "Real and Practical Relations between Psychology and Sociology," in Mauss 1979: 32.

GLOSSARY

Akiba Sanshakubō Daigongen — 秋
葉三尺坊大権現
ako — 下火
Amaterasu — 天照
Amida (Nyorai) — 阿彌陀(如來)
Ankokuji — 安國寺
Anza tengen — 安坐点眼
Anzan Kichidō — 案山吉道
Arakan — 阿羅漢
Ashikaga — 足利
Ashikaga Takauji — 足利高氏
Atago(yama) — 愛宕山
Ayuwang shan — 阿育王山

Baizhang Huaihai — 百丈懷海
bao — 寶
Baozhi — 寶誌
Bassui oshō gyōjitsu — 抜隊和尙行
實
Bassui Tokushō — 抜隊得勝
Bendōwa — 辨道話
Benzai (ten) — 辨才(天)
Beppō Daiju — 別峰大殊
Bidatsu (Emperor) — 敏達天皇
bikuni — 比丘尼
Bishamon — 毗沙門
Biyan lu — 碧巖錄
bodaiji — 菩提寺
bodai(mon) — 菩提(門)
bosatsukai — 菩薩戒
Budai (J. Hotei) — 布袋
Bukke ichi daiji yawa — 佛家一大事
夜話
Bunpo (era) — 文保
busshō — 佛性
butsuden — 佛殿
Butsuge shariki — 佛牙舍利記
Butsuji Zenji — 佛滋禪師

Caodong (J. Sōtō) — 曹洞
Caoshan Benji — 曹山本寂
Caoxi — 曹溪
Chan (J. Zen) — 禪

Chang'an — 長安
Chanyuan qinggui — 禪苑淸規
Chewu Jixing — 徹悟際醒
chigo — 稚児
Chikuhō — 竹峰
chinju — 鎭守
Chinju kirigami — 鎭守切紙
chinkasai — 鎭花祭
chinsō (var. *chinzō*) — 頂相
Chinsō kirigami — 頂相切紙
Chinsō no daiji — 頂相大事
Chitō Shōgen — 智燈照玄
Chixiu Baizhang qinggui — 敕修百
丈淸規
Chōnen — 奝然
Chōri yurai ki — 長吏由来記
chōsō (see *chinsō*)
Chūgan Engetsu — 中巖圓月
chuzui — 除罪
Cuiwei Wuxue — 翠微無學

Da fangdeng tuoluoni jing — 大方等
陀羅尼經
Dahui Zonggao — 大慧宗杲
Daibutsu — 大佛
Daichi — 大智
Daigenshuri — 大権修利
daiji — 大事
Daijiji — 大滋寺
Daijōji — 大乘寺
daimyōjin — 大明神
Dainichi (Nyorai) — 大日 (如來)
Dainichi[bō] Nōnin — 大日房能忍
Daizong (Emperor) — 代宗
Dakiniten — 茶枳尼天
Damei Fachang — 大梅法常
Damei shan — 大梅山
Damo lun — 達磨論
danshi — 斷紙
Danxia Tianran — 丹霞天然
daochang — 道場
Daoji — 道濟
Daoxin — 道信

Daoxuan — 道宣

Daruma — 達磨

Darumashū — 達磨宗

Dayang Jingxuan — 大陽警玄

Dayang shan — 大陽山

Den'e — 傳衣

Denkōroku — 傳光錄

Dentōin — 傳燈院

Dōgen — 道元

Dōjōji — 道成寺

Dōkyō — 道鏡

Dongming Huiri — 東明慧日

Dongshan (J. Tōzan) — 洞山

Dongshan Liangjie — 洞山良介

Dongyang Dehui — 東陽德輝

Dōryō — 道了

Dunhuang — 敦煌

Echizen — 越煌

Eifukuan — 永福庵

Eihei (Dōgen) — 永平(道元)

Eiheiji — 永平寺

Eiheiji sanko ryōzuiki — 永平寺三箇靈瑞記

Eihei kaisan goyuigon ki — 永平開山御遺言記

Eihei kōroku — 永平廣錄

Eihei shingi — 永平清規

Eikan — 永觀

Eikandō — 永觀堂

Eisai (see Yōsai)

Eizon — 睿尊

Ejō (see Koun Ejō)

Ejō shōjōsha — 懷弉証状寫

Ekan (nun) — 慧觀

Ekan (Darumashū) — 懷鑒

ekō — 廻向

Ekyū (nun) — 慧球

Emei (shan) — 峨眉山

Engakuji — 圓覺寺

engi — 緣起

En'i (nun) — 圓意

Enni Ben'en — 圓爾辨圓

Ennin — 圓仁

En no Gyōja — 役行者

enoki — 榎

Enpō dentōroku — 延寶傳燈錄

Enryakuji — 延曆寺

Enzūin — 圓通院

Eshinni — 慧信尼

Famensi — 法門寺

Fanwang jing — 梵網經

Fazang — 法藏

fengshui — 風水

Fengxiang — 鳳翔

foxiang (J. *butsuzō*) — 佛像

Fozhao Deguang — 佛照德光

Fozu tongji — 佛祖統記

fu — 符

Fudō (Myōō) — 不動明王

Fugen (Bosatsu) — 普賢菩薩

Fugen (Kōmyō) — 普賢光明

fuhao — 符號

Fujiwara no Iekata — 藤原家方

Fujiwara no Tanetsugu — 藤原種継

funzōe — 糞掃衣

fuqi — 符契

fuxin — 符信

Gaki-emaki — 餓鬼絵巻

Gakudō yōjinshū — 學道用心集

gandō — 龕堂

Ganjin (Ch. Jianzhen) — 鑑眞

Ganzan Daishi — 元三大師

garanjin — 伽藍神

Gasan Jōseki — 峨山紹碩

Gedatsu Shōnin — 解脱上人

gedō — 外道

Genji monogatari — 源氏物語

genjō kōan — 現成公案

Genka — 眼可

Genkō (era) — 元亨

Genkō shakusho — 元亨釋書

Gennō (era) — 元應

Gennō Shinshō — 源翁心昭

Genshō Chinzan — 源照珍山

Genso (*jisha*) — 源祖侍者

genze riyaku — 現世利益

Gidaji — 祇陀寺

Gien — 義演

Giin — 義尹

Gijun — 義準

Gikai (see Tettsū Gikai)

Gishin — 義眞
Go-Daigo (Emperor) — 後醍醐
gofu — 護符
Gofuin sahō — 合符印作法
gohōjin — 護法神
gongen — 權現
gorin(no)tō — 五輪塔
Gorōhō — 五老峯
goryō — 御靈
goryō-e — 御靈會
Gozan — 五山
Guan Di — 關帝
Guanxin lun — 觀心論
Guanxiu — 貫休
Guanyin (see Kannon)
Guifeng Zongmi — 圭峰宗密
Guze Kannon — 救世觀音
Gyōki — 行基

Hachiman — 八幡
Hajakuji — 波著寺
Hakurakuten — 白楽天
Hakusan — 白山
Hakusan Gongen — 白山權現
Hakusan Myōjin — 白山明神
Hakusan Myōri Daigongen — 白山
妙理大權現
Hannya shingyō — 般若心經
Hanshan — 寒山
Hanshan Deqing — 憨山德清
Han Yu — 韓愈
hanza — 半座
Hasedera — 長谷寺
Hatano Yoshishige — 波多野義重
Hatsuu — 鉢盂
hattō — 法堂
Heisenji — 平泉寺
Hekizan nichiroku — 碧山日錄
hetong — 合同
Hetou — 河図
Hiei(zan) — 比叡(山)
hinin — 非人
Hirata Atsutane — 平田篤胤
hiya — 火屋
Hōe sōdensho — 法衣相傳書
Hōjō Masako — 北条正子
Hōjō Tokimune — 北条時宗

Hōjō Tokiyori — 北条時頼
Hōkyōintō — 寶篋印塔
Hōkyōki — 寶慶記
hōmyaku — 法脈
Honchō kōsōden — 本朝高僧傳
Hōnen — 法然
hongaku — 本覺
Honganji — 本願寺
Hongren — 弘忍
honji — 本地
honji suijaku — 本地垂迹
honzon — 本尊
Hōōji — 寶應寺
Hōō Nōshō zenji tōmei — 法王能照
禪師塔銘
Hōryūji — 法隆寺
Hōshō (Nyōrai) — 寶生(如來)
Hōshōji — 法勝寺
hosshin(mon) — 發心門
hosshin seppō — 法身說法
hossu — 拂子
Hottō Kokushi — 法燈國師
Huangbo Xiyun — 黃檗希運
Huayan (J. Kegon) — 華嚴
Huike — 慧可
Huineng — 慧能
Huisi — 慧思
Huiyuan — 慧遠
Hundun — 混沌
Hyakurenshō — 百練抄

Ichinomiya — 一ノ宮
Ichiya Hekiganshū — 一夜碧巖集
Idaten — 韋駄天
ihai — 位牌
Ikkei Eishū — 一径永就
ikki — 一揆
ikkō ikki — 一向一揆
Ikkyū Sōjun — 一休宗純
Inari — 稲荷
ino (Ch. *weina*) — 維那
Ippen (Shōnin) — 一遍(上人)
Ishiyamadera — 石山寺
isshinkai — 一心戒
Isurugiyama (Sekidōzan) — 石動山
Izanagi (no mikoto) — 伊弉諾命
Izanami (no mikoto) — 伊弉冊命

Jakuen — 寂圓
Jakushitsu Ryōkō — 寂室了光
ji/tera — 寺
Jianzhen (see Ganjin)
Jiashan — 夾山
Jien — 慈圓
Jigong — 濟公
Jingde chuandeng lu — 景德傳燈錄
jinushigami — 地主神
jinzū (riki) — 神通力
jiriki — 自力
jisetsu innen — 時節因緣
jisha — 侍者
jitō — 地頭
Jixiangdan — 吉祥旦
jixin shifo — 即心是佛
Jiyuan (see Jakuen)
Jizō — 地藏
Jochū Tengin — 如仲天誾
Jōdo shinshū — 淨土眞宗
Jōjin — 成尋
Jōjūji — 淨住寺
Jōkei — 貞慶
Jōmanji — 城萬寺
Jōsai daishi zenshū — 常濟大師全集
Jōshun (*jisha*) — 承順(侍者)
Jōtō shōgakuron — 成等正覺論
Jōzan Ryōkō — 定山良光
Jūichimen Kannon — 十一面觀音
jun/gyaku — 順逆
Jūroku rakan genzuiki — 十六羅漢現瑞記
Juzhi (J. Gutei) — 俱胝

Kaga — 加賀
Kagerō nikki — 蜻蛉日記
kaigen — 開眼
Kaiyuansi — 開元寺
kaji kitō — 加持祈禱
kajō zanmai — 火定三昧
Kakunichi — 覺日
Kakunyo — 覺如
kakurei — 覺靈
Kakushin (nun) — 覺心
Kakushin (see Shinchi Kakushin)
kami — 神
Kammu (Emperor) — 桓武天皇

Kaneie (Fujiwara) — 藤原兼家
Kangiten — 歡喜天
kanjō — 灌頂
Kannon (Ch. Guanyin) — 觀音
kansu — 簡都
Kanzeon (var. for Kannon) — 觀世音
karagokoro — 唐心
Karaten — 迦羅天
Kasuga — 春日
Kasuisai — 可睡斎
Katoku Shōkun — 火德聖君
kawaramono — 河原者
kechimyaku — 血脈
kechimyakubukuro — 血脈袋
Kechimyaku no san — 血脈參
Kegon — 華嚴
Keidō — 慶道
Keiran shūyōshū — 溪嵐拾葉集
Keizan Jōkin — 瑩山紹瑾
Keizan shingi — 瑩山清規
Kenninji — 建仁寺
Kenzei — 建撕
Kenzei ki — 建撕記
kesa — 袈裟
Kesa mandara kirigami — 袈裟曼茶羅切紙
Kichijōsan — 吉祥山
Kikudō Soei — 菊堂祖英
Kinben shigai — 金鞭指街
kirigami (var. kirikami) — 切紙
Kissa yōjōki — 喫茶養生記
kitō jiin — 祈禱寺院
Kiyomizu(dera) — 清水(寺)
kōan — 公案
Koan Shikan — 壺庵至簡
Kōchi Hōin — 弘智法印
Kōei — 珖瑛
Kohō Kakumyō — 孤峰覺明
Kōjin — 荒神
Kokan Shiren — 虎關師鍊
Kōkōji — 光孝寺
Kokūzō — 虛空藏
komonjo — 古文書
komori — 籠り
Kōshōji — 興聖寺
Kōshū — 光宗
Koun Ejō — 孤雲懷弉

Kōya(san) — 高野(山)
Kōzanji — 高山寺
Kōzen gokokuron — 興禪護國論
Kudenshō — 口傳抄
Kuginuki Jizō — 釘抜き地藏
Kūkai — 空海
Kukurihime — 菊理媛
Kumano — 熊野
Kyōkai (var. Keikai) — 景戒
Kyōō Unryō — 恭翁雲良

Laozi — 老子
Lengqie shizi ji — 楞伽師資記
Liandeng huiyao — 聯燈會要
Liang Wudi — 梁武帝
Liezi — 列子
Li Longmin — 李龍眠
ling — 靈
lingbao — 靈寶
lingshen — 靈神
lingwei — 靈位
lingwu — 靈屋
lingxiang (J. *reizō*) — 靈像
lingyan — 靈驗
lingying — 靈應
Lingyun Zhiqin — 靈雲志勤
linian — 離念
Linji (see Rinzai)
Linji Yixuan — 臨濟義玄
Luofu — 洛浦
Luoshu — 洛書

Mangen Shiban — 卍元師蛮
manji hankei — 滿字半形
man'yōgana — 万葉仮名
Manzan Dōhaku — 卍山道白
Manzan oshō Tōmon ejōshū — 卍山
和尚洞門衣袖集
mappō — 末法
masa yume — 眞夢
Mazu Daoyi — 馬祖道一
Meihō Sotetsu — 明峰素哲
Meikyoku Sokushō — 明極即証
Menzan Zuihō — 面山瑞方
Miidera — 三井寺
Minamoto no Sanetomo — 源實朝
Ming'an Dashi — 明安大師

Mingzan — 明瓚
Miroku — 彌勒
missanchō — 密参帳
mogari — 殯
Mokufu Sonin — 默譜祖忍
Mokuren (Ch. Mulian) — 目蓮
mondō (see *wenda*)
Monju — 文殊
Morookadera — 諸岡寺
mōshigo — 申し子
Muchū mondō — 夢中問答
Muchū setsumu — 夢中說夢
Mugai Chikō — 無涯知洪
Mugaku Sogen (Ch. Wuxue Zuyuan)
— 無學祖元
Mujaku Dōchū — 無着道忠
mujō bodai — 無上菩提
mujō seppō — 無情說法
Mujū Ichien — 無住一圓
Mulian (see Mokuren)
Mumako (var. Umako) no Sukune
(Soga no) — 蘇我馬子宿禰
Murasaki Shikibu — 紫式部
mushi dokugo — 無師独悟
mushi-okuri — 虫送り
Musō nikki — 夢想日記
Musō Soseki — 無窓疎石
Mutan Sokan — 無端祖環
Mutei Ryōshō — 無底良詔
myō — 妙
Myōchi — 明智
Myōe (Shōnin) — 明恵(上人)
Myōgonji — 妙嚴寺
Myōshō Enkan (nun) — 明照圓觀
Myōzen — 明全

nadebotoke — 撫で佛
Nanhuasi — 南華寺
Nanyue Huairang — 南岳懷讓
Nanzenji — 南禪寺
Nasu (Mt.) — 那須
nehan(mon) — 涅槃門
nehan myōshin — 涅槃妙心
nenbutsu — 念佛
Nengrensi (J. Nōninji) — 能仁寺
Nichiiki Tōjō shosoden — 日域洞上
諸祖傳

Nichira — 日羅
Nichiren — 日蓮
Nichizō Shōnin — 日藏上人
Nihon ryōiki — 日本靈異記
Nihon shoki — 日本書記
Nihon Tōjō rentōroku — 日本洞上
聯燈錄
ningyō — 忍行
Nōnin (see Dainichi Nōnin)
nyogen zanmai — 如幻三昧
Nyorai ha shari denrai — 如來齒舍
利傳来
Nyoshin — 如心
Nyū Myōjin (var. Nifu Myōjin) — 丹
生明神
nyusshitsu — 入室

Ōbaku — 黃檗
Ōbaku Kōsen — 黃檗高泉
Oda Nobunaga — 織田信長
okibumi — 置文
Ōnin no Ran — 応仁 の 乱
Onjōji — 園城寺
Onmyōdō — 陰陽道
onryō — 怨靈
Ōshō — 應照
Osorezan — 恐山

Paekche — 百濟
Pei Xiu — 裴休
Pozao Duo — 破竈墮
Puhua — 普化
Puji — 普寂

qi — 契
Qinglongsi — 清龍寺
Qingyuan (see Qingyuan Xingsi)
Qingyuan Xingsi — 青原行思
Quan Tang wen — 全唐文

Raihai tokuzui — 礼拝得髓
rakan (Ch. luohan) — 羅漢
Rakanji — 羅漢寺
Rakan kuyō shikimon — 羅漢供養
式文
Rakan ōkenden — 羅漢應驗傳
Rakanshō — 羅漢松
reiken (see *lingyan*)

Rennyo — 蓮如
Renzong — 仁宗
rinka — 林下
Rinzai (Ch. Linji) — 臨濟
rishōtō — 利生塔
rissō — 立僧
rissō nyūsshitsu — 立僧入室
rissō shuso — 立僧首座
Rokkakudō — 六角堂
Rozanji — 盧山寺
Rujing (see Tiantong Rujing)
Ryōan Emyō — 了庵慧明
Ryōgen — 良源
Ryūtakuji — 龍鐸寺
ryūten — 龍天
Ryūten jukai kirigami — 龍天授戒切
紙

Saga (Emperor) — 嵯峨天皇
Saichō — 最澄
Saigyō — 西行
Saijōji — 最乘寺
Saishōden — 最勝殿
Saishōōkyō — 最勝王經
Sakai Norikane — 酒井章兼
Sakai Toshitada — 酒井利忠
Sakawa (Sakō) (no Hachirō)
  Yorichika — 酒勾(八郎)頼親
Sakawa (Sakō) (no Heihachi)
  Yorimoto — 酒勾(平八)頼基
Sakingo Tomosada — 左金吾朝定
Sanbō Daikōjin — 三寶大荒神
Sanbōekotoba — 三寶繪詞
Sanbōji — 三寶寺
Sanbyaku soku — 三百則
sandai sōron — 三代相論
Sanemori — 實盛
Sanemori-*okuri* — 實盛送り
Sangai isshinki — 三界一心記
Sankon zazensetsu — 三根禪說
sanmon — 山門
Sansuikyō — 山水經
sanwa — 參話
Sarashina — 更級
Sarashina nikki — 更級日記
Sawara (Prince) — 早良親王
segaki — 施餓鬼

Seimen (var. Shōmen) dōji — 靑面童子

Seiryōji — 清凉寺

Seiwa (Emperor) — 淸和天皇

Sekidōzan — 石動山

Sengcan — 僧璨

Sengqie — 僧伽

Sennyūji — 泉湧寺

sesshōseki — 殺生石

Shaka — 釋迦

Shaka hankei — 釋迦半形

Shakadō — 釋迦堂

shakujō — 釋杖

Shanmiao (J. Zenmyō) — 善妙

Shaoshi — 少室

shari — 舍利

Shari sōdenki — 舍利相傳記

Shasekishū — 沙石集

Shenhui — 神會

Shenseng zhuan — 神僧傳

shentong — 神通

Shenxiu — 神秀

shenzuo — 神座

shi — 勢

Shiban — 師蛮

shichidō garan — 七堂伽藍

Shide — 拾得

Shigeno Nobunao — 滋野信直

Shikan (see Koan Shikan)

shikan taza — 只管打坐

Shimazu Atsutada — 島津敦忠

shin (mind/heart) — 心

shin (portrait) — 眞

Shinchi Kakushin — 心地覺心

Shingon — 眞言

shinjin datsuraku — 身心脱落

Shinjinmei nentei — 信心銘拈提

shinkoku — 神國

Shinnyodō — 眞如堂

Shinran — 親鸞

Shinran yume no ki — 親鸞夢記

shinsen — 神仙

shippei — 竹箆

Shiragi (var. Shinra) Myōjin — 新羅明神

Shirayamahime (no mikoto) — 白山比咩命

shisho — 嗣書

Shitou [Xiqian] — 石頭希遷

Shōbōgenzō — 正法眼藏

Shōbōgenzō Zuimonki — 正法眼藏隨聞記

Shōbōji — 正法寺

Shōchū (era) — 正中

Shoekō shingi shiki — 諸回向清規式

Shōgen — 昭元

Shōgun Jizō — 将軍地藏

Shōhō Shichirō (Ch. Zhaobao Qilang) — 招寶七郎

Shōkokuji — 相國寺

shōmono — 抄物

Shōmu (Emperor) — 聖武天皇

shōmyaku — 正脈

Shōrenji — 勝蓮寺

Shōshitsu (see Shaoshi)

Shōten — 聖天

Shōtoku Taishi — 聖德太子

Shoulengyan jing — 首楞嚴經

Shōwa (era) — 正和

Shōzen (nun) — 性禪

Shugendō — 修驗道

shugyō(mon) — 修行門

shuilu — 水陸

shujō — 扛杖

Shūmon mujintōron — 宗門無盡燈論

Shungi — 舜義

Shunjō — 俊芿

Shuryōgon-kyō — 首楞嚴經

shushō ittō — 修證一等

shuso — 首座

Soan Shien — 松岸旨淵

sōhei — 僧兵

Sōjiji — 総持寺

Sōjiji chūkō engi — 総持寺中興緣起

Sokei — 祖溪

Song gaoseng zhuan — 宋高僧傳

Song shan — 嵩山

Sonin (see Mokufu Sonin)

Sōtō — 曹洞

sotoba — 卒塔婆

Sōtōshū komonjo — 曹洞宗古文書

Sōtōshū zensho — 曹洞宗全書

Ssanggye-sa — 雙溪寺

Sudō (Emperor) — 崇道天皇
Sugawara no Michizane — 菅原道眞
suijaku — 垂迹
Sujun (var. Sushun) (Emperor) — 崇峻天皇
Sumiyoshi Myōjin — 住吉明神
Susano-ō — 須佐之男
Suzuki Bokushi — 鈴木牧之

Tachikawa — 立川
Taichō — 泰澄
Taigen Sōshin — 太源宗眞
Taikyūji — 退休寺
tainai — 胎內 (體內)
Taira no Kiyomori — 平清盛
Taira no uji — 平氏
taizōkai mandara — 胎藏界曼荼羅
Taizu (Emperor) — 太祖
Takauji (see Ashikaga Takauji)
Tamamo no mae — 玉藻前
tanden — 丹田
tariki — 他力
Tateyama — 立山
Tendai — 天臺
tengu — 天狗
Tenkai Kūkō — 天海空廣
Tenkei Denson — 天桂傳尊
Tenman Daijizai Tenjin — 天滿大自在天神
Tenryūji — 天龍寺
Tettsū Gikai — 徹通義介
Tiantai shan — 天臺山
Tiantong Rujing — 天童如淨
Tiantong shan (J. Tendōzan) — 天童山
Tōdaiji — 東大寺
Tōfukuji — 東福寺
Togashi Iekata — 富樫家方
Tōjiin — 等持院
Tōjō shitsunai danshi kenpi shiki — 洞上室內斷紙揀非私記
Tōkeiji — 東慶寺
Tōkokki (Tōkoku ki) — 洞谷記
Tōkoku — 洞谷
Tōkoku goso gyōjitsu — 洞谷五祖行實
Tōkoku shingi — 洞谷清規

Tōkokuzan — 洞谷山
Tōrei Enji — 東嶺圓滋
Tōshōdaiji — 唐招提寺
Touzi — 投子
Toyokawa Inari — 豐川稻荷
Tōzan (see Dongshan)
Tōzan jinmiraisai okibumi — 當山盡未來際置文
Tōzan Ryōkai (see Dongshan Liangjie)
Tsūgen Jakurei — 通幻寂靈
Tsūhō Meidō — 通方明道
Tsuno Daishi — 角大師
tsusu — 都寺

Ŭisang — 義湘
uji — 氏
ujidera — 氏寺
ujigami — 氏神
ujiko — 氏子
Unjuji — 雲樹寺
Unno Saburō — 海野三郎
unsui — 雲水
Ususama (Myōō) — 烏蒭沙摩(明王)

Weituo — 韋馱
wenda (J. *mondō*) — 問答
Wu (Emperor, see Liang Wudi)
Wulou — 無漏
wunian — 無念
Wutai shan — 五臺山
wuwei — 五位
wuxiang — 無相
Wuxue Zuyuan — 無學祖元
Wuzhun Shifan — 無準師範
Wuzu Fayan — 五祖法演

Xiangguosi — 相國寺
xiang (J. *sō*) — 相
Xiangyan Zhixian — 香嚴智閑
xin (heart/mind) — 心
xin (pledge) — 信
Xinxinming — 信心銘
xinzong — 心宗
Xiuyao jing (J. *Shukuyō kyō*) — 宿曜經
Xuanzang — 玄奘
Xuanzong (Emperor) — 玄宗

Xuemo lun — 血脈論
Xu Yun — 虛雲

Yahata no kami — 八幡神
Yakushi (Nyorai) — 藥師(如來)
Yang Guifei — 楊貴妃
Yangshan Huiji — 仰山慧寂
Yao Chong — 姚崇
Yi jing — 易經
Yijing — 義淨
yixin chuanxin — 以心傳心
Yōkōji — 永光寺
Yōkōji kirigami — 永光寺切紙
Yongming Yanshou — 永明延壽
Yorichika — 賴親
Yōsai (var. Eisai) — 榮西
Yoshino — 吉野
Yoshitoshi — 芳年
Yōtakuji — 永澤寺
Yōtakuji Tsūgen zenji gyōgō — 永澤
寺通幻禪師行業

Yuangui — 元珪
yume-awase — 夢合わせ
Yumedono — 夢殿
Yuquan shan — 玉泉山

Zanning — 贊寧
Zaojun — 竈君
Zazen yōjinki — 座禪用心記
Zenkōji — 善光寺
Zenmyō — 善妙
Zenmyōji — 善妙寺
Zenran — 善鸞
Zenrinji — 禪林寺
Zenrin shōkisen — 禪林象器箋
Zhenxie — 眞歇
Zhenzong (Emperor) — 眞宗
Zhiyi — 智顗
Zhuangzi — 莊子
Zhuoan Deguang — 拙菴德光
Zōga — 增賀
Zonkaku — 存覺

BIBLIOGRAPHY

PRIMARY SOURCES

Collections

Dai Nihon bukkyō zensho (*DNBZ*). 151 vols. Tokyo: Bussho kankōkai, 1911–22.

Dai Nihon zokuzōkyō (*ZZ*). 150 vols. Nakano Tatsue, ed. Kyoto: Zōkyō Shoin. 1905–12. Reprint Taibei: Xinwenfeng, 1968–70.

Dōgen zenji zenshū (*DZZ*). Ōkubo Dōshū, ed. 2 vols. Tokyo: Chikuma shobō, 1969–70.

Gunsho ruijū. Comp. Hanawa Hokinoichi (1779–1819). Shinkō Gunsho Ruijū. 24 vols. Tokyo: Naigai Shoseki, 1937.

Jōsai daishi zenshū (*JDZ*). Kohō Chisan, ed. 1937. Rept. Yokohama: Daihonzan Sōjiji, 1976.

Sōtōshū komonjo. Ōkubo Dōshū, ed. 3 vols. Tokyo: Chikuma shobō, 1972.

Sōtōshū zensho (*SZ*). 1929–35. Sōtōshū zensho kankōkai, ed. Re-ed. 18 vols. Tokyo: Sōtōshū shūmuchō, 1970–73.

Taishō shinshū daizōkyō (*T*). Takakusu Junjirō, Watanabe Kaigyoku, et al., eds. 85 vols. Tokyo: Taishō issaikyō kankōkai, 1924–34.

Zenmon shōmono sōkan. Komazawa daigaku kokubungaku kenkyūshitsu, ed. 15 vols. Tokyo: Kyūko shoin, 1973–76.

Zoku gunsho ruijū. Hanawa Hokinoichi and Hanawa Tadatomi, eds. 1150 fasc., 1822. Rept. 19 vols. Tokyo: Keizai zasshisha, 1902.

Zoku Sōtōshū zensho. Zoku Sōtōshū zensho kankōkai, ed. 10 vols. Tokyo: Sōtōshū shūmuchō, 1974–77.

Primary Works

Biyan lu. By Xuetou Chongxian (980–1052). Commentary by Yuanwu Keqin (1063–1135). *T.* 48, 2003.

Chanlin sengbao zhuan. By Juefan Huihong (1071–1128). ZZ 1, 2B: 10, 3. (Taibei ed., vol. 137)

Chanmen shizi chengxi tu. By Guifeng Zongmi (780–841). ZZ 1, 2, 15. (Taibei ed., vol. 110)

Chanyuan qinggui, by Changlu Zongze. ZZ 1, 2, 16, 5. (Taibei ed., vol. 111). See also *Yakuchū Zen'en shingi.* Kagamishima Genryū, Satō Tatsugen, and Kosaka Kiyū, eds. Tokyo: Sōtōshū shūmuchō, 1972.

Chanyuan zhuquanji duxu. By Guifeng Zongmi. T. 48, 2015.

Chixiu Baizhang qinggui. By Dongyang Dehui. T. 48, 2025.

Chuan fabao ji. By Du Fei (n. d.). In *Shoki no zenshi 1.* Yanagida Seizan, ed. Tokyo: Chikuma shobō, 1971.

Chuanfa zhengzong ji. By Qi Song (1007–1072). T. 51, 2078.

Chuanxin fayao. By Pei Xiu (797–870). T. 47, 2012a. See also ed. Taibei: Fojiao chubanshe, 1976.

Da fangguang fo huayan jing (Avataṃsaka-sūtra). Trans. Buddhabhadra (359–429): *T.* 9, 278; trans. Śikṣānanda (652–710): *T.* 10, 279.

Dahui Pujue chanshi yulu. *T.* 47, 1998a.

Dahui shuwen. In *Daie sho.* Araki Kengo, ed. Tokyo: Chikuma shobō, 1969.

Dahui wuku. *T.* 47, 1998b.

Damo dashi xuemo lun. Attr. to Bodhidharma. ZZ 1, 2, 15, 5. (Taibei ed., vol. 110)

Dasheng qixin lun. Apocryphon. *T.* 32, 1666.

Dasheng wusheng fangbian men. *T.* 85, 2834.

Da zhidu lun. Attr. to Nāgārjuna. Trans. Kumārajīva. *T.* 25, 1509.

Denjutsu isshinkaimon. By Kōjō (779–858). *T.* 74, 2379.

Denkōroku. By Keizan Jōkin (1268–1325). *T.* 82, 2585. See also *Keizan.* Tajima Hakudō, ed. Tokyo: Kōdansha, 1978.

Dongshanlu (Dongshan Liangjie chanshi yulu). *T.* 47, 1986a.

Eiheiji sanko ryō zuiki. By Dōgen (1200–1253). *DZZ* 2: 398.

Eihei kōroku (Dōgen oshō kōroku). *DZZ* 2: 7–200.

Eihei shingi. By Dōgen. *T.* 82, 2584.

Eihei shitsuchū kikigaki. *DZZ* 2: 496–507.

Enpō dentōroku. By Mangen Shiban. *DNBZ* 69–70.

Erru sixing lun. Attr. to Bodhidharma. In *Daruma no goroku: Ninyū shigyō ron.* Yanagida Seizan, ed. Tokyo: Chikuma shobō, 1969.

Fanwang jing. Apocryphon. *T.* 24, 1484.

Fayuan zhulin [668]. By Daoshi. *T.* 53, 2122.

Fozu lidai tongzai [1344]. By Meiwu Nianchang (1282–?). *T.* 49, 2036.

Fozu tongji [ca. 1258–69]. By Zhipan. *T.* 49, 2035.

Fu fazang yinyuan zhuan. *T.* 50, 2058.

Fukan zazengi. By Dōgen. *T.* 82, 2580.

Gakudō yōjinshū. By Dōgen. *T.* 82, 2581.

Genkō shakusho [1322]. By Kokan Shiren (1278–1346). *DNBZ* 62, 470 (1931 ed., vol. 101).

Guang hongming ji. By Daoxuan (596–667). *T.* 52, 2103.

Guanxin lun [Poxiang lun]. Attr. to Shenxiu (606–706). *T.* 85, 2833.

Hanshan dashi mengyu quanji. ZZ 1, 2, 32. (Taibei ed., vol. 127)

Hōkyōki. By Dōgen. *DZZ* 2: 371–88.

Honchō kōsōden. By Shiban (1626–1710). *DNBZ* 63, 472 (1931 ed., vols. 102–103).

Hongzhi chanshi guanglu. *T.* 48, 2001.

Hōonhen. By Tenkei Denson (1648–1735). *T.* 82, 2600.

Ishiyamadera engi. *DNBZ* 117.

Jingang banruo bolomi jing (Vajracchedikā). Trans. Kumārajīva. *T.* 8, 235.

Jingang sanmei jing. Apocryphon. *T.* 9, 273.

Jingde chuandeng lu [1004]. By Daoyuan. *T.* 51, 2076.

Jōtō shōgakuron. Anon. In *Kanazawa bunko shiryō zensho: Butten I, Zensekihen.* Shinagawa Kenritsu Kanazawa Bunko, ed. Yokohama: Kanazawa Bunko, 1974.

Jūroku rakan genzuiki [1249]. By Dōgen. *DZZ* 2: 399.

Jusshu chokumon sōtaishū. By Keizan Jōkin. *T.* 82, 2588.

Kakuzen shō. By Kakuzen. *DNBZ* 45–51 (1931 ed., vol. 45–51). T. 89–90, 3022.

Kanmuki. By Enchi. *DNBZ* 113: 296.

Keiran shūyōshū. By Kōshū (1276–1350). *T.* 76, 2410.

Keizan shingi (*Tōkoku shingi*). By Keizan Jōkin. *T.* 82, 2589.

Kenzei ki. By Kenzei [ca. 1472] *DNBZ* 73, 587 (1931 ed., vol. 115). *Sōtōshū zensho*, 17, *Shiden*, 2, rev. ed., Tokyo: Sōtōshū Shūmuchō, 1970–73.

Kissa yōjōki. By Yōsai (1141–1215). *DNBZ* 115. See also *Nihon no Zen goroku: Yōsai*. Furuta Shōkin, ed. Tokyo: Kōdansha.

Kōzen gokoku ron. By Yōsai. *T.* 80, 2543.

Kyōjijō, by Annen (841–?). *T.* 75, 2395(a).

Kyōjijōron. By Annen. *T.* 75, 2395(b).

Kyōun shū. By Ikkyū Sōjun (1394–1481). In *Ikkyū. Ryōkan*. Yanagida Seizan, ed. Tokyo: Chūō kōron, 1987.

Laozi. Sibu congkan, ed. Shanghai: Shangwu yinshuguan, 1937–38.

Lengqie shizi ji. By Jingjue (683–ca. 750). *T.* 85, 2837.

Lidai fabao ji (ca. 774). *T.* 51, 2075.

Linjian lu. by Juefan Huihong (1071–1128). *ZZ* 1, 2B, 21, 4. (Taibei ed., vol. 148).

Linji lu (*Zhenzhou Linji Huizhao chanshi yulu*). *T.* 47, 1985.

Liuzu dashi fabao tanjing. Attr. to Huineng (638–713). *T.* 48, 2008.

Mengqi bitan. By Shen Gua (1031–1095). Umehara Kaoru, ed., *Mukei hitsudan*. 3 vols. Tokyo: Heibonsha, 1978–81.

Miaofa lianhua jing (*Saddharmapuṇḍarīka-sūtra*). Trans. Kumārajīva. *T.* 9, 262.

Muchū mondō. By Musō Soseki (1275–1351). Satō Taishun, ed. 1934. Tokyo: Iwanami shoten, 1974.

Nichiiki Tōjō Shosoden. By Tangen Jishō. *DNBZ* 110.

Nihon Tōjō rentoroku (1727), *DNBZ* 111.

Ojō yōshū. By Genshin (942–1017). *T.* 84, 2682.

Quan Tangwen 262. Dong Gao, ed. Taibei: Huawen shuju, 1965.

Rakan kuyō shikimon. By Dōgen. *DZZ* 2: 402–4.

Rakan ōkenden, by Menzan Zuihō. Ms., 3 fasc. Komazawa University Library.

Rujing heshang yulu. *T.* 48, 2002a.

Sanbōekotoba. By Minamoto Tamenori. *DNBZ* 111.

San Tendaisan Godaisanki. By Jōjin (1011–1081). *DNBZ* 114.

Sennyūji Fukaki hōshi den. By Shinzui (d. 1279). *DNBZ.* 115 (1931 ed., vol. 115).

Shari sōdenki (by Dōgen). *DZZ* 2: 395–96.

Shasekishū. By Mujū Ichien (1226–1312). Watanabe Tsunaya, ed. 1966. Tokyo: Iwanami shoten, 1975.

Shinjinmei nentei. By Keizan Jōkin. *T.* 82, 2587.

Shōbōgenzō. By Dōgen (1200–1253). *T.* 82, 2582.

Shōbōgenzō sanbyakusoku. *DZZ* 2: 201–52.

Shōbōgenzō zuimonki. By Ejō Koun (1198–1290). *DZZ* 2: 419–95. See *Shōbō-genzō zuimonki*. Watsuji Tetsurō, ed. Iwanami bunko 310. Tokyo: Iwanami shoten, 1990 [1929].

Shōbōzan shi. By Mujaku Dōchū. Tokyo: Shibunkaku, 1935.

Sho ekō shingishiki. By Tenrin Fūin (n.d.). *T.* 81, 2578.

Shōsōrin shingi. By Mujaku Dōchū. *T.* 82, 2579.

Shoulengyan jing (*Śūraṃgama-sūtra*). Apocryphon. *T.* 19, 945.

Shūmon mujintōron. By Tōrei Enji. T. 81, 2575.

Shutsujō kōgo. By Tominaga Nakamoto (1715–46). Kyōdo Jikō, ed. Tokyo: Ryōbunkan, 1982.

Song gaoseng zhuan. By Zanning (919–1001). T. 50, 2061.

Songyue Gui chanshi yingtang ji. By Xu Chou. *Quan Tang wen* 790, vol. 17: 10435–36.

Sōtōshū Komonjo. Ed. Ōkubo Dōshū. 3 vols. Tokyo: Chikuma Shobō, 1972.

Tōjō shitsunai danshi kenpi shiki [1749]. By Menzan Zuihō (1683–1769). In *SZ* 15, *Shitsuchū.*

Tōkoku ki. By Keizan Jōkin. In *Jōsai Daishi zenshū.* 1937. Rept. Yokohama: Daihonzan Sōjiji, 1976, 392–463. See also *Sōtōshū zensho,* Shūgen 2. Sōtōshū shūmuchō, ed. Tokyo: Sōtōshū shūmuchō, 1970–73; and "Daijōji hihon *Tō-kokki.*" Ōtani Teppu, ed. Rept. of 1432 Daijōji Ms. *Shūgaku kenkyū* 16 (1974): 231–48.

Weimojie jing (Vimalakīrti-nirdeśa). Trans. Zhi Qian (fl. 3rd. c.). T. 14, 474.

Xu gaoseng zhuan. By Daoxuan. T. 50, 2060.

Youyang zazu. By Duan Chengshi. Imamura Yoshio, ed., *Yuyō zasso.* 5 vols. Tokyo: Heibonsha, 1980–81.

Zazen yōjinki. By Keizan Jōkin. T. 82, 2586.

Zhengfa yanzang. By Dahui Zonggao (1089–1163). ZZ 1, 2, 23. (Taibei ed., vol. 118).

Zenkaiketsu. By Manzan Dōhaku (1636–1715). T. 82, 2599.

Zenrin shōkisen [1741]. By Mujaku Dōchū (1653–1744). Kyoto: Kaiyō Shoin, 1909. Rept. Tokyo: Seishin Shōbō, 1963; and *Zenrin shōkisen; Kattō gosen jikkan; Zenrin kushū benmyō.* Yanagida Seizan, ed. Vol. 1. Kyoto: Chūbun shuppansha, 1979.

Zoku honchō kōsōden. DNBZ 104.

Zuting shiyuan [1108]. By Muan Shanqing. ZZ 1, 2, 18, 1. (Taibei ed., vol. 113). See also *Chanxue dacheng.* Xieguan Shengti, ed. Vol. 3. Taibei: Zhonghua fo-jiao wenhua guan, 1969.

SECONDARY SOURCES

Akamatsu Toshihide, and Philip Yampolsky. 1977. "Muromachi Zen and the Gozan System." In *Japan in the Muromachi Age.* John Whitney Hall and Toyoda Takeshi, eds. Berkeley: University of California Press, 313–29.

Amino Yoshihiko. 1978. *Muen, kugai, raku: Nihon chūsei no jiyū to heiwa.* Heibonsha sensho 58. Tokyo: Heibonsha.

———. 1983. "Some Problems Concerning the History of Popular Life in Medieval Japan." *Acta Asiatica* 44: 77–97.

———. 1993. *Igyō no ōken.* Heibonsha raiburarī. Tokyo: Heibonsha.

Andō Kōsei. 1961. *Nihon no miira.* Tokyo: Mainichi shinbunsha.

Ariès, Philippe. 1974. *Western Attitudes toward Death: From the Middle Ages to the Present.* Trans. Patricia M. Ranum. Baltimore: Johns Hopkins University Press.

Arntzen, Sonja. *Ikkyū and the Crazy Cloud Anthology.* Tokyo: University of Tokyo Press, 1986.

Augé, Marc. 1982. *Génie du paganisme*. Bibliothèque des Sciences Humaines. Paris: Gallimard.

———. 1988. *Le Dieu objet*. Paris: Flammarion.

Azuma Ryūshin. 1974. *Keizan zenji no kenkyū*. Tokyo: Shunjūsha.

———. 1982. *Tōkokki ni manabu: Nihon shoki Sōtōshū sōdan no taidō*. Tokyo: Sōtōshū shūmuchō.

Bareau, André. 1975. "Les Récits canoniques des funérailles du Buddha et leurs anomalies: Nouvel essai d'interprétation." *BEFEO* 62: 151–90.

Barthes, Roland. 1975 *The Pleasure of the Text*. Trans. Richard Miller. New York: Hill and Wang.

———. 1982. *Empire of Signs*. Trans. Richard Howard. New York: Hill and Wang.

Bastide, Roger. 1972. *Le Rêve, la transe, la folie*. Paris: Flammarion.

Bataille, Georges. 1988. *The Accursed Share: An Essay on General Economy*. 3 vols. Trans. Robert Hurley. New York: Urzone.

Baudrillard, Jean. 1988. *Selected Writings*. Mark Poster, ed. Stanford: Stanford University Press.

Bazin, Jean. 1991. "Les Fantômes de Mme du Deffand (Exercices sur la croyance)." *Critique* 529–30: 492–511.

Benveniste, Emile. 1969. *Le Vocabulaire des institutions indo-européennes*. 2 vols. Paris: Minuit.

Beyer, Stephen. 1977. "Notes on the Vision Quest in Early Mahāyāna." In *Prajñāpāramitā and Related Systems: Studies in Honor of Edward Conze*. L. Lancaster, ed. Berkeley: Buddhist Studies Series, University of California, 329–40.

Bielefeldt, Carl. 1985. "Recarving the Dragon: History and Dogma in the Study of Dōgen." In *Dōgen Studies*. William R. LaFleur, ed. Honolulu: University of Hawaii Press, 21–53.

———. 1988. *Dōgen's Manuals of Zen Meditation*. Berkeley: University of California Press.

Birnbaum, Raoul. 1986. "The Manifestation of a Monastery: Shen-ying's Experiences of Mount Wu-t'ai in T'ang Context." *JAOS* 106: 119–37.

Bloch, Marc. 1983. *Les Rois thaumaturges*. Paris: Gallimard.

Bloch, Maurice. 1992. *Prey into Hunter: The Politics of Religious Experience*. Lewis Henry Morgan Lectures. Cambridge: Cambridge University Press.

Bloch, Maurice, and Jonathan Parry, eds. 1982. *Death and the Regeneration of Life*. Cambridge: Cambridge University Press.

Blonski, Marshall, ed. 1985. *On Signs*. Baltimore: Johns Hopkins University Press.

Bodiford, William M. 1991. "Dharma Transmission in Sōtō Zen: Manzan Dōhaku's Reform Movement." *Monumenta Nipponica* 46, 4: 423–51.

———. 1992. "Zen in the Art of Funerals: Ritual Salvation in Japanese Buddhism." *History of Religions* 32, 2: 146–64.

———. 1993. *Sōtō Zen in Medieval Japan*. Kuroda Institute, Studies in East Asian Buddhism 8. Honolulu: University of Hawaii Press.

———. 1993–94. "The Enlightenment of Kami and Ghosts: Spirit Ordinations in Japanese Sōtō Zen." *Cahiers d'Extrême-Asie* 7: 267–82.

Boon, James A. 1982. *Other Tribes, Other Scribes: Symbolic Anthropology in the Comparative Study of Cultures, Histories, Religions, and Texts*. Cambridge: Cambridge University Press.

Boucher, Daniel. 1990. "The *Pratītyasamutpādagāthā* and Its Role in the Medieval Cult of Relics." *JIABS* 14, 1: 28–72.

Bouchy, Anne-Marie. 1976. "Comment fut révélée la nature véritable de la divinité du Mont Atago." *Cahiers d'études et de documents sur les religions du Japan* 1: 9–48.

Bourdieu, Pierre. 1977. *Outline of a Theory of Practice*. Cambridge: Cambridge University Press.

———. 1990. *The Logic of Practice*. Trans. Richard Nice. Stanford: Stanford University Press.

Boureau, Alain. 1988. *Le simple corps du roi: L'Impossible sacralité des souverains français, XVe-XVIIIe siècle*. Paris: Editions de Paris.

———. 1991. "La Croyance comme compétence," *Critique* 529–30: 512–26.

Braverman, Arthur, trans. 1989. *Mud and Water: A Collection of Talks by the Zen Master Bassui*. San Francisco: North Point.

Brock, Karen. 1990. "Chinese Maiden, Silla Monk: Zenmyō and Her Thirteenth-Century Japanese Audience," in *Flowering in the Shadows: Women in the History of Chinese and Japanese Painting*. Marsha Weidner, ed. Honolulu: University of Hawaii Press, 205–11.

Brown, Carolyn T., ed. 1988. *Psycho-Sinology: The Universe of Dreams in Chinese Culture*. Lanham: University Press of America.

Brown, Delmer M., and Ichirō Ishida. 1979. *The Future and the Past: A Translation and Study of the Gukanshō, an Interpretative History of Japan Written in 1219*. Berkeley: University of California Press.

Brown, Peter. 1981. *The Cult of the Saints: Its Rise and Function in Latin Christianity*. Chicago: University of Chicago Press.

———. 1988. *The Body and Society: Men, Women, and Sexual Renunciation in Early Christianity*. New York: Columbia University Press.

Bynum, Caroline Walker. 1991. *Fragmentation and Redemption: Essays on Gender and the Human Body in Medieval Religion*. New York: Urzone.

Caillet, Laurence. 1991. "Espaces mythiques et territoire national." *L'Homme* 117: 10–33.

Caillois, Roger, and G. E. von Grunebaum, eds. 1967. *Le Rêve et les sociétés humaines*. Paris: Gallimard.

Campany, Robert F. 1990. "Notes on the Devotional Use and Symbolic Functions of *Sūtra* Texts as Depicted in Early Chinese Buddhist Miracle Tales and Hagiographies." *JIABS* 14, 1: 28–72.

———. 1993. "The Real Presence." *History of Religions* 32, 3: 232–72.

Camporesi, Piero. 1981. *Le Pain Sauvage: L'Imaginaire de la faim de la Renaissance au XVIIIe siècle*. Paris: Le Chemin vert.

Certeau, Michel de. 1982. *La Fable mystique: XVIe-XVIIe siècle*. Paris: Gallimard.

———. 1985. "What We Do When We Believe." In *On Signs*. Marshall Blonski, ed. Baltimore: Johns Hopkins University Press, 192–202.

———. 1986. *Heterologies: Discourse on the Other*. Trans. Brian Massumi. Theory and History of Literature, vol. 17. Minneapolis: University of Minnesota Press.

———. 1988. *The Practice of Everyday Life*. Trans. Steven Randall. Berkeley: University of California Press.

Chenet, François. 1990. "L'Hindouisme, mystique des images ou traversée de l'image?" In *L'Image divine*. André Padoux, ed. Paris: C.N.R.S., 151–68.

Christin, Olivier. 1991. *Une Révolution symbolique: L'Iconoclasme huguenot et la reconstruction catholique*. Paris: Minuit.

Chu Kun-liang. 1991. *Les Aspects rituels du théâtre chinois*. Institut des Hautes Etudes Chinoises. Paris: Collège de France.

Cleary, Thomas, and J. C. Cleary. 1977. *The Blue Cliff Record*. 3 vols. Boulder and London: Shambala.

Clifford, James, and George E. Marcus, eds. 1986. *Writing Culture: The Poetics and Politics of Ethnography*. Berkeley: University of California Press.

Colas, Gérard. 1989. "L'Instauration de la puissance divine dans l'image du temple en Inde du sud." *Revue de l'Histoire des Religions* 206, 2: 129–50.

———. 1990. "*Le Dévot, le prêtre et l'image Vishnouiste en Inde méridionale*" In *L'Image divine*. André Padoux, ed. Paris: C.N.R.S., 99–114.

Collcutt, Martin. 1981. *Five Mountains: The Rinzai Zen Monastic Institution in Medieval Japan*. Cambridge, Mass.: Harvard University Press.

———. 1982. "The Zen Monastery in Kamakura Society." In *Court and Bakufu in Japan: Essays in Kamakura History*. Jeffrey P. Mass., ed. New Haven: Yale University Press, 191–220.

———. 1983. "The Early Ch'an Monastic Rule: *Ch'ing kuei* and the Shaping of Ch'an Community Life." In *Early Ch'an in China and Tibet*. Whalen Lai and Lewis Lancaster, eds. Berkeley: Asian Humanities Press, 165–84.

———. 1990. "Zen and the Gozan." In *The Cambridge History of Japan*. Vol. 3: *Medieval Japan*. Yamamura Kozo, ed. Cambridge: Cambridge University Press, 583–652.

Conze, Edward. 1974. "The Intermediary World in Buddhism." *The Eastern Buddhist* (n.s.) 7, 2: 22–31.

Corbin, Henri. 1958. *L'Imagination créatrice dans le soufisme d'Ibn' Arabî*. Paris: Flammarion.

———. 1967. "Le Songe visionnaire en spiritualité islamique." In *Le Rêve et les sociétés humaines*. R. Caillois et G. E. von Grunebaum, eds. Paris: Gallimard 1967, 380–406.

Croissant, Doris. 1990. "Der Unsterbliche Leib: Ahneffigies und Reliquienporträt in der Porträtplastik Ostasiens." In *Das Bildnis in der Kunst der Orients*. Martin Kraatz, Jürg Meyer zur Capellen, and Dietrich Seckel, eds. Stuttgart: Franz Steiner, 235–68.

Delahaye, Hubert. 1981. *Les Premières Peintures de paysage en chine: Aspects religieux*. Paris: Ecole Française d'Extrême-Orient.

———. 1983. "Les Antécédents magiques des statues chinoises." *Revue d'esthétique* (n.s.) 5: 45–53.

Delehaye, Hippolyte. 1962 [1905]. *The Legends of the Saints*. Trans. Donald Attwater. New York: Fordham University Press.

Demiéville, Paul. 1927. "Sur la mémoire des existences antérieures." *BEFEO* 27: 283–98.

———. 1965. "Momies d'Extrême-Orient." *Journal des savants*, 144–70. Rept. in Demiéville 1973a (listed below), 407–32.

———. 1972. *Entretiens de Lin-tsi*. Paris: Fayard.

———. 1973a. *Choix d'études bouddhiques (1929–1970)*. Leiden: E. J. Brill.

———. 1973b. *Choix d'études sinologiques (1929–1970)*. Leiden: E. J. Brill.

———. 1973c. "Adieu maman." *Bulletin of the School of Oriental and African Studies* 36, 2: 271–86.

———. 1974. "L'Iconoclasme anti-bouddhique en Chine." In *Mélanges d'Histoire des Religions offerts à H. C. Puech*. Paris: Presses Universitaires de France, 17–25.

———. 1976. "Une descente aux enfers sous les T'ang: La Biographie de Houang Che-k'iang." In *Etudes d'histoire et de littérature chinoises offertes au professeur Jaroslav Prušek*. Paris: Presses Universitaires de France, 71–84.

Derrida, Jacques. 1970. "Structure, Sign, and Play in the Discourse of Human Sciences." In *The Structuralist Controversy: The Languages of Criticism and the Sciences of Man*. Richard Macksey and Eugenio Donato, eds. Baltimore: Johns Hopkins University Press, 247–72.

———. 1984. *Of Grammatology*. Trans. Gayatri Chakravorty Spivak. Baltimore: Johns Hopkins University Press.

———. 1992. *Given Time: 1. Counterfeit Money*. Trans. Peggy Kamuf. Chicago: University of Chicago Press.

Didi-Huberman, Georges. 1990. *Devant l'image: Question posée aux fins d'une histoire de l'art*. Paris: Minuit.

———. 1992. *Ce que nous voyons, ce qui nous regarde*. Paris: Minuit.

Dobbins, James C. 1986. "From Inspiration to Institution: The Rise of Sectarian Identity in Jōdo Shinshū." *Monumenta Nipponica* 41, 3: 331–43.

———. 1989. *Jōdo Shinshū: Shin Buddhism in Medieval Japan*. Bloomington and Indianapolis: Indiana University Press.

———. 1990. "The Biography of Shinran: Apotheosis of a Japanese Buddhist Visionary." *History of Religions* 30, 2: 179–96.

Drège, Jean-Pierre. 1981a. "Notes d'onirologie chinoise." *BEFEO* 70: 271–89.

———. 1981b. "Clefs des Songes de Touen-houang." In *Nouvelles contributions aux études de Touen-houang*. Michel Soymié, ed. Geneva: Droz, vol. 3, 205–49.

Dubs, Jomer. 1946. "Han Yü and the Buddha's Relic: An Episode in Medieval Chinese Religion." *The Review of Religion* 11: 5–17.

Duby, Georges. 1988. *Mâle Moyen Age*. Paris: Flammarion.

Dumoulin, Heinrich. 1990. *Zen Buddhism: A History*. Vol. 2: *Japan*. New York: Macmillan.

Dupont, Florence. 1989. "The Emperor-God's Other Body." In *Fragments for a History of the Human Body*. Michel Feher, ed. New York: Urzone, 3: 397–420.

Duquenne, Robert. Forthcoming. "Daishōkangiten." In *Hōbōgirin*, vol. 8. Paris: Adrien Maisonneuve.

Durt, Hubert. 1983. "Daigenshuri." In *Hōbōgirin*, vol. 6, 599–609. Paris: Adrien Maisonneuve.

Dykstra, Yoshiko K., trans. 1976. "Tales of the Compassionate Kannon: The *Hasedera Kannon Genki.*" *Monumenta Nipponica* 31, 2: 113–43.

———, trans. 1983. *Miraculous Tales of the Lotus Sutra from Ancient Japan: The Dainihon Hokekyōkenki of Priest Chingen.* Honolulu: University of Hawaii Press.

Ebrey, Patricia. 1990. "Cremation in Sung China." *American Historical Review* 95, 2: 406–28.

Eck, Diana. 1985. *Darśan: Seeing the Divine Image in India.* Chambersburg, Pa.: Anima Books.

Eckel, Malcolm David. 1990. "The Power of the Buddha's Absence: On the Foundations of Mahāyāna Buddhist Ritual." *Journal of Ritual Studies* 4, 2: 61–95.

———. 1992. *To See the Buddha: A Philosopher's Quest for the Meaning of Emptiness.* San Francisco: Harper.

Eco, Umberto. 1989. *Foucault's Pendulum.* Trans. William Weaver. San Diego, New York, London: Harcourt, Brace, Jovanovich.

Elias, Norbert. 1982 [1939]. *Power and Civility.* Trans. Edmund Jephcott. The Civilizing Process, vol. 2. New York: Pantheon Books.

Elster, Jon. 1983. *Sour Grapes: Studies in the Subversion of Rationality.* Cambridge: Cambridge University Press.

Falk, Nancy. 1977. "To Gaze on the Sacred Traces." *History of Religions* 16, 4: 281–93.

Faure, Bernard. 1986. *Le Traité de Bodhidharma: Première anthologie du bouddhisme Chan.* Aix-en-Provence: Le Mail.

———. 1987a. *La Vision immédiate: Nature, éveil et tradition selon le Shōbōgenzō.* Aix-en-Provence: Le Mail.

———. 1987b. "The Daruma-shū, Dōgen and Sōtō Zen." *Monumenta Nipponica* 42, 1: 25–55.

———. 1987c. "Space and Place in Chinese Religious Traditions." *History of Religions* 26, 4: 337–56.

———. 1988. *La Volonté d'orthodoxie dans le bouddhisme chinois.* Paris: C.N.R.S.

———. 1989. *Le Bouddhisme Ch'an en mal d'histoire: Genèse d'une tradition religieuse dans la Chine des T'ang.* Paris: Ecole Française d'Extrême-Orient.

———. 1991 *The Rhetoric of Immediacy: A Cultural Critique of the Chan/Zen Tradition.* Princeton: Princeton University Press.

———. 1993. *Chan Insights and Oversights: An Epistemological Critique of the Chan Tradition.* Princeton: Princeton University Press

———. 1994. *Sexualités bouddhiques: Entre désirs et réalités.* Paris: Le Mail.

———. 1995. "Quand l'habit fait le moine: The Symbolism of the *kāṣāya* in Sōtō Zen." *Cahiers d'Extrême Asie* 8: 335–69.

———. Forthcoming. "*Dato*: Le Culte des reliques dans le bouddhisme." In *Hōbōgirin*, vol. 8. Paris: Adrian Maisonneuve.

Favret-Saada, Jeanne. 1980. *Deadly Words: Witchcraft in the Bocage.* Cambridge: Cambridge University Press.

Feher, Michel, ed. 1989. *Fragments for a History of the Human Body.* 3 vols. New York: Urzone.

Foard, James H. 1977. "Ippen Shōnin and Popular Buddhism in Kamakura Japan." Ph.D. Dissertation, Stanford University.

Fontein, Jan. 1993. "The Epitaphs of Two Chan Patriarchs." *Artibus Asiae* 53, 1–2: 98–106.

Foucault, Michel. 1974. *The Order of Things: An Archeology of the Human Sciences*. London: Routledge.

Foulk, T. Griffith. 1987. "The 'Ch'an School' and Its Place in the Buddhist Monastic Tradition." Ph.D. dissertation, University of Michigan.

Foulk, T. Griffith, and Robert H. Sharf. 1993–94. "On the Ritual Use of Ch'an Portraiture in Medieval China." *Cahiers d'Extrême-Asie* 7: 149–219.

Frank, Bernard. 1958. "Kata-imi et kata-tagae: Etude sur les interdits de direction à l'époque Heian." *Bulletin de la Maison Franco-Japonaise 5*, 24. Paris: Presses Universitaires de France.

———. 1968. *Histoires qui sont maintenant du passé*. Connaissance de l'Orient 26. Paris: Gallimard.

———. 1988. "Vacuité et corps actualisé: Le Problème de la présence des 'Personnages Vénérés' dans leurs images selon la tradition du bouddhisme japonais." *JIABS* 11, 2: 53–86.

———. 1989. "L'Expérience d'un malheur absolu: Son refus et son dépassement. L'Histoire de la mère de Jōjin." *Académie des Inscriptions et Belles-Lettres*. Paris: Diffusion de Boccard, 472–88.

———. 1991. *Le Panthéon bouddhique au Japon: Collections d'Emile Guimet*. Paris: Réunion des musées nationaux.

Freedberg, David. 1989. *The Power of Images: Studies in the History and Theory of Response*. Chicago: University of Chicago Press.

Fujii Masao, ed. 1977. *Bukkyō girei jiten*. Tokyo: Tōkyōdō.

Funaoka Makoto. 1987. *Nihon zenshū no seiritsu*. Chūsei kenkyū sensho. Tokyo: Yoshikawa kōbunkan.

Furuta Shōkin. "'Keizan oshō shitsuchū okibumi' ni tsuite." In *Keizan zenji kenkyū*. Tokyo: Keizan zenji hōsan kankōkai, 781–99.

Geary, Patrick. 1978. *Furta Sacra: Thefts of Relics in the Central Middle Ages*. Princeton: Princeton University Press.

Geertz, Clifford. 1973. *The Interpretation of Cultures*. New York: Basic Books.

Gennep, Arnold van. 1960. *Rites of Passage*. Chicago: University of Chicago Press.

Gernet, Jacques. 1959. "Les Suicides par le feu chez les bouddhistes chinois du Ve au Xe siècle." In *Mélanges publiés par l'Institut des Hautes Etudes Chinoises*. Paris: Presses Universitaires de France, vol. 2, 528–58.

Giesey, Ralph E. 1960. *The Royal Funeral Ceremony in Renaissance France*. Geneva: Librairie E. Droz.

———. 1987. *Cérémonial et puissance souveraine: France, XVe–XVIIe siècles*. Paris: Armand Colin.

Girard, Frédéric. 1990a. *Un Moine de la secte Kegon à l'époque de Kamakura, Myōe (1173–1232) et le "Journal de ses rêves."* Paris: Ecole Française d'Extrême-Orient.

———. 1990b. "Le Journal des rêves de Myōe, moine japonais de l'école Kegon." *Journal Asiatique*, 278: 167–93.

Girardot, Norman J. 1983. *Myth and Meaning in Early Taoism: The Theme of Chaos (Hun-tun)*. Berkeley: University of California Press.

Goble, Andrew. 1989. "Truth, Contradiction and Harmony in Medieval Japan: Emperor Hanazono (1297–1348) and Buddhism." *JIABS* 12, 1: 21–64.

Godelier, Maurice. 1986. *The Mental and the Material*. London and New York: Verso.

Gombrich, Richard. 1966. "The Consecration of a Buddhist Image." *Journal of Asian Studies* 26, 1: 23–36.

Gonda, J. 1970. *Eye and Gaze in the Veda*. Amsterdam: Verhandelingen der Koninklijke Nederlandse Akademie van Wetenschappen.

Goodwin, Janet R. 1994. *Alms and Vagabonds: Buddhist Temples and Popular Patronage in Medieval Japan*. Honolulu: University of Hawaii Press.

Gorai, Shigeru. 1983. "Sō to kuyō." *Tōhōkai* 112: 34–42.

Goux, Jean-Joseph. 1990. *Symbolic Economies: After Marx and Freud*. Trans. Jennifer Curtis Gage. Ithaca: Cornell University Press.

Granet, Marcel. 1968. *La Pensée chinoise*. Paris: Albin Michel.

Grapard, Allan G. 1982. "Flying Mountains and Walkers of Emptiness: Toward a Definition of Sacred Space in Japanese Religion." *History of Religions* 21, 3: 195–221.

———. 1987. "Linguistic Cubism: A Singularity of Pluralism in the Sannō Cult." *Japanese Journal of Religious Studies* 14, 2–3: 211–34.

———. 1991. "Visions of Excess and Excesses of Vision: Women and Transgression in Japanese Myth." *Japanese Journal of Religious Studies* 18, 1: 3–22.

———. 1992. *The Protocol of the Gods: A Study of the Kasuga Cult in Japanese History*. Berkeley: University of California Press.

———. 1994. "Rite de voyage: Redressing Hachiman's appearance." In *Mélanges offerts à René Sieffert à l'occasion de son soixante-dixième anniversaire*. François Macé, ed. Paris: Institut National des Langues et Civilisations Orientales, Centre d'études japonaises, 335–52.

Groner, Paul. 1984. *Saichō: The Establishment of the Japanese Tendai School*. Berkeley: Asian Humanities Press.

Gyatso, Janet. 1992. *In the Mirror of Memory: Reflections on Mindfulness and Remembrance in Indian and Tibetan Buddhism*. Albany: SUNY Press.

Hakeda, Yoshito S. 1972. *Kūkai: Major Works*. New York: Columbia University Press.

Hall, John W., and Jeffrey P. Mass, eds. 1974. *Medieval Japan: Essays in Institutional History*. Stanford: Stanford University Press.

Hansen, Valerie. 1990. *Changing Gods in Medieval China*. Princeton: Princeton University Press.

Hanuki Masai. 1962. "Tōmon zensō to shinjin kedo no setsuwa." *Komazawa shigaku* 10: 44–51

Harada Kōdō. 1988. "Chūsei Sōtōshū to rakan shinkō." *IBK* 37, 1: 232–38.

Harrison, Paul. 1992. "Is the *Dharma-kāya* the Real 'Phantom Body' of the Buddha?" *JIABS* 15, 1: 44–94.

Hartog, François. 1980. *Le Miroir d'Hérodote: Essai sur la représentation de l'autre*. Bibliothèque des Histoires. Paris: Gallimard.

310 BIBLIOGRAPHY

Heine, Steven. 1994. *Dōgen and the Kōan Tradition: A Tale of Two Shōbōgenzō Texts*. Albany: SUNY Press.

Herrenschmidt, Olivier. 1982. "Sacrifice: Symbolique or Effective?" In *Between Belief and Transgression: Structuralist Essays in Religion, History, and Myth*. Michel Izard and Pierre Smith, eds. Trans. John Leavitt. Chicago: University of Chicago Press, 24–42.

Hertz, Robert. 1960. *Death and the Right Hand*. Trans. Rodney and Claudia Needham. Glencoe, Ill.: Free Press.

————. 1970. *Sociologie religieuse et folklore*. Paris: Presses Universitaires de France.

Hibe Noboru. 1984. "Aru shū no Tōmon shōmono: Noto Yōkōjizō kirigamirui kara." *Tsuru bunka daigaku bungaku ronkō* 20: 89–95.

Hirose Ryōkō. 1983. "Sōtō ni okeru shinjin kedo akuryō. chin'atsu." *IBK* 31, 2: 233–36.

————. 1988. *Zenshū chihō tenkaishi no kenkyū*. Tokyo: Yoshikawa kōbunkan.

Hōbōgirin: Dictionnaire encyclopédique du bouddhisme d'après les sources chinoises et japonaises. Paul Demiéville et al., eds. Vols. 1–6. Paris: Adrien Maisonneuve, 1927–83.

Hoopes, James, ed. 1991. *Peirce on Signs: Writings on Semiotics by Charles Sanders Peirce*. Chapel Hill and London: University of North Carolina Press.

Hori Ichiro. 1962. "Self-Mummified Buddhas in Japan: An Aspect of the Shugendō ('Mountain Asceticism') Sect." *History of Religions* 1, 2: 222–42.

————. 1974 [1968]. *Folk Religion in Japan: Continuity and Change*. Joseph Kitagawa and Alan L. Miller, eds. Midway Reprint. Chicago: University of Chicago Press.

————. 1975. "Shamanism in Japan." *Japanese Journal of Religious Studies* 2, 4: 231–87.

Hou Chin-lang. 1975. *Monnaies d'offrande et la notion de trésorerie dans la religion chinoise*. Paris: Institut des Hautes Etudes Chinoises.

Hsü Sung-peng. 1979. *A Buddhist Leader in Ming China: The Life and Thought of Han-shan Te-ch'ing, 1546–1623*. University Park: Pennsylvania State University Press.

Hubert, Henri, and Marcel Mauss. 1981 [1964]. *Sacrifice: Its Nature and Functions*. Trans. W. D. Halls. Midway Reprint. Chicago: University of Chicago Press.

Huntington, Richard, and Peter Metcalf. 1979. *Celebrations of Death: The Anthropology of Mortuary Ritual*. New York: Cambridge University Press.

Ichikawa Hakugen, Iriya Yoshitaka, and Yanagida Seizan, eds. 1972. *Chūsei zenke no shisō*. Tokyo: Iwanami shoten.

Imaeda, Aishin. 1962. *Zenshū no rekishi*. Nihon rekishi shinsho. Tokyo: Shibundō.

————. 1974. "Keizan zenji no rekishiteki chii: Hakusan Tendai to no kanren to shite." In *Keizan zenji kenkyū*. Tokyo: Keizan zenji hōsan kankōkai, 82–99.

Imamura Yoshio, ed. 1980–81. *Yuyō zasso*. 5 vols. Tokyo: Heibonsha.

Ishida Jūshi, ed. 1972. *Kamakura bukkyō seiritsu no kenkyū: Shunjō Risshi*. Kyoto: Hōzōkan.

Ishii Shūdō. 1974. "Busshō Tokkō to Nihon Darumashū." *Kanazawa bunko kenkyū* 20, 11: 1–16; 20, 12: 1–20.

———. 1987. *Sōdai zenshūshi no kenkyū: Chūgoku Sōtōshū to Dōgen zen.* To-kyo: Daitō shuppan.

Ishikawa Rikizan. 1982. "Chūsei Sōtōshū no chihō tenkai to Gennō Shinshō." *IBK* 31, 1: 227–31.

———. 1983–94. "Chūsei Sōtōshū kirigami no bunrui shiron." (1) *KDBK* 41 (1983): 338–50; (2) *KDBR* 14 (1983): 123–55; (3) *KDBK* 42 (1984): 82–96; (4) *KDBR* 15 (1984): 152–69; (5) *KDBK* 43 (1985): 94–116; (6) *KDBK* 16 (1985): 102–52; (7) *KDBK* 44 (1986): 250–67; (8) *KDBR* 17 (1986): : 179–213; (9) *KDBK* 45 (1987): 167–98; (10) *KDBR* 18: (1987): 163–92; (11) *KDBK* 46 (1988): 128–55; (12) *KDBR* 19 (1988): 159–97; (13) *KDBK* 47 (1989): 157–89; (14) *KDBR* 20 (1989): 108–34; (15) *KDBK* 48 (1990): 22–41; (16) *KDBR* 21 (1990): 142–68; (17) *KDBK* 49 (1991): 1–19; (18) *KDBR* (1991): 24–34; (19) *KDBK* 50 (1992): 29–50; (20) *KDBR* 23 (1992): 95–126.

———. 1984. "Chūsei Zenshū to shinbutsu shūgō: Toku ni Sōtōshū no chihōteki tenkai to kirigami shiryō o chūshin ni shite." *Nihon bukkyō* 60–61: 41–56.

———. 1985. "Chūsei Sōtōshū to reizan shinkō." *IBK* 33, 2: 26–31.

———. 1987. "Chūsei Zenshū to sōsō girei." *IBK* 35, 2: 299–304.

———. 1989. "Chūsei Sōtōshū ni okeru jukai girei ni tsuite: Iroiro no jukai girei shinansho no hassei to sono shakaiteki kinō." *Bukkyō shigaku kenkyū* 32, 1: 60–80.

———. 1992–93. "Chūsei bukkyō ni okeru ama no isō ni tsuite: Toku ni sho Sōtō shūkyōdan no jirei o chūshin to shite." Pt 1: *Komazawa daigaku zen kenkyūjo nenpō* 3 (1992): 141–53; Pt. 2: ibid., 4 (1993): 63–80.

Iyanaga Nobumi. 1983. "Daijizaiten." In *Hōbōgirin*, vol. 6, 713–65. Paris: Adrien Maisonneuve.

Izard, Michel, and Pierre Smith, eds. 1982. *Between Belief and Transgression: Structuralist Essays in Religion, History, and Myth.* Chicago: University of Chicago Press.

Jameson, Fredric. 1985. "The Realist Floor-Plan." In *On Signs.* Marshall Blonski, ed. Baltimore: Johns Hopkins University Press, 373–83.

Jan Yün-hua. 1965. "Buddhist Self-Immolation in Medieval China." *History of Religions* 4, 2: 243–68.

———. 1966. *A Chronicle of Buddhism in China (580–960 A.D.): Translations of the Monk Chih-p'an's Fo-tsu t'ung-chi.* Santiniketan: Visva Bharati.

Jorgensen, John. 1987. "The 'Imperial' Lineage of Ch'an Buddhism: The Role of Confucian Ritual and Ancestor Worship in Ch'an's Search for Legitimation in the Mid-T'ang Dynasty." *Papers on Far Eastern History* 35: 89–133.

Jullien, François. 1984. "L'Oeuvre et l'univers: Imitation ou déploiement (Limites à une conception mimétique de la création littéraire dans la tradition chinoise)." *Extrême-Orient, Extrême-Occident* 3: 37–88.

———. 1986. "Naissance de l'"imagination': Essai de problématique au travers de la réflexion littéraire de la Chine et de l'Occident." *Extrême-Orient, Extrême-Occident* 7: 23–81.

———. 1992. *La Propension des choses: Pour une histoire de l'efficacité en Chine.* Paris: Seuil.

Kabanoff, Alexander M. 1993. "Zen and Chinese Culture in Japan: Discrimination or Selection." In *Modulations in Tradition: Japan and Korea in a Chang-*

ing World. Jorma Kivistö, Mika Merviö, Takahashi Mutsuko and Mark Waller, eds. Tampere: University of Tampere, 49–64.

Kagamishima Genryū, ed. 1961. *Dōgen zenji to sono monryū*. Tokyo: Seishin shobō.

———. 1978. *Manzan. Menzan*. Nihon no Zen goroku 18. Tokyo: Kōdansha.

Kagamishima Genryū, Satō Tatsugen, and Kosaka Kiyū, eds. 1972. *Yakuchū Zen'en shingi*. Tokyo: Sōtōshū shūmuchō.

Kageyama Haruki. 1977. "Shari shinkō no hensen." *Kokugakuin zasshi*, 78, 9: 85–105.

———. 1986. *Shari shinkō: Sono kenkyū to shiryō*. Tokyo: Tōkyō bijutsu.

Kaltenmark, Max. 1960. "*Ling-pao*: Note sur un terme du taoïsme religieux." In *Mélanges publiés par l'Institut des Hautes Etudes Chinoises*. Paris: Presses Universitaires de France, 1: 559–88.

Kamata Shigeo, and Tanaka Hisao, eds. 1971. *Kamakura kyū bukkyō*. Tokyo: Iwanami shoten.

Kamens, Edward, trans. 1988. *The Three Jewels: A Study and Translation of Minamoto Tamenori's Sanbōe*. Ann Arbor: Center for Japanese Studies, The University of Michigan.

Kanda, Christine Guth. 1985. *Shinzō: Hachiman Imagery and its Development*. Harvard East Asian Monographs 119. Cambridge, Mass.: Council on East Asian Studies, Harvard University.

Kaneda Hiroshi. 1976. *Tōmon shōmono to kokugo kenkyū: Shiryō*. 6 vols. Tokyo: Ōfūsha.

Kaneko, Sachiko, and Robert E. Morrell. 1983. "Sanctuary: Kamakura's Tōkeiji Convent." *Japanese Journal of Religious Studies* 10, 2–3: 195–228.

Kantorowicz, Ernst H. 1957. *The King's Two Bodies: A Study in Medieval Political Theology*. Princeton: Princeton University Press.

Kawai Hayao. 1992. *The Buddhist Priest Myōe: A Life of Dreams*. Trans. Mark Unno. Venice, Ca.: Lapis.

Kawamura Kōdō, and Ishikawa Rikizan, eds. 1985. *Dōgen zenji to Sōtōshū*. Tokyo: Yoshikawa kōbunkan.

Keirstead, Thomas. 1992. *The Geography of Power in Medieval Japan*. Princeton: Princeton University Press.

Keizan zenji hōsan kankōkai, ed. 1974. *Keizan zenji kenkyū*. Tokyo: Keizan zenji hōsan kankōkai.

Kelsey, W. Michael. 1981. "Salvation of the Snake, the Snake of Salvation: Buddhist-Shinto Conflict Resolution." *Japanese Journal of Religious Studies* 8, 1–2: 83–113.

Kidder, J. Edward. 1992. "Busshari and Fukuzō: Buddhist Relics and Hidden Repositories of Hōryū-ji." *Japanese Journal of Religious Studies* 19: 217–44.

Kieschnick, John. 1995. "The Idea of the Monk in Medieval China: Asceticism, Thaumaturgy, and Scholarship in the *Biographies of Eminent Monks*." Ph.D. dissertation, Stanford University.

Kōhō Chisan, ed. 1976 [1937]. *Jōsai daishi zenshū*. Yokohama: Daihonzan Sōjiji.

Kosugi Kazuo. 1937. "Nikushinzō oyobi yuikaizō no kenkyū." *Tōyō gakuhō* 24, 3: 93–124.

Kuo Li-ying. 1994. *Confession et contrition dans le bouddhisme chinois du V*^{e}* au*

Xe siècle. Publications de l'Ecole Française d'Extrême-Orient. Paris: Ecole Française d'Extrême-Orient.

Kuroda Toshio. 1980. *Jisha seiryoku*. Iwanami shinsho 117. Tokyo: Iwanami shoten.

———. 1981. "Shintō in the History of Japanese Religion." Trans. James C. Dobbins and Suzanne Gay. *Journal of Japanese Studies* 7, 1: 1–21.

———. 1989. "Historical Consciousness and *Hon-jaku* Philosophy in the Medieval Period on Mount Hiei." Trans. Allan G. Grapard. In *The Lotus Sūtra in Japanese Culture*. George J. Tanabe, Jr., and Willa Jane Tanabe, eds., Honolulu: University of Hawaii Press, 143–58.

Kuriyama Taion. 1980 [1938]. *Sōjijishi*. Yokohama: Daihonzan Sōjiji.

LaFleur, William R. 1983. *The Karma of Words: Buddhism and the Literary Arts in Medieval Japan*. Berkeley: University of California Press.

———, ed. 1985. *Dōgen Studies*. Honolulu: University of Hawaii Press.

Lamotte, Etienne, trans. 1944–1980. *Traité de la Grande vertu de Sagesse*. 5 vols. Louvain: Institut Orientaliste. (1: 1944; 2: 1949; 3. 1970; 4: 1976; 5: 1980).

———, trans. 1966. *L'Enseignement de Vimalakīrti*. Louvain: Institut Orientaliste.

Lefebvre, Henri. 1984 [1974]. *The Production of Space*. Trans. Donald Nicholson-Smith. Cambridge, Mass.: Basil Blackwell.

Le Goff, Jacques. 1980. *Time, Work, and Culture in the Middle Ages*. Trans. Arthur Goldhammer. Chicago: University of Chicago Press.

———. 1982. "Saint Louis et les corps royaux." In *Le Temps de la réflexion* 3: 255–84.

———. 1984. *The Birth of Purgatory*. Trans. Arthur Goldhammer. Chicago: University of Chicago Press.

———. 1985. "Mentalities: A History of Ambiguities." In Jacques Le Goff and Pierre Nora, eds., *Constructing the Past*. Cambridge: Cambridge University Press, 166–80.

———. 1986. "Qu'est-ce que l'histoire de l'imaginaire? Exemple: l'imaginaire de la société féodale médiévale." In *Sens et place des connaissances dans la société*. Paris: Centre National de la Recherche Scientifique, 217–50.

———. 1988. *The Medieval Imagination*. Trans. Arthur Goldhammer. Chicago: University of Chicago Press.

Levering, Miriam. 1982. "The Dragon Girl and the Abbess of Mo-shan: Gender and Status in the Ch'an Buddhist Tradition." *JIABS* 5, 1: 19–35.

———. 1987. "Ta-hui and Lay Buddhists: Ch'an Sermons on Death." In *Buddhist and Taoist Practice in Medieval Chinese Society*. David W. Chappell, ed. *Buddhist and Taoist Studies* 2. Honolulu: University of Hawaii Press, 181–206.

Lévi, Sylvain. 1966. *La Doctrine du sacrifice dans les Brāhmanas*. Paris: Presses Universitaires de France.

Lévi, Sylvain, and Edouard Chavannes. 1916. "Les Seize Arhat protecteurs de la Loi." *Journal Asiatique* 8: 5–48, 189–304.

Lévi-Strauss, Claude. 1963 [1958]. *Structural Anthropology*. Trans. Claire Jacobson and Brooke Grundfest Schoepf. New York: Doubleday.

————. 1981 [1971]. *The Naked Man: Introduction to a Science of Mythology: 4.* Trans. John and Doreen Weightman. New York: Harper and Row.

————. 1987 [1950]. *Introduction to the Work of Marcel Mauss.* London: Routledge and Kegan Paul.

Liebenthal, Walter. "Shi Hui-yüan's Buddhism as Set Forth in His Writings." *JAOS* 70 (1950): 258.

Lopez, Donald S., Jr. 1990. "Inscribing the Bodhisattva's Speech: On the *Heart Sūtra*'s Mantra." *History of Religions* 29, 4: 351–72.

Macé, François. 1986. *La Mort et les funérailles dans le Japon ancien.* Paris: Presses Orientalistes de France.

MacWilliams, Mark W. 1990. "*Kannon-engi*: The *Reijō* and the Concept of *Kechien* as Strategies of Indigenization in Buddhist Sacred Narratives." *Transactions of the Asiatic Society of Japan*, 4th ser., 5: 53–70.

Malamoud, Charles. 1980. "La Théologie de la dette dans le brāhmanisme." *Puruṣārtha* 4:39–62. Reprinted in Malamoud, 1989 (listed below): 115–66. English translation in *Debt and Debtors.* Charles Malamoud, ed. Delhi: Vikas, 1983.

————. 1989. *Cuire le monde: Rite et pensée dans l'Inde ancienne.* Paris: La Découverte.

Mannoni, Octave. 1969. *Clefs pour l'imaginaire ou L'Autre Scène.* Paris: Seuil.

Marin, Louis. 1981. *Le Portrait du roi.* Paris: Minuit.

Marra, Michele. 1993. *Representations of Power: The Literary Politics of Medieval Japan.* Honolulu: University of Hawaii Press.

Maspero, Henri. 1955. *La Chine antique.* New ed. Paris: Presses Universitaires de France.

Mass, Jeffrey P. 1989. *Lordship and Inheritance in Early Medieval Japan: A Study of the Kamakura Sōryō System.* Stanford: Stanford University Press.

Mather, Richard. 1986. "Hymns on the Devotee's Entrance into the Pure Life." *JAOS* 106, 1: 79–98.

Matsuda Fumio. 1970. "Keizan zenji no jinmiraisai okibumi ni tsuite: Yōkōji kaibyaku no haikei." *Shūgaku kenkyū* 12: 130–42.

————. 1974. "*Tōkokki* no kenkyū." In *Keizan zenji kenkyū.* Tokyo: Keizan zenji hōsan kankōkai, 824–73.

Matsumoto Akira. 1985. *Nihon no miirabutsu.* Tokyo: Rokkō shuppan.

Matsunaga, Alicia. 1969. *The Buddhist Philosophy of Assimilation: The Historical Development of the Honji-Suijaku Theory.* Rutland: Charles E. Tuttle.

Matsuura Shūkō. 1976. *Zenshū kojitsu sonzō no kenkyū.* Tokyo: Sankibō busshorin.

————. 1985. *Sonshuku sōhō no kenkyū.* Tokyo: Sankibō busshorin.

Mauclaire, Simone. 1991. "Serpent et féminité, métaphores du corps réel des dieux." *L'Homme* 117: 66–95.

Mauss, Marcel. 1950. *Sociologie et anthropologie.* Paris: Presses Universitaires de France.

————. 1967. *The Gift: Forms and Functions of Exchange in Archaic Societies.* Trans. Ian Cunnison. New York and London: W. W. Norton.

————. 1968–69. *Oeuvres.* 3 vols. Paris: Minuit.

————. 1972 [1950]. *A General Theory of Magic.* Trans. Robert Brain. New York: W. W. Norton.

———. 1979. *Sociology and Psychology.* Trans. B. Brewster. London: Routledge and Kegan Paul.

McCallum, David. 1994. *The Zenkōji Icon.* Princeton: Princeton University Press.

McFarland, H. Neil. 1987. *Daruma: The Founder of Zen in Japanese Art and Popular Culture.* Tokyo and New York: Kōdansha International.

McMullin, Neil. 1987. "The Enryaku-ji and the Gion Shrine-Temple Complex in the Mid-Heian Period." *Japanese Journal of Religious Studies* 14, 2–3: 161–84.

———. 1988. "On Placating the Gods and Pacifying the Populace: The Case of the Gion Goryō Cult." *History of Religions* 27, 3: 270–93.

Merleau-Ponty, Maurice. 1968. *The Visible and the Invisible: Followed by Working Notes.* Trans. Alphonso Lingis. Northwestern Studies in Phenomenological and Existential Philosophy. Evanston: Northwestern University Press.

Michihata Ryōshū. 1983. *Rakan shinkōshi.* Tokyo: Daitō shuppansha.

Mills, D. E., trans. 1970. *A Collection of Tales from Uji: A Study and Translation of Uji Shūi Monogatari.* Cambridge: Cambridge University Press.

Miyata Noboru. 1972. *Kami no minzokushi.* Tokyo: Iwanami shoten.

———. 1994. *Shiro no fōkuroa: Genshoteki shikō.* Heibonsha raiburarī. Tokyo: Heibonsha.

Mōri Hisashi. 1977. *Japanese Portrait Sculpture.* Tokyo and New York: Kōdansha International.

Morrell, Robert E. 1982. "Passage to India Denied: Zeami's *Kasuga Ryūjin.*" *Monumenta Nipponica* 37, 2: 179–200.

———, trans. 1985. *Sand and Pebbles (Shasekishū): The Tales of Mujū Ichien, A Voice for Pluralism in Kamakura Buddhism.* Albany: SUNY Press.

———. 1987. *Early Kamakura Buddhism: A Minority Report.* Berkeley: Asian Humanities Press.

Morris, Ivan., ed. 1970. *Madly Singing in the Mountains: An Appreciation and Anthology of Arthur Waley.* New York: Walker.

———, trans. 1975. *As I Crossed a Bridge of Dreams.* London: Penguin.

Mujaku Dōchū. 1963 [1908]. *Zenrin shōkisen.* Murayama Mudō, ed. Rept. Tokyo: Seishin shobō.

Mus, Paul. 1928. "Le Buddha paré." *BEFEO* 28, 1–2: 153–278.

———. 1937. "La Tombe vivante: Esquisse d'une série ethnographique naturelle." *La Terre et la vie* 4:117–27.

———. 1990 [1935]. *Barabuḍur: Esquisse d'une histoire du bouddhisme fondée sur la critique archéologique des textes.* Rpt. Paris: Arma Artis.

Nagahara Keiji. 1979. "The Medieval Origins of the 'Eta-Hinin.'" Trans. Yamamura Kozo. *Journal of Japanese Studies* 5, 2: 385–403.

Nagai Masashi. 1985. "Chūgoku zen no minshū kyōke ni tsuite: Chōrō Sōsaku no baai." *IBK* 34, 1: 291–98.

Naitō Masatoshi. 1974. *Miira shinkō no kenkyū.* Tokyo: Yamato shobō.

Nakamura, Kyoko Motomochi. 1973. *Miraculous Stories from the Japanese Buddhist Tradition: The Nihon ryōiki of the Monk Kyōkai.* Harvard-Yenching Institute Monograph Series 20. Cambridge, Mass.: Harvard University Press.

Nara Yasuaki. 1990. "'Puissent les morts atteindre l'illumination: Points de vue sur l'insertion du bouddhisme au Japon." In *Bouddhisme et sociétés asiatiques*. Léon Vandermeersch et al., eds. Paris: L'Harmattan, 75–109.

Needham, Joseph, ed. 1974–83. *Science and Civilization in China 5*: 2–5. Cambridge: Cambridge University Press.

Nihon bukkyō kenkyūkai, ed. 1991 [1970]. *Nihon shūkyō no genze riyaku*. Tokyo: Daizō shuppan.

Nihon miira kenkyū gurūpu, ed. 1993. *Nihon, Chūgoku miira shinkō kenkyū*. 2 vols. Tokyo: Heibonsha.

Nishiguchi Junko. 1987. *Onna no chikara: Kodai no josei to bukkyō*. Heibonsha sensho 110. Tokyo: Heibonsha.

———. 1993. "Jōbutsu to josei: 'Nyobonge' made." *Nihon kenkyūshi* 366: 20–38.

O'Flaherty, Wendy Doniger. 1984. *Dreams, Illusions, and Other Realities*. Chicago: University of Chicago Press.

Ōkubo Dōshū. 1966. *Dōgen zenji den no kenkyū*. Tokyo: Chikuma shobō.

———, ed. 1971. *Kohon kōtei Shōbōgenzō*. Tokyo: Chikuma shobō.

Ong, Robert K. 1985. *The Interpretation of Dreams in Ancient China*. Bochum (Germany): Studienverlag Brockmeyer.

Ōsumi Kazuo. 1990. "Buddhism in the Kamakura Period." In *The Cambridge History of Japan*. Vol. 3: *Medieval Japan*. Yamamura Kozo, ed. Cambridge: Cambridge University Press, 544–82.

Ōtani Teppu. 1974. "*Tōkokki*: Sono genkei ni tsuite ichi shiron." *Shūgaku kenkyū* 16: 105–16.

Ōwa Iwao. 1989. *Jinja to kodai minkan saiki*. Tokyo: Hakusuisha.

Padoux, André, ed. 1990. *L'Image divine: Culte et méditation dans l'hindouisme*. Paris: C.N.R.S.

Pedersen, Kusumita Priscilla, trans. 1975. "Jishōki." *The Eastern Buddhist* (n.s.) 8, 1: 96–132.

Pirandello, Luigi. 1977–85. *Sogno* [*ma forse no*]. French trans. by Michel Arnaud: *Je rêve* [*mais peut-être que non*]. In Pirandello, *Théâtre complet*. Bibliothèque de la Pléiade, vol. 2. Ed. André Boissy et al. Paris: Gallimard.

Plutschow, Herbert E. 1990. *Chaos and Cosmos: Ritual in Early and Medieval Japanese Literature*. Leiden and New York: E. J. Brill.

Pokora, Timoteus. 1985. " 'Living Corpses in Early Medieval China: Sources and Opinions." In *Religion und Philosophie in Ostasien: Festschrift für Hans Steininger*. Gert Naundorf, Karl-Heinz Pohl and Hans-Hermann Schmidt, eds. Würzburg: Königshausen and Neumann, 343–57.

Pollack, David. 1986. *The Fracture of Meaning: Japan's Synthesis of China from the Eighth through the Eighteenth Centuries*. Princeton: Princeton University Press.

Rasmus, Rebecca, trans. 1982. "The Sayings of Myōe Shōnin of Togano-o," *The Eastern Buddhist* (n.s.) 15, 1: 87–105.

Reischauer, Edwin O., trans. 1955a. *Ennin's Diary: The Record of a Pilgrimage to China in Search of the Law*. New York: Reginald Press.

———. 1955b. *Ennin's Travels in T'ang China*. New York: Reginald Press.

Robinet, Isabelle. 1993. *Taoist Meditation: The Mao-shan Tradition of Great Purity*. Trans. Julian Pas and Norman J. Girardot, Albany: SUNY Press.

Rosset, Clément. 1976. *Le Réel et son double: Essai.* Paris: Gallimard.

Rotours, Robert des. 1952. "Les insignes en deux parties (*fou*) sous la dynastie des T'ang (618–907)." *T'oung Pao* 41: 1–148.

Rouget, Gilbert. 1980. *La Musique et la transe: Esquisse d'une théorie générale des relations de la musique et de la possession.* Paris: Gallimard.

Sahashi Hōryū. 1979. *Keizan: Nihon Sōtōshū no botai—Keizan Jōkin no hito to shisō.* Tokyo: Shunjūsha.

Saigō Nobutsuna. 1993. *Kodaijin to yume.* Tokyo: Heibonsha.

Sanford, James H., and Alexander Kabanoff. 1994. "The Kangi-ten (Gaṇapati) Cult in Medieval Japanese Mikkyō," in *Esoteric Buddhism in Japan.* Ian Astley, ed. SBS Monographs 1. Copenhagen and Arhus: The Seminar for Buddhist Studies.

Sanford, James H., William R. LaFleur, and Masatoshi Nagatomi, eds. 1992. *Flowing Traces: Buddhism in the Literary and Visual Arts of Japan.* Princeton: Princeton University Press.

Sano Kenji. 1991. *Kokūzō shinkō.* Minshū shūkyōshi sōsho 24. Tokyo: Yūzankaku.

Sasaki, Ruth Fuller. 1975. *The Recorded Sayings of Ch'an Master Lin-chi Hui-chao of Chen Prefecture.* Kyoto: The Institute for Zen Studies.

Satō Shunkō. 1985. "Sekidōzan shinkō to Noto Keizan kyōdan." *Shūkyōgaku ronshū* 12: 73–102.

———. 1986–87. "Sōtōshū kyōdan ni okeru 'Hakusan shinkō' jūyōshi no mondai." *Shūgaku kenkyū* 28: 148–51; 29: 157–60.

Schafer, E. 1977. *Pacing the Void: T'ang Approaches to the Stars.* Berkeley: University of California Press.

Schmitt, Jean-Claude. 1990. *La Raison des gestes dans l'Occident médiéval.* Paris: Gallimard.

———. 1994. *Les Revenants: Les Vivants et les morts dans la société médiévale.* Bibliothèque des Histoires. Paris: Gallimard.

Schopen, Gregory. 1987. "Burial 'Ad Sanctos' and the Physical Presence of the Buddha in Early Indian Buddhism: A Study in the Archeology of Religions." *Religion* 17: 193–225.

———. 1988. "On the Buddha and His Bones: The Conception of a Relic in the Inscription of Nāgārjunikoṇḍa." *JAOS* 108: 527–37.

———. 1992. "On Avoiding Ghosts and Social Censure: Monastic Funerals in the Mūlasarvāstivāda-vinaya." *Journal of Indian Philosophy* 20: 1–39.

Seidel, Anna. 1983a. "Imperial Treasures and Taoist Sacraments: Taoist Roots in the Apocrypha." In *Tantric and Taoist Studies in Honour of R. A. Stein.* Michel Strickmann, ed. Brussels: Institut Belge des Hautes Etudes Chinoises, vol. 2, 291–371.

———. 1983b. "Dabi." *Hōbōgirin.* Paris: Adrien Maisonneuve, vol. 6, 578–82.

———. Forthcoming. "Den'e." *Hōbōgirin*, vol. 9. Paris: Adrien Maisonneuve.

Seidensticker, Edward, trans. 1964. *The Gossamer Years (Kagerō Nikki): The Diary of a Noblewoman of Heian Japan.* Tokyo and Rutland, Vt.: Charles E. Tuttle.

Sharf, Robert. 1992. "The Idolization of Enlightenment: On the Mummification of Ch'an Masters in Medieval China." *History of Religions* 32, 1: 1–31.

Shibata Minoru. 1984. *Goryō shinkō*, Minshū shūkyōshi sōsho 5. Tokyo: Yūzankaku.

Shinagawa Kenritsu Kanazawa Bunko, ed. 1974. *Kanazawa bunko shiryō zensho: Butten, zensekihen I.* Yokohama: Shinagawa Kenritsu Kanazawa Bunko.

Smith, Jonathan Z. 1978. *Map Is Not Territory: Studies in the History of Religions.* Leiden: E. J. Brill.

———. 1982. *Imagining Religion: From Babylon to Jonestown.* Chicago: University of Chicago Press.

———. 1987. *To Take Place: Toward Theory in Ritual.* Chicago: University of Chicago Press.

Sōtōshū Nisōshi Hensakai, ed. 1955. *Sōtōshū nisō shi.* Tokyo: Sōtōshū nisōdan honbu.

Soymié, Michel. 1961. "Sources et sourciers en Chine." *Bulletin de la Maison Franco-Japonaise* (n.s.) 7, 1: 1–56.

———. 1984. "Quelques représentations de statues miraculeuses dans les grottes de Touen-houang." In *Contributions aux Etudes de Touen-houang.* M. Soymié, ed. Paris: Ecole Française d'Extrême-Orient, vol. 3: 77–102.

Sperber, Dan. 1975. *Rethinking Symbolism.* Trans. Alice L. Morton. Cambridge Studies in Social Anthropology. Cambridge: Cambridge University Press.

Sponberg, Alan, and Helen Hardacre, eds. 1988. *Maitreya, the Future Buddha.* Cambridge: Cambridge University Press.

Stein, Rolf A. 1986. "Avalokiteśvara/Kouan-yin, un exemple de transformation d'un dieu en déesse." *Cahiers d'Extrême Asie* 2: 17–77.

———. 1988. *Grottes-matrices et lieux saints de la déesse en Asie orientale.* Publications de l'Ecole Française d'Extrême-Orient 151. Paris: Ecole Française d'Extrême-Orient.

———. 1990. *The World in Miniature: Container Gardens and Dwellings in Far Eastern Religious Thought.* Trans. Phyllis Brooks. Stanford: Stanford University Press.

———. 1991. "The Guardian of the Gate: An Example of Buddhist Mythology, from India to Japan." In *Asian Mythologies.* Yves Bonnefoy, ed. Chicago: University of Chicago Press, 122–36.

Strickmann, Michel, ed. 1985. *Tantric and Taoist Studies in Honor of R. A. Stein.* Brussels: Institut Belge des Hautes Etudes Chinoises.

———. 1988. "Dreamwork of Psycho-Sinologists: Doctors, Taoists, Monks." In *Psycho-Sinology: The Universe of Dreams in Chinese Culture.* Carolyn T. Brown, ed. Lanham: University Press of America, 25–46.

———. 1996. *Mantras et mandarins: le bouddhisme tantrique en Chine.* Paris: Gallimard.

Strong, John S. 1979. "The Legend of the Lion-Roarer: A Study of the Buddhist Arhat Piṇḍola Bhāradvāja." *Numen* 26,1: 50–88.

———. 1994. "Buddhist Relics in Comparative Perspective: Beyond the Parallels." Unpublished ms.

Strong, John S., and Sarah Strong. 1995. "A Tooth Relic of the Buddha in Japan: An Essay on the Sennyū-ji Tradition and a Translation of Zeami's Nō Play 'Shari.'" *Japanese Religions* 20, 1: 1–33.

Sugimoto Shunryū 1982 [1938]. *Zōtei Tōjō shitsunai kirigami narabini sanwa no kenkyū.* Tokyo: Sōtōshū shūmucho.

Suzuki Bokushi. 1986. *Snow Country Tales: Life in the Other Japan*. Trans. Jeffrey Hunter. New York: Weatherhill.

Suzuki Shōkun. 1987. "Rinzai zen no jingi shisō." *Nihon bukkyō gakkai nenpō* 52: 219–30.

Suzuki Taisan. 1983 [1942]. *Zenshū no chihō hatten*. Tokyo: Yoshikawa kōbunkan.

Tada Michitarō. 1981. "Sacred and Profane: The Division of a Japanese Space." *Zinbun: Memoirs of the Research Institute for Humanistic Studies* 17: 17–38.

Takagi Yutaka. 1988. *Bukkyōshi no naka no nyonin*. Heibonsha sensho 126. Tokyo: Heibonsha.

Takahashi Shūei. 1984. "Sanbōji no Darumashū monto to rokuso Fugen shari." *Shūgaku kenkyū* 26: 116–21.

Takase Shigeo, ed. 1977. *Hakusan. Tateyama to Hokuriku shugendō*. Tokyo: Meicho shuppan.

Takatori Ayumi. 1993. *Shintō no seiritsu*. Heibonsha raiburarī. Tokyo: Heibonsha.

Takemi Momoko. 1983. "'Menstruation Sutra' Belief in Japan." Trans. W. Michael Kelsey. *Japanese Journal of Religious Studies* 10, 2–3: 229–46.

Tamamuro Taijō. 1963. *Sōshiki bukkyō*. Tokyo: Daihōrinkaku.

Tambiah, Stanley J. 1981. "A Performative Approach to Ritual." In *Proceedings of the British Academy*, 65: 113–69.

———. 1985. *The Buddhist Saints of the Forest and the Cult of Amulets: A Study in Charisma, Hagiography, Sectarianism, and Millenial Buddhism*. Cambridge: Cambridge University Press.

Tanabe, George J., Jr. 1992. *Myōe the Dreamkeeper: Fantasy and Knowledge in Early Kamakura Buddhism*. Harvard East Asian Monographs. Cambridge, Mass.: Harvard University Press.

Tanabe, George J., Jr., and Willa Jane Tanabe, eds. 1989. *The Lotus Sūtra in Japanese Culture*. Honolulu: University of Hawaii Press.

Tedlock, Barbara, ed. 1992 [1987]. *Dreaming: Anthropological and Psychological Interpretations*. Santa Fe, N.M.: School of American Research Press.

Teiser, Stephen. 1988. *The Ghost Festival in Medieval China*. Princeton: Princeton University Press.

Togawa Anshō. 1974. *Dewa sanzan no miirabutsu*. Tokyo: Chūō shoin.

Tominaga Nakamoto. 1990. *Emerging from Meditation*. Trans. Michael Pye. Honolulu: University of Hawaii Press.

Trainor, Kevin M. "The Relics of the Buddha: A Study of the Cult of Relic Veneration in the Theravāda Buddhist Tradition of Sri Lanka." Ph.D. dissertation, Columbia University.

Tsunoda Ryūsaku, Wm. Theodore de Bary, and Donald Keene, eds. 1958. *Sources of Japanese Tradition*. 2 vols. New York: Columbia University Press.

Tyler, Royall. 1990. *The Miracles of the Kasuga Deity*. New York: Columbia University Press.

Tyler, Susan C. 1992. *The Cult of Kasuga Seen through Its Art*. Ann Arbor: Center for Japanese Studies, University of Michigan.

Ury, Marian Bloom. 1971. "*Genkō Shakusho*: Japan's First Comprehensive History of Buddhism: A Partial Translation, with Introduction and Notes." Ph.D. dissertation, Berkeley.

Verdú, Alfonso. 1966. "The 'Five Ranks' Dialectics of the Sōtō-Zen School in the Light of Kuei-fêng Tsung-mi's 'Ariya-shiki' Scheme." *Monumenta Nipponica* 21, 1–2: 125–70.

Vernant, Jean-Pierre. 1965. *Mythe et pensée chez les Grecs: Etudes de psychologie historique.* 2 vols. Paris: Maspero.

———. 1990. *Figures, idoles, masques.* Paris: Julliard.

———. 1991. *Mortals and Immortals: Collected Essays.* Froma I. Zeitlin, ed. Princeton: Princeton University Press.

Veyne, Paul. 1988. *Did the Greeks Believe in Their Myths? An Essay on the Constitutive Imagination.* Trans. Paula Wissing. Chicago: University of Chicago Press.

Visser, Marinus Willem de. 1923. *The Arhats in China and Japan.* Berlin: Oesterheld.

Wata Kenju. 1960. "Minzokugakuteki tachiba kara mita Sōtōshū no hatten ni tsuite." *Shūgaku kenkyū* 2: 124–31.

Watson, Burton, trans. 1993. *The Zen Teachings of Master Lin-chi.* Boston and London: Shambala.

Watson, James L., and Evelyn S. Rawski, eds. 1988. *Death Rituals in Late Imperial and Modern China.* Berkeley: University of California Press.

Weber, Max. 1978. *Economy and Society: An Outline of Interpretive Sociology.* Berkeley and Los Angeles: University of California Press.

Weinstein, Stanley. 1974. "The Beginnings of Esoteric Buddhism in Japan: The Neglected Tendai Tradition." *Journal of Asian Studies* 34, 1: 177–91.

Wen Fong. 1958. *The Lohans and a Bridge to Heaven.* Washington, D.C.: Smithsonian Institution.

Whitfield, Roderick. 1990. "Esoteric Buddhist Elements in the Famensi Reliquary Deposit." *Etudes Asiatiques/Asiatische Studien* 44, 2: 247–66.

Wittgenstein, Ludwig. 1971. "Remarks on Frazer's *Golden Bough.*" *The Human World* 3: 18–41.

———. 1979. *Remarks on Frazer's Golden Bough.* Rush Rhees, ed., A. C. Miles, trans. Doncaster: Brynmill Press.

———. 1982. *Remarques sur le Rameau d'Or de Frazer.* Trans. Jean Lacoste. Paris: L'Age d'Homme.

Xu Hengbin. 1993. "Nankaji no 'rokuso Enō no shinjin' kō. In *Nihon, Chūgoku miira shinkō kenkyū.* Nihon mira kenkyū gurūpu, ed. Tokyo: Heibonsha, 217–57.

Yamaori Tetsuo. 1973. *Nihon bukkyō shisōron josetsu.* Tokyo: San'ichi shobō.

Yampolsky, Philip B., trans. 1967. *The Platform Sūtra of the Sixth Patriarch: The Text of the Tun-huang Manuscript.* New York: Columbia University Press.

Yanagida Seizan. 1967. *Rinzai no kafū.* Nihon no bukkyō 9. Tokyo: Chikuma shobō.

———, ed. 1979. *Zenrin shōkisen; Kattō gosen jikkan; Zenrin kushū benmyō.* 2 vols. Kyoto: Chūbun shuppansha.

———. 1984. "Dōgen to Chūgoku bukkyō." *Zen bunka kenkyūjo kiyō* 13: 3–128.

Yates, Frances A. 1966. *The Art of Memory*. Chicago: University of Chicago Press.

Yetts, W. Perceval. 1911. "Notes on the Disposal of Buddhist Dead in China." *Journal of the Royal Asiatic Society* 43: 699–725.

Yokoi Yuhō. 1976. *Zen Master Dōgen: An Introduction with Selected Writings*. New York and Tokyo: Weatherhill.

Yü Chün-fang. 1981. *The Renewal of Buddhism in China: Chu-hung and the Late Ming Synthesis*. New York: Columbia University Press.

Zürcher, Erik. 1959. *The Buddhist Conquest of China: The Spread and Adaptation of Buddhism in Early Medieval China*. 2 vols. Leiden: E. J. Brill.

INDEX

Abhidharmakośa (śāstra), 76, 147
abhijñā, 73, 74
abhiṣeka, 61, 122
ako ("lowering the torch"), 151
Amaterasu (goddess), 105; and Beppō
Daiju, 107; as Dainichi, 105; and Haku-
san god, 105; mirror as symbol of, 270;
and Shinchi Kakushin, 107
Amida (Buddha), icon of, 244n20
amulets, Buddhist, 254-55
Ānanda, 47, 175n91
aniconism, 267
Arhat: image of, 238n4, 244; Keizan as,
30; Piṇḍola, 89-90, 205; Subhūti, 89;
Suvinda, 89; Vajraputra, 89
Arhats, 88, 91-92, 266; at Eiheiji, 92-93;
Five hundred, 94n34; Four Great, 90;
Sixteen, 92; on Tiantai shan, 92-93;
Yōsai and the, 91, 92
Ashikaga, 158n58. See also Takauji
Aśoka (King), 102; and the Arhat Piṇḍola,
252; and relics, 160
astrology (Indian and Chinese), 230
Aśvaghoṣa, 78-79
Augé, Marc, 15, 224, 282
Avalokiteśvara. See Kannon
Ayuwang shan (Mt. King Aśoka), 160,
165

Bai Juyi, 108
Baizhang Huaihai, and the fox, 11, 30,
174
bao (dynastic treasure), 69, 226; robe as,
49
Baozhi, 75, 207-8
Barthes, Roland, 9, 16, 121, 224
Basiasita (Indian patriarch), 159, 202
Bassui Tokushō, 66, 172, 221
Bataille, Georges, 142
Bazin, Jean, 22, 23
Beppō Daiju, 107
Bhadrapāla, 83
Bimbisāra (King), 33
Bishamon, 84, 96
Biyan lu (Emerald Cliff Record), 97, 102

blood symbolism, 67
bodaiji, 154, 158
Bodhidharma, 32; avatar of Kannon, 75;
in the cave, 128; dolls, 263; and Huike,
57; Keizan on, 22; in Keizan's dream,
32; and Liang Wudi, 75; poisoning of,
63; portrait of, 259
bodhimaṇḍa, 10, 215, 216, 217
Bodhisattva(s): career of the, 229; Five,
203. See also Kannon; Kokūzō; Mañjuśrī; Miroku; Samantabhadia
Bodhisattva Precepts, 65, 245; and the
conversion of the mountain god, 103
Bodhisena, 249
body: adamantine, 206; in Christianity,
205; in Daoism, 204; as illusory, 201;
as microcosm, 203-4; and mind, 199;
mutilation of, 204; perfect, 200; symbolism of, 195; ten metaphors for, 201
bonsai (miniature garden), 228
Borobuḍur, 195
Bourdieu, Pierre, 25-26, 54, 211, 217,
276; on the habitus, 281; on the logic
of practice, 223; on rites of passage,
279
bowl, symbolism of, 234
Budai, 87, 205
Buddha(s): five, 203; footprints of the,
200; thirteen, 146
Buddha nature, 209
Butsuge shariki, 164

Can (Lazy), 199
Castoriadis, Cornelius, 236
center, symbolism of the, 229
Certeau, Michel de, 23, 111
Chanyuan qinggui, 147-48
Chewu Jixing, 119
chinju (tutelary god), 100
Chinju kirigami, 154-55
Chinkasai (Blossom-Appeasing Festival),
157n42
chinsō (portrait), 201, 243, 259-62;
Dōgen's, 172
Chinsō kirigami, 261-62

Lightning Source UK Ltd.
Milton Keynes UK
09 September 2010

159673UK00001B/27/A